THE BOOK OF WISDOM

Dropsie College Edition

JEWISH

APOCRYPHAL LITERATURE

THE BOOK OF

WISDOM

An English Translation with Introduction
and Commentary
by
JOSEPH REIDER

Published for

THE DROPSIE COLLEGE

FOR HEBREW AND COGNATE LEARNING

by

HARPER & BROTHERS, NEW YORK

THE BOOK OF WISDOM

Library of Congress catalog card number: 53-5114

Dedicated to

WILLIAM AND IDA ROSENTHAL

ABRAHAM A. NEUMAN

With the appearance of this volume, the Book of Wisdom, the Dropsie College series of Jewish Apocryphal Literature is introducing to its readers a work which is more than a repository of ancient wisdom and a venerable text of moral religious philosophy which prevailed in the Jewish-Hellenistic world two thousand years ago. The Book of Wisdom is undoubtedly intrinsically important as an historic religious work in the twilight zone during which Judaism reached maturity and also gave birth to Christianity. However, in common with all the inspired works of Scripture it has a value and significance that transcend the limitations of the time and circumstances which gave birth to this religious classic.

From earliest time to the present, the Book of Wisdom attracted the attention of scholars and learned pietists who sought to fathom the secrets of its origin, its influence and inspiration. The literature centering around this work is considerable. The most important books on this subject are treated critically in the Introduction by Doctor Joseph Reider, the editor and translator of this volume. No unanimity of opinion exists regarding its many facets: its authorship, its birthplace, the original language in which it was composed, the date of its origin, the authenticity of its theological tenets or its relationship to the philosophical currents then prevailing in the Hellenistic milieu. Doctor Reider marshals the various conflicting scholarly opinions and after carefully weighing all the evidence and opinions, pro and con, advances his own conclusions.

The resultant picture may not be entirely clear but its outlines are firmly drawn. The author, who is anonymous, was an Alexandrian Jew: Greek in speech and thought, and a Jew in

religion and in moral sensitivity. He was a citizen of two con-
trasting worlds. He lived and had his being in two competing
civilizations. On the one hand there was the Greek world, intel-
lectually alluring, worshipful of beauty and art, hedonistic and
sensuous; on the other hand, there was deeply rooted in his soul
the Hebrew conscience, a pervading sense of duty inspired by
godliness, a feeling of holiness, and a conviction of divine
destiny.

The author was at home in the Greek surroundings. He loved
beauty; he was versed in the various schools of philosophic
thought without adhering to any one system consistently. His
religious ideas were colored by Hellenistic concepts. But the
garb of Hellenism was merely the outward garment that covered
his inner being. In depth and in truth, he was the offspring of
Biblical wisdom. His wisdom was the distillation of Hebraic
experiences and insights. His love of beauty may have been
Hellenistically inspired, but his Hebraic conscience revolted
against its sublimation and the moral decadence which was its
consequence. To the author, beauty as a creation of the divine
was uplifting. As an end in itself—as the incorporation of
divinity—it was idolatry, the denial of the true God, the Author
of all.

Steeped as he was in Greek philosophy, his interest was not
in intellectual speculation. A vision captivated his heart and
soul, the vision of Wisdom; wisdom not in the mundane sense
pertaining to human relationships, but wisdom as a mystic
creation, an emanation of the divine essence, existent before
the creation of the world and participating with God in its
formation.

The title of the book is obviously derived from this pro-
foundly mystic concept; but even more so, the entire book is
inspired by its religious motivation. Notwithstanding the lofty
supra-human altitude in which the author's concept of Wisdom
is poised, the author is not writing in a vacuum. The tormenting
questions concerning life and death, how to explain evil and
injustice in a world created by a god of love and justice, or the

nature of divine retribution, immortality of the soul, the ultimate destiny of humanity and Israel—these are the problems
to which the author applies the canons derived from Hebrew
wisdom.

The author was directing himself in the first instance to his
co-religionists in Alexandria and throughout the Hellenistic
diaspora because so many of his brethren were falling prey to
the allurements of Hellenism. Loss of faith in Israel's religion
and destiny, and outright apostasy constituted mortal danger to
the continued existence of the Jewish people. He laid bare the
moral weaknesses and fallacies on which the glamorous idolatrous civilization rested. Living in an Egyptian environment, he
boldly invokes the testimony of history in denunciation of
Egypt and in glorification of Israel. While Israel is portrayed
under favored divine providence, the author, like the preceding
Hebrew prophets, firmly held on to the universal vision of God
as the Father of all men and all creation.

The detailed analysis of the Book of Wisdom by many
scholars has proved amply rewarding in relation to the history
of Judaism and Christianity. In its general overtones, this
classic bears relevance also to our times. To the perplexed
generation of the author's kin, who are being lured away from
Jewish loyalties by the more glamorous trappings of a material-
istic civilization, the appeal of the Book of Wisdom is prophetic.
Equally so does the voice of Wisdom speak forcefully to the
nations of the world:

> Love righteousness, you that be judges of the earth,
> Think of the Lord in goodness,
> And in simplicity of heart seek you him.

It is fitting to conclude with a few words of appreciation: to
Doctor Solomon Zeitlin, Editor-in-Chief of the Jewish Apocryphal Literature series, thanks are due for seeing the work
through editorially in all its stages; to Doctor Harry L. Levy
and Edwin Wolf II for careful proofreading and many valuable
suggestions. Of a different order, we are beholden with thanks

and appreciation to Mr. and Mrs. William Rosenthal who have generously defrayed the costs of this publication in honor of their golden wedding anniversary. This act is in true consonance with the dictate of Jewish wisdom to celebrate epochal events in life not through lavish display but by aiding in the production of enduring cultural creations.

⊷§ CONTENTS §⊶

Foreword: Abraham A. Neuman................ vii

Introduction................................. 1

I. Title..................................... 1

II. Contents................................ 2

III. Text................................... 5

IV. Purpose................................ 9

V. Date of Composition...................... 12

VI. Authorship............................. 15

VII. Language.............................. 22

VIII. Theology and Philosophy................ 29

IX. Wisdom Literature....................... 38

X. Rabbinic Sources........................ 40

XI. Bibliography........................... 43

Text, Translation, Commentary and Critical Notes 47

Index................................... 227

THE BOOK OF WISDOM

❧ INTRODUCTION ❧

I

TITLE

The all but universal title "Wisdom of Solomon" derives from the original Greek title Σοφία Σαλωμῶνος in MS.B, or Σοφία Σαλωμῶντος in MS. א, or Σοφία Σολομῶντος in MS.A of the Septuagint. The Syriac Version known as Peshitta entitles it *Hokmeta rabbati di-Shelomo*, "The Great Wisdom of Solomon," but the Syriac in Walton's Polyglot[1] adds the following remark "concerning which there is doubt whether some other Hebrew sage, writing in the spirit of prophecy, did not compose it in the name of Solomon, and it was so accepted." The Old Latin Version known as Itala has simply *Liber Sapientiae*, "Book of Wisdom", which is acceptable to modern critics.

Of the Greek Church Fathers, Epiphanius[2] and Pseudo-Athanasius[3] call it πανάρετος Σοφία, "The all-virtuous Wisdom"; Clement of Alexandria[4] and Origen[5] ἡ θεία Σοφία, "The divine Wisdom." Of the Latin Church Fathers, Augustine[6] called it *Liber Christianae Sapientiae*, "Book of Christian Wisdom"; Jerome[7] characterizes it as *Pseudepigraphus* and says it was entitled *Sapientia Salomonis*, "The Wisdom of Solomon."

---

[1] Issued in London in 1657.
[2] *De Ponder. et Mens.*, § 4.
[3] *Synopsis Scripturae*, II, 173 D.
[4] Strom., IV.16.
[5] *Epist. ad Rom.*, VII.14.
[6] *Epist.* 130; *De Doctr. Christ.*, II.8.
[7] In his Preface to the Books of Solomon.

1

The most extraordinary title of the Book of Wisdom is found in the Muratorian Canon: *Sapientia Salomonis ab amicis Salomonis in honorem ipsius scripta.* Tregelles[8] suggested ingeniously that *ab amicis* might stand for ὑπὸ Φίλωνος in the Greek original,[9] which was mistaken for ὑπὸ φίλων, "by the friends."

II

Contents

According to subject matter the Book of Wisdom may be divided into two main parts, each of which may be further subdivided. 1) Chapters 1–9 expatiate on the role of Wisdom in human life and experience: 1–5 enumerate in detail the moral demands of Wisdom and her corresponding rewards; 6–9 describe in glowing colors the nature of Wisdom and her supernal powers. 2) Chapters 10–19 furnish illustrations of Wisdom's power from the ancient history of Israel: 10 f. deal with the patriarchs and the exodus from Egypt; 12 is devoted to the Canaanites; 13–15 constitute a digression on idolatry; 16–19 contrast God's treatment of Israel with His treatment of the Egyptians.

Bretschneider[10] divided the book into three distinct parts: ch. 1–6.8 which he styled Book of Eschatology[11]; ch. 6.9–10 Paean or Panegyric on Wisdom[12]; ch. 11–19 Historical Retrospect with a tract on idolatry or polytheism.[13] This threefold division, or

---

[8] *Canon Murat.*, p. 53.

[9] The book being erroneously attributed to Philo.

[10] *De Libri Sapientiae parte priore cap. I–XI e duobus libellis diversis conflata.* Viteb. 1804.

[11] So called because it stresses the different destinies which await the righteous sufferers and the ungodly oppressors.

[12] Containing the claim to Solomonic authorship and references to Platonic philosophy.

[13] Different in contents and style from the other two parts; sometimes characterized as a Passover sermon.

something similar to it[14] is most generally adopted by commentators and exegetes.

The first ten chapters are far superior to the rest of the book in point of thought. True, the thought is not that of a systematic or consistent thinker, yet it evinces the strong convictions of a great religious spirit, who was aware of the stress and strain of life and yet refused to abandon his ancestral belief in a God of righteousness. It is in these first chapters that the writer boldly enunciates the doctrine of immortality immediately after death, denies that suffering presupposes sin, refuses to admit that early death is necessarily a calamity, or that childlessness is a mark of divine displeasure. Compared to them the last nine chapters, which are homiletic and haggadic in character, weaving a pattern of salvation for Israel the God-intoxicated and destruction for Egypt the idolatrous, are far inferior with their labored diction and dragging periods, with their repetitions and wordiness.

In a more detailed way the book opens with an address to kings and potentates of the world, whom evidently the author wishes to influence in favor of the Jews, but apparently the discourse is intended for all men, of whatever station in life. First comes an appeal to love righteousness, which is the only way leading to Wisdom, unrighteousness being alien to it and leading to death and destruction unwilled by God (ch. 1). Then a vivid picture is drawn of the wicked, who, observing the absence of just compensation in this world and denying future retribution, abandon themselves to sensual enjoyment here; moreover, they hate and persecute the righteous because they are reproved by them for their wicked deeds (ch. 2). There follows a contrast between the righteous, whose sufferings in this world are only a chastening and whose hope is full of immortality and transcendental happiness, and the wicked, whose life even here is miserable and whose offspring are cursed (3.1–12). Here the observation is made that happiness does not consist in children and old age, for virtue without children is better than vice with chil-

[14] Namely ch. 1–5; ch. 6–9; and ch. 10–19.

dren, and the truly venerable age is wisdom and probity (3.13–4.9).

The general argument is resumed and it is stressed that the value of righteousness will be shown hereafter, when good men, here despised by the wicked, will be blessed, whilst the wicked, pursued by divine wrath, will be forced to acknowledge the folly of their course (4.10–5.23). Here comes a renewal of the address to kings to heed Wisdom so that they may govern worthily and be assured of immortality (6.1–21), followed by the personal experience of King Solomon, who had prayed for wisdom and it was granted him, and an enumeration of the great virtues of wisdom and the benefits derived therefrom (6.22–9.18).

At this point begins a historical retrospect purporting to show how the past generations were guided by Wisdom, specifically the patriarchs, from Adam to Joseph, but especially Moses, who led the Israelites victoriously out of Egypt (ch. 10). Contrasted to the Israelites are the Egyptians and Canaanites, who in defiance of wisdom worshipped false gods, and consequently were punished grievously, though they were not wholly destroyed, giving them a chance for repentance. The Egyptians especially were punished by means of their own animal gods in order to make them acknowledge the true God, whom they formally denied (11.1–12–27).

The argument is interrupted by a lengthy discourse on idolatry, its nature, its origin, its many varieties, such as the worship of the forces of nature, or beasts, or stones and images fashioned by human hands. This idolatry, which originated in a desire to honor dead children and kings, and was abetted by skilled artists who carved attractive images, led to moral corruption and all the frightful vices of society, from which Israel kept free, whilst its enemies were engulfed by it (ch. 13–15).

After this digression the historical retrospect is resumed and a contrast is drawn between the punishments of the Egyptians and those of the Israelites: God did indeed send plagues on Is-

rael as on Egypt, but whereas the former came as chastisement only and were not altogether destructive, the latter were utterly devastating, culminating in the destruction of the Egyptian firstborn (ch. 16–18). Finally, an account is given of the passage of the Red Sea, when the Egyptians were drowned for their treachery to strangers, whilst the Israelites waded through safely and proceeded to fresh conquests. Thus in all things God magnified and glorified His people, in spite of its enemies (ch. 19).[15]

III

TEXT

The Greek text of the Septuagint is paramount, and all of it is found in the great uncials ‫א‬ (Sinaiticus), A (Alexandrinus) and B (Vaticanus). It is incomplete in C (Codex Ephraimi rescriptus). As to cursives, there are about a dozen listed in the classic edition of Holmes and Parsons,[16] the most important of which appears to be 248 embodying very ancient elements and frequently quoted by Margoliouth in his article on our book.[17]

There is no critical edition of the original Greek text. The edition of Holmes and Parsons quoted above, though based on numerous manuscripts, is far from accurate and is, besides, quite antiquated. The larger Cambridge edition of the Septuagint by Brooke and McLean,[18] which is supposed to replace it, has not yet reached the Book of Wisdom. Swete's admirable shorter Cambridge edition,[19] though based on all the important

[15] A very detailed analysis of the contents of the Book of Wisdom is given by Rev. J. A. F. Gregg in the introduction to his Commentary in the *Cambridge Bible for Schools and Colleges*, pp. xlix–lii.

[16] *Vetus Testamentum Graecum cum variis lectionibus* (Oxford 1798–1827), vol. V.

[17] In the *Journal of the Royal Asiatic Society* for 1890, pp. 263–297.

[18] Has been appearing since 1906.

[19] Began to appear in 1887 and has been reprinted many times.

uncials, is confined to only a limited number of cursive manuscripts. Many interesting variants in the cursives are given by
Grimm, Holtzmann, and especially Feldmann in their commen-
taries and treatises. The latest edition of the Septuagint by A.
Rahlfs[20] gives an arbitrarily corrected text based of course on
variae lectiones but sometimes also on the individual judgment
of the editor. Yet it seemed both feasible and practical to use
this text in the present edition of the Book of Wisdom, together
with the most important critical notes. As a matter of fact in this
particular book it differs only very slightly from the text of
Swete, and never in essential matters.

There are scholars who doubt that the Greek text as it is has
been preserved pure and pristine. On the contrary, as in many
other ancient texts, which had gone through various vicissitudes,
they are convinced that here too are some interpolations. Thus,
for example, Graetz[21] believed that the Book of Wisdom had
been manipulated by some Christian scribe, who interpolated in
it at least the following four passages: 2.24 φθόνῳ δὲ διαβόλου
θάνατος εἰσῆλθεν εἰς τὸν κόσμον, "by the envy of the devil
death entered into the world"; 3.13 ἥτις οὐκ ἔγνω κοίτην ἐν
παραπτώματι, "she who has not conceived in transgression"; 4.1
κρείσσων ἀτεκνία μετὰ ἀρετῆς, "better than this is childlessness
with virtue"; and 14.7 εὐλόγηται γὰρ ξύλον, δι' οὗ γίνεται
δικαιοσύνη, "blessed has been wood through which comes
righteousness." For a discussion of these passages see our Commentary ad loc.

The Old Latin version (Itala) seems to be of North African
origin and belongs to the second century CE. Many words
found in it occur only in African writers, such as Tertullian and
Augustine. It is certain that Jerome, in preparing the Vulgate,
did not revise the already existing Latin translation of Wisdom.[22]

---

[20] Published by the Privilegierte Württembergische Bibelanstalt in
Stuttgart 1935.

[21] *Geschichte der Juden*, III, 444.

[22] Comp. P. Thielmann, "Über den Charakter der 'Vetus Latina' des
Buches der Weisheit," in *Archiv für lateinische Lexicographie und Gram-*

This version is generally faithful to the Greek, but contains also some additions,[23] glosses, paraphrases, or variant renderings.

The Syriac version seems to have been made from the Greek and corrected from some other sources, notably the Old Latin. This version exists in three different recensions: the Peshitta, printed in Walton's Polyglot,[24] and also, with slight differences, from a British Museum manuscript by Lagarde[25]; the Syro-Hexaplaric text, published by A. M. Ceriani[26]; and the fragment of a Palestinian version from a Bodleian manuscript made known by George Henry Gwilliam.[27] With regard to the Peshitta, it is paraphrastic down to the end of chapter 10, but from that point onwards, according to Goodrick, "it would almost seem that another interpreter had taken the task in hand, who had little or no knowledge of Greek." For purposes of textual criticism, therefore, this portion of the translation is almost valueless.[28] The Hexaplaric text, which is a translation of the Septuagint text of Origen's Hexapla, executed by Paul, bishop of Tella in Mesopotamia, about 617 CE., is slavishly faithful to the letter of the Septuagint, even at the expense of sense, though accompanied by marginal notes and later annotations. The Syriac of this version is much later than the Syriac of the Peshitta. As to the Palestinian version, it is understood that it is the text of the Malkite (or Greek) Church in Palestine and Egypt and that it is written in a dialect more akin to that of the Jewish Targums.[29]

matik, VIII (1893), 235 ff.; also D. de Bruyne, "Étude sur le texte latin de la Sagesse," in *Revue Bénédictine*, XLI (1929), 101 ff.

[23] See 1.15, 2.8, 2.17, 5.14, 6.1, 8.11, 9.19, 10.1, 11.5, 17.1.

[24] *Biblia Sacra Polyglotta . . . Edidit Brianus Waltonius*, London, 1657.

[25] *Libri Apocryphi Vet. Test. Syriace*, Leipzig 1861.

[26] In *Monumenta Sacra et Profana*, vol. VII, Milan 1874.

[27] In *Anecdota Oxoniensia*, Oxford 1893.

[28] Comp. further Joseph Holtzmann, *Die Peshitto zum Buche der Weisheit*, Freiburg im Breisgau 1903.

[29] On this version generally comp. Burkitt in *Journal of Theological Studies*, II (1901), 175.

An Aramaic translation of Wisdom is mentioned by Nahman-ides (13 cent.) in the preface to his Commentary on the Penta-teuch.[30] Also Azariah dei Rossi[31] attests to the existence of an Aramaic version. But since such a version has not come down to us it is quite possible that these references are to the Syriac version transcribed in Hebrew characters.[32]

An Egyptian Sahidic version of Wisdom was published by Lagarde,[33] and there is also an Ethiopic version; but these are of little critical value.

The Arabic version, which is said to be of the twelfth century or later, is often paraphrastic, like the Peshitta, yet it never de-parts much from the Greek text, and is occasionally more ac-curate than the Old Latin.

The Armenian version is "word-true," according to Cony-beare.[34] Reusch made a collation of this version, but this has been declared inaccurate and imperfect. Margoliouth made good use of it in his article on the Hebrew origin of the Book of Wisdom.[35]

The Authorized English version is fairly good and accurate, but the English is at times too diffuse, at times quite inadequate

---

[30] וראיתי הספר המתורגם הנקרא חכמתא רבא דשלמה וכתוב בו ולא ממתום הות תולדתא
חדיתא למלך או לשליט דחדיו מעלנא דכל נש לעלמא ומפקאנא שריאת חדיו מטול כן צלית
ואתיהיבת לי רוחא דחכמתא וקרית ואתת לי רוחא דאידעתא צבית בה יתיר מן שבטא וכורסוותא
(אמר כי לא מדבר תהיה תולדת מיוחדת למלך או לשליט אחד הוא ובא לי רוח דעת בחרתי בה
שוה לכלם יחד ובעבור כן התפללתי ונתן לי רוח חכמה וקראתי ובא לי רוח דעת בחרתי בה
יותר מן השבט והכסא) ונאמר שם והוא דיהב אדעתא דלא לגלוחא למידיע היכן קם עלמא
ועובדיהון דמזאלתא שריא ושולמא ומצעתהון דזבני שולחפי דזנבותא ודהיכן עבדי זבני ריהטהון
דשמיא וקבעיהון דכוכבא מתנא דבעירא וחימתא דחיותא עזויהון דרוחי ומחשבתהון דבני נשא
גינסי דנצבתא וחיליהון דעקרי כל מדם דכסי וכל מדם דגלי ידעית. The quotation is from chapter 7.5–8, 17–21. Comp. also דרשת הרמב'ן על דברי
דשלמה קהלת, ed. A. Z. Schwartz, Vienna 1913, p. 9: ומצינו עוד ספר שנקרא חכמתא רבתא
דשלמה והוא בלשון תרגום חמור מאד והגוים העתיקו[הון] מן הלשון ההוא ואני חושב שלא העתיקוהו
אנשי חזקיהו מלך יהודה אלא ירד עמהם לבבל על פה ושם אמרוהו בלשונם כי היו חכמות ולא
נאמר ברוח הקודש. See further Alexander Marx, "An Aramaic Fragment of
the Wisdom of Solomon," in JBL., XL (1921) 57 ff.

[31] In his מאור עינים, section ימי עולם, chapter 57.

[32] See Grimm in his Commentary, p. 9.

[33] In his *Aegyptiaca*, Gottingae 1883.

[34] In Hastings' *Dictionary of the Bible*, I, 151 ff.

[35] See note 2 above.

to express the meaning of the Greek. The same may be said also of the English Revised version.

German translations of Wisdom are numerous, but one with notes by M. Gutmann[36] is particularly valuable for its numerous references to rabbinical literature.

A Hebrew version with an extensive commentary was published by Hartwig Wessely,[37] but Wessely failed because, not being familiar with Greek, he prepared his version from German and French texts; and besides he could not find Hebrew words to express adequately the philosophical and theological concepts of Wisdom. Also Seckel (Isaac) Fraenkel rendered into Hebrew the Book of Wisdom among other apocrypha,[38] with similar results. In fact this is too free and paraphrastic to be called a translation. A new and much better version into Hebrew was made directly from the Greek by Menahem Stein for Abraham Kahana's edition of the Apocrypha and Pseudepigrapha.[39]

IV

PURPOSE

Various motives have been advanced for the writing of the Book of Wisdom. Some thought that it constituted an attempt to controvert the teaching of Ecclesiastes.[40] For instance, the writer of Wisdom 2.1–9 certainly had Ecclesiastes in mind: 2.1 can only have reference to Eccl. 2.23 and 5.1; 2.2 is reminiscent of Eccl. 3.19; 2.3 recalls Eccl. 12.7; 2.4 is reflected in Eccl. 1.11, 2.16, 9.5, and 2.11; 2.5 is based on Eccl. 6.12 and 8.8; 2.6 is

---

[36] Published in Altona in 1841.

[37] ספר חכמת שלמה . . . אני הצעיר, נפתלי הירץ וייזל . . . עשיתי הפי' רוח חן, Berlin 1780. Reissued with an abbreviated commentary, Zolkiew 1805; and with a German translation by M. E. Stern, Prague 1853.

[38] כתובים אחרונים הנודעים בשם אפוקריפא, Leipzig 1830, and frequently reissued.

[39] הספרים החיצונים לתורה לנביאים ולכתובים ושאר ספרים חיצונים, עם מבואות ופירושים ערוכים בהשתתפות כמה למדנים ע"י אברהם כהנא. Tel-Aviv 1937. Vol. I, pp. 463–514.

[40] Nachtigal and many others.

founded on Eccl. 2.24; 2.7 refers to Eccl. 9.7; 2.8 alludes to Eccl. 9.8; and 2.9 looks like an allusion to Eccl. 3.22, 5.18, and 9.8. But while this opposition to Ecclesiastes may have been one of the writer's motives, it could not have been the chief and only motive: for this something more positive and urgent is required.

Somewhat better is the suggestion of Siegfried[41] that the main purpose of the book is an attempt to reconcile Jewish and Greek philosophy. But this too is only partly true. Naturally, the reconciliation between Jewish thought and Greek philosophy was always before the eyes of Jewish authors in Alexandria writing in Greek, but this was by no means their chief consideration, certainly not before the days of Philo, who was the first to go about it in a systematic and thorough way.

Others, like Bertholet,[42] maintained that the Book of Wisdom was written for the purpose of attracting proselytes to Judaism from among the cultured Greeks. This may be seen from the following considerations: first, that it is permeated by Platonic and Stoic philosophy, and secondly, that it endeavors to explain away in an allegorical manner those signs and wonders of the Old Testament which might arouse incredulity in Gentiles. We know that these were precisely the methods employed by the Jewish intellectuals in Alexandria in order to attract Greeks to their religion: they either explained away every point of Jewish history which might give umbrage to a cultured Greek, as Philo did, or they boldly affirmed that Hellenic civilization was borrowed from that of the Jews, as Pseudo-Aristobulus did. But again this cannot have been the main issue: actual conversion of pagans to Judaism never was of paramount importance to the Jews, who often enough pleaded for sympathy and tolerance but not for the acceptance of their beliefs and tenets.

There can be no doubt that the purpose of the Book of Wisdom is primarily to strengthen the faith of the pious Jews,[43] to

[41] *Philo von Alexandria als Ausleger des Alten Testaments*, p. 23.
[42] In Budde's *Althebräische Litteratur*, p. 413.
[43] This becomes quite evident from a perusal of chapters 6–12 and 16–19.

convert the apostate or renegade Jews to such a faith,[44] and to convince the heathen of the folly of their idolatry.[45] It will be recalled that Alexandrine-Jewish literature generally aimed at keeping the Jews loyal to their ancestral beliefs and practices and at convincing the pagans of the folly of their own polytheism and idolatry. In the conception of these writers the Jews alone had a very great light, while over the heathen was spread a heavy night.[46] Hence the apotheosis of the God of Israel and His surrogate Wisdom, the promise of reward for virtue, if not in this then in the next world, and the denunciation of materialism, scepticism and idolatry.

Judaism in Alexandria was passing through a severe crisis. Having been imported by early Jewish settlers from Palestine and remaining in its pristine purity for some time, it soon came into conflict with the mighty Greek civilization and its alluring splendors, particularly its over-emphasis of materialism over spiritualism and its accentuation of hedonism as against temperance and self-restraint. To some cultured but weak-minded Jews the beauties and attractions of the Hellenistic civilization were too potent to withstand, and these naturally yielded to its blandishments sooner or later. First imitation would set in, followed by partial and then complete assimilation, and this would inevitably lead to alienation and apostasy. The situation became very alarming, since these Hellenizers and apostates generally entered government service and strove to annoy and harass their former coreligionists by agitating and proselytising among them. There are numerous instances of such inner destructive forces in Alexandrian Jewry. To counteract this nefarious activity of the Hellenizers and apostates and to contradict it thoroughly and effectively became the imperative task of the loyal and learned Jews, such as the author of the Book of Wisdom, who knew both the Jewish Scripture and

[44] See especially chapters 1–5.
[45] Comp. chapters 13–15.
[46] Comp. Wisdom 17.21 f.

Greek philosophy and could readily discern the advantages of the one and the disadvantages of the other.

Thus the Book of Wisdom is really a polemic work, the first six chapters directed against the recalcitrant and apostate Jews, the last ten chapters against vicious idolatry or paganism then dominant in the Greek world. In accordance with this plan the author addresses himself specifically to Jews in ch. 1–5 and to Gentiles in the rest of the book. In the former he undoubtedly had in mind the Epicurean Jews who under the impress of Greek civilization apostatized and mingled with the pagans, sometimes to the detriment of their fellow Jews. For these Epicureans he extols in sonorous phrases the beauties and marvels of the Jewish faith and its great superiority over any other belief of antiquity, and to them he passionately appeals to return to the belief of their ancestors and to abandon their worldly philosophy. He was grieved to see that his countrymen in Egypt were losing their ancient faith while being tolerated by the Egyptians. His aim was to console and strengthen his people by showing them the bankruptcy of materialism and the futility of idolatry and by recommending to them the pursuit of wisdom, which to him, generally meant all sorts of virtue, everything noble and sublime, the *summum bonum* of moralists and philosophers, but essentially the doctrines of Pharisaic Judaism superimposed on a veneer of Greek philosophical terminology. This and this alone is the chief purpose of our book.

V

DATE OF COMPOSITION

Like everything else in the Book of Wisdom, its date is quite controversial. Thus M. Friedländer[47] ascribes it to the beginning of the second century BCE. Deane[48] places it between 217 and 145, that is "between the epoch marked by the religious op-

[47] *Griechische Philosophie im Alten Testament*, pp. 182 ff.
[48] In his Commentary, p. 32.

pression under Philopator and that rendered memorable by the enormities of the bloated sensualist Physkon." Grimm[49] hovers between 145, when the Jews of Egypt were subject to severe public persecution, and 50 BCE, since it must have come into existence before Philo. Thackeray[50] fixes it at 130–100 BCE; Gregg[51] at 125–100 BCE; Gfrörer[52] at 100 BCE; Siegfried[53] at 100–50 BCE. Schürer[54] argues as follows: "With reference to the time of the author it should be clear beyond doubt that he was younger than Ben Sira but older than Philo. For his standpoint is a preliminary step to that of Philo. This in itself would not yet prove a higher age, but in view of the close relationship of both it is indeed unthinkable that our author would have remained untouched by Philo had he been younger than the latter." P. Heinisch[55] infers from the allusions to the persecution of pious Jews by apostate Jews with the connivance of the Ptolemies (2.10–20; 5.3 f.), that the book was written about 88–30 BCE; as does F. Focke.[56] Samuel Holmes[57] inclines to a date between 50 and 30 BCE. for the first part of the book, and 30 BCE to 10 CE. for the second part. Others thought that Wisdom was composed in the reign of Caligula (37–41 CE.). Thus Graetz[58] saw in 14.16–20 a clear reference to the command of Caligula that his statue should be placed in the Temple of Jerusalem and in the synagogues of Alexandria. Accordingly he believed that the author was a contemporary of Philo, that "his book was intended at once as a defense of his suffering brethren, a panegyric on Judaism and a polemic against paganism and the

---

[49] In his Commentary, pp. 34 f.
[50] *Grammar of Old Testament Greek*, p. 62.
[51] In his Commentary, p. XIII.
[52] *Philo und die jüdisch-alexandrinische Theosophie*, II, 200 ff.
[53] In Kautzsch's *Die Apokryphen und Pseudepigraphen des Alten Testament*, I, 479.
[54] *Geschichte des jüdischen Volkes im Zeitalter Jesu Christi* III (1909), 508.
[55] In his Commentary, pp. XX–XXIII.
[56] *Die Entstehung der Weisheit Salomos*, pp. 74 ff.
[57] In Charles' *Apocrypha and Pseudepigrapha*, I, 520 f.
[58] *Geschichte der Juden*, III, Note 3.

apotheosis of Caesar." Similarly Dean Farrar[59] thought "that it was written in the decade after the death of Christ." This late date is endorsed also by Goodrick.[60]

What is one to draw from this mass of contradictory dates? Evidently neither the language, nor the context, nor the purpose of the book, so far as it reveals itself, is of any appreciable assistance in determining its exact age, and no matter what ingenuities or subtleties we may employ to worm out a plausible conclusion we can never be quite satisfied that we obtained the desired end. All we can say with reasonable assurance is that the Book of Wisdom is later than Ben Sira[61] (circa 180 BCE) and the Septuagint of the Prophets and Hagiographa[62] (about the middle of the second century BCE), which it quotes in a version that differs from the Hebrew; and earlier than Philo's writings[63] and the New Testament books,[64] since the latter presuppose its existence. These two points of contact give us a *terminus a quo* and a *terminus ad quem*. Somewhere between these two points, some time during the last pre-Christian century, the Book of Wisdom must have come into being.

[59] In his Commentary, p. 422.

[60] In his Commentary, pp. 5 ff.

[61] We find no direct quotation from Ecclesiasticus in our book, but there is some similarity of tone between such Wisdom-passages in Ecclus. as 4.11–15; 6.18–28; 15.1–8 and Wisd. ch. 6 and 8. Comp. also Wisd. 4.3 and Ecclus. 23.25; Wisd. 6.18 and Ecclus. 1.26; Wisd. 15.7 f. and Ecclus. 33.10–13.

[62] Comp. Wisd. 2.12 with the Septuagint of Isa. 3.10, and Wisd. 15.10 with the Septuagint of Isa. 44.20. Comp. further Wisd. 12.12 with the Septuagint of Job 9.12 and 19. Moreover, it is difficult to believe that the author of the first ten chapters of Wisdom was not well acquainted with the Septuagint of the Book of Proverbs.

[63] With regard to Philo, comp. Schürer, *loc. cit.*; also Grimm points out that the writer's apparent ignorance of the Alexandrine doctrine of the Logos points to a date earlier than Philo.

[64] As to the New Testament, some close resemblances in diction have been discovered between the Epistle to the Hebrews, and the Book of Wisdom, similarly between 1 Peter and our book.

VI

Authorship

The ascription of the Book of Wisdom to King Solomon, it is generally admitted, is a fiction and has no factual basis whatsoever. Solomonic authorship is a purely literary artifice, in keeping with biblical usage which depicts the great Solomon as a kind of collective name for all sapiential Hebrew literature. In truth, the Book of Wisdom, as will be demonstrated in the course of this introduction, was written in the midst of the Hellenistic period, in a Greek-speaking country, by a Jew well versed in Greek speech and thought.

With regard to the period, it is naturally conditioned by the language in which the book was originally written and which we believe to have been Greek. There can be little doubt that the book originated in the Hellenistic period, when the Jews of Alexandria used Greek as their medium of speech and literary expression. The arguments in favor of this claim are set forth in the proper place.[65]

The locale is evidently Egypt, more specifically Greek-speaking Alexandria, with its speculative thought of a theological or philosophical nature. The entire atmosphere of the book is Hellenistic and Alexandrian. In the first place, there is a close connection between the language of the Book of Wisdom and that of the Septuagint or the Alexandrian version of the Old Testament. Similarly there is a close resemblance between the Book of Wisdom and other Jewish-Alexandrian works of the same period, such as the Third Book of Maccabees. Then the historical and religious treatment of Egypt[66] is expert and apparently based on first-hand experience. The emphasis on Egypt and its relationship to Israel, the description of the Egyptian pantheon and the numerous allusions to animal worship practiced in the country of the Nile,[67] all point in the same direction.

[65] See the chapter on "Language," pp. 22 ff.
[66] In chapters 11, 16–19.
[67] Comp. 15.18 f., 16.1.9, etc.

Again, sympathy with Hellenic thought, with Platonic and Stoic doctrines, and above all affinity with the allegorism and eclecticism of Philo of Alexandria, all make it clear that the Book of Wisdom could have originated nowhere else but in Alexandria.

Not so clear is the matter of authorship, on which *quot homines tot sententiae*. Aside from the fantastic claim of Solomonic authorship, mentioned above, the book has been attributed to Zerubbabel,[68] Ben Sira,[69] Aristobulus or Pseudo-Aristobulus,[70] the older Philo,[71] Philo,[72] et al. There is also a hypothesis that the Book of Wisdom was composed by an Essene or his equivalent in Egypt, one of the Therapeutae.[73] Another hypothesis[74] claims that a Christian was the author of the book. Needless to say, all of these suppositions are far-fetched or at least very doubtful.

Of all the supposed authors mentioned above only two could really come into consideration, namely Aristobulus and Philo. But the former could not be the author, for being a friend of Ptolemy Philometor he would not have written the passages in which kings are reproached for their abuse of authority (6.1–5), while under that king the Jews enjoyed many privileges. As to Philo, there are numerous reasons why he could not have been the author. Philo is abstract and unemotional throughout, whereas the author of Wisdom is laconic and sententious like the gnomic poets of the Old Testament in the first part and quite emotional and impetuous in the last part. Philo is an ac-

[68] J. M. Faber in *Prolusiones de libro Sapient.*, Onoldi 1776 f., Part V.

[69] Augustine, *De doctrina christ.*, 2.8. In justice to him it should be stated that he later retracted this opinion (*Retract.* 2.4)

[70] Lutterbeck, *Die neutestamentliche Lehrbegriffe*, I, 407 ff.

[71] Who was a heathen, according to Josephus, *Contra Apion.*, I, 218.

[72] So some ancient writers before Jerome, Nicolaus de Lyra, Luther, et al.; similarly Gedaliah ben Joseph Ibn Yahya in his Hebrew chronicle entitled *Shalshelet ha-Kabbalah*, ed., Amsterdam 1697, fol. 85a.

[73] See Gfrörer, *Philo*, II, 265.

[74] Propounded by Noack and Dean Plumptre. Against this theory suffice it to quote the judgment of Farrar in the introduction to his Com-

curate thinker, but the author of Wisdom lacks precision of thought. Philo is a philosopher, the author of Wisdom is a rhetorician. As Farrar puts it: Philo allegorises rather than exaggerates; Pseudo-Solomon exaggerates rather than allegorises. More specifically, Philo's famous Logos is foreign to Wisdom, where the word occurs three times in the ordinary sense of ῥῆμα and is identified with σοφία, which is absent in Philo. It is quite apparent that the Logos, which is the foundation of Philo's philosophical system, is entirely wanting in Wisdom, nor is divine wisdom ever identified with the Logos. Moreover, the two differ considerably in their theology. Philo does not recognize a spirit of evil, but the author of Wisdom plainly speaks of it in 224. Philo adheres strictly to the Platonic idea of the natural evil character of the body, which he even calls "utterly polluted prison,"[75] while the author of Wisdom acknowledges that there may be "a body undefiled,"[76] though elsewhere[77] the statement is made that "a corruptible body weighs down the soul." Quite consequentially, Philo does not believe in resurrection, but the author of Wisdom does. Again, Philo's trichotomy of the soul is wanting in Wisdom. Note also that Wisdom's strange approval of the eunuch in 3.14 is contradictory to Philo and Jewish feeling generally. Of course, there are cases in which Wisdom and Philo coincide, but then they are both most likely dependent on Palestinian sources.

Assuming then that Wisdom differs from Philo the question remains: Is Wisdom pre-Philonic or post-Philonic? Farrar[78] was of the opinion that Wisdom was post-Philonic, but his argu-

mentary, p. 414, col. 1: "There is no trace in the book of any knowledge of Christ, nor of the Incarnation, nor of the Atonement, nor of the Resurrection, nor indeed of any doctrine distinctly Christian"; also the verdict of Goodrick in the introduction to his Commentary, p. 46, that of nine texts adduced to support such a view (3.5, 4.2, 10, 5.17, 7.26, 9.8.15 ff., 11.10.24) not a single one shows distinct marks of Christian origin.

[75] *De Migr. Abr.*, 2.
[76] See 8.20.
[77] In 9.15.
[78] In Wace's *Apocrypha*, I, 421.

ments cannot be said to be cogent and convincing. The opposite view recommends itself much better. The author of Wisdom is not an advanced Alexandrian like Philo. He is quite clumsy in his handling of the principles of Greek philosophy and in his allegorising method with regard to the Hebrew Scriptures. Grimm[79] is probably right in maintaining that Wisdom presents an earlier stage of development in the type of thought whose ripened fruit appears in Philo. Schürer[80] is quite positive that the author of Wisdom precedes Philo, since "his standpoint is a preliminary step to Philo's."

The author of Wisdom must have been an Hellenistic Jew, yet pious and loyal to the Law, who lived in Egypt, presumably in Alexandria.[81] He had considerable acquaintance with the poetry and philosophy of Greece, and was conversant with the religious controversies raging in Alexandria. That he belonged to the intellectual and cultured group of Alexandrian Jews may be seen from the fact that he lays great stress on form, that he is sensitive to the euphony and harmony of the language he employs, that he uses many compounded words and even attempts the formation of new expressions and turns of speech. He may have been somewhat confused in his theological and philosophical system, but he was clear and concise in his diction and a master of Greek grammar and syntax. Apparently he wrote the book because he was grieved to see that his countrymen in Egypt were weakened by unfaithfulness within and harassed by

[79] In the introduction to his Commentary, p. 23.

[80] *Geschichte des jüdischen Volkes*, II, 3.234.

[81] Professor Margoliouth (l.c. p. 295), on the contrary, argues that the author of the Book of Wisdom was a Palestinian Jew. His chief argument is the ignorance manifested on the part of the author with regard to the land of Egypt. "He knows," he says, "nothing of Egypt beyond what he might have got from the Bible." He points out especially that "Wisdom does not refer to the scarcity of water, but speaks of the 'ever-flowing river,' which is an incorrect description." However, Margoliouth was answered effectually by Freudenthal in the *JQR.* for 1891. The flimsiness of Margoliouth's arguments may be seen from the following, that because the writer of Wisdom refers with affection to Jerusalem and never once to the rival temple of Onias at Leontopolis, he therefore did not dwell in Egypt.

oppression from without, to the extent of apostatizing from their true religion and becoming idolators like the Egyptians. So he composed the book for the purpose of showing them the bankruptcy of materialism and the futility of idolatry and recommending to them the pursuit of Almighty Wisdom. It is against these apostates and renegades that the first five chapters are directed.[82]

However, not all scholars are convinced of the unity and homogeneity of the book, and quite a few believe in composite or multiple authorship. Thus Nachtigal,[83] Bretschneider,[84] Bertholet,[85] Engelbreth,[86] Kohler,[87] Gärtner,[88] Holmes,[89] Focke,[90] and Weber[91] advocated composite authorship. Following Houbigant,[92] Eichhorn[93] pointed out (1) that in the earlier chapters the history of Israel was treated with sobriety and restraint, in the last chapters with gross exaggeration; (2) that first freethinking is the cause of all evil, then idolatry; (3) that first virtue is the basis of immortality, then the recognition of God; (4) that the first section has no sign of particularism, while the last is full of it; (5) that σοφία is the mainspring of the first part, but plays no part whatever in the last part. Ex-

---

[82] For an account of apostasy in Palestine under Antiochus Epiphanes see I Macc. 1.11–16.43–64; II Macc. 4.10; and for that in Egypt under Physcon see III Macc. 2.31. Comp. also Philo, *Mos.*, I.6: "They despise countrymen and friends, they transgress the laws under which they were born and brought up, they change their national customs against which no fault can be alleged, and they live under an alien rule and for the sake of present advantages forget all their old associations."

[83] *Das Buch der Weisheit*, Halle 1799, pp. 1 ff.

[84] *De libri Sap. parte priore Cap. I–XI e duobus libellis diversis conflata* (Viteb. 1804), I, 9 ff.

[85] *Einleitung in sämtl. Schriften des A.N.T.*, V, 2261, especially 2276 ff.

[86] *Libr. Sap. Sal. interpretandi specimina* (Havn. 1816), pp. 9 ff.

[87] In *Jewish Encyclopedia*, XII, 540, col. 1 below.

[88] *Komposition und Wortwahl des Buches der Weisheit*, pp. 61 ff.

[89] In *Apocrypha and Pseudepigrapha*, ed. Charles, I, 524.

[90] *Die Entstehung der Weisheit Salomos* (Göttingen, 1913), pp. 21 ff.

[91] In *Zeitschrift für wissenschaftliche Theologie*, XLVII (1904), 145 ff.

[92] *Notae criticae in omnes V. T. libros* (Frankf. a.M., 1777), I, CCXVI ff.

[93] *Einleitung in die apokryphischen Schriften des A.T.* (Leipzig, 1795), pp. 86 ff.

pressly Focke attributes chapters 1–5 and 6–19 to different authors, for the following reasons: (1) Wisdom, with a few exceptions, plays no role in 1–5; (2) Greek philosophical terms are absent in 1–5; (3) the deity is ethical in 1–5 but nationalistic in 6–19; (4) resurrection is implicit in 1–5 but the insignificance of the body and the immortality of the soul are taught in 6–19; (5) 1–5 contrasts Pharisees and Sadducees, while 6–19 contrasts Israelites and heathen. He consequently concludes that the first part is Palestinian and the second Alexandrian, explaining the uniformity of the Greek diction by the supposition that the author of the second part translated the first from the Hebrew. Weber traces four different hands in the book, and in this theory he is followed by Gärtner.

But against these scholars there are many who defend the unity of the book, such as Heydenreich,[94] Bauermeister,[95] Gfrörer,[96] Grimm,[97] Farrar,[98] Bois,[99] Siegfried,[100] Goodrick,[101] and Feldmann.[102] Grimm especially is adamant in his defense, marshalling such cogent arguments that he almost lays the critics low. Siegfried called the book "the well-arranged product of a single author." Feldmann contended most vigorously against Weber and his fantastic hypothesis of quadruple authorship. Goodrick is convinced of the unity of authorship, but thinks that the "Solomonic chapters" (7–9) may have been added by the same man after the rest of the book had been completed. As he puts it[103]: "It is possible that a writer who had laid aside his work, dictated in the beginning by irritation at apostasy and persecution, gave it a new colour by adapting it to

[94] In Tzschirner's *Memorabilia*, V, 2, 29 ff.
[95] *Commentar. in libros Sapientiae*, pp. 3 ff.
[96] *Philo*, II (1831), 200 ff.
[97] In his Commentary of 1860, pp. 9 ff.
[98] In *Apocrypha*, ed. Henry Wace (London, 1888), I, 415.
[99] *Essai sur les origines des la philosophie Judéo-Alexandrine*, pp. 211 ff.
[100] In Kautzsch's *Die Apokryphen und Pseudepigraphen*, I, 479.
[101] *The Book of Wisdom* (New York, 1913), pp. 37 ff.
[102] In a brilliant article entitled "Zur Einheit des Buches der Weisheit" in *Biblische Zeitschrift* for 1909, pp. 140 ff.
[103] Loc. cit. p. 39.

philosophic ideas which he had only lately assimilated, and, its original interest having passed with the times of persecution which suggested it, should endeavour to obtain a vogue for it by the direct ascription of it to Solomon."

Here are some arguments in favor of composite authorship:

1) The difference in style and tone between the first and last parts of the book.

2) The absence of references to Wisdom and the doctrine of immortality of the soul in the last part of the book.

3) Elimination of the transcendental view of God in the last part. But most important of all is

4) A number of striking linguistic differences, especially in the use of particles and choice of words.[104]

The arguments for the unity of the book are as follows:

1) The same extensive vocabulary throughout, including poetical and rhetorical figures as well as rhythmical structure.

2) The use of Greek philosophic doctrines throughout, e.g. the Stoic doctrine of the world-soul at the beginning of the book, and the Stoic doctrine of the metabolism of the four elements at the end.

3) Omission of proper names throughout the book. But most important of all is

4) The use of certain unusual words and expressions throughout.[105]

There is still another possibility, a compromise between uniform and composite authorship, namely that the book may have been written by one and the same person, but on different occasions, at different times of his life. Assuming that the Book of Wisdom is not a homogeneous whole, this does not have to

---

[104] For details comp. Holmes in Charles' *Apocrypha and Pseudepigrapha*, I, 522 ff.

[105] Such as μεταλλεύειν in 4.12 and 16.25; ἀπότομος in 5.20, 6.5, 11.10, 12.9 and 18.15; ἀνυπόκριτος in 5.18 and 18.16; κίβδηλος in 2.16 and 15.9; συγγνωστός in 6.6. and 13.8; παντοδύναμος in 7.23, 11.17 and 18.15; γεώδης in 9.15 and 15.13; διέπειν in 9.3 and 12.15; διερευνᾶν in 6.3 and 13.7; κακότεχνος in 1.4 and 15.4; ἐν ὄψει in 3.4, 7.9, 8.11, 14.17 and 15.19; θηρίων θυμοί in 7.20 and 16.5; λογισμοὶ ἀσύνετοι in 1.5 and 11.15.

mean that the book was composed by more than one person. It is quite possible that one and the same writer may have composed different parts of the book at different times, under different circumstances, and perhaps even with a different object in view. This was the view of Houbigant and after him Eichhorn, both of whom believed that there was a world of difference in language and style between the first and last part of the book, and consequently conjectured that the last part was composed by our author in his youth and the first part in his mature years. This view is plausible and appeals to conservative minds.

VII

LANGUAGE

Ever since the Book of Wisdom came to be attributed to Solomon it was natural to assume that it was originally composed in Hebrew. Thus the Church Fathers Clement of Alexandria, Tertullian, Cyprian, Hippolytus, and Lactantius, ascribed it to Solomon and assumed a Hebrew origin.[106] Similarly some medieval rabbis, such as Gedaliah ben Joseph Ibn Yahya[107] and Azariah dei Rossi.[108]

In modern times critics modified their claim of Hebrew origin, so as to cover only part of the book. Thus Charles Francois Houbigant[109] claimed that only ch. 1–9 are genuinely Solomonic, hence were written originally in Hebrew; the rest, ch. 10–19, were composed in Greek, possibly by the same man who trans-

---

[106] Comp. Schürer, *Geschichte des jüdischen Volkes im Zeitalter Jesu Christi*,[4] III, 509 f.

[107] In *Shalshelet ha-Kabbalah*, p. 104.

[108] In *Meor Ennayim*, p. 175 b.

[109] In the Preface to his edition of the Book of Wisdom, which appeared in the third volume of his *Biblia Hebraica*, Paris, 1753. See further his *Notae Criticae*, Frankfort 1777, p. CCXVI: *Nec tamen putandum est Librum Sapientiae totum esse unius ejusdemque autoris, sed potius partem priorem in qua extant et vaticinationes et sententiae Salomonis Proverbiis fere similes esse ipsius Salomonis, partem posteriorem alterius scriptoris; forte ejus qui priorem Graece converterat quique addiderat de suo partem posteriorem.*

lated the first nine chapters from Hebrew into Greek. Another critic, Karl Gottlieb Bretschneider,[110] limited the Hebrew original to chapters 1, 1–6.8. Engelbreth[111] further reduced it to chapters 1.1–5. 23s. F. Focke[112] reached the conclusion that only the first five chapters of the book were originally written in Hebrew, in Jerusalem, about the time of Alexander Jannaeus, by a Pharisee arguing against the Sadducees. This part was later translated into Greek by an Alexandrian Jew and added to the rest of the book which is a denunciation of the Egyptian king Ptolemy (Soter II) who persecuted the Jews. It will be noticed that Focke really reverted to Houbigant's theory in general, though he mentioned only three cases of mistranslation from the supposed Hebrew: 5.7, 1.3, and 2.6. Worth mentioning is the fact that N. Peters,[113] following the deductions of Focke, has reconstructed a Hebrew psalm with an alphabetic acrostic out of ch. 9 of the Book of Wisdom.

In recent years Professor Margoliouth was a staunch advocate of a Hebrew original of the Book of Wisdom. In a brilliant article entitled "Was the Book of Wisdom written in Hebrew?",[114] he adduced a goodly number of Greek expressions from our book which he stamped as Hebraisms or else reduced to Neo-Hebrew locutions. He argued that many passages in the Book of Wisdom could be better explained through the assumption of a Hebrew original, which was often misunderstood, and, further, that a part at least of the variants of the Peshitta of Wisdom may be explained by the hypothesis that it was made or corrected from a Hebrew original, and as a corollary that the old Latin version often agrees with the Syriac and not with the Greek. Naturally he was forced to argue also that the book was of Palestinian, not Egyptian, origin; that "the writer shows no acquaintance with Egypt beyond what he might have got from the Bible, and that

[110] *De libri Sapientiae parte priore*, Wittenberg 1804.
[111] *Libri qui vulgo inscribitur Sapientia Salomonis*, Havniae 1816.
[112] *Die Entstehung der Weisheit Solomos*, pp. 82 f.
[113] In *Biblische Zeitschrift*, XIV (1916), 1 ff.
[114] Published in the *Journal of the Royal Asiatic Society* for 1890, pp. 263 ff.

he shows a familiarity with the interpretation of the Midrash
which points to the Palestinian School."

It should be stated, however, that Margoliouth's thesis has
been thoroughly confuted by Freudenthal,[115] by adducing numerous specimens of Greek rhetoric and also cases of paronomasia which it would hardly be possible for a translator to con-
struct. In addition, he stressed the prevalence of Greek ideas
and philosophical terms in the book which hardly have an equivalent in the Hebrew language. He also pointed out that the
Hebrew reconstructions and assumed originals of Margoliouth
were not always on a par and beyond criticism from a purely
Hebrew standpoint.

History repeats itself, and once more, in spite of Freudenthal's cogent arguments, scholars come forth to battle for a Hebrew original in at least part of the Book of Wisdom. Following
Margoliouth's lead E. A. Speiser[116] and C. E. Purinton[117] argued
for an Hebrew origin of the first 10 chapters. Speiser in fact
thought to have found eleven cases of mistranslation from Hebrew; while Purinton claimed that the translation from Hebrew
ends with 11.1 and that the Greek original begins with 11.2.

In support of a Hebrew original many arguments have been
adduced, such as Wisdom's imitation of *parallelismus membro-
rum*, occasional asyndetic and paratactic constructions, use of
the same stem in verb and noun, Hebraic modes of thought and
expression, above all a number of undeniable Hebraisms.[118]

---

[115] In the *Jewish Quarterly Review*, III (1891), 722 ff.

[116] In *JQR*., N.S., XIV (1923–24), 455 ff.

[117] In *JBL*., XLVII (1928), 276 ff.

[118] Such as the following: ἁπλότης καρδίας (1.1) = לבב חֹם; μερίς and
κλῆρος (2.9) = חלק and חבל respectively; τρίβοι ~ (2.15, 5.7, 9.18, 10.10) =
ארחות חיים; λογίζεσθαι εἴς τι (2.16) = 'הֶחְשֵׁב ל; ἐν χειρί τινος (3.1, 7.16, 11.1)
= בְּיַד; πληροῦν χρόνον (4.13) = מָלֵא יָמִים; θέντες ἐπὶ διανοίᾳ (4.14) = שׂם עַל
לֵב; ὅσιοι τοῦ θεοῦ (4.15) = קָדְשֵׁי אֵל; ὑποστελεῖται πρόσωπον (6.7) = נָשׂא
פָנִים; εὑρίσκεσθαι (7.29, 8.11) = הִמָּצֵא; ἐξ ὅλης καρδίας (8.21) = בְּכָל לֵב;
εὐθύτης ψυχῆς ~ (9.3) = טוֹב לֵב or יְשַׁר לֵב, and κρίσιν κρίνῃ (ibid.) = מִשְׁפָּט
שָׁפַט; υἱοὶ ἀνθρώπων (9.6) = בְּנֵי אָדָם; ἄριστον ἐν ὀφθαλμοῖς τινος (9.9) =
יְשַׁר בְּעֵינֵי; αἰών (13.9, 18.4) = עוֹלָם; πλήττειν ἀορασίᾳ (19.17) = ~ הִכָּה בַּסַּנְוֵרִים.

However, one must not forget that these Hebraisms are part
and parcel of Hellenistic Greek, as proved conclusively by
Adolf Deissmann,[119] and do not have to come from a Hebrew
original. Through contacts with the Semitic peoples, especially
the Hebrews, specifically through the Septuagint or the Greek
version of the Old Testament, Hellenistic Greek became Semi-
tized or Hebraized to a great extent, that is, it became suffused
with Hebrew forms and expressions, exactly as modern English
became suffused with biblical forms and expressions since the
King James Version of the Bible. Hebrew modes and expressions were mingled with the Greek of Alexandria to suit the
new theology and philosophy of the period. We have the testimony of Jerome in his preface to the Book of Wisdom that the
book was composed in Greek.[120] Abundant evidence in support
of a Greek original is presented by Grimm[121]; and Freudenthal[122]
has shown conclusively that the Book of Wisdom was composed
in Greek by an Alexandrian Jew. Indeed, it cannot be empha-
sized too much that the book of Wisdom was composed in
Greek, not in Hebrew, and that its character is Hellenistic
throughout. Naturally, dealing with subject-matter that is
Hebraic, there are bound to be many allusions to Hebrew
thoughts and concepts, but there is a far cry from this to the assumption of a Hebrew original. Its affectation of Greek eloquence, its reminiscences of Greek authors, its allusions to Greek
manners and customs, speak clearly against a Hebrew origin.
According to the best authorities, it is written in the purest
form of Alexandrian Greek, free from the Hebraisms and
anomalies of the Septuagint, and full of passages which combine

To these Margoliouth adds the following: ἡ κτίσις (2.6) = בריאה;
στενοχωρία πνεύματος (5.3) = קצר רוח; τὸ διάδημα τοῦ κάλλους (5.16) = תפארת
עטרת; γηγενοῦς πρωτοπλαστοῦ (7.1) = יליד עפר יציר קדם; σύστασις κόσμου (7.17)
= סדר התבל.

[119] *Die Hellenisierung des semitischen Monotheismus,* Leipzig 1903. See
also his *Bibelstudien,* Marburg 1895, and *Neue Bibelstudien,* Marburg 1897.

[120] *Liber qui Sapientia Salomonis inscribitur apud Hebraeos nusquam est,
quin et ipse stylus Graecam eloquentiam redolet.*

[121] In his learned Commentary, pp. 5–9.

[122] In his rebuttal of Margoliouth in *JQR.,* III (1891), 722 ff.

the richest vocabulary with genuine rhetorical eloquence.[123] Compared with the Septuagint, Wisdom appears to be an original and independent work: it is written not in the impotent κοινή, but in vigorous classical Greek, which only at times appears to be labored and artificial. Evidently it was written in Greek by an Alexandrian Jew who was also familiar with the Greek Bible or the Septuagint, especially the Wisdom literature. Hence some phrases seem to be Hebraic, especially since they are couched in the form of parallelism. True, the Book of Wisdom is encumbered with idiotisms and solecisms, Hebraisms and Semitisms, but so are the writings of Philo, and yet no one would think of claiming a Hebrew origin for Philo's works.

Here are some cogent reasons and arguments for a Greek original:

1) The Greek of Wisdom is generally spontaneous and free from the constraint which is inevitable in a translation.

2) The book is full of poetical words and rare usages found only in the early Greek poets. In fact, Epiphanius[124] speaks of the book as written stichometrically, and critics have ascertained that it is divided in our Greek manuscripts into 1098 stichs. Its author is sometimes claimed to have been a Jewish Isocrates, and Bois[125] even makes him out to be a poet.

3) The book exhibits a number of unusual compound words, which are characteristic of Alexandrian Greek.[126]

4) All sorts of rhetorical devices make their appearance in the Book of Wisdom: alliteration, assonance, juxtaposition of similarly sounding words, paronomasia, chiasmus (1.1.4.8; 3.15,

---

[123] Comp. William J. Deane, *The Book of Wisdom*, p. 27, col. 1.

[124] *De Mens. et Pond.*, ch. IV.

[125] *Essai sur les origines de la philisophie Judéo-Alexandrine*, p. 212. See further on Wisdom's dexterity of rhythm H. St. John Thackeray in *Journal of Theological Studies*, VI, 232 ff. Comp. also the lyrical outbursts about the vanity of life in 2.1–9 and 5.8–13 with Ecclesiastes, who expressed similar thoughts in Hebrew.

[126] Comp. the following: ἀκηλίδωτος (4.9), ἀναποδισμός (2.5), βραχυτελής (15.9), γενεσιάρχης (13.3), γηγενής (7.1), εἰδέχθαια (16.3), εὐδράνεια (13.19), κακόμοχθος (15.8), μετακιρνᾶσθαι (16.21), νηπιοκτόνος (11.7), πρωτόπλαστος (7.1 and 10.1); τεκνοφόνος (14.23), ὑπέρμαχος (10.20 and 16.17).

etc.), sorites (6.17–20), multiple epithets (7.22–23).[127] This rhetorical and idiomatic style of the Greek precludes the possibility of its being a translation from some other language.

5) Moreover, the Book of Wisdom contains technical Greek terms which could hardly be expressed in the Hebrew of that period.[128]

6) The book shows an acquaintance and familiarity with Greek customs and mores,[129] which can only be predicated of a writer who wrote in Greek.

7) There are at least two passages in Wisdom, 2.12 and 15.10, in which the Septuagint version of Isa. 3.10 and 44.20 is quoted in a widely different form than that of the Masoretic Hebrew.[130]

8) Another argument against a Hebrew original is the fact that some of the least Hebraic ideas occur in the first ten chapters of the book, for whose Hebraic origin most evidence has been adduced so far.[131]

Yet, after all is said and done, we must admit that our author exhibits also some ignorance and poverty of diction, which

[127] For numerous examples see Gregg in the introduction to his Commentary, p. XVI.

[128] See especially 5.22, 7.17.22–26, 8.1.7.19 f., 9.15.

[129] Thus 2.8 probably refers to the use of garlands at banquets; 4.2 refers to the crowning of victors at a contest; 8.4 tells about mysteries and those initiated into them; 13.15 deals with little shrines set up for domestic gods; 14.1 may be an allusion to the ancient heathen custom of placing images of protecting gods at the prow of vessels, and so on.

[130] 2.12 ἐνεδρεύσωμεν δὲ τὸν δίκαιον, ὅτι δύσχρηστος ἡμῖν ἐστι appears to be a quotation from an erroneous Septuagint version of Isa. 3.10 כי טוב: אמרו צדיק δήσωμεν τὸν δίκαιον ὅτι δύσχρηστος ἡμῖν ἐστι (the only difference being in the first word: "lie in wait" instead of "bind" = אסרו). 15.10 σποδὸς ἡ καρδία αὐτοῦ, which is the Septuagint reading of Isa. 44.20, seems to be a mistranslation of the Hebrew אפר לב, the second word being erroneously included in the first member of the sentence. Both these examples point to a Greek original.

[131] Passages like 4.2, Greek in thought and experience, are a potent argument against the assumption of a Hebrew original. I might add that chapter 17 is of such poetical character and plastic beauty that W. Headlam (*A Book of Greek Verse*, Cambridge 1907) considered it worth while to translate it into English metre together with other pieces of the Greek Bible.

justifies perhaps Freudenthal's dictum that he was writing in a
foreign language which he really did not know thoroughly. This
poverty of diction manifests itself in various ways and places.
Thus we find some thirty pet expressions used too frequently,
such as ἀπότομος 7 times, παροδεύειν 5 times, εὐεργετεῖν 4
times, καταδυναστεύειν 3 times.[132] More serious is misunder-
standing of Greek words, such as μεταλλεύειν "to mine," which
is used in lieu of μεταλλάσειν "to change" in 4.12 and 16.25;
ἀγερωχία "haughtiness, insolence," which is used in 2.9 in the
sense of "revelry which knows no old age," as if associating it
with the root of γέρων; πάχνη "hoar-frost, rime," which seems
to be used in 5.14 in the sense of ἀράχνη "spider's web"; βραβεύειν
meaning "to act as umpire in a contest" is employed in 10, 12 in
the sense of "giving the victory to a competitor"; the composite φιλόψυχος meaning "cowardly" is used in 11.26 literally
as "lover of souls," and so on. Again, the author of the Book of
Wisdom sometimes uses a word in one sense in one line and in
another in the next, comp. ἐλέγχειν meaning once "confute" and
then "convict," or ἐπισκοπή meaning once "inspection" and
then "visitation." A very good example of lack of clarity and
confusion of diction is 17.6 τῆς μὴ θεωρουμένης ἐκείνης ὄψεως
ἡγοῦντο χείρω τὰ βλεπόμενα, on which scholars differ considerably.[133] Certainly the last chapters show turgid and grotesque
diction, justifying Grimm's verdict[134]: "The writer's effort to
produce a lively and picturesome representation here breaks
away from his formal arguments, and he commits the error of
tricking out historical material, intended for doctrinal instruction, with fantastic adornments and exaggerations; those additions to the Mosaic account which the author permits himself
cannot in all cases be even justified by later tradition. The parallel drawn between the Egyptians' sins and their punishment,
and also that between their plagues and the Israelites' blessings,
are overstated and wearisome and at times degenerate into
trifling and childishness."

[132] See Grimm in the introduction to his Commentary, p. 6.
[133] See Commentary ad loc.
[134] In the introduction to his Commentary, p. 7.

It should be pointed out also that the connecting particles seem to be used by the writer of Wisdom in the most haphazard way, and that it is useless to found arguments upon them. The constant repetition of καί often renders it advisable, both for the sake of variety and to emphasize its intensive use, to translate it "yea" or "yea, and."[135]

But these flaws and shortcomings, with all their unseemliness, do not impair in the least the probability, nay the certainty, that the Book of Wisdom was written originally in Greek. We simply have to assume that it was composed by an Alexandrian Jew who was well versed in the Greek language, classical and otherwise, but to whom not all its secrets had been revealed. Add to this the Semitic or Hebraic background, and the result is exactly a literary product of the type of the Book of Wisdom, with all its superior and inferior qualities.

VIII

THEOLOGY AND PHILOSOPHY

The theology of the Book of Wisdom is thoroughly Alexandrian, a coordination of Hellenistic thought with Hebrew revelation, an amalgam of Greek philosophy with Jewish religion. This theology, evolved by Hellenistic Judaism in the course of centuries, was a sort of logosophic theology, i.e. an interlacing of the Scriptural concept of wisdom with the Greek logos of Heraclitus and the Stoic philosophers.[136] From Aristobulus to Philo Jewish scholars and writers in Alexandria, well aware of the beauty and charm of Greek culture but convinced of the religious and ethical superiority of Judaism, endeavored to reconcile Hebrew doctrine with Greek philosophy through the allegorical interpretation of the Scriptures.[137] This mode of interpretation led to the sublimation of the biblical narratives and their crystallization into universal principles. The concrete be-

[135] Comp. Goodrick in his Commentary, p. 110.
[136] Comp. Menahem Stein in the introduction to his Hebrew translation of the Book of Wisdom, in Kahana's הספרים החיצונים, vol. I.
[137] See Wolfson, *Philo*, I, 1 ff., and especially 115 ff. dealing with the allegorical method.

came abstract, the particular was universalized, and thus a point of contact was established between two different civilizations. Through the process of symbolization and especially through dexterous manipulation of the Scriptures and the Greek philosophers it became possible to equate even some of their diametrically opposed doctrines. In this way Aristobulus undertook to show that the Peripatetic philosophy of Aristotle was influenced by the Pentateuch and the Hebrew Prophets.[138] In fact, he maintained that all the Greek philosophers and many Greek poets borrowed their ideas from the Pentateuch. His followers and disciples, whose aim was forever to glorify Judaism in the eyes of the pagans, did not hesitate to proclaim that the entire Greek culture was derived from the Old Testament, which they regarded as the source of all knowledge and the fountain-head of all wisdom.

This allegorizing tendency, which is so characteristically Alexandrian and reached its acme of perfection in Philo, is quite evident in our book: 10.7 the pillar of salt represents incredulity; 10.17 the cloud stands for wisdom; 16.5–7 the brazen serpent points to salvation; 16.28 the manna stands for prayer; 17.21 the Egyptian darkness is equivalent to hell; 18.24 Aaron's ephod represents the whole world,[139] and so on. From this process of symbolization to the identification of some biblical principles with some concepts or ideas of the Greek philosophers was only a short step, dependent on the acumen and will to compromise of the particular scholar.

Thus the author of Wisdom adopted from Plato and his followers the doctrine that matter is eternal (11.17); that it is essentially evil, and that therefore an evil nature attaches to the human body (1.4); that the soul pre-exists (8.20) and finds in the body a temporary prison-house (9.15). From the Stoics he derived the four cardinal virtues which wisdom teaches, namely temperance, prudence, justice and fortitude (8.7), and probably also his idea of a world-soul (11.7, 7.24, 12.1). As pointed out by

[138] Clement of Alexandria, *Stromata*, V. 14.97.
[139] The Greek κόσμος meaning both "ornate garment" and "universe."

Gregg,[140] the author "makes no effort to disguise his sympathy with Hellenic thought. He is a Euhemerist in his account of the origin of idol-worship (xiv); he is a Platonist in his sense of the beauty of the world, and in his argument that its beauty points to a supreme First Cause. He draws on Plato for his doctrine of pre-existing matter (xi.17), of the pre-existence of the soul (viii.19), and of the body as an obstacle in the path to spiritual knowledge (ix.15). The teaching of the Stoics suggested to him the penetrating quality of Wisdom (vii.24), and her quickness of understanding (vii.22). The doctrine of Providence (xiv.3) and the conception of the four cardinal virtues (viii.7), were a loan partly from Plato and partly from the Stoics." Menzel[141] lists 135 places where connection between the Book of Wisdom and Greek philosophy has been traced by one scholar or another. According to Edmund Pfleiderer,[142] the writer of Wisdom had an intimate knowledge of Greek philosophy and especially a direct acquaintance with Heraclitus. He proves this especially through the metabolism of the elements at the end of our book, which the Stoics adopted from Heraclitus. It is true that Paul Heinisch[143] criticizes this contention and endeavors to prove that the writer of Wisdom did not have even a superficial knowledge of the system of Heraclitus, but his point is not well taken and there are loopholes in his argument.[144]

Among the philosophical doctrines enunciated in our book are the following:

[140] *The Wisdom of Solomon*, p. XVII.
[141] *Der griechische Einfluss auf Prediger und Weisheit Salomos*, pp. 39–70.
[142] *Die Philosophie des Heraklitus*, pp. 289–348.
[143] *Die griechische Philosophie im Buche der Weisheit*, pp. 18–30.
[144] Heinisch maintains (*ibid.* p. 156) that the writer of Wisdom "taught nothing which contradicted the faith inherited from his fathers. That which was new, which he expounded in his speculations on Wisdom and in his Eschatology, made no breach with the ideas of the Old Testament . . . and if it has found acceptance in the New Testament, that is only a proof that the sacred writer in his literary activity was under the guidance of divine inspiration." Surprisingly enough he admits that the writer of Wisdom had read Xenophon's *Memorabilia*: he quotes 2.1 from the latter side by side with Wisdom 8.2–18, and points out that in nearly every one of these verses there is an echo of the passage in the *Memorabilia*.

1) Pre-existence of the individual soul. 8.19 f. is unmistakable about this point: "Now I was a child of fine parts, and to my lot fell a good soul, or rather being good I came into a body un-defiled." This is consonant with Plato's teaching on the pre-existence of the soul, as summed up by Zeller.[145] There are two more passages, 15.8 and 15.11, which seem to be based on the belief of the pre-existence of the soul, but these reflect the dictum of Gen. 2.7: "Then the Lord God formed man of the dust of the ground, and breathed into his nostrils the breath of life; and man became a living soul." According to this, the *neshamah* or soul is in existence with God before man is created. From this undoubtedly evolved the midrashic statement that in the seventh heaven God kept the souls of those whom He intends to send on earth.[146] R. Simlai, an Amora of the third century, advances the same concept of the pre-existence of the soul, for he speaks of the soul as a being of the highest intelligence, which sees before birth all things throughout the world, but forgets all at birth, so that all subsequent learning is only a recollection.[147] It should be stated that Porter[148] attacks the prevalent view that the author of Wisdom accepted the Greek doctrine of the pre-existence of soul. The soul, he states, "is not the man's self, the person, but is an individualisation and personification of that breath or spirit of God, which is the life of the man, and uniting

---

[145] In his *Outlines of Greek Philosophy*, pp. 152 f.: "The soul of man is in its nature homogeneous with the soul of the universe, from which it springs. Being of a simple and incorporeal nature it is by its power of self-movement the origin of motion in the body; inseparably connected with the idea of life, it has neither end nor beginning. As the souls have descended from a higher world into the earthly body, they return after death, if their lives have been pure and devoted to higher objects, to this higher world, while those who need correction in part undergo punishments in another world, and in part migrate through the bodies of men and animals. In its earlier existence our soul has seen the ideas of which it is reminded by the sight of their sensuous copies."

[146] Midrash Sifre. 143 b.

[147] Tractate Nid. 30 b.

[148] "The Pre-Existence of the Soul in the Book of Wisdom and in the Rabbinic Writings," in *Old Testament and Semitic Studies in Memory of William Rainey Harper*, pp. 208 ff.

with the earthly body, makes him a living being. The pre-existence of the *neshamah* was no doubt thought of as real; but since it was not the man himself, its pre-existence was of more significance for the conception of God than for that of man. It expressed the idea that God foreknows and has predetermined the number and lot of all men; and it is substantially the same idea, and not a different one, that is expressed when it is said that God has fixed the number of men who are to be born, so that at conception or during the prenatal period of each man's existence He creates or forms the *neshamah* within him." But this argument, remarkable for its subtlety, is hardly convincing.

2) Immortality of the soul. This doctrine is expressed in 1.12 f. and 3.1, and is strictly Platonic.[149] But at the same time this doctrine, decried by the Sadducees, was appropriated by the Pharisees, who derived it from Deut. 31.16 "and this people will rise up," Isa. 26.19 "thy dead shall live," and Dan. 12.2 "and many of them that sleep in the dust of the earth shall awake, some to everlasting life." Thus the Mishnah[150] declares: "He who says that there is no resurrection of the dead shall have no share in the world to come."

3) Resurrection of the soul, not of the body. This doctrine too was derived by the Pharisees from the Scriptures, namely Ezek. ch. 37 dealing with the revivification of the dry bones.[151] One of the earliest prayers in the Jewish liturgy[152] is that of

[149] Comp. Zeller, op. cit., p. 155; Menzel, op. cit., p. 58.

[150] Sanh. X. 1. The expression עולם הבא is post-biblical and occurs first in Tannaitic literature. The relation of the future world to this world is expressed in the dictum of Abot 4.21: "This world is like an antechamber to the world to come; prepare thyself in the antechamber that thou mayest enter the hall." And the rabbinic conception of the future world is given in the following dictum of Raba (Ber. 17 d): "In the future world there is neither eating nor drinking nor marrying nor business, but the righteous sit with their crowns on their heads feasting on the brightness of the Divine Presence."

[151] In spite of negative statements such as Job 7.9 "he who goes down to the grave shall come up no more."

[152] Probably going back to Maccabean times.

34 THE BOOK OF WISDOM

"resurrecting the dead," at the beginning of the Amidah, or the Eighteen Benedictions. As might have been expected, the Sadducees denied the doctrine of resurrection.[153]

4) Corruption of the body. This doctrine is expressed in 9.15 and is probably based on Plato's teaching.[154] Judaism never regarded the body as impure. According to it, "the whole human personality, including both soul and body, is divine, just so far as it asserts its freedom and molds its motives toward a divine end. In recognition of this fact Hillel claimed reverence for the human body as well as mind, comparing it to the homage rendered to the statue of a king, for man is made in the image of God, the king of all the world."[155]

5) Creation of the world out of primordial and eternal formless matter. This doctrine about creation ἐξ ἀμόρφου ὕλης (11.17) was taught by both Plato and the Stoics,[156] but it is contrary to the prevalent Jewish view of *creatio ex nihilo*, which is voiced in II Maccabees in the appeal made by the heroic mother to the youngest of her seven sons.[157]

6) Stoicism versus Epicureanism. Endorsement of all the virtues preached by the Stoics and warning against the vices practiced by the Epicureans. The following Stoic doctrines are emulated in our book: 1) The idea of *anima mundi* or world soul (1.7); 2) the all-pervading character of Wisdom (7.22 ff.); 3) metabolism of the elements through which the second part of the book endeavors to rationalize the miracles of the Exodus (19.18 ff.); 4) the four cardinal virtues, which the Stoics borrowed from Plato (8.7). Some commentators[158] claim that there is a direct attempt in the book to controvert the Epicurean teachings of Koheleth or Ecclesiastes.

[153] See p. Sanh. 16.4.
[154] *Phaedo* 81 C. Comp. Zeller, op. cit., p. 155.
[155] Kohler, *Jewish Theology*, p. 209.
[156] Comp. Zeller, op. cit., p. 147.
[157] II Macc. 7.28. Comp. also Gen. r. I, 12; X, 3; and Hag. 11b–13a, where R. Gamaliel II scornfully rejects the suggestion of a heretic that God used primeval substances already extant in creating the world.
[158] Like Nachtigal and others.

7) Opposition to paganism and idolatry of all sorts (ch. 13–15). In this, Greek philosophy was at one with Jewish doctrine. According to Jewish tradition the basis of all moral evil is idolatry,[159] and similarly Greek philosophy considered idolatry a hindrance to moral development, a sure guide to debauchery. There is even an allusion in our book to the theory of Euhemerus that idolatry arose from the worship of deceased heroes (14.15).

8) Divine providence. This doctrine is expressed in 6.7, 14.3 and 17.2, and the Greek term for it, $\pi\rho\acute{o}\nu o\iota a$, occurs here for the first time in the Greek Bible, although it is found in early Greek authors.[160] Pythagoras as well as Plato taught divine providence.[161] Philo[162] says: "From the creation-story we learn that God exercises a providence over the world. By the laws of nature the maker must always care for the thing made, even as parents take thought for their offspring." Bois[163] sees in $\pi\rho\acute{o}\nu o\iota a$ only another designation of Wisdom.

9) Divine retribution for human deeds before or after death. Nothing escapes the ken of God, and just as every good deed is followed by an appropriate reward so every crime is accompanied by an adequate punishment, which may be disciplinary and remedial.[164] The age-old problem of the prosperity of the wicked and the sufferings of the righteous is resolved by the assumption that retribution may be exacted beyond death, in the hereafter.

10) Concept of Wisdom. Though derived primarily from Prov. ch. 8 and Job ch. 28, the term *sofia* was naturally colored by Greek ideas and concepts.[165] Wisdom is throughout the book repeatedly apotheosized and personified, to the extent of

---

[159] Sifre on Num. § 111; ed. Friedmann, pp. 31 b f.
[160] On providence in Greek philosophy see Wolfson, *Philo*, I, 434; II, 283 f.
[161] See Diog. Laert. I, 3, 24 and II, 8, 27.
[162] *Opif.* 61.
[163] *Essai*, pp. 238 and 264.
[164] Comp. Moore, *Judaism*, II, 239 f.; see also Wolfson, *Philo*, II, 279 ff.
[165] Comp. the twenty-one attributes of Wisdom listed in 7.22 f.

becoming an omnipotent and omniscient intermediary of God
in His dealings with men. Wisdom is an emanation from God
rather than a mere creation (7.25 f.), and lives in such close
association with God (8.3 f.) that she seems to be a manifestation of God (9.9 f.). Nay, Wisdom existed before the creation of
the world (9.9),[166] though God alone created the world through
His word (9.1).[167] After creation Wisdom became an artificer of
all things ($\pi\acute{a}\nu\tau\omega\nu$ $\tau\epsilon\chi\nu\acute{\iota}\tau\eta s$ 7.22). This term makes it clear that
Wisdom was the assistant of God at the creation.[168] In fact Wis-
dom is conceived as the $\pi\acute{a}\rho\epsilon\delta\rho os$ or "throne partner" of God
(6.14; 9.4). That Wisdom is a $\pi\nu\epsilon\hat{v}\mu a$ is stated expressly in 1.6,
and in 9.17 $\sigma o\varphi\acute{\iota}a$ is parallel to $\pi\nu\epsilon\hat{v}\mu a$ $\ddot{a}\gamma\iota o\nu$. In 7.22 $\pi\nu\epsilon\hat{v}\mu a$
$\nu o\epsilon\rho\grave{o}\nu$, "an understanding spirit," applied to the spirit of Wis-
dom, reflects the Stoic definition of God as $\pi\nu\epsilon\hat{v}\mu a$ $\nu o\epsilon\rho\grave{o}\nu$.

The eschatology of our book is not as elaborate as in some
other apocryphal books, such as Enoch and IV Maccabees.[169]
Like Philo, Wisdom has no consistent eschatology. Thus there is
no allusion to a personal Messiah, though there is an expectation of a realm where the righteous will have dominion and
judge the nations (3.7 f.). As stated above, this includes the resurrection of the soul, but not of the body, immortality of the
soul, and, of course, also the pre-existence of the soul.

In a way, the Book of Wisdom reflects the Neo-Platonic
philosophy of pre-Christian Alexandria. In it we find the prevailing syncretism of different systems of Greek philosophy.
Any doctrine that could buttress the Jewish faith became grist
to its mill. It becomes evident at a glance that the author of
Wisdom is not a consistent thinker. He often contradicts himself, as when advocating universalism in 11.23–26, but particularism in 12.10 f. He makes no reference to the Messiah, but
there is to be a theocratic kingdom in which the surviving

[166] See Prov. 8.24 ff. and Ecclus. 1.4.
[167] Comp. Gen. ch. 1.
[168] Comp. אמון (אומן?) in Prov. 8.30, for which G, however, reads $\dot{a}\rho\mu\acute{o}\zeta o\nu\sigma a$.
[169] It should be stated that IV Maccabees discloses a deeper knowledge of
Greek philosophy than all other Hellenistic-Jewish writings, except
Philo's.

righteous will judge the nations and have dominion over peoples (3.7 f.). He adheres to the Alexandrian belief in the transcendence of God and His vicarious intermediary Wisdom, but he also voices the Stoic doctrine of the immanence of God in nature.

Sometimes it appears that Wisdom only plays with Greek philosophical terms, but does not adopt their ideas. These terms were what Wendland[170] calls "trivial wisdom, as was then current in the street." As Wolfson[171] puts it, the Hellenization of the Alexandrian Jews was in language only, not in religious belief or cult. The Jews often used Greek words inaccurately or in a wrong sense, as pointed out here and there in our commentary.

The theological teachings of our book may be summarized as follows: God is one, omnipresent, omniscient, and omnipotent. He created the world not out of nothing, but out of formless matter. He is the possessor of wisdom, justice and kindness, and takes providential care of the world, but especially of Israel. Israel He chastens, but other nations warring on Israel He punishes, though for the purpose of leading them to repentance (ch. 12). The Greek term $\dot{\alpha}\nu\dot{\alpha}\gamma\kappa\eta$ of 19.4 is the destiny determined by God, probably the idea of divine predestination of the Old Testament. The word of God is not the Logos of Philo, but the utterance of God's will (9.1; 16.12.26). Further, man is not a three-divisional entity, a trichotomy into body, soul and spirit, as taught by the Greeks, but a two-divisional entity, a dichotomy into body and soul or spirit (1.4). The soul or spirit is represented as breathed into the body by God (15.11), exactly as in Gen. 2.7, and at death received into the other world never to return. Although created in God's image, man is said to be foolish by nature, unable by himself to know God

---

[170] *Kultur*, p. 204.

[171] *Philo*, I, 13: "Alexandrian Jews like Philo used the terminology of pagan religions without recognizing the truth of the pagan ideas expressed therein. In general, they approved of Greek religious philosophy as opposed to Greek popular religion, and saw in the Greek philosophers the spiritual kindred of the Jews, though, of course, they held that the whole truth was to be found only in biblical revelation."

(12.10; 13.1). Freewill is assumed in 1.16, where it is stated that wicked men call down destruction on themselves, and in 5.6.13, where they attribute their wretchedness to their own folly. Sin, according to 2.24, was introduced into the world by the devil, but, according to 14.27, it is the result of idolatry. Suffering is meant to test the righteous and prove them worthy of immortality and communion with God. There is a Book of Remembrance before the Lord in which all deeds of man, good and bad, are recorded (1.9). The wicked get their retribution in this life (3.10 ff., 4.3), but the righteous may be recompensed in the future life. The wicked will be punished with death (1.12.16; 2.24); they will be bereft of hope (3.11.18; 5.14); they will be utterly destroyed (4.19), yet not annihilated, for they will be subject to pain and be aware of the blessedness of the righteous (5.1 f.).

IX

Wisdom Literature

Wisdom literature, which serves as a corrective of legalism, is of many lands and many kinds. It was not confined to the Hebrews, but was common to the East. The men of Edom were famous for their sagacity.[172] Collections of parables and proverbs are known to have been current among the Egyptians and Accadians, and some of these have come down to us.[173] As to form, there seem to have been fables,[174] riddles,[175] parables,[176] and proverbs.[177] Among the Israelites these seem to have attained their greatest development in the post-exilic period, when a bounteous historical experience, replete with successes and vic-

[172] Comp. Jer. 49.7 and Obad. verse 8.
[173] Comp. Hugo Gressmann, *Altorientalische Texte zum Alten Testament*, Berlin 1926, pp. 33–46; also James B. Pritchard, *Ancient Near Eastern Texts relating to the Old Testament*, Princeton, New Jersey, 1950, pp. 412–430.
[174] Comp. Jud. 9.8 ff.
[175] As in Jud. 14.14.
[176] See II Sam. 12.1 ff.
[177] See Ezek. 18.2.

tories but more so with frustrations and disappointments, offered a broad stratum on which to weave variegated patterns of
moral observations and ethical instruction. It was then that
some portions of the Book of Proverbs came into existence, as
well as Ecclesiastes, Ecclesiasticus, Ahikar, Tobit, and The
Book of Wisdom.

The latter, strictly speaking, is not a book of wisdom, but a
book about wisdom, or a book in praise of wisdom, which
brings salvation to the pious Jews (ch. 1–5), is of divine essence
(ch. 6–9), and always brought blessing to the Israelites and
calamities to the heathen (ch. 10–19). It apotheosizes wisdom
and raises it to the high rank of God's mate and coadjutor, with
numerous synonyms, attributes, and functions, that sometimes
give the appearance as if wisdom were usurping the prerogatives
of God Himself. More than the books of Proverbs and Ecclesiasticus it personifies, nay hypostatizes wisdom,[178] reifying an ab-
straction into something concrete or objective and making
palpable the benefits accruing from steady intercourse with her.

Like most wisdom books our book is anonymous and entirely
impersonal. Not only is the name of the author not mentioned,
but even the proper names of the historical characters dealt with
in the book are carefully omitted. There is a studied attempt at
dealing with abstract ideas and avoiding personalities as much
as possible, as is perhaps natural to apocryphal literature.
Various reasons have been advanced for this anonymity, but
none of them is quite plausible. For instance, Stade[179] thought
that it was not necessary to name the Jewish personalities because the book was addressed to the Jews of Alexandria, who
were more or less familiar with the history of their people.
Others, like Siegfried[180] and Bertholet,[181] who believed that the

[178] On the hypostatization of wisdom see Helmer Ringgren, *Word and
Wisdom, Studies in the Hypostatization of Divine Qualities and Functions in
the Ancient Near East*, Lund 1947. For Albright's suggestions concerning
Ugaritic influences upon the figure of personified wisdom in Prov. 8–9, see
his *From the Stone Age to Christianity*, pp. 283 f.

[179] *Geschichte des Volkes Israel*, II, 436.

[180] *Philo*, p. 23.

[181] In Budde's *Althebräische Litteratur*, p. 413.

book was written with the view of attracting proselytes to Judaism from among the cultured Greeks, ascribed anonymity to some sort of simulation or affectation. I am rather inclined to think that this was done in order to heighten the mystic strain of the book and thus intensify its paramount message.

The Book of Wisdom differs also from its predecessors in that it is an exposition and elaboration of certain parts or passages of the Bible. Not only its historical background but also its ideational contents are based largely on the Scriptures. Seizing upon an idea in the Bible it elaborates it in great detail, as, for instance, 9.9 f., which is nothing more than a summary of Prov. 8.22 ff. In fact, the entire eighth chapter of the Book of Proverbs served as a substratum for our author on which to weave and embroider his thoughts on wisdom in ch. 7–9. In this sense it is not an independent work, but rather a commentary, a sort of Midrash, on the wisdom books of the Bible.

X

RABBINIC SOURCES

Although written in an immaculate Greek and touching upon profound philosophical problems the sentiment of the author of the Book of Wisdom remains Jewish throughout, orthodoxly and Pharisaically Jewish.[182] Not only does he base himself on the books of the Bible, specifically on Psalms, Proverbs, Job, Ecclesiastes, and Ecclesiasticus, besides the Pentateuch,[183] but he also seems to draw from the same sources as the interpretations of the Talmud and Midrash.[184] As a matter of fact the last

---

[182] Comp. Wolfson, *Philo*, I, 56: "Alexandrian Judaism at the time of Philo was a collateral branch of Pharisaic Judaism, which flourished in Palestine at that time, both of them having sprung from that pre-Maccabean Judaism which had been molded by the activities of the Scribes."

[183] It cannot be denied that the writer was aware of the existence of these books, nay that he knew them in one form or another.

[184] See Margoliouth, loc. cit., p. 296 top; also infra.

ten chapters of the book have been characterized by some
critics as a sort of Midrash, or remnants of an Alexandrian
Passover Haggadah, or a Passover sermon.[185] Here we meet with
an intransigent construction of Judaism, sometimes bordering
on fanaticism; here we are amazed to be confronted with an ar-
rogant and undisguised particularism[186] which is strongly in contrast with the universalism of the great literary prophets. God
appears as a tribal god who is partial to the Jews and inimical to
their enemies. The sufferings which afflicted the Jews were but a
fatherly correction, but the sufferings of the heathen meant out-
pourings of divine wrath and a sign of judgment. Sinning Jews
are freed from evil by punishment, but God hates the sinning
Canaanites and exterminates them for their sins. This matches
the narrow-mindedness of Mal. 1.2 f. "I have loved Jacob and
hated Esau," though it is somewhat mitigated by the universalism of 11.23 ff. Thus the author often halts between two opinions, but his leanings towards Pharisee doctrines are unmistakable.

Numerous examples of adherence to rabbinic interpretation
could be pointed out in this part of the book. Suffice it to mention only a few (the rest will be found in the Commentary ad
loc. 16.7), such as that of those bitten by the writhing serpents
who were saved by appealing to God, not to the serpent, had its
counterpart in the Talmud R. H. 29a: "Does a serpent kill
or keep alive? But when the Israelites were looking on high and
were pledging their hearts to their Father in heaven they were
healed, and if not they were decayed." 16.20, speaking of the
manna as "sufficient for all pleasure and fitted for every taste,"
is corroborated by Yoma 75a, with reference to Num. 11.8:
"Said Rabbi Abbahu: Just as a child tastes many tastes in the
breast (of his mother), so also the Israelites experienced many
tastes in the manna as long as they were eating it." Further, the
idea enunciated in this part of the book that God punishes with
painful justice but also with loving mercy has its counterpart in

[185] See Kaufman Kohler in *Jewish Encyclopedia*, s. v. Wisdom.
[186] See especially 11.10 ff. and 12.1 ff.

the Talmudic interpretation of the various divine names, namely that אלהים expresses the divine attribute of justice, while יהוה represents the divine attribute of mercy.[187]

But even the first part of the book, which is more akin to Hellenistic thinking, harks back to rabbinic teachings and Pharisaic norms. For example, the passage 1.13 stating that God made not death is reflected in Sifra on Par. Behukkotai, section 4: "Evil never goes forth from me, as stated[188]: Out of the mouth of the Most High proceeds not evil, but good." Again, 3.1 δικαίων δὲ ψυχαὶ ἐν χειρὶ θεοῦ has its equivalent in tractate Shab. 152b: "the souls of the righteous are hidden under the throne of glory." On 4.9 stating that understanding is old age to men one should compare Kid. 32b: "only he who acquires wisdom may be styled an old man." 5.15 ff. claiming that the righteous will live forever in bliss and glory has its counterpart in Ber. 17a: "The righteous are sitting with crowns on their heads and enjoy of the splendor of the *Shekinah*." The figure of Wisdom depicted in chapters 7–9 as a sort of consultant of God finds its analogy in the angels of the Midrash and the Talmud with whom God consulted at the creation of man.[189] Even more striking is the following similarity: the twenty-one attributes of wisdom enumerated in 7.22 f. have their parallel in Sifre for *Haazinu* § 306: "For I will proclaim the name of the Lord" (Deut. 32.3). We learn from this that Moses mentioned the name of the Lord only after twenty-one words.[191] From whom did he learn this? From the ministering angels, who only mention the name of the Lord after a threefold *kadosh* (holy), as it is written (Isa. 6.3) "and one called to another, and said: holy, holy, holy, is the Lord of hosts." Moses said: it is enough that I be in somewhat less than seven[192] like the ministering angels."

---

[187] Comp. e.g. Talm. Yerush. Ber. IX. 5.

[188] In Lam. 3.38. The verse reads somewhat differently: עליון לא תצא הרעות והטוב מפי

[189] Genesis rabba 8.3 ff.; Sanh. 38b. Comp. Wolfson, *Philo*, I, 289.

[190] Ed. Friedmann, fol. 132a f.

[191] Counting from the beginning of chapter 32 of Deuteronomy.

[192] Seven times three being twenty-one.

In our book we find twenty-one attributes before the mention of Wisdom, and in the Midrashic passage we have twenty-one words before the mention of the divine name.

XI

Bibliography

Blakeney, E. H., *The Praises of Wisdom*, Oxford, 1937.
Bois, H., *Essai sur les origines de la philosophie Judéo-Alexandrine*, Toulouse, 1890.
Bousset, W., *Die Religion des Judentums im späthellenistischen Zeitalter*, 3 Aufl. hrsgbn. von H. Gressman, Tübingen, 1926.
Charles, R. H. ed., *Apocrypha and Pseudepigrapha of the Old Testament*, 2 vols., Oxford, 1913.
Charles, R. H., *A Critical History of the Doctrine of a Future Life In Israel, In Judaism, and in Christianity, or Hebrew, Jewish, and Christian Eschatology from Pre-Prophetic Times till the close of the New Testament Canon*. London, 1913.
Churton, W. R., *In the Uncanonical and Apocryphal Scriptures*, published by the Society for the Promotion of Christian Knowledge.
Cornely, R., *Commentarium in Librum Sapientiae, Cursus Scripturae Sacrae*, Parisiis, 1910.
Deane, W. J., *The Book of Wisdom*. The Greek Text, the Latin Vulgate and the Authorised English Version, with an introduction, critical apparatus and a Commentary. Oxford, 1881.
Dähne, August Ferdinand, *Geschichtliche Darstellung der jüdisch-alexandrinischen Religions-Philosophie*.
Deissmann, Adolf, *Die Hellenisierung des Semitischen Monotheismus*. 1903.
Deissmann, Adolf, *Licht vom Osten*, 1908.
Drummond, J., *Philo Judaeus*, 2 vols., London, 1888. Vol. I, pp. 177–229, deals with Book of Wisdom.
Farrar, F. W., *The Wisdom of Solomon* (Speaker's Commentary on the Apocrypha). London, 1888.
Feldmann, F., *Textkritische Materialen zum Buch der Weisheit*, Freiburg i. B., 1902.
Feldmann, F., *Das Buch der Weisheit* (HSAT, VI, 4), Bonn, 1926.
Fichtner, Johannes, Die Weisheit Salomos, Tübingen, 1937.
Fichtner, Johannes, *Die Altorientalische Weisheit in ihrer Israel-*

itisch-Jüdischen Ausprägung. Eine Studie zur Nationalisierung der Weisheit in Israel von Johannes Fichtner. Giessen, 1933.

Focke, F., *Die Entstehung der Weisheit Salomos,* Göttingen, 1913.

Friedländer, Moriz: *Griechische Philosophie im Alten Testament,* Berlin, 1904.

Freudenthal, J., What is the Original Language of the Wisdom of Solomon? in: *Jewish Quarterly Review,* III, 1891, pp. 722–53.

Fuchs, L. *Die Juden Aegyptens,* Vienna, 1924.

Gärtner, E., *Komposition und Wortwahl des Buch der Weisheit,* Berlin, 1913.

Gfrörer, A. Fr.: *Philo und die jüdisch-alexandrinische Theosophie,* 2 vols. 1830.

Ginzberg, Louis H.: *Legends of the Jews,* Philadelphia, 1909–1938.

Goodrick, A. T. S., The Book of Wisdom, New York, 1913.

Gregg, J. A. F., *The Wisdom of Solomon.* In the Revised Version (With Introduction and Notes. The Cambridge Bible for Schools and Colleges). Cambridge 1909.

Grimm, C. L. W., *Das Buch der Weisheit erklärt* (Kurzgefasstes exegetisches Handbuch zu den Apokryphen des Alten Testamentes). Leipzig, 1860.

Gutmann, M. *Die Apokryphen des Alten Testaments, auf's Neue aus dem griechischen Texte übersetzt und durch Einleitungen und Anmerkungen erläutert.* Altona, 1841.

Heinemann, I., Die griechische Quelle der "Weisheit Salomos" in: *Jahresbericht des jüdisch-theologischen Seminars Frankelscher Stiftung für* . . . 1920 (Breslau), pp. viii-xxv.

Heinemann, I., *Philons griechische und jüdische Bildung.* Breslau, 1929–1932.

Heinemann, Isaac: *Altjüdische Allegoristik,* Breslau, 1936.

Heinisch, P. *Die Griechische Philosophie im Buche der Weisheit* (ATAbhandlungen, I), Münster i. W., 1908.

Heinisch, P. *Das Buch der Weisheit* (EH), Münster i. W., 1912.

Heinze, *Die Lehre vom Logos in der griechischen Philosophie,* 1872.

Hesselgrave, Charles Everett, *The Hebrew Personification of Wisdom,* New York, 1910.

Holtzmann, Joseph: *Die Peshitta zum Buche der Weisheit.* Freib. i. Br. 1903.

Humbert, Paul: *Recherches sur les Sources Égyptiennes de la Littérature Sapientiale d' Israel,* Neuchatel, 1929.

Klasen, F. *Die alttestamentliche Weisheit und der Logos der jüdisch-alexandrinischen Philosophie,* Freiburg i. B., 1878.

Krauss, Samuel, *Talmudische Archäologie,* Leipzig, 1910–1912.

à Lapide, C., *Commentaria in Sacram Scripturam Tomi* I–XIX, Mediolani, 1857–1870.

Margoliouth, D. S., Was the Book of Wisdom Written in Hebrew? in: *Journal of the Royal Asiatic Society*, N. S., XXII (1890), 263–297.

Menzel, P.: *Der griechische Einfluss auf Prediger und Weisheit Salomos*, 1889. Criticized by Heinisch, pp. 9 ff.

Meyer, Eduard: *Ursprung und Anfänge des Christentums*, Stuttgart, 1921–1923.

Moore, George Foot: *Judaism in the First Centuries of the Christian Era*. Cambridge, 1927–1930.

Oesterley, W. O. E.: *The Books of the Apocrypha. Their Origin, Teaching and Contents*. London, 1915.

Oesterley, W. O. E., *The Wisdom of Solomon*, London, 1917.

Oesterley, W. O. E.: *The Wisdom of Egypt and The Old Testament in the light of the newly discovered "Teaching of Amen-em-ope."* London, 1927.

Oesterley, W. O. E.: *An Introduction to the Books of the Apocrypha*, New York, 1935.

Pfeiffer, Robert H.: *History of New Testament Times. With an Introduction to the Apocrypha*. New York, 1949.

Pfleiderer, Edmund: *Die Philosophie des Heraklit von Ephesus nebst einem Anhang über heraklitische Einflüsse im Alttestamentlichen Koheleth und besonders im Buch der Weisheit*, 1886.

Philo: *Philo with an English translation* by F. H. Colson and H. G. Whitaker, London, 1929.

Porter, F. C.: The Pre-existence of the Soul in the Book of Wisdom and in the Rabbinical Writings in: *Old Testament and Semitic Studies in Memory of W. R. Harper*, Chicago, 1908, vol. I. pp. 205–70.

Preisigke, E.: *Wörterbuch der griechischen Papyrusurkunden*, Bde. 1–3, Berlin, 1925–31.

Purinton, C. E.: Translation Greek in the Wisdom of Solomon, in: *Journal of Biblical Literature*, vol. 47, 1928, pp. 276–304.

Rahlfs, A., ed., *Septuaginta, id est Vetus Testamentum graece* . . . 2 vol., Stuttgartiae, 1935.

Ranston, Harry: *Ecclesiastes and the Early Greek Wisdom Literature*. London [1925].

Rostovtseff: *The Social and Economic History of the Hellenistic World*, Oxford, 1941.

Schleusner, J. F., *Novus Thesaurus . . . sive Lexicon in LXX et reliquos Veteris Testamenti* . . . vol. I–V, Lipsiae, 1820–21.

Schürer, Emil: *Geschichte des jüdischen Volkes im Zeitalter Jesu Christi*[3]. Leipzig, 1901–1911.

Schütz, Rodolphe: *Les Idées eschatologiques du Livre de la Sagesse*, Strasbourg, 1935.

Siegfried, Karl: *Die Weisheit Salomos*. (Die Apokryphen und Pseudepigraphen des Alten Testaments, herausgegeben von E. Kautzsch). Tübingen, 1900.

Speiser, E. A., The Hebrew Origin of the First Part of the Book of Wisdom, in: *Jewish Quarterly Review*, N. S., xiv (1923–24), 455–482.

Stein, Edmund: *Alttestamentliche Bibelkritik in der späthellenistischen Literatur*. Lwow, 1935. Sonderabdruck aus "Collectanea Theologica" Societatis Theologorum Polonorum. XVI (1935).

Stein, Menahem: ספר חכמת שלמה (הספרים החיצונים . . . ערוכים בהשתתפות כמה למדנים ע"י אברהם כהנא]. Tel-Aviv, 1937.

Swete, H. B. ed., The Old Testament in Greek, 3 vols., Cambridge, 1909–13–22.

Tarn, W. W.: *Hellenistic Civilization*[2], London, 1930.

Tscherikower, Vigdor: היהודים והיונים בתקופה ההלניסטית. Tel-Aviv, 1930. היהודים במצרים בתקופה ההלניסטית-הרומנית לאור הפאפירולוגיה — Jerusalem, 1945.

Tscherikower, Vigdor: *The Jews in Egypt in the Hellenistic-Roman Age in the Light of the Papyri*. Jerusalem, 1945.

Weber, Ferdinand: *Jüdische Theologie auf Grund des Talmud und verwandter Schriften gemeinfässlich dargestellt von F. W.* . . .Nach des Verfassers Tode herausugegeben von Franz Delitsch und Georg Schnedermann[2]. Leipzig, 1897.

Wessely, Naphtali Hirtz (Hartwig): ספר חכמת שלמה עם פי' רוח חן. Berlin, 1780.

Wolfson, Harry Austryn: *Philo. Foundations of Religious Philosophy in Judaism, Christianity, and Islam*. 2 volumes. Cambridge, Massachusetts, 1947.

The book opens in medias res, lacking even the slightest preface or introductory formula. There is no mention of author nor time nor purpose. The only hint we get is the address to the "judges of the earth," repeated 6.1, which may be a purely rhetorical device hiding the real purpose of the book, which consists in warning and encouraging the faithful Jews; or may be a reference to rulers in general, in keeping with the hypothesis of Solomonic authorship, which assumes that one king would naturally appeal to other kings (there is a specific reference to kings in 6.20–25); or to Roman rulers in particular who are known to have perpetrated injustices against the Jews of Alexandria; or to powerful personages in the Jewish environment of Alexandria who had apostatized and attached themselves to the heathen government, vexing and harassing their former brethren (Siegfried in Hastings' *Dictionary of the Bible*, s.v. Wisdom). The latter seems to be the most plausible assumption.

It is well known that in the days of Philo the Jews in Egypt amounted to a million souls, half or even more of whom probably lived in Alexandria. Some of these, especially the wealthy and ruling classes, were of the Sadducean type and prone to Hellenization. Philo speaks of apostate Jews in *Conf. Ling.*, ch. II: "Those who are discontented at the constitution under which their fathers have lived, being always eager to blame and accuse the laws, say: Do you boast of your precepts as if they contained truth itself? Behold, the books which you call sacred scriptures contain fables at which you are accustomed to laugh when you hear others relating them." Comp. also *Mos.* I.6. Undoubtedly these apostates took every opportunity to vex and persecute the pious Jews (2.10 and elsewhere), and it is against them and their like that the author of our book sets out to polemize, and endeavors to prove that true religion leads to a blessed immortality, while irreligion and apostasy lead to utter destruction.

ᚕᚄ ΣΟΦΙΑ ΣΑΛΩΜΩΝΟΣ ᚃᚃ

1 ¹ Ἀγαπήσατε δικαιοσύνην, οἱ κρίνοντες τὴν γῆν,
φρονήσατε περὶ τοῦ κυρίου ἐν ἀγαθότητι
καὶ ἐν ἁπλότητι καρδίας ζητήσατε αὐτόν.
²ὅτι εὑρίσκεται τοῖς μὴ πειράζουσιν αὐτόν,
ἐμφανίζεται δὲ τοῖς μὴ ἀπιστοῦσιν αὐτῷ.
³σκολιοὶ γὰρ λογισμοὶ χωρίζουσιν ἀπὸ θεοῦ,
δοκιμαζομένη τε ἡ δύναμις ἐλέγχει τοὺς ἄφρονας.
⁴ὅτι εἰς κακότεχνον ψυχὴν οὐκ εἰσελεύσεται σοφία
οὐδὲ κατοικήσει ἐν σώματι κατάχρεῳ ἁμαρτίας.

Sap.: BSA. — Fr.=Libri apocryphi
V. T. graece ed. Fritzsche (Lips.
1871).

Inscr. σαλωμωνος B*†] -μων Bᶜ†, σαλομωντος S†, σολομωντος A: cf.
subscr. et Regn. III **1** 10

1. LOVE RIGHTEOUSNESS: Identical with Ps. 45.8, which is likewise addressed to a royal personage. *Zedek* is often synonymous with *mishpat* in the Bible and opposed to *resha*. Cf. Kautzsch, *Über die Derivate des Stammes* צדק *im alttestamentlichen Sprachgebrauch*, Tübingen 1881. It should be stated that righteousness here is used in a general sense of conforming in thought and deed to the will of God. JUDGES OF THE EARTH: Similarly 6.1; cf. Ps. 2.10 and elsewhere. Judges here is used as a synonym for rulers, one of whose functions is to dispense justice, see I Ki. 3.9. IN SIMPLICITY OF HEART, see Gen. 20.5 f. The antithesis is "crooked thoughts" in verse 3 below. The heart is the repository of the intellect in Hebrew.

2. HE IS FOUND: Similarly 6.12. For the idea cf. Prov. 8.17, also Isa. 65.1. TEMPT HIM NOT: Namely through immoral conduct.

3. FOR: The next few verses are in contrast to the preceding verse: God is readily accessible to the pious, but definitely inaccessible to the impious. CROOKED THOUGHTS: For the former cf. Deut. 32.5 and Prov. 21.8; as to the latter, Gr. *logismoi*, it is used in Hellenistic Greek mostly in a bad sense, somewhat like "wicked thoughts" in Prov. 6.18. The reference is undoubtedly to the turnings and twistings by which the Jewish renegades or apostates endeavored to argue themselves out of their allegiance to the God of their fathers. SEPARATE FROM GOD: Similarly Isa. 59.2, 7–9. Cf. also Philo, *Mut. Nom.* § 46: "God stands afar off from sinners, but He

1 ¹ Love righteousness, you that be judges of the earth
Think of the Lord in goodness,
And in simplicity of heart seek you him.
²For he is found of them that tempt him not,
And is manifested to them that do not distrust him.
³For crooked thoughts separate from God,
And his power being put to proof confutes the fools.
⁴For wisdom will not enter into a soul that devises evil,
Nor abide in a body that is subject to sin.

---

walks within the souls of the upright." HIS POWER: *i. e.* God's power, the supreme power of R.V., though the Greek text is non-committal, reading "the power." Early commentators, following the Old Latin's *provata virtus corripit insipientes*, referred the expression to human excellence. Some construe it as a synonym for wisdom, which is seen being brought to proof in the following two verses (Gregg). On Philo's use of power see Bois, *Essai sur les origines de la philosophie Judéo-Alexandrine*, p. 237. BEING PUT TO PROOF: or "being tested," *cf.* Ps. 95.9. CONFUTES: The Greek word *elenchein* has different shades of meaning: put to shame, confute, prove. In biblical Greek it means "to convict." See further on v. 5 below. THE FOOLS: In a moral sense. The word is sometimes used euphemistically in the Old Testament to express the folly of immoral living that ignores God, *cf.* Ps. 14.1.

4. DEVISES EVIL: κακότεχνος, here and 15.4, is poetic and Homeric. The term is very appropriate if applied to the evil intentions of the Jewish renegades against their faithful fellow-countrymen. WISDOM: Our author's conception of wisdom seems to be vague and indeterminate. To him wisdom means everything: providence, destiny, justice, virtue, truth, etc. He identifies wisdom with the spirit of the Lord (9.17), the word of the Lord (9.1), power (1.3), providence (14.3), hand of God (14.6), justice (1.8), angel of the Lord (18.15), etc. The attributes he ascribes to wisdom are numerous: intelligence, holiness, omnipotence, omniscience, beneficence, mobility, penetrativeness, etc. (7.22–24). Wisdom is limned as a cosmic figure concerned with nature and man (9.2 ff.), though the emphasis is on the latter. Indeed, wisdom is personalized and pictured as being very near to God Himself (9.4.9), yet it is not hypostatized and remains forever

51

5   ⁵ἅγιον γὰρ πνεῦμα παιδείας φεύξεται δόλον
    καὶ ἀπαναστήσεται ἀπὸ λογισμῶν ἀσυνέτων
    καὶ ἐλεγχθήσεται ἐπελθούσης ἀδικίας.
    ⁶φιλάνθρωπον γὰρ πνεῦμα σοφία
    καὶ οὐκ ἀθῳώσει βλάσφημον ἀπὸ χειλέων αὐτοῦ·
    ὅτι τῶν νεφρῶν αὐτοῦ μάρτυς ὁ θεὸς
    καὶ τῆς καρδίας αὐτοῦ ἐπίσκοπος ἀληθὴς
    καὶ τῆς γλώσσης ἀκουστής.

5¹ παιδ.] σοφιας A   6⁵ γλωσσης]+αυτου A
6¹ σοφιας A

---

subordinate to all-powerful God. Like the Logos of the Stoics it is a sort of intermediary between transcendental God and earthly man. In the words of Drummond (*Philo Judaeus*, I, 225): "Wisdom is a self-adaptation of the inviolable spirituality of God to material conditions, an assumption of the necessary community of nature, in order to bring the infinite and eternal into those relations of space and time which are implied in the creation and government of the world of sense." See, further, Introduction, p. 35. NOR ABIDE: In the same vein Philo, *Somn.*, I.23: "Strive to be a house of God, a holy temple, a fair dwelling-place for Him."   SUBJECT TO SIN: So the Peshitta. The Greek phrase denotes "mortgaged to sin," hence Farrar very aptly renders "impawned to sin." R.V. "held in pledge by sin." Margoliouth (in *JRAS*. for 1890, p. 286) speaks of it as an ordinary Rabbinic expression for "sinful," which he claims is also the rendering of the Coptic version. Goodrick (p. 30) opposes Eccl. 2.1–8 to this verse. According to this verse both soul and body are liable to sin, but in 9.15 corruption is ascribed to the body alone, "that loathsome prison-house" in the words of Philo (*Migr.* § 2). The dichotomy of human nature into body and soul is strictly Jewish and is reflected also in II Macc. 7.37 and 15.30, and in Philo (*Mos.*III 39), though elsewhere Philo insists on the Platonic trichotomy of body, soul, and spirit. See further Moore, *Judaism*, I, 486 ff.; II, 384.

5. A HOLY SPIRIT: having nothing in common with what is sinful and impure. There is no personification here of the Holy Spirit or the Holy Ghost, as maintained by some commentators. The Septuagint uses the same expression *to pneuma to hagion* in Isa. 63.10 f. and Ps. 50 (51).13. The Hebrew term is *ruah ha-kodesh*, which is on a par with the spirit of prophecy. In rabbinical Hebrew the term *shekinah*, "Divine Presence," is often used with the same intent.   DISCIPLINE: Gr. *paideias*, for which A has a variant *sofias*. Bois (*Essai*, p. 234) claims that this expression is a paraphrase for Wisdom, just as she is characterized as a spirit in v. 6 below, as a holy spirit in 7.22, and as a spirit of discipline in 6.11.   PUT TO CONFUSION: So R.V., with "convicted" on the margin, which is the more common meaning of *elegxein* in our book. However, *elegxtysetai* is a very difficult word here, so much so that some commentators did not hesitate to declare it corrupt and suggest emendations (Schultess et al.).

5   ⁵For a holy spirit of discipline will flee deceit
      And hold aloof from witless thoughts
      And will be put to confusion when unrighteousness has
         set in.
      ⁶For wisdom is a spirit that loves man,
      And will not hold a blasphemer guiltless of his lips;
      Because God is witness of his reins,
      And a true inspector of his heart,
      And a hearer of his tongue.

A.V. "will not abide"; Gfrörer "cannot live where iniquity rules." Grimm, basing himself on Byzantine Greek, renders "is scared away," which is followed by Holmes in Charles' *Apocrypha*. Siegfried's "will be filled with a spirit of reproof" is admirable, but hardly justifiable and quite forced. Some might render "put to shame," like purity in the presence of iniquity. Finally Bois (*Essai*, p. 379) would even remove the line altogether and place it between v. 8 and v. 9, reading: "justice convicting will not pass him by, but he will be convicted under the weight of his iniquity."
6. FOR: Gfrörer, who sees no connection between this verse and the one preceding, renders "although." However, this is hardly necessary. As Grimm construes it, "Wisdom is a spirit that loves mankind, and for that very reason will not leave wickedness unpunished." Siegfried removes this line and places it between v. 13 and v. 14; similarly Bois. Holmes suggests that the line may be an interpolation on the basis of 7.22 f., where wisdom is said to be a *pneuma* and *filanthrôpos*. WISDOM: *sofia*, so B, but A, Itala, Peshitta and others have *sofias*, probably to avoid hypostatization of wisdom (so Goodrick: "the spirit of wisdom"). LOVES MAN: Earlier commentators construed *filanthropon* in the sense of "mild, gentle" and connected it with the preceding verse thus: Wisdom will be put to confusion when wickedness comes on fast, because it is a mild spirit and will not abide in the same abode as injustice. On the humanitarian aspect of wisdom *cf*. Prov. 8.17 ff. BLASPHEMER: This word, which in classical Greek meant simply "evil-speaking," assumed in Hellenistic Greek the special meaning of "reviling God." Examples of such blasphemy may be found in 2.1–20. GUILTLESS OF HIS LIPS: A.V. more explicitly "will not acquit a blasphemer of his words." But the implicit expression is characteristic of the Scriptures and may be illustrated through *peh* in Jud. 9.38, Num. 14.41, I Sam. 15.24, etc. REINS: or kidneys, though in later Greek it assumed the sense of "the inmost dwelling of thought" (comp. *frenes*, "the midriff," then "heart" and "mind"). In Hebrew psychology the kidneys are sometimes paralleled with the heart (*cf*. Ps. 7.10, Jer. 11.20, and elsewhere), but this does not mean that they are synonymous, since the kidneys are known to be the seat of feelings and affections, while the heart is the source of thoughts and ideas. According to the rabbis (Ber. 61a) man has two kidneys, one urging him to good, the other to evil. INSPECTOR: Itala *scrutator*, which is nearer

⁷ὅτι πνεῦμα κυρίου πεπλήρωκεν τὴν οἰκουμένην,
καὶ τὸ συνέχον τὰ πάντα γνῶσιν ἔχει φωνῆς.
⁸διὰ τοῦτο φθεγγόμενος ἄδικα οὐδεὶς μὴ λάθῃ,
οὐδὲ μὴ παροδεύσῃ αὐτὸν ἐλέγχουσα ἡ δίκη.
⁹ἐν γὰρ διαβουλίοις ἀσεβοῦς ἐξέτασις ἔσται,
λόγων δὲ αὐτοῦ ἀκοὴ πρὸς κύριον ἥξει
εἰς ἔλεγχον ἀνομημάτων αὐτοῦ·
10 ¹⁰ὅτι οὖς ζηλώσεως ἀκροᾶται τὰ πάντα,
καὶ θροῦς γογγυσμῶν οὐκ ἀποκρύπτεται.
¹¹ Φυλάξασθε τοίνυν γογγυσμὸν ἀνωφελῆ

---

to *episcopos* here than "beholder" of A.V. and "overseer" of R.V. The Greek word is generally used in the Septuagint in the sense of "taskmaster" or "captain," but here it is used as in Philo, *Somn.* I.15: "God is the overseer of all, to whom all things are open, even all that is done invisibly in the depths of the heart." Cicero (*de Nat. Deor.* I.15, 39) writes of the Stoic deity "holding together nature and all things." The Stoic God was soul, spirit, reason of the world, providence, destiny, universal law.

7. THE SPIRIT OF THE LORD: This may stand for God or the wisdom of God. For the omnipresence of wisdom see 8.1. HAS FILLED: *Cf.* Jer. 23.24: "Do not I fill heaven and earth?"; see also Ps. 139.7. Philo likewise states (*Leg. All.* III.2): "God has filled all things, and has passed through all things, and has left nothing void or unoccupied by Himself." THE WORLD: Strictly speaking *oikoumene* signifies "habitable earth," and it is only in later Greek that it assumed the larger meaning of *kosmos*. EMBRACES ALL THINGS: So Reuss and Goodrick, others "holds all things together." The purpose of the writer is to express the omnipresence and omniscience of God, exactly the way it is expressed in Ps. 139.7 quoted above. However, nearly all commentators see in *sunechon* the idea of permeation as reflected in Platonic or Stoic philosophy. THE VOICE: Literal rendering of *phone*, for which Goodrick has "the spoken word."

8. THEREFORE NO MAN: Similarly Jer. 23.24 of false prophets. *Cf.* further Job 34.21 ff. UNRIGHTEOUS THINGS: Such as quoted by Philo in *Conf. Ling.*, ch. II, as given above in note on v. 1. JUSTICE: Personified here as in 11.20 "pursued by justice." Similarly Philo personifies *dikē* in *Flac.* § 18 and elsewhere. PASS HIM BY: *parodeuein*, found in Theocritus in the intransitive sense of "to pass along," is used in our book five times (here and 2.7, 5.14, 6.22, 10.8), and in four of these in the unnatural sense of "to pass over," in which it is found in later Greek authors.

9. PLOTS: So Goodrick, but A.V. and R.V. have "counsels" for *diabouliai*, which admittedly is used in a bad sense, approaching "craftiness," like Heb. *mezimmot* in Ps. 10.2. The Greek word is a favorite with LXX, perhaps because of its resemblance to *diabolos*. THE WICKED MAN: An allusion to the apostate or renegade Jews whose aim was to oppress their

⁷For the spirit of the Lord has filled the world,
  And that which embraces all things has knowledge of
    the voice.
⁸Therefore no man speaking unrighteous things shall
    escape notice,
  Nor shall convicting justice pass him by.
⁹For into the plots of the wicked man a searching shall
    be made,
  And the sound of his words shall come unto the Lord,
  For a conviction of his lawless deeds.
10 ¹⁰For the ear of jealousy overhears all,
  And the muttering of murmurings is not hidden.
  ¹¹Beware you therefore of unprofitable murmuring,

---

fellow-countrymen.   A SEARCHING: Somewhat like R.V. Others render
more forcibly by "inquisition" (A.V. et al.).   SOUND: Goodrick, following Reuss, has "echo." On the general sense *cf.* Mal. 3.13 ff.   SHALL
COME: According to Jewish tradition there is a Book of Remembrance
(Mal. 3.16) before the Lord, wherein all the deeds of man, good and bad,
are meticulously recorded. The Book of Jubilees 30.20 ff. speaks of two
heavenly books: a Book of Life for the righteous, and a Book of Death for
the unrighteous. According to *ibid.* 36.10, one who contrives evil against
his neighbor will be blotted out of the Book of Remembrance of men, and
will not be written in the Book of Life, but in the Book of Perdition. *Cf.*
also Enoch 47.3, 104.1, 108.3. The Jewish liturgy of the High Holidays is
permeated with this idea of a Book of Life or Book of Remembrance
before the Lord, from which He judges the deeds of men.   LAWLESS
DEEDS: literally "lawlessnesses," referring to the plots and words mentioned in the preceding lines. Philo, *Dec.* § 17, is to the point: "The conviction that is innate in and inhabits each man, at once his accuser and his
judge, wages a truceless war with the disobedient."
10. THE EAR OF JEALOUSY: an imitation of the Hebrew adjectival genitive,
which is not lacking in the Septuagint, *cf. e. g.* Num. 5.14 *pneuma zēlōseōs*
for *ruah kin'ah.* God's jealousy is manifested in the Old Testament either
on behalf of His chosen people, as *e. g.* Joel 2.18, or for His own honor, as
e. g. Ex. 20.5. It is in the latter sense, in the sense of *theos zylotys,* that the
phrase is used here: God is jealous as He watches the words and thoughts
of men.   THE MUTTERINGS OF MURMURINGS: an unusual expression, but
perhaps θροῦς was used deliberately because of its resemblance to οὖς in the
line above (Grimm). *Gongusmos* is not classical, but quite effective, and
occurs in Ex. 16.8 and Num. 17.5 ff., where it is used of the murmuring of
the Israelites against Moses. The sense is that even the unuttered murmurings of the heart are overheard.
11. BEWARE: This address is quite cogent if, as assumed by most commen-

καὶ ἀπὸ καταλαλιᾶς φείσασθε γλώσσης·
ὅτι φθέγμα λαθραῖον κενὸν οὐ πορεύσεται,
στόμα δὲ καταψευδόμενον ἀναιρεῖ ψυχήν.
¹²μὴ ζηλοῦτε θάνατον ἐν πλάνῃ ζωῆς ὑμῶν
μηδὲ ἐπισπᾶσθε ὄλεθρον ἐν ἔργοις χειρῶν ὑμῶν·
¹³ὅτι ὁ θεὸς θάνατον οὐκ ἐποίησεν
οὐδὲ τέρπεται ἐπ' ἀπωλείᾳ ζώντων.
¹⁴ἔκτισεν γὰρ εἰς τὸ εἶναι τὰ πάντα,
καὶ σωτήριοι αἱ γενέσεις τοῦ κόσμου,
καὶ οὐκ ἔστιν ἐν αὐταῖς φάρμακον ὀλέθρου

12² εν> B S

tators, it is directed to the renegade Jews of Alexandria, who openly expressed their cavillings and criticisms against the God of their fathers and His multiple laws.   SLANDER: R.V. has "backbiting," and Deane suggests "blasphemy." The Greek word *katalalia* is used in the New Testament in the sense of speaking evil of men, but the corresponding verb is employed in LXX in the sense of speaking evil of God, *cf.* Num. 21.5 and Ps. 78.19.   A MOUTH THAT BELIES: Meaning a mouth that speaks falsely against God.   DESTROYS THE SOUL: This does not imply, as some maintain, absolute annihilation of the wicked, since this would conflict with 4, 20, but rather condemnation to a continued miserable existence, as expressed in Enoch ch. 100 ff. and in our book 4.19. Hence the Greek phrase may mean nothing more than "committing the soul to torments beyond the grave," for which Tatian ch. 13 is often cited: *thanatos* signifies the eternal punishment to be assigned to the wicked on the Day of Judgment. And this is also the view of the Rabbis: the souls of the good go straight to God; those of the wicked wander to and fro, chased by angels from one end of the world to the other, but they are not annihilated, they still exist (*cf.* Weber, *Jüdische Theologie*, p. 338). It should be added that the same expression is used of physical death in Ecclus. 21.2.

12. This verse is undoubtedly based on Prov. 8.36, where wisdom says "All they that hate me love death." Contrast with this verse Eccl. 6.4 f., which seems to contain the thought that death is preferable to life. IN THE ERROR OF YOUR LIFE: *i. e.* by your epicurean vagaries that lead you astray. Similarly 12.23.   DRAW DESTRUCTION: *Cf.* Isa. 5.18, where LXX uses the same word as here, for *mashak*.   WORKS OF YOUR HANDS: *Cf.* Philo, *Det. Pot.*, § 32: "Moses says it is not God who is the author of our evils, but our own hands, by which he intends the voluntary preference of our minds for the worse course." See also Enoch 98.4: "Sin has not been sent upon the earth, but man of himself has created it."

13. GOD MADE NOT DEATH: God is not the author of death; *cf.* Ezek. 33.11. "I have no pleasure in the death of the wicked, but that the wicked turn

And refrain from slander of the tongue,
Because no secret utterance shall go on its way void
And a mouth that belies destroys the soul.
¹²Seek not death in the error of your life,
Neither draw destruction upon yourselves by the works
    of your hands.
¹³For God made not death,
Nor does he delight in the destruction of the living.
¹⁴For he created all things that they might have being,
And all the races of the world are wholesome,
And there is not in them the poison of destruction,

---

from his way and live; turn ye, turn ye from your evil ways; for why will ye die, O house of Israel?" See also *ibid.* 18.32. The doctrine that God is altogether good and cannot produce anything evil is a Philonic doctrine, see *Mut.* § 4 and *de Conf. Ling.* § 35 f. It implies absolute free-will with regard to sin, as stated in Deut. 30.19: "I have set before thee life and death, the blessing and the curse; therefore choose life." *Cf.* also Ecclus. 15.17: "Before man is life and death; and whichsoever he likes it shall be given him." But it is reflected also in the Midrash, see Sifra on *Behukkothai* 4: "evil never goes forth from me, as it is written (Lam. 3.38): out of the mouth of the Most High proceeds not evil."

14. ALL THINGS: rational as well as irrational.   BEING: God created all things to partake of His own nature, which is basically Being, *cf.* Ex. 3.14. *Eis to einai* can hardly mean everlasting existence: perhaps it denotes that the creatures were to carry out the laws of their proper existence, which would include the growth and decay of plants and brutes and the immortality of man (Deane).   RACES: So margin of R.V. "races of creatures," following the Itala *nationes terrae*, "products of the earth." R.V. itself has "the generative powers" (so Goodrick), but it is doubtful whether *geneseis* can have an active sense. The Greek word is used in various ways in the Septuagint and Apocrypha: birth, the process of coming into being, a generation, a tribe or species; but only two come into consideration here: "races of creatures" and "generative powers." Most commentators follow the former (Wahl, Gfrörer, Siegfried, Grimm, Deane, Farrar, et al.); the latter is adopted by a few, among them Goodrick, who justifies it on the logical ground that all creatures are not full of health and that some of them have the poison of death in them.   POISON OF DESTRUCTION: Strictly "medicine of destruction," as rendered by Itala *medicamentum exterminii*, for there is no implication of evil in *farmakon* itself. Some endeavor to see here a reference to the tree of knowledge of good and evil (Gfrörer, *Philo*, II, 208). The general sense is that the physical world in which men are placed is perfect and without blemish,

οὔτε ᾅδου βασίλειον ἐπὶ γῆς.
15   ¹⁵δικαιοσύνη γὰρ ἀθάνατός ἐστιν.
       ¹⁶ Ἀσεβεῖς δὲ ταῖς χερσὶν καὶ τοῖς λόγοις προσεκαλέ-
         σαντο αὐτόν,
       φίλον ἡγησάμενοι αὐτὸν ἐτάκησαν
       καὶ συνθήκην ἔθεντο πρὸς αὐτόν,
       ὅτι ἄξιοί εἰσιν τῆς ἐκείνου μερίδος εἶναι.

2 ¹εἶπον γὰρ ἐν ἑαυτοῖς λογισάμενοι οὐκ ὀρθῶς
    Ὀλίγος ἐστὶν καὶ λυπηρὸς ὁ βίος ἡμῶν,

14⁴ γης] pr. της A^t | post 15 add. Fr.   *mortis est acquisitio*
   ex La stichum *iniustitia autem*

---

but that the moral evil within men poisons everything.   KINGDOM OF DEATH: So A.V. and R.V., following Itala, Peshitta and Syrohexapla. But in classical Greek *basileion* stands for "palace" (so LXX in Prov. 18.19), hence R.V. margin "a royal house," referring perhaps to the idea of *Sheol* as the royal house of Hades. Many commentators see here a personification of Hades, corresponding to the Greek Pluto, the god of the lower regions. But Grimm stoutly opposes this view, arguing that it cannot be proved that Hades here denotes a personal existence as prince or angel of death, as in Rev. 6.8 and 20.14, or even a rhetorical personification of the lower world, as in Hos. 13.14 and Isa. 5.14. On the other hand, Isa. 38.18 and Hos. 13.14 clearly prove that death and Hades are identical. The sense conveyed by this passage is that death has no power over created beings on earth, nor did death form part of God's original scheme.
15. RIGHTEOUSNESS IS IMMORTAL: Meaning that either righteousness leads its adherents to immortality, or the righteous people are immortal (abstr. for concr., in contrast with "the impious" of the next verse). Righteousness comes in quite abruptly, hence A.V. puts this line in a parenthesis. According to Gregg we should expect a link between v. 14 and v. 15, such as "For (God destined His creation for righteousness, and) righteousness is immortal." However, there is an additional line in the Sixtine Vulgate and the Complutensian: *iniustitia autem mortis acquisitio est,* "but injustice is the very attainment of death." This completes the parallelism and furnishes the desired connection both with what follows and what precedes, and hence its genuineness is endorsed by Fritzsche and Grimm, the latter even conjecturing the Greek original as follows: ἀδικία δὲ θανάτου περιποίησις ἐστίν. Nevertheless, the line is spurious, chiefly because it occurs in no Greek manuscript whatever, nor in the Itala, and it is quite evident that it was introduced by some scribe to complete the parallelism. Itala has a slight addition to the Greek text: *justitia autem perpetua et immortalis est,* which may or may not go back to a different

Nor is the kingdom of death upon earth.

15   [15]For righteousness is immortal.

[16]But the impious summoned him by their hands and
    words;
Deeming him a friend they pined for him,
And made a covenant with him,
Because they are worthy to be of his portion.

2   [1]   For they said within themselves, reasoning not aright,
    Short and sorrowful is our life,

---

original. For the life-bestowing power of wisdom see Prov. 3.18; *cf.* also
Philo, *Plant.* § 27: "the nature of the good is incorruptible."
16. This verse seems to be based on Isa. 28.15, though the context is not
exactly the same.   IMPIOUS: or ungodly or simply wicked, all of which
are included in *asebeis*.   HIM: very vague, but evidently it has reference
to Hades or death, both of which are personified.   THEIR HANDS:
Really the work of their hands, or deeds, see above v. 12.   THEY PINED:
the Greek word means primarily "melted away," then in the abstract
"pined or wasted away," as here and 6.23. For the wasting effects of love it
is attested from Theocritus II, 28. Accordingly Pfleiderer and Bois take
this verse to refer to the pagan mysteries, especially to the identification
of Hades the god of death with Dionysus the god of life. Incidentally,
Pfleiderer thinks that the Book of Wisdom was composed by one who
desired to attack the pagan mysteries and that this verse was specially
directed against the initiated.   MADE A COVENANT: Pfleiderer (*Heraklit*,
p. 319) is of the opinion that an actual marriage contract is here involved.
Bois takes *sunthêkê* to refer to initiation into the pagan mysteries.
WORTHY: The wicked are worthy of Hades and deserve the fate of death.
PORTION: Similarly 2.24. The Greek *meros* means "a possession," especially
by inheritance.

The words here put into the mouth of the impious read very much like
a catalogue of Epicurean tenets or principles. Naturally, many of them
find their counterpart in the Book of Ecclesiastes, which is largely based on
the hedonistic philosophy of Epicurus. Comp. also Isa. 22.13 "Let us eat
and drink, for tomorrow we shall die." For similar sentiments in the
mouth of the ungodly see Enoch 102.6 ff.
1. WITHIN THEMSELVES: So R.V.; A.V. "reasoning with themselves,"
following Itala *cogitantes apud se.* R.V. margin has "among themselves,"
like Grimm "with one another," which is a classical use, but out of place
here, where reflections in times of distress are involved, not deliberations
of a council. Besides, there is a clear allusion here to Eccl. 2.1: "I said in
my heart etc."   SHORT AND SORROWFUL: *Cf.* Job 10.20 and 14.1, Eccl.

60 ΣΟΦΙΑ ΣΑΛΩΜΩΝΟΣ 2 2-4

καὶ οὐκ ἔστιν ἴασις ἐν τελευτῇ ἀνθρώπου,
καὶ οὐκ ἐγνώσθη ὁ ἀναλύσας ἐξ ᾅδου.
²ὅτι αὐτοσχεδίως ἐγενήθημεν
καὶ μετὰ τοῦτο ἐσόμεθα ὡς οὐχ ὑπάρξαντες·
ὅτι καπνὸς ἡ πνοὴ ἐν ῥισὶν ἡμῶν,
καὶ ὁ λόγος σπινθὴρ ἐν κινήσει καρδίας ἡμῶν,
³οὗ σβεσθέντος τέφρα ἀποβήσεται τὸ σῶμα
καὶ τὸ πνεῦμα διαχυθήσεται ὡς χαῦνος ἀήρ.
⁴καὶ τὸ ὄνομα ἡμῶν ἐπιλησθήσεται ἐν χρόνῳ,

2.23 and 5.17.   NO HEALING: or no cure, cf. Jer. 14.19, Nah. 3.19, and
elsewhere. Itala *refrigerium* may be due to theological considerations. The
meaning of the passage seems to be that there is no remedy or escape from
death, cf. 16.14 "the spirit that is gone forth he turns not again" and
Eccles. 8.8 "there is no man that has power over the spirit; neither has he
power over the day of death." Some commentators, like Grimm, give it a
different sense: In a man's end there is no remedy for his earthly troubles,
i. e. there is immortality as a reward for this world's evils.   RETURNED:
Taking *analuein* as an intransitive, but R.V. "gave release" takes it as a
transitive, perhaps because it is used transitively in 16.14 and in the passive in 5.12. But Grimm on II Macc. 8.25 quotes eight places where the
word means "to return." In view of the liberties that our author is known
to take with the Greek language, it is not impossible that he used the
active and passive forms of an intransitive verb without any difference of
meaning. The sense is quite clear: None of the dead have returned to tell
of a life beyond the grave; therefore let us enjoy the present life (Churton).
Similarly Job 7.9 f.   HADES: LXX's common rendering of *Sheol*, the
common abode of the departed, the unseen world into which men pass at
death. The Old Testament conception of *Sheol* as a dark underworld in
which the deceased continue to exist, though without the usual activity
and substantiality of real life, without joy and hope for better days, became modified later on, as reflected in rabbinical, apocryphal, and especially apocalyptic literature. Here, as in our Book of Wisdom, we light
upon the ideas of immortality of the soul, resurrection of the body, and
other benefits or rewards for the dead; while in the apocalyptic book of
Enoch we find Hades as an intermediate state, with relative rewards for
the good and penalties for the evil. The latter is further developed by the
Rabbis whose belief in resurrection became all but universal, cf., for
example, Abot 4.29: "Those who are dead are to be brought to life again."
2. BY MERE CHANCE: So R.V., but A.V. renders "at all adventure" and
Goodrick "at random." Incomprehensible is Itala's *ex nihilo*, which savors
of philosophizing. This passage resembles closely Eccles. 3.19 which is
generally rendered "that which befalls the sons of men befalls the beasts,"
but which may as well be translated "a mere chance are the sons of men

And there is no healing at the end of man,
And none was ever known that returned from Hades.
²For by mere chance were we begotten,
And hereafter we shall be as though we had never been,
For smoke is the breath in our nostrils,
And reason but a spark in the beating of our heart,
³Which being extinguished, the body shall turn into
    ashes,
And the spirit be dispersed as thin air;
⁴And our name shall be forgotten in time,

---

and a mere chance the beasts" (so R.V. margin). This tenet of Epicurean philosophy is illustrated from Lactantius, *Instit.* II.I.2, where men are described as *supervacuos et frustra omnino natos quae opinio plerosque ad vitia compellit.*   WE SHALL BE: Similarly Obad. 16. *Cf.* also Job 10.19. SMOKE: A symbol for something unsubstantial, see Ps. 102.4.   THE BREATH IN OUR NOSTRILS: As in Gen. 2.7 and Job 27.3. As Reuss puts it, this is a well formulated expression of materialism: breath does not prove the existence of a soul; it is produced by the play of the organs.   REASON BUT A SPARK: *logos* here stands for "reason" and not "speech." As stated by Siegfried, the ancients had no idea of the functions of the brain, and conceived of thought as a fiery matter. This idea is not only that of Heraclitus, who believed that fire was the origin of all things, but was common to Stoics and Epicureans alike. Zeno held that the soul was a fiery principle with which we are inspired and by which we move (*Diog. Laert,* VII, § 157).   THE BEATING OF OUR HEART: The idea conveyed in *kinêsei* seems to be that as two bodies rubbed together produced heat, so perpetual motion in the heart produced sparks which within meant "thought," without, in the form of breath, emitted vapor (Goodrick). The Greek philosophers supposed that the beating of the heart produced thought in the form of gleams or sparks from the fire-substance of the soul. "Breath" and "thoughts" to them are merely the results of mechanism (Farrar).

3. THE BODY etc.: This looks like an adaptation of Job 13.12 in LXX: "your boasting shall become like ashes, and your body clay." The idea expressed here is that life is a spark of fire which gradually consumes the body and leaves only ashes (Deane).   THIN AIR: Itala *mollis aer,* followed by A.V., but R.V. has "thin air," which is hardly justified. *Cf.* Ps. 144.4 "man is like to a breath," and Job 7.7 "remember that my life is wind."

4. OUR NAME SHALL BE FORGOTTEN: So also 4.19. *Cf.* Deut. 9.14, Ps. 109.13, Job 18.17, Eccl. 2.16 and 9.5. Such oblivion was considered a great calamity to man in ancient times, when the idea of personal immortality

καὶ οὐθεὶς μνημονεύσει τῶν ἔργων ἡμῶν·
καὶ παρελεύσεται ὁ βίος ἡμῶν ὡς ἴχνη νεφέλης
καὶ ὡς ὁμίχλη διασκεδασθήσεται
διωχθεῖσα ὑπὸ ἀκτίνων ἡλίου
καὶ ὑπὸ θερμότητος αὐτοῦ βαρυνθεῖσα.
5 ⁵σκιᾶς γὰρ πάροδος ὁ καιρὸς ἡμῶν,
καὶ οὐκ ἔστιν ἀναποδισμὸς τῆς τελευτῆς ἡμῶν,
ὅτι κατεσφραγίσθη καὶ οὐδεὶς ἀναστρέφει.
⁶δεῦτε οὖν καὶ ἀπολαύσωμεν τῶν ὄντων ἀγαθῶν
καὶ χρησώμεθα τῇ κτίσει ὡς ἐν νεότητι σπουδαίως·
⁷οἴνου πολυτελοῦς καὶ μύρων πλησθῶμεν,
καὶ μὴ παροδευσάτω ἡμᾶς ἄνθος ἔαρος·
⁸στεψώμεθα ῥόδων κάλυξιν πρὶν ἢ μαρανθῆναι·

5¹ καιρος] βιος B*Aᶜ
6² κτησει A | εν νεοτητι compl.]
εν > BSᶜ, νεοτητος S*A

7² ημας] με S*† | εαρος] αερος BS ‖
post 8 add. Fr. ex La stichum
*nullum pratum sit quod non per-
transeat luxuria nostra*

---

had not yet emerged and when future life meant no more than remembrance by future generations. *Cf.* II Sam. 18.18, Ps. 49.12.   OUR WORKS: Our good as well as our bad deeds will be forgotten, *cf.* Eccl. 9.6 "As well their love as their hatred and their envy is now perished."   TRACES OF A CLOUD: For comparison of life to a cloud see Hos. 13.3 and Job 7.9. Grimm takes the phrase as "the remains of a cloud" which pass away more quickly than the main mass of it. Churton renders "the mist which is the last vestige of a cloud."   WEIGHED DOWN: *Baruntheisa* is an awkward word to employ here, hence Arnold, on the basis of a single MS., suggested *marantheisa* (withered), but this is evidently a gloss. Itala has *aggravata*, R.V. "overcome." Gregg suggests *kathartheisa*: "as a mist is cleaned away from the sky by the sun's heat, so the name perishes."
5. OUR LIFE: so B; but ℵ A have *kairos* instead, so Itala *tempus nostrum*, and this is followed by R.V. "our allotted time."   THE PASSING OF A SHADOW: So also 5.9. For this metaphor *cf.* Ps. 102.12, 144.4, Job 8.9, 14.2, Eccl. 8.13, I Chron. 29.15. Gregg suggests that the shadow is that of a sun-dial, *cf.* Ecclus. 46.4 and 48.23.   RETREAT: This is the literal rendering of *anapodismos*, hence Itala *non est reversio finis nostri* and R.V. margin "no putting back of our end" (*cf.* Isa. 38.8). To render "repetition" and explain that no man can die twice (Grimm, Siegfried, *et al.*) is hardly feasible, since it is known that man can only die once, *cf.* Heb. 9.27. Goodrick, basing himself on تعويق of the Arabic version, which leads

back to *empodismos,* "hindering," and supported also by the Armenian version, renders the line "there is no prevention of our end," *i.e.* there is no

And none shall remember our works;
And our life shall pass away as the traces of a cloud,
And as mist shall it be dispersed,
Chased by the sun's rays,
And weighed down by the heat thereof.
5 ⁵For our life is the passing of a shadow,
And there is no retreat from our end,
For it has been sealed and none reverses it.
⁶Come therefore and let us enjoy the good things that are,
And earnestly make use of creation as in youth.
⁷Let us fill ourselves with costly wine and perfumes,
And let not a flower of the spring pass us by.
⁸Let us crown ourselves with rosebuds ere they wither,

---

preventing death.   SEALED: *I. e.* the end is pre-determined, *cf.* Job
14.17, Dan. 6.18 and 12.9.   REVERSES IT: R.V. "turns it back." The
verb *anastrefein* is transitive here and in 16.14, but it occurs also in an
intransitive sense in II Sam. 12.23 and Ecclus. 40.11, hence R.V. margin
"comes again." On the sense of the passage see Ecclus. 38.21.

6. COME THEREFORE etc.: This and the following verses are reminiscent of
Isa. 22.13 and 56.12, Eccl. 2.24, 3.12 and 9.7. According to Farrar, they
represent "the dregs of Epicurean theory."   THE GOOD THINGS THAT
ARE: *I. e.* that have real being: not clouds or shadows or imaginary delights like those of virtue, but tangible sources of enjoyment, sensual
pleasures of the hedonist or Epicurean. This evidently is directed against
Koheleth and his hedonistic philosophy. A.V. "are present" and R.V.
"that now are" refer to things ready at hand or easily obtainable.
CREATION: Namely the aggregate of created things, as usual in our book
and in Ecclesiasticus.   AS IN YOUTH: *neotêti* is difficult of interpretation,
so is the variant *neotêtos* of ℵ A. Our reading follows Itala *tanquam in
iuventute*, "as in youth," when pleasure is keenest and energy most
abounding. Pal. Syr. "in our youth," Arab. "as long as youth lasts."
Grimm, with the support of some manuscripts and the Complutensian
Polyglot, would read *nôs en neotêti*; similarly Siegfried with particular
reference to Eccl. 11.9.

7. WINE AND PERFUMES: *Cf.* Isa. 25.6 and Am. 6.6. By hendiadys this may
stand for "perfumed wine," *cf.* Cant. 8.2 G and see numerous examples in
Goodrick *ad loc.*   A FLOWER OF THE SPRING: *anthos earos*, so A, supported by Itala *flos temporis;* but ℵB have *aeros*, "a flower that scents the
air." The former seems to be the original reading, since it is not likely that
a copyist would have changed *aeros* into *earos* but rather vice versa.

8. ROSEBUDS: Off hand, crowning with roses seems to be a Greek rather
than Jewish custom, but undoubtedly the Jewish renegades in Alexandria
practiced such pagan customs, bedecking themselves with flowers and

⁹μηδεὶς ἡμῶν ἄμοιρος ἔστω τῆς ἡμετέρας ἀγερωχίας,
  πανταχῇ καταλίπωμεν σύμβολα τῆς εὐφροσύνης,
  ὅτι αὕτη ἡ μερὶς ἡμῶν καὶ ὁ κλῆρος οὗτος.
10 ¹⁰καταδυναστεύσωμεν πένητα δίκαιον,
  μὴ φεισώμεθα χήρας
  μηδὲ πρεσβύτου ἐντραπῶμεν πολιὰς πολυχρονίους·
  ¹¹ἔστω δὲ ἡμῶν ἡ ἰσχὺς νόμος τῆς δικαιοσύνης,
  τὸ γὰρ ἀσθενὲς ἄχρηστον ἐλέγχεται.
  ¹²ἐνεδρεύσωμεν τὸν δίκαιον, ὅτι δύσχρηστος ἡμῖν ἐστιν
  καὶ ἐναντιοῦται τοῖς ἔργοις ἡμῶν

9¹ εστω] -τε S⸍ i. e. -ται (sic pau.)   10³ πρεσβυτερου A
9³ ουτος] ημων A⸍

garlands as symbols of rejoicing. *Cf.* on this heathenish custom Isa. 28.1, Ezek. 23.42, Judith 15.13; see also Josephus, *Antiq.*, XIX. IX.1. Greek and Latin sources are numerous and can hardly be quoted here. Suffice it to mention Plutarch, quoted by Grimm, to the effect that "warm flowers opened the pores and provided an exit for the spirit and vapour of the wine."

The second part of this verse, wanting in Greek, is supplied from the Old Latin version: *nullum pratum sit quod non pertranseat luxuria nostra.* Goodrick holds that this line is almost certainly genuine: "It must have fallen out at an early date, for none of the versions recognize it; but (1) it restores the balance of periods so carefully maintained in the rest of the paragraph; (2) it makes up one, at least, of the two *stichs* which are presumed to have fallen out: Nicephorus (Deane, *Proleg.*, 28) reckoned 1100 *stichs* in 'Wisdom', and at present there are but 1098; (3) an ancient glossary attached to Cod. Coislinianus, CCCXCIV, gives the word λειμών as occurring in 'Wisdom'; it is nowhere to be found if not here." But against these cogent considerations Gregg adduces the following acute argument: "It does not seem to have been noticed that Vulg. is simply a rendering of the first line of verse 9, with λειμών substituted for ἡμῶν Either this line was introduced to complete the apparently unfinished verse 8, or it is the original reading, and verse 9a is the interpolation. Verse 9a as it stands is somewhat pointless, and adds nothing to the sense."

9. OVERWEENING REVELRY: *agerochia* occurs nowhere else in the Bible except in II Macc. 9.7 and III Macc. 2.3, where it signifies "rude insolence" or "overweening arrogance." Here the word is variously rendered: A.V. "voluptuousness," R.V. "proud revelry," Goodrick "insolent revelry." Curious is the rendering of the Palest. Syr. "Let none of us be without pleasure until our old age," evidently connecting the word with *geron* "an old man," and surmising it meant "revelry which knows no old age." Bois (*Essai*, p. 295) is of the opinion that the word may be an allusion to

[And let there be no meadow uncoursed by our debauch].

⁹Let none of us go without his share in our overweening
    revelry;

Let us leave everywhere tokens of our mirth,

For this is our portion, and such is our lot.

10 ¹⁰Let us oppress the righteous poor,

Let us not spare the widow,

Nor reverence the old man's gray hairs full of years.

¹¹Let our strength be the rule of our righteousness,

For weakness is proved to be unprofitable.

¹²But let us lie in wait for the righteous, because he is of
    disservice to us,

And he is opposed to our doings,

---

the heathen mysteries.   TOKENS OF OUR MIRTH: So R.V., and similarly
Grimm, Goodrick and others. These imply abuses of ordinary decencies
of life, oppression of the poor, and destruction of property.   OUR
PORTION . . . OUR LOT: Cf. Isa. 57.6; see also Jer. 13.25, Eccl. 2.10, 3.22,
9.9. The sense is: "Let us enjoy life while it lasts: we have nothing else to
do and nothing more to expect" (Grimm). Cornely explains it somewhat
differently: "Let there be no concealment and no hypocrisy about our
debauches: let every one see our revelry and the tokens of it."
10. OPPRESS: A reference perhaps to the wealthy and apostate Jews of
Alexandria, who persecuted their humbler fellow-countrymen because
they refused to abandon their faith. For oppression of the righteous and
the poor see Ezek. 18.12, Hab. 1.4, Zech. 7.10, etc. It is interesting to
note a cleavage here between Wisdom and Koheleth, since the latter
speaks of oppression with abhorrence (4.1). But perhaps Goodrick is right
"that in most of the passages where *katadynastevein* is used (15.14, 17.2,
Ecclus. 48.12, Ezek. 22.29, Acts 10.38) it is used not of one private person
wronging another, but of men in authority misusing their power."   THE
WIDOW: The widow and the orphan were particularly exposed to injustice,
cf. Isa. 10.2, Jer. 22.3, Mal. 3.5.   THE OLD MAN'S GRAY HAIRS: On this
point cf. the story of Eleazar in II Macc. 6.18 ff., though there the
agents were heathen soldiers.
11. OUR STRENGTH etc.: Meaning: let might be right! Less effectively R.V.
"let our strength be to us a law of righteousness."   UNPROFITABLE: R.V.
"of no service." The sense of the passage seems to be: Weakness is not
only contemptible; it is unprofitable and therefore should be exterminated
(Goodrick).
12. LIE IN WAIT: Cf. Ps. 10.8 and 9. This line appears to be a quotation
from an erroneous LXX version of Isa. 3.10, the only difference being in
the first word: "lie in wait" instead of "bind." It should be noted that this
mistranslation was adopted by the Church Fathers, following its citation

καὶ ὀνειδίζει ἡμῖν ἁμαρτήματα νόμου
καὶ ἐπιφημίζει ἡμῖν ἁμαρτήματα παιδείας ἡμῶν·
¹³ἐπαγγέλλεται γνῶσιν ἔχειν θεοῦ
καὶ παῖδα κυρίου ἑαυτὸν ὀνομάζει·
¹⁴ἐγένετο ἡμῖν εἰς ἔλεγχον ἐννοιῶν ἡμῶν,
βαρύς ἐστιν ἡμῖν καὶ βλεπόμενος,
15   ¹⁵ὅτι ἀνόμοιος τοῖς ἄλλοις ὁ βίος αὐτοῦ,
καὶ ἐξηλλαγμέναι αἱ τρίβοι αὐτοῦ·
¹⁶εἰς κίβδηλον ἐλογίσθημεν αὐτῷ,
καὶ ἀπέχεται τῶν ὁδῶν ἡμῶν ὡς ἀπὸ ἀκαθαρσιῶν·
μακαρίζει ἔσχατα δικαίων
καὶ ἀλαζονεύεται πατέρα θεόν.

12⁴ επιφημιζεται Bᵒ   16¹ ελογισθημεν] εγενηθ. S*

in Ep. Barnab. 6.7, and taken by them as an allusion to the sufferings of Jesus. Incidentally, this passage goes to prove that Greek was the original language of Wisdom.   SINS AGAINST THE LAW: *I.e.* the actual law of Moses. Grimm endeavors to prove that in Jewish writings "law" without the article stands always for the law of Moses, and consequently he insists that this line proves that the enemies of the righteous are apostate Jews.   SINS AGAINST OUR DISCIPLINE: Parallel in meaning and construction to the preceding "sins against the law," hence may imply sins against traditional observances. Grimm and Siegfried render "sins against morality," Weber "sins of our method of life." Lastly, Gregg is inclined to omit this line altogether, with Cyprian (*Testim.* II.14), as an ineffective addition.

13. KNOWLEDGE OF GOD: of His will and requirements, what He rewards and what He punishes (Deane). Knowledge of God is equivalent to true religion and may be attained through a strictly ethical life. *Cf.* Isa. 11.2 and 9, Hos. 4.1.   SERVANT OF THE LORD: So R.V., but margin has "child" (so Goodrick). In favor of the former are the facts that *pais* in classical Greek denotes "servant" as well as "child" and that the phrase *pais theou* is often employed in LXX for "Servant of the Lord." The latter finds its support in v. 16 below "and vaunts that God is his father" and in v. 18 below "if the righteous be God's son he will uphold him." The two expressions are employed interchangeably in 9.4-7 and 12.19 f. Ever since the Epistle of Barnabas this passage has been adduced by Church Fathers as a Messianic prophecy foretelling the coming of Jesus, *cf.* Justin, *Dial. cum Tryph.*, XVII; Eusebius, *Praeparatio Evangelica*, XIII, 13; Clem. Alexandr., *Stromata*, V, Z4. Of the Latin Fathers quoting it Augustine is very explicit (*de Civit. Dei*, XVII, 20): *In uno (libro) qui*

And reproaches us with sins against the law,
And lays to our charge sins against our discipline.
[13]He professes to have knowledge of God,
And calls himself servant of the Lord.
[14]He became to us a reproach of our thoughts,
Grievous is he to us even to look upon.

15   [15]For his life is unlike to others,
And his paths are peculiar.
[16]As base metal were we accounted by him,
And he abstains from our ways as from impurities,
He blesses the end of the righteous,
And vaunts that God is his father.

---

appellatur sapientia Salomonis passio Christi apertissime prophetatur. Impii quippe interfectores ejus commemorantur dicentes Circumveniamus justum. This even led some critics to treat the passage as a Christian interpolation, and others to argue that the whole Book of Wisdom was the work of a Christian. But such deductions are highly problematical, since they lack a factual foundation. It must be borne in mind that whenever the sonship of Jesus is mentioned elsewhere the word used is *Vios*, not *pais*. Moreover, the figure "servant of the Lord" is so well-known to us from the Second Isaiah that it hardly needs corroboration. Undoubtedly, the reference here is to the poor righteous man of ordinary life, and the term "righteous man," like "servant of the Lord," might be a collective formula standing for the whole community.

14. A REPROACH: Not that the righteous actually rebuked the apostates, but the mere sight of their piety and probity would be enough of a reproach for them.

15. UNLIKE TO OTHERS: This is a literal rendering of a Greek idiom known as *comparatio compendiaria*. The real meaning is "unlike to others' lives," hence A.V. and R.V. have "unlike other men's." PECULIAR: The Greek word means primarily "changed," *i. e.* abnormal, then "strange, peculiar." R.V. renders "of strange fashion." The freethinkers reckon all piety and observance of the law as a fancy of eccentric persons (Grimm).

16. A BASE METAL: So R.V., A.V. "counterfeits," Goodrick "false coin." Itala *nugaces* seems to point to a different text, so also Pal. Syr. "filthiness," which occurs only in the second line. THE END: *I. e.* the end of life, or death, *cf.* Ecclus. 1.13, 7.36, 51.14. R.V. has "the latter end." Grimm thinks that *ta eschata* may refer to this life, to the good fortune of the righteous upon earth, *cf.* Job 42.12. VAUNTS: The Greek word is probably used in scorn: he boasts, he brags. GOD IS HIS FATHER: *Cf.* Ecclus. 23.1 and 4.

^{17}ἴδωμεν εἰ οἱ λόγοι αὐτοῦ ἀληθεῖς,
καὶ πειράσωμεν τὰ ἐν ἐκβάσει αὐτοῦ·
^{18}εἰ γάρ ἐστιν ὁ δίκαιος υἱὸς θεοῦ, ἀντιλήμψεται αὐτοῦ
καὶ ῥύσεται αὐτὸν ἐκ χειρὸς ἀνθεστηκότων.
^{19}ὕβρει καὶ βασάνῳ ἐτάσωμεν αὐτόν,
ἵνα γνῶμεν τὴν ἐπιείκειαν αὐτοῦ
καὶ δοκιμάσωμεν τὴν ἀνεξικακίαν αὐτοῦ·
20   ^{20}θανάτῳ ἀσχήμονι καταδικάσωμεν αὐτόν,
ἔσται γὰρ αὐτοῦ ἐπισκοπὴ ἐκ λόγων αὐτοῦ.
^{21} Ταῦτα ἐλογίσαντο, καὶ ἐπλανήθησαν·
ἀπετύφλωσεν γὰρ αὐτοὺς ἡ κακία αὐτῶν,
^{22}καὶ οὐκ ἔγνωσαν μυστήρια θεοῦ
οὐδὲ μισθὸν ἤλπισαν ὁσιότητος

19³ δοκιμασωμεν] δικασ. B†   21² απετυφλ.] απ>S†
21¹ ελογισθησαν S*†   22¹ θεου] αυτου B*†

17. AT HIS DEPARTURE: Goodrick "at his going forth." Less effective A.V. "in the end of him" and R.V. "in the ending of his life." The word *ekbasis* occurs in the same sense also in 11.14. A parallel to it is *exodos*, similarly used of death in Luke 9.31 and II Pet. 1.15.

18. The similarity between this verse and Matt. 27.43 has led some commentators to suspect a Christian interpolation here, as in v. 13 above; but we must not overlook the fact that verbal agreement between two passages may be due to a common source, and such a source has been found in Ps. 22.9, see also Isa. 42.1. As Reuss pointed out: 1) the following chapter, which is closely connected with this, employs "just man" and "just men" indiscriminately; 2) the persecutors of Jesus were not materialists, but rather idealists; 3) a Christian interpolator could not have omitted an allusion to the purpose of Jesus' death.

19. WANTON VIOLENCE: R.V. has "outrage," Goodrick "insult."   TEST HIM: This is a euphemism for "torture him." The verb is so used also in Acts 22.24.   REASONABLENESS: A.V. "meekness," R.V. "gentleness," Goodrick "tolerance." The Greek word denotes self-restraint in relation to others. Itala *reverentia* is inexplicable.   ENDURANCE OF EVIL: So Goodrick, rendering literally. R.V. "patience under wrong." Examples of sufferings for the Jewish faith are numerous in the books of Maccabees.

20. A SHAMEFUL DEATH: The dative points to late Greek, see Winer's Grammar, p. 263, and Moulton's note. À Lapide sees here a direct allusion to the crucifixion of Jesus.   HIS EXAMINATION etc.: So Goodrick. This is a literal rendering of the Greek, but the line is interpreted in various ways. A.V. has "by his own saying he shall be respected," which no doubt is based on Itala *erit enim ei respectus ex sermonibus illius*. R.V. "he shall be visited according to his words," that is visited by God, in a

¹⁷Let us see if his words be true,
And let us try what will happen at his departure.
¹⁸For if the righteous be God's son, he will uphold him,
And save him from the hand of his adversaries.
¹⁹With wanton violence and torture let us test him,
That we may know his reasonableness,
And judge of his endurance of evil.

20   ²⁰Let us condemn him to a shameful death,
For his examination will be made from his own words.
²¹Thus reasoned they, and were led astray,
For their wickedness blinded them.
²²And they knew not the mysteries of God,
Neither hoped they for the reward of holiness,

---

favorable sense, but margin has "there shall be a visitation of him out of his words," in a bad sense. Grimm renders "there shall be an ἐπισκοπή in accordance with his words"; similarly Churton "there shall be an inquiry into the truth of his words." The general sense seems to be that a severe examination, by God Himself, will be made on the ground of the man's own professions.

21. THUS REASONED THEY etc: *Cf.* 2.1 "reasoning not aright." The text might seem to convey the idea that their going astray was the result of their false reasoning, but this can hardly be true: on the contrary, their false reasoning was the result of their evil deeds. Graetz, on the basis of resemblance to John 9.40 f. and Luke 23.34, singled out this verse as a Christian interpolation, but really the resemblance is only linguistic and does not involve Christian sentiment or dogma. In the words of Bissell: "What is here said of the relations between the pious and worldly-minded has always been true and the similarity of the language used to that used by the Jews against Christ arises solely from a natural similarity of circumstances."　BLINDED THEM: Through evil living they had lost the eye for spiritual things, *cf.* Isa. 56.10.

22. THE MYSTERIES OF GOD: B has μυστήρια αὐτοῦ. *Cf.* "the mysteries of wisdom" in 6.22. What these mysteries are is a subject for contention. Some claim that they refer to the esoteric doctrine of immortality (so Bois, *Essai*, p. 297; Gfrörer, *Philo*, II, 234), but others characterize them as the mysterious dealing of God with the righteous upon earth—their troubles to be succeeded by future happiness (Goodrick), that suffering is not necessarily punishment, but is often a test of goodness which will be rewarded after death by immortality (Holmes). Itala *sacramenta Dei* means the same thing, as clearly expressed in 4.17, and not what this term implies in the New Testament.　REWARD OF HOLINESS: *hosiotês* occurs also in 5.19, 9.3, and 14.30, while *hosios* occurs in 4.15, 6.10, 7.27, 10.15, 18.1.5.9. This emphasis on "holiness" and "holy," which in the Psalms

οὐδὲ ἔκριναν γέρας ψυχῶν ἀμώμων.
²³ὅτι ὁ θεὸς ἔκτισεν τὸν ἄνθρωπον ἐπ' ἀφθαρσίᾳ
καὶ εἰκόνα τῆς ἰδίας ἀϊδιότητος ἐποίησεν αὐτόν·
²⁴φθόνῳ δὲ διαβόλου θάνατος εἰσῆλθεν εἰς τὸν κόσμον,
πειράζουσιν δὲ αὐτὸν οἱ τῆς ἐκείνου μερίδος ὄντες.

3 ¹ Δικαίων δὲ ψυχαὶ ἐν χειρὶ θεοῦ,
καὶ οὐ μὴ ἅψηται αὐτῶν βάσανος.
²ἔδοξαν ἐν ὀφθαλμοῖς ἀφρόνων τεθνάναι,
καὶ ἐλογίσθη κάκωσις ἡ ἔξοδος αὐτῶν

---

always corresponds to the Heb. *hasid*, led some commentators to see here an allusion to the Hasidim or Hasidaeans, a religious sect in Palestine during the Second Commonwealth (I Macc. 2.42, 7.13), and others to the hypothesis that the author of Wisdom himself belonged to an ascetic or mystic sect, such as the *Therapeutae*, known to have existed in the vicinity of Alexandria in the days of Philo.

23. INCORRUPTION: A literal rendering of *aftharsia*, so R.V. following Itala *inexterminabilem*. Similarly in 6.19. Although this word alludes primarily to the elevated spiritual life of man without particular reference to the present or future life, yet undoubtedly it includes also the notion of blessed immortality, on a par with *athanasia* in 3.4, 8.13.17, 15.3.   AN IMAGE OF HIS OWN PROPER BEING: So R.V., reading ἰδιότητος, in imitation of Gen. 1.26. This certainly implies immortality. However, there is a variant reading ἀϊδιότητος "everlastingness" (see the quotations in Goodrick), which constitutes a direct statement in favor of immortality. The latter is followed by A.V. and Goodrick. Comp. also Philo, *Opif.*, § 13: "God gave them a share in His everlastingness." Contrary to this view is Ecclus. 17.1 ff., which evidently negates the immortality of man.

24. THE DEVIL'S ENVY: *diabolos* is regularly used by LXX in rendering Heb. *Satan*. Both words originally meant "adversary," *cf.* Ps. 109.6 and I Macc. 1.36. Their metaphysical implications belong to the post-exilic period of Jewish history. The reference here, according to most expositors, is to the temptation of Eve by the serpent; comp. I Enoch 69.6, Ecclus. 25.24; see also Josephus, *Antiq.*, I.I.4. The Talmud and Midrash likewise identify the serpent with the devil, named Satan or Sammael, *cf. Pirke de R. Eliezer*, 13; *Zohar, Ber.*; Rev. 2:9; 20.2. But Bois (*Essai*, p. 297) suggests that it may refer to Cain, the first murderer, and Gregg adduces a number of arguments in favor of this view, among them that the Fall is treated as of small account in 10.1 ff. while all the stress is laid on the sin of Cain, the first unrighteous man, and that the root of his sin was indeed envy and jealousy. Gregg also avers that the identification of the serpent with the devil is not known to Alexandrian literature of this date.   DEATH: *I. e.* physical death, *cf.* v. 20 above.   HIS: Namely the devil's.   PARTY: So Goodrick, R.V. "portion" with

Nor estimated the prize of blameless souls.
²³Because God created man for incorruption,
  And made him an image of his own proper being.
²⁴But through the devil's envy death entered into the
  world,
  And they that belong to his party experience it.

3   ¹   But the souls of the righteous are in the hand of God,
          And no torment shall touch them.
      ²In the eyes of the foolish they seemed to have died,
          And their departure was accounted a misfortune,

Pal. Syr. *meris* has the same force here as in 1.16. In Ecclus. 17.15 Israel is called *meris Kuriou*. EXPERIENCE IT: Namely death. So Goodrick, R.V. renders "make trial thereof."
   This verse too is considered by Graetz (*Geschichte*, III, 444) as a Christian interpolation, for the following reasons: (1) the verse disturbs the connection of the passage; (2) the last few words have no sense; (3) in the Jewish writings of this period no analogy can be found to the doctrine of the cosmical power of the devil.

1. THE SOULS OF THE RIGHTEOUS: The aim here is to teach immortality of the soul, not resurrection of the body. Freed from the coils of the body the soul is delivered from the pains that are inevitable in a material world (Gregg). *Cf.* Philo, *Jos.*, § 43: "There is not one good man, but shall live hereafter ageless and deathless, with a soul constrained no longer by the fetters of the body"; see also *Moses*, III.39. *Cf.* also b. Shab. 152b: "The souls of the righteous are concealed under the throne of glory."   TOR-MENT: Itala *tormentum mortis. Basanos* undoubtedly means "torment after death," and not the sufferings inflicted by the wicked upon earth (Good-rick). This idea of punishment of the wicked after death may be said to have become current by the time of the Book of Wisdom, though, as pointed out by Farrar, the nature and continuance of their future torment are not defined, and were not clearly recognized. Of course, the idea of such torment is incompatible with the notion of the annihilation of the wicked.
2. IN THE EYES OF: *I. e.* in the judgment of, as frequently in the Bible. FOOLISH: or wicked, as in 1.3. *Afrôn* is supposed to correspond to Heb. *nabal*, as in II Sam. 13.13, see also I Sam. 25.25. For a different meaning see v. 12 below.   THEY SEEMED TO HAVE DIED: But in truth they were alive, or at least their souls were alive. This paradox is illustrated from Philo, *Fug.*, § 10: "Enquiry taught me that some living men are dead and some dead men are alive: the wicked who live to be old men are mere corpses devoid of the life of virtue, but the good, though they are parted from the body live for ever, enjoying an immortal destiny." *Cf.* also *Q.D.P.I.S.*,

³καὶ ἡ ἀφ᾽ ἡμῶν πορεία σύντριμμα,
οἱ δέ εἰσιν ἐν εἰρήνῃ.
⁴καὶ γὰρ ἐν ὄψει ἀνθρώπων ἐὰν κολασθῶσιν,
ἡ ἐλπὶς αὐτῶν ἀθανασίας πλήρης·
5 ⁵καὶ ὀλίγα παιδευθέντες μεγάλα εὐεργετηθήσονται,
ὅτι ὁ θεὸς ἐπείρασεν αὐτοὺς
καὶ εὗρεν αὐτοὺς ἀξίους ἑαυτοῦ·
⁶ὡς χρυσὸν ἐν χωνευτηρίῳ ἐδοκίμασεν αὐτοὺς
καὶ ὡς ὁλοκάρπωμα θυσίας προσεδέξατο αὐτούς.
⁷καὶ ἐν καιρῷ ἐπισκοπῆς αὐτῶν ἀναλάμψουσιν

---

§ 15: "The wise man who appears to have departed from this mortal life lives in a life immortal." This spiritual idea of life and death is evident also in 5.13 and 10.3.

3. THEIR GOING FROM US: *Cf*. Eccl. 12.5. R.V. has "their journeying." A RUIN: *Suntrimma* in this sense occurs in Isa. 22.4, 59.7, Ecclus. 40.9, I Macc. 2.7. For the verb in the sense of "break to pieces" see Ps. 2.9. IN PEACE: εἰρήνη here may be synonymous with ἀνάπαυσις, meaning "rest from toil and earthly care," as in Isa. 57.2 and Job 3.17, or may refer to the blessedness of the soul of the righteous under God's protection, as in Enoch 102.10. For the various views on this subject see Charles, *Eschatology*, and Barney, *Israel's Hope of Immortality*.

4. Gregg calls attention to the apocalyptic character of this and the following verses, which hinge on the difficulties concerning the righteousness of God and the suffering of His righteous servants upon earth. "Apocalyptic was the refuge of those who found that the traditional view of God's dealings with His people was unsatisfying. Earthly life did not provide a full opportunity for justice and vengeance. It is not to be wondered at that the inevitable rebound from a conception of life limited to the earthly lives of a man and his descendants to one in which physical death was merely an incident, was accompanied by wildly exaggerated promises and hopes. This passage exhibits unusual reticence. It dismisses in one line the old view that suffering was an indication of God's wrath and punishment. It is only 'in the sight of men' that the righteous are forsaken: what looks like punishment is education." MEN: Meaning unreasoning people at large, not the freethinkers only, as Bois maintains (*Essai*, p. 383). FULL: *Plêrês* may be conjoined either with *elpis* ("their sure hope is that of immortality") or with *athanasia* ("their hope is full of immortality"), but the latter seems to be preferable, whether the reference be to hopes they cherished on earth or to expectations entertained now that they are in the hand of God.

5. CHASTENED BUT A LITTLE: *Cf*. II Macc. 6.12–7.33, see also Ps. 119.75 and Prov. 3.11 f. Itala varies: *in paucis vexati in multis bene disponentur*. Pal. Syr. paraphrases "a little he inquired of them, a little he tried them, much shall they inherit." TRIED THEM: in the sense of testing, *cf*. Gen. 22.1 and Ps. 26.2, see also I Enoch 108.9: the righteous "were much

³And their going from us a ruin;

But they are in peace.

⁴For even if they shall have been punished in the sight of
men,

Their hope is full of immortality.

5   ⁵And having been chastened but a little, they shall be
benefited greatly,

For God tried them,

And found them worthy of himself.

⁶As gold in a smelting-furnace he tested them,

And as a whole burnt offering he accepted them.

⁷And in the time of their visitation they shall shine
forth,

---

tried by the Lord and their spirits were found pure." WORTHY: *Cf.*
6.16 "Wisdom goes about seeking them that are worthy of her." Grimm,
remarking that Pseudo-Solomon would find the righteous to be rewarded
only among the Jews, discovers here a narrow particularism, which is in
striking contrast with the love of God for all His creatures as stated in
11.23 f. Goodrick adduces further proof for this particularism, quoting
especially II Macc. 6.14 ff. Herein, states Goodrick, lay a fatal fault of the
Jewish Alexandrine School—in the attempt to hold at once with philan-
thropic universalism and Jewish particularism.

6. AS GOLD IN A SMELTING-FURNACE: This metaphor is frequent in the
Bible, *cf.*, for example, Isa. 40.19, Zech. 13.9, Mal. 3.3, Ps. 66.10, Prov.
17.3 and 27.21. χωνευτήριον is found only in LXX and in ecclesiastical
literature.   TESTED THEM: to prove that they are not base metal, like
the persecutors in 2.16.   AS A WHOLE BURNT OFFERING: So R.V., but
Goodrick has "as the whole offering of a burnt sacrifice." It appears that
holokarpôma had lost its etymological connection with fruits of the earth
and was applied to flesh offerings, especially the whole burnt offering. Not
so Syroh. which has "like fruits of an offering of slaughter."

Itala has an addition here *et in tempore erit respectus illorum*, which is
followed by *Fulgebunt justi* etc. It is quite evident that the Latin originally
read *et in tempore respectus illorum fulgebunt justi*, which is the first line of
v. 7, but *respectus* being mistaken for a nominative *erit* was added unnecessarily (Reusch quoted by Deane).

7. VISITATION: So R.V., but Goodrick has "inspection." Some critics, in
their anxiety to prove that the author of Wisdom could not have believed
in a Judgment Day or in the resurrection of the body, have endeavored to
show that this and the next verse have reference to the righteous who shall
be found alive when God shall come to judge the earth. But as Deane
points out, "as the whole passage evidently refers to the life beyond the
grave, it is a mistake to understand the time of visitation as referring to
this world."   SHINE FORTH: The souls of the righteous shall shine forth

καὶ ὡς σπινθῆρες ἐν καλάμῃ διαδραμοῦνται·
⁸κρινοῦσιν ἔθνη καὶ κρατήσουσιν λαῶν,
καὶ βασιλεύσει αὐτῶν κύριος εἰς τοὺς αἰῶνας.
⁹οἱ πεποιθότες ἐπ᾽ αὐτῷ συνήσουσιν ἀλήθειαν,
καὶ οἱ πιστοὶ ἐν ἀγάπῃ προσμενοῦσιν αὐτῷ·
ὅτι χάρις καὶ ἔλεος τοῖς ἐκλεκτοῖς αὐτοῦ.
10   ¹⁰ Οἱ δὲ ἀσεβεῖς καθὰ ἐλογίσαντο ἕξουσιν ἐπιτιμίαν
οἱ ἀμελήσαντες τοῦ δικαίου καὶ τοῦ κυρίου ἀποστάντες·
¹¹σοφίαν γὰρ καὶ παιδείαν ὁ ἐξουθενῶν ταλαίπωρος,
καὶ κενὴ ἡ ἐλπὶς αὐτῶν, καὶ οἱ κόποι ἀνόνητοι,
καὶ ἄχρηστα τὰ ἔργα αὐτῶν·

9³ εκλεκτοις] οσιοις S | post 9³ ad-   οσιοις (Sεκλεκτοις) αυτου SA : ex 4 15
dunt stichum και επισκοπη εν τοις   11² κοποι]+αυτων S†

---

in glory. *Cf.* Dan. 12.3, Enoch 104.2.   AS SPARKS IN THE STUBBLE: This metaphor is quite frequent in the Bible, *cf.* Isa. 1.31, Joel 2.5, Obad. 18, Zech. 12.6, Mal. 4.1 (3.19). According to Farrar it expresses the victorious and consuming power of the righteous hereafter. This idea is elaborated by Philo in *Migr.*, § 21.

8. THEY SHALL JUDGE etc.: This verse is best illustrated through Dan. 7.22: "judgment was given for the saints of the Most High; and the time came, and the saints possessed the kingdom." *Cf.* also Ecclus. 4.15. THEIR LORD etc.: So Itala, A.V., Goodrick, but R.V. has "the Lord shall reign over them for evermore." That the former is more appropriate may be seen from Ps. 10.16. As Goodrick puts it, the question is not whether God will reign over the righteous, for He is already their king; "what is promised here is that he shall be king not only over them, but over all the world, in which his sway is certainly at present disowned."

9. THEY THAT TRUST IN HIM: *Cf.* Prov. 28.5. The author wants to convey the idea that adherence to God constitutes wise living and improvement of character, see Ps. 111.10. For the opposite see 1.3 above.   SHALL UNDERSTAND TRUTH: Not intellectual truth of the philosophers, but rather the truth of God's mysterious dealings with men, or, as Holmes puts it, God's methods in governing the world.   ABIDE WITH HIM IN LOVE: Meaning they shall be loved by God. For heaven as the everlasting home of the good see also *Assumptio Mosis*, 10.9. Enoch 104.6 pictures them as companions of the heavenly host; the Apocalypse of Baruch 51.10 makes them like unto the angels; and the Similitudes of Enoch 41.2 and 51.4 make it clear that they are actually to become angels. *Cf.* on this subject Charles, *Eschatology*, p. 235.   BECAUSE GRACE AND MERCY etc: This line, which occurs again in the first part of 4.15, is found in all MSS. and versions (only Itala has "peace" instead of "mercy"), and is adopted as genuine by R.V., Siegfried, and others. But some MSS., such as א A, and all the versions, Complutensian and A.V., add also the second line of

And as sparks in the stubble they shall run to and fro.
⁸They shall judge nations and have dominion over peoples,
And their Lord shall reign over them for ever.
⁹They that trust in him shall understand truth,
And the faithful shall abide with him in love,
Because grace and mercy are to his chosen.

10 ¹⁰But the impious shall receive punishment in accord with their reasonings,
They that heeded not the righteous and revolted from the Lord.
¹¹For he that sets at naught wisdom and discipline is miserable,
And vain is their hope and their labours unavailing,
And their works unprofitable.

4.15, with some minor variations. Because of these and other differences Grimm suspects the entire passage as an early interpolation, and Goodrick omits it altogether as spurious. On the contents *cf.* I Enoch 5.7.

10. PUNISHMENT: ἐπιτιμία in this sense occurs only in ecclesiastical Greek. In classical Greek it denotes "enjoyment of civil rights and privileges" or "citizenship." It is surmised that the error arose from confusion with the constantly used plural of the real word ἐπιτίμιον (Goodrick).   IN ACCORD WITH THEIR REASONINGS: According to their crooked thoughts (1.3 and 2.1). This appears to be the first mention of the theory of punishment of like offenses by like chastisements, which is elaborated with such great detail in the last chapters of our book. Its origin may be traced to Prov. 1.31; *cf.* also Ps. 109.17 f. and Job 34.11.   THE RIGHTEOUS: *tou dikaiou* may be either masculine or neuter, hence Itala has *iustum*, but Augustine renders *iustitiam*, and similarly R.V. "the righteous man" and Goodrick "the right." In favor of the former Gregg argues that the righteous man has been the leading thought of ch. 2, to which this verse recalls attention. The latter is supported by Bois (*Essai*, p. 385) on account of the parallel in v. 11, and on the commonsense ground that the wicked did not neglect the righteous at all.   REVOLTED FROM THE LORD: An allusion either to apostasy from Judaism (10.3) or the moral apostasy of sensuality (2.10).

11. The first line is in the singular, though the entire passage is couched in the plural, hence Bois and the R.V. prefer to put it in a parenthesis.   SETS AT NAUGHT etc.: This line is almost a verbal reproduction of Prov. 1.7b. Wisdom is internal compliance with divine commands and therefore corresponds to moral law; discipline is the observance of statutes and ordinances and therefore coincides with ceremonial law. MISERABLE: In a moral sense. *Talaiporôs* is a rare word, but it occurs again in 13.10 in connection with false hopes.

^{12}αἱ γυναῖκες αὐτῶν ἄφρονες,
   καὶ πονηρὰ τὰ τέκνα αὐτῶν,
   ἐπικατάρατος ἡ γένεσις αὐτῶν.
^{13}ὅτι μακαρία στεῖρα ἡ ἀμίαντος,
   ἥτις οὐκ ἔγνω κοίτην ἐν παραπτώματι,
   ἕξει καρπὸν ἐν ἐπισκοπῇ ψυχῶν,
^{14}καὶ εὐνοῦχος ὁ μὴ ἐργασάμενος ἐν χειρὶ ἀνόμημα

13³ fin.] + αυτων A†

---

12. LIGHTMINDED: So Goodrick, A.V. margin "light or unchaste." This rendering of *afrones* is preferable to "foolish" of R.V. because it expresses the idea not only of folly but also of wantonness, which is evidently intended here. See Prov. 5.5, where LXX describes the feet of the harlot as *podes afrosunês*. Hence Bretschneider simply renders "adulterous." THEIR CHILDREN: This seems to follow the old doctrine of heredity, which is clearly enunciated in a proverb quoted in Ezek. 16.44 "as is the mother so is the daughter," in Ecclus. 41.5 "the children of sinners are abominable sinners," in II Esdr. 9.17 "like as the field is so is also the seed," etc. But this fateful doctrine was later superseded by the healthier doctrine of personal responsibility. Ezekiel himself vehemently protests against any inflexible law of heredity in 18.1 ff.: after quoting the proverb "The fathers have eaten sour grapes and the children's teeth are set on edge" he goes on to say: "Ye shall not have occasion any more to use this proverb in Israel. Behold, all souls are Mine; as the soul of the father, so also the soul of the son is Mine; the soul that sinneth, it shall die." This is in line with modern educational theory which stresses environment as against heredity: though it is proper to speak of a "bad stock," yet bad training is a more potent factor. GENERATION: So Goodrick, who adopts this ambiguous word because both the Greek *genesis* and Itala *creatura* are equally capable of the two renderings, "their begetting" (R.V.) and "their off-spring" (A.V., Pal. Syr., Grimm, Siegfried).

13. The primary purpose of this and the following verse appears to be to rebuke mixed marriages between Jewesses and Gentiles, of the sort practiced by the renegade Jews of Alexandria, and then also to refute the popular idea that a numerous progeny was a blessing and a proof of divine favor. With regard to the former, it should be noted that mixed marriages are denounced in Mal. 2.11, Ezra 9 and 10, Neh. 13.23, and elsewhere. As to the latter, a numerous offspring is exalted as a supreme blessing in Ps. 127 and 128 and elsewhere (see Cornely *ad loc.*); yet curiously enough Isa. 54.1 and 56.4 make it evident that parentage is not a necessary condition of human happiness on earth: sterility, if pure, may be compensated by fertility of the soul. Cf. further Ecclus. 16.1. THE BARREN: στεῖρα can have reference only to a married woman, not to a virgin (*cf.*

¹²Their wives are lightminded,
   And wicked their children;
   Accursed is their generation.
¹³For happy is the barren that is undefiled,
   She who has not conceived in transgression,
   She shall have fruit in the visitation of souls.
   ¹⁴And the eunuch who has not wrought unlawfulness with
      his hand,

---

the evidence in Cornely *ad loc.*). Hence the attempt of some commentators
to construe it as referring to a virgin and see here a defense of celibacy and
asceticism as practiced especially by the Therapeutae (Philo, *Vit. Con.*,
§ 8) is unfounded and far from true. For the same reason there is hardly
any support to Graetz's conjecture (*Gesch.d. Juden.*, III, 495) that this
and the following verse refer to conventual life and hence are Christian
interpolations of late date.   UNDEFILED: Goodrick prefers "unstained"
for the reason that the meaning is apparently moral rather than physical
and refers to a mixed not an adulterous union. The word is further explained by the following line "she who has not conceived in transgression."
WHO HAS NOT CONCEIVED: So R.V. *ouk egnô koitên* is an euphemism for
sexual intercourse adopted from biblical Hebrew (classical Greek employs *eunê* and *lechos* instead of *koitê*). Goodrick follows the Greek more
closely by rendering "that hath not known wedlock," but then he misses
the act of conception which seems to be the point involved here.
TRANSGRESSION: A reference to the unlawful marriages with the heathen,
comp. Jubilees 30.7.   FRUIT: A distinct allusion to Ps. 127.3. Evidently
karpos is used in the sense of reward or compensation.   WHO HAS NOT
WROUGHT etc.: Physical debility in itself is not sufficient for future bliss
and divine grace: it should be accompanied by clean hands and a loyal
heart.   VISITATION OF SOULS: A vague and mysterious phrase, without
any delimitation of time and place. Undoubtedly the writer himself had no
clear conception about this spiritual visitation, which could take place at
any time here or hereafter.
14. THE EUNUCH etc.: The adjective ("happy is the eunuch etc.,") *makar*,
of the preceding verse being understood also here. Although under the old
covenant a eunuch was excluded from the community of Yahweh (Deut.
23.2), yet Isa. 56.3 ff. strikes a different note: "Neither let the eunuch say:
Behold I am a dry tree. For thus saith the Lord concerning the eunuchs
that keep my sabbaths, and choose the things that please me, and hold
fast by my covenant: Even unto them will I give in my house and within
my walls a monument and a memorial better than sons and daughters."
Those who are inclined to see here a glorification of celibacy are compelled
to take *eunouchos* in the sense of voluntary celibate, which is hardly the
case here. The word no doubt refers to a person who from natural causes is
incapable of begetting children: such a person, if blameless in deed and

μηδὲ ἐνθυμηθεὶς κατὰ τοῦ κυρίου πονηρά,
δοθήσεται γὰρ αὐτῷ τῆς πίστεως χάρις ἐκλεκτὴ
καὶ κλῆρος ἐν ναῷ κυρίου θυμηρέστερος.
15 ¹⁵ἀγαθῶν γὰρ πόνων καρπὸς εὐκλεής,
καὶ ἀδιάπτωτος ἡ ῥίζα τῆς φρονήσεως.
¹⁶τέκνα δὲ μοιχῶν ἀτέλεστα ἔσται,
καὶ ἐκ παρανόμου κοίτης σπέρμα ἀφανισθήσεται.
¹⁷ἐάν τε γὰρ μακρόβιοι γένωνται, εἰς οὐθὲν λογισθήσονται,
καὶ ἄτιμον ἐπ' ἐσχάτων τὸ γῆρας αὐτῶν·
¹⁸ἐάν τε ὀξέως τελευτήσωσιν, οὐχ ἕξουσιν ἐλπίδα
οὐδὲ ἐν ἡμέρᾳ διαγνώσεως παραμύθιον·

18¹ ουκ εχουσιν B†

---

thought, shall obtain inner consolation.   FAITH'S PECULIAR GRACE: So
Goodrick following Itala and A.V. But R.V. renders "there shall be given
him for his faithfulness a peculiar favor" and on the margin "the grace of
God's chosen," evidently construing *pisteôs* as genitive of price. The
phrase is indefinite and its exact meaning is far from certain. According to
Grimm, it is "the gift of true faith."   MORE PLEASING: θυμηρέστερος is an
unusual word not found elsewhere in the Greek Bible. The sense is of
course spiritual, somewhat like Deut. 10.9 "Levi hath no portion nor inheritance with his brethren; the Lord is his inheritance." Since the idea
expressed here is taken from Isa. 56.5, R.V. imitates that passage closely
by rendering here "more delightsome than wife or children."   TEMPLE
OF THE LORD: Probably heaven, *cf.* Ps. 11.4 (repeated in Heb. 2.20)
and 18.7.

15. Margoliouth (*op. cit.*, p. 287) discovers a connection between this and
the preceding verses by quoting from Midr. Tanhuma on Gen. 6.9: "At
the time a man departs childless from this world he is grieved and cries.
Says God to him: "Why art thou crying that thou hast not raised fruit in
this world, when thou hast fruit more beautiful than children." Says man
before God: "Oh, Lord, what kind of fruit have I raised?" Says God:
"The Torah, of which it is written (Prov. 11.30): "The fruit of the
righteous is a tree of life." The text does not say "children," but "fruit of
the righteous." And so the achievements of man are nothing but his "good
deeds."   GOOD LABOURS: Properly good deeds.   GLORIOUS: An allusion to the old Jewish notion of subjective immortality (*cf.* Ps. 112.6 and
Prov. 10.7), from which the writer somehow cannot divest himself; or
perhaps he aims to contradict Eccl. 1.11, 2.16, and 9.5 that there is no
remembrance of the dead, whether righteous or unrighteous. The verse
appears to be a variation of 1.15 "For righteousness is immortal" and
4.1. "for there is immortality in its remembrance."   THE ROOT OF
UNDERSTANDING: The Greek phrase does not denote "the origin of understanding," but rather "the root, which is understanding." Holmes renders
more explicitly "wisdom's root." For root as an indication of permanence

Nor devised evil things against the Lord,
For to him shall be given faith's peculiar grace,
And a more pleasing portion in the temple of the Lord.
15   ¹⁵For the fruit of good labours is glorious,
And the root of understanding is infallible.
¹⁶But children of adulterers shall not reach maturity,
And seed from unlawful wedlock shall vanish away.
¹⁷For even if they be long lived, they shall be reckoned
for naught,
And at the end their old age shall be without honour.
¹⁸And if they die quickly, they have no hope,
Nor consolation in the day of decision.

---

cf. Prov. 12.3 and 12.

16. ADULTERERS: In contrast to *amiantos* of v. 13 above are those who had contracted unlawful marriages, as becomes evident from the next line and also from 4.6. An earlier view, expressed by Luther and others, was to the effect that the word signified "sinners" in general and referred to the renegade Jews of Alexandria, and this is supported by Siegfried who points out that since the days of Hosea adultery had been a common image for unlawful dealings with the heathen.   SHALL NOT REACH MATURITY: This is the natural meaning of *atelesta estai* and it agrees very well with the preceding line. But very curiously A.V. margin has "shall not be partakers of holy things," which seems to be based on a secondary sense of *atelesta* "uninitiated in the mysteries." Some support this rendering through a reference to Deut. 23.2 "a bastard shall not enter into the assembly of the Lord." However, the real meaning is made evident by *klônes atelestoi* in 4.5. For the severe condemnation *cf.* Jer. 18.21 f.

17. LONG LIVED: *makrobioi* refers of course to the children and not to the adulterers, as some think.   FOR NAUGHT: In spite of Jeremiah's (31.28 f.). and Ezekiel's (ch. 18) mitigation of the doctrine of hereditary sin, that ruthless doctrine is maintained here as also in Ecclus. 41.5: "The children of sinners are abominable children." *Cf.*, however, 11.23 in our book "But thou hast mercy on all because thou hast power over all etc."   AT THE END: *ep' eschatôn* is generally rendered "at the end of life," but, according to Siegfried, it refers to the final judgment, corresponding to *hemera diagnoseôs* of the next verse.

18. QUICKLY: The Greek word primarily means "sharply," then also "quickly," as in 16.11. Here it really denotes "early" or "suddenly." CONSOLATION: *paramuthion* means "comfort, relief," but it may also denote "address, exhortation," hence Itala renders *allocutio*.   DAY OF DECISION: *I. e.* day of judgment. *Diagnôsis* is a technical word for the "decision" of a suit, but it does not occur elsewhere in the Greek Old Testament. Here it is used of the day of visitation of the righteous, *cf.* 5.15 ff., when the impious shall be separated with the storm.

¹⁹γενεᾶς γὰρ ἀδίκου χαλεπὰ τὰ τέλη.

4 ¹κρείσσων ἀτεκνία μετὰ ἀρετῆς·
　ἀθανασία γάρ ἐστιν ἐν μνήμῃ αὐτῆς,
　ὅτι καὶ παρὰ θεῷ γινώσκεται καὶ παρὰ ἀνθρώποις.
²παροῦσάν τε μιμοῦνται αὐτὴν
　καὶ ποθοῦσιν ἀπελθοῦσαν·
　καὶ ἐν τῷ αἰῶνι στεφανηφοροῦσα πομπεύει
　τὸν τῶν ἀμιάντων ἄθλων ἀγῶνα νικήσασα.
³πολύγονον δὲ ἀσεβῶν πλῆθος οὐ χρησιμεύσει
　καὶ ἐκ νόθων μοσχευμάτων οὐ δώσει ῥίζαν εἰς βάθος

1¹ κρεισσων]+γαρ S*†　　　　　　2¹ μιμουνται] τιμωσιν A mu.

19. FOR THE ENDS etc.: So margin of R.V., following the Greek very closely. This line appears to be a summary of the doctrine of hereditary sin enunciated in the preceding lines, based on Ex. 20.5, 34.7, and Deut. 5.9. But, as pointed out above on v. 17, this doctrine is reversed in Jer. 31.28 f. and Ezek. ch. 18.　　GENERATION: Very peculiarly Itala renders the Greek word here by *natio*, which in classical Latin is used of foreign or barbarian hordes.

1. CHILDLESSNESS WITH VIRTUE: Reverting to 3.13 f. Virtue here is synonymous with wisdom, as in Philo, *Cong.*, § 3. The singular rendering of Itala *O quam pulera est casta generatio cum claritate* apparently aims to glorify celibacy, in support of which Philo, *Vita Cont.*, § 8 is often adduced. But Cyprian's version in *Sing. Cler.*, § 40 *melius est esse sine filiis* militates against it, as does that of Ambrosius *Virg.* I *melior est sterilitas cum virtute*. For the idea expressed here comp. Eccles. 6.3 and Ecclus. 16.3. There is a far cry from this exhortation of childlessness to the old Hebrew ideal of abundance of offspring.　　IMMORTALITY: The reference is to the earlier Jewish conception of immortality, which involved long life and numerous posterity. *Cf.* Ps. 112.6, Prov. 10.7, and Ecclus. 44.8 ff. See also comment on 2.4 above.　　ITS REMEMBRANCE: *I. e.* in remembrance of virtue, not of childlessness. To avoid ambiguity R.V. renders explicitly "in the memory of virtue" and Goodrick "in the remembrance of her." RECOGNIZED BOTH etc.: *Cf.* Prov. 3.4 and Ps. 1.6 "The Lord regards the way of the righteous." To be known by God involves a measure of immortality, for any thing that has existed in the mind of God and has been approved by Him can never become as though it had not been.

2. MEN IMITATE IT: In recognizing virtue (see preceding verse) men gradually come to imitate it or to identify themselves with it.　　WHEN IT IS GONE etc.: Grimm very appropriately quotes Horace, *Odes*, III, XXIV.31 *Virtutem . . . sublatam ex oculis quaerimus invidi.*　　CROWNED IN POMP: Virtue is described as marching in a festival procession, along a Via Sacra, crowned with a wreath of flowers as the reward of a victor in

¹⁹For the ends of an unrighteous generation are grievous.

4   ¹   Better is childlessness with virtue,
       For there is immortality in its remembrance,
       Since it is recognized both with God and with men.
       ²When it is present men imitate it,
       And when it is gone they long for it,
       And for ever it marches crowned in pomp,
       Victorious in the contest for prizes that are undefiled.
       ³But the prolific multitude of the impious shall be of no
            profit,
       And with bastard slips it shall not send its root deep,

---

public games, see II Macc. 6.7 and IV Macc. 17.15. The picture is figurative and of course Greek, not Jewish, though it was common enough in later Jewish life as a sign of rejoicing or festivity, *cf.* above 2.8, Ecclus. 1.11, 6.30, 15.6. For garlands in rejoicings *cf.* Judith 15.13.   CONTEST: *agōn* is primarily "an assembly," like *agora*, especially an assembly convened to watch games; then it came to mean "the contest" for a prize at the games. Metaphorically it is used by Philo of the "conflict of life" (*Somn.* II.21).   PRIZES THAT ARE UNDEFILED: So A.V. and R.V., deriving *athlōn* from the neuter noun *athlon* meaning the "prize" of a contest; but Goodrick, basing himself on Itala and Pal. Syr., renders "stainless struggles" by deriving the Greek word from the masculine noun *athlos* denoting "contest" for a prize (so also Grimm). Both renderings are admissible, the first signifying "perfect rewards, unstained by unfairness of winning or savage passions on the part of the competitors," as in earthly contests; the second is characterized as "the struggles of the virtuous life, unstained by selfishness or sin."

3. BASTARD SLIPS: Or better spurious offshoots, *i. e.* children born of hated mixed marriages, *cf.* above 3.16. The Heb. equivalent is *mamzer*, which, according to the Talmud (Yeb. 76b), is composed of two words, *mum zar* "a strange blemish," but, according to Geiger (*Urschrift*, p. 52), is made up of *me'am zar* "of a foreign people." Itala has *spuria vitulamina*, the latter evidently coined from *vitulus* = μόσχος, of which Augustine disapproves (*Doctr. Christ.*, II.12), hence the substitution *adulterinae plantationes* by some Latin translators. However, Cornely (p. 149) adduces an ancient glossary quoted by Ducange *vitilamen planta illa infructuosa qui nascitur a radice vitis.*   SHALL NOT SEND ITS ROOT DEEP: *Cf.* Ecclus. 23.25 "Her children shall not spread into roots." Lévi (*Ecclésiastique*, I.22) observes that this verse constitutes an imitation to a certain degree of Ecclus. 40.15, though the two do not agree in their Greek expressions; and for this reason he is inclined to think that the author of

οὐδὲ ἀσφαλῆ βάσιν ἑδράσει·
⁴κἂν γὰρ ἐν κλάδοις πρὸς καιρὸν ἀναθάλῃ,
ἐπισφαλῶς βεβηκότα ὑπὸ ἀνέμου σαλευθήσεται
καὶ ὑπὸ βίας ἀνέμων ἐκριζωθήσεται.

5   ⁵περικλασθήσονται κλῶνες ἀτέλεστοι,
καὶ ὁ καρπὸς αὐτῶν ἄχρηστος, ἄωρος εἰς βρῶσιν
καὶ εἰς οὐθὲν ἐπιτήδειος·
⁶ἐκ γὰρ ἀνόμων ὕπνων τέκνα γεννώμενα
μάρτυρές εἰσιν πονηρίας κατὰ γονέων ἐν ἐξετασμῷ αὐτῶν.

7   Δίκαιος δὲ ἐὰν φθάσῃ τελευτῆσαι, ἐν ἀναπαύσει ἔσται·

4² βεβιωκοτα S*†   5¹ κλωνες] pr. αυτων S*

Wisdom had a Hebrew rather than a Greek text before him. However, variation of language where thoughts resemble may also be due to other causes, such as e. g. to a conscious effort on the part of the author to cover up the traces of imitation.

4. BLOSSOM: The Greek word might be better rendered with Grimm "put forth buds and leaves" (cf. R.V. "put forth boughs"), since no real flourishing can be meant here.   STANDING UNSTABLY: literally rendered by Syroh. "they walk not safely," is an awkward expression in our context, but Deane quotes Archil., 52. Some commentators would render "growing up unstably." As to the sense, cf. Ps. 92.8. If the reference is to children of mixed marriages, the author may have wished to allude here to their want of firm grounding in the religion of their fathers.   VIOLENCE OF THE WINDS: bia is curiously rendered by Itala nimietas "superfluity, redundancy," instead of "violence." Anemos "wind" is used tautologically in this and the preceding line, and this usage becomes more frequent in the last chapters of our book.

The simile of a richly developed tree but with few roots, and hence incapable of withstanding a storm, which is applied here to the impious, is found also in Pirke Abot 3.22, only there it is applied to one whose wisdom exceeds his deeds.

5. THEIR TWIGS etc.: Comparisons of the pious to flourishing and of the impious to decaying trees are numerous in the Bible (Jer. 17.8, Ps. 1.3, 37.35 f., 92.13 f., 128.3; Isa. 1.29 f., Job 15.32 f., 18.16). Perhaps our author had in mind Ecclus. 23.25: "Her children shall not spread into roots and her branches shall bear no fruit."   USELESS: with reference to v. 3 above.   UNRIPE: aōros is used of untimely death in Prov. 11.30 and Job 22.16.

6. CHILDREN etc.: Meaning children of mixed marriages, not actual bastards, as maintained by Farrar.   WEDLOCK: hupnos is a euphemism, like koite in 3.13.   WITNESSES: Children prove wickedness in their parents when they suffer misfortune. Not that the existence of the children is a reproof of the parents' lust, but the misfortunes of children argue a parental sin, cf. Ecclus. 41.5 ff. (Gregg).   WHEN THEY ARE EXAMINED:

Nor establish a firm foundation.

⁴For even if in their shoots they blossom for a season,
Standing unstably they shall be shaken by the wind,
And be rooted out by the violence of winds.

5   ⁵Their twigs shall be broken off ere they be full grown,
And their fruit useless, unripe for eating,
And fit for nothing.

⁶For children born of unlawful wedlock,
Are witnesses of wickedness against their parents when
they are examined.

⁷But a righteous man, though he die before his time, shall
be at rest,

I. e. when the parents are put on their trial and inquiry is made after them. The reference is apparently to the final judgment, *exetasmos* being used in the same sense as *episkopê*. Some exegetes, like Grimm and Gregg, argue that *autōn* is used of the children and that *exetasmos* implies the traditional view that children were actually punished for the sins of the parents. This verse, they claim, is without point if it does not lay stress upon the misfortunes threatened in verses 3–5. There is still another view, that of Cornely, that both parents and children are involved in the trial or examination: "for the words clearly show," he avers, "that the children are referred to, who, displaying their own wretched condition, rise up as witnesses against their wicked parents; but again, as the sin of the parents is made manifest by the witness of the children, their trial is also necessarily implied."

7. THOUGH HE DIE BEFORE HIS TIME: So R.V., but A.V. has "though the righteous be prevented with death," following Itala. *Fthanein* is generally followed by a participle, the infinitive being very unusual. Here, too, the author is combating the traditional view that longevity was a sign of God's favor and early death a severe punishment.   AT REST: The righteous man is compensated by the profound rest he enjoys after trials and tribulations, *cf.* Isa. 57.1 f. and Job 3.17. Itala renders *in refrigerio*, which led early Catholic commentators to find here a reference to the lightening of the pains of purgatory by the prayers of the living and the comfort of the angels. However, later Catholic authorities regard this as absurd, though admitting that heaven in the language of the ancient church is *locus refrigerii* (Goodrick). Farrar is probably right when he says that "it is unlikely that these general expressions correspond to any rigid or detailed system of eschatology in the mind of the writer, and it is idle to quote them as authorities for purgatory, the intermediate state, etc."

Pal. Syr. adds here another line to complete the apparently defective verse: " And if he die in length of days, he shall be found in honour," but this is evidently a gross interpolation, since it is inconsistent with the context.

^{8}γῆρας γὰρ τίμιον οὐ τὸ πολυχρόνιον
οὐδὲ ἀριθμῷ ἐτῶν μεμέτρηται,
^{9}πολιὰ δέ ἐστιν φρόνησις ἀνθρώποις
καὶ ἡλικία γήρως βίος ἀκηλίδωτος.
10   ^{10}εὐάρεστος θεῷ γενόμενος ἠγαπήθη
καὶ ζῶν μεταξὺ ἁμαρτωλῶν μετετέθη·
^{11}ἡρπάγη, μὴ κακία ἀλλάξῃ σύνεσιν αὐτοῦ
ἢ δόλος ἀπατήσῃ ψυχὴν αὐτοῦ·
^{12}βασκανία γὰρ φαυλότητος ἀμαυροῖ τὰ καλά,

11^1 αυτου> S*

---

8. OLD AGE etc.: The meaning apparently is that old age is valued not by years but by the righteousness of the man who lives and dies. Grimm and Goodrick quote numerous passages from Greek and Latin literature stressing this idea. Very interesting is what Philo writes of the Therapeutae (*Vita Cont.*, § 8): "For they do not regard those as elders who are advanced in years and aged, but as mere youths if they have only lately devoted themselves to the vocation; but they call those elders who from their earliest years have spent time and strength in the contemplative part of philosophy," *Cf.* also *Abr.*, § 46.   MEASURED BY NUMBER OF YEARS: Having already departed from the traditional view that life without offspring cannot be regarded as happy, the author now departs from the belief that longevity is necessary to the happiness of a pious man. *Cf.* Job 32.7 ff. in LXX.

9. UNDERSTANDING IS GRAY HAIRS: This thought, too, is abundantly illustrated from classical sources, *cf.* Goodrick *ad loc.* Suffice it to quote Philo, *Plant.*, § 40: "Those who are gray, not through time, but in goodness of counsel." This thought is reflected also in the Talmud, *cf.* Kid. 32b: "no one is old but he who acquired wisdom."   RIPE OLD AGE: The Greek expression appears pleonastic at first glance, hence some suggested rendering it by "stature of old age" (so indeed Syroh.), *hêlikia* denoting also "stature" or "bulk" of body. The sense is that old age is not the measure of life, but rather inward character, *cf.* Isa. 65.20 and Ps. 84.11.

10. WELL-PLEASING TO GOD etc.: Undoubtedly the reference is to Enoch, *cf.* Gen. 5.24. Similarly Ecclus. 44.16. This is the first instance of anonymity so characteristic of the Book of Wisdom. The reason for it is not quite apparent. Various theories have been suggested (see Goodrick), but none is quite plausible. Perhaps the most acceptable is that of Stade (*Geschichte des Volkes Israel*, II, 436), that it was unnecessary to name the Jewish saints because the book was addressed to Jewish renegades and apostates. Grimm, on the other hand, has an exactly opposite explanation, viz. that the pagan princes to whom the book is addressed would not care to know the names of the Hebrew characters. Elsewhere Grimm attributes this trait of anonymity to some sort of affectation. Gregg thinks that the person referred to is not Enoch, but the righteous man of verse 7, whose

⁸For honourable old age is not so by reason of length of
time,
Nor is it measured by number of years.
⁹But understanding is gray hairs unto men,
And an untarnished life is ripe old age.
10   ¹⁰Being well-pleasing to God he was cherished,
And living among sinners was translated.
¹¹He was plucked away, lest wickedness should alter his
understanding,
Or guile deceive his soul.
¹²For the fascination of meanness obscures things that
are good,

---

death is spoken of in terms used to recount the translation of Enoch, a
typical instance. Accordingly he would render μετετέθη not "was translated" but "was transferred," i. e. killed and received into a happier state.
CHERISHED: The idea that death may be a mercy was not first introduced
by Christianity; with the Greeks a dead man was makaritês, "an in-
habitant of the Islands of the Blessed." Cf. also Midr. Ber. rabba 9.7:
"As long as the righteous are alive they contend with their desire, but as
soon as they die they are at peace."   LIVING AMONG SINNERS: Cf. Isa.
57.1 in LXX "The righteous is taken away from the presence of iniquity."
WAS TRANSLATED: There are numerous stories and legends about the
translation of Enoch and Elijah to heaven without intervening death. See
Ginzberg, Legends, I, 137 ff. (on Enoch), and IV, 202 ff. (on Elijah).
11. PLUCKED AWAY: Itala raptus est, shows clearly that more than natural
causes were responsible for his demise. A.V. "speedily was he taken
away" intends to express the element of suddenness contained in the
Greek word. Grimm notes that there is a connection between the case of
Enoch and the verses preceding it, proving that even an untimely death
may be a positive blessing, a gift of God, a release.   LEST WICKEDNESS
etc.: It is surprising that the motive given here for the removal of Enoch
differs from that assumed in both the Greek and the Hebrew of Ecclus.
44.16: in the former the reason is "being an example of repentance to all
generations," in the latter "a sign of instruction to future generations."
Cf., however, Midr Ber. rabba. 25.1, which agrees with our passage. R.V.
margin has "malice" instead of "wickedness."   UNDERSTANDING: Used
here in the sense of moral insight.
12. THE FASCINATION OF MEANNESS: or wickedness, as Goodrick puts it.
This is an exact rendering of the Greek phrase on a par with Itala fas-
cinatio nugacitatis. R.V. has "the bewitching of naughtiness," which may
overcome the righteous man in spite of himself.   OBSCURES: It should be
noticed that the verb amauroein was used by Greek philosophers to express the darkening of the moral sense.   THINGS THAT ARE GOOD: Refers

καὶ ῥεμβασμὸς ἐπιθυμίας μεταλλεύει νοῦν ἄκακον
¹³τελειωθεὶς ἐν ὀλίγῳ ἐπλήρωσεν χρόνους μακρούς·
¹⁴ἀρεστὴ γὰρ ἦν κυρίῳ ἡ ψυχὴ αὐτοῦ,
διὰ τοῦτο ἔσπευσεν ἐκ μέσου πονηρίας·
οἱ δὲ λαοὶ ἰδόντες καὶ μὴ νοήσαντες
μηδὲ θέντες ἐπὶ διανοίᾳ τὸ τοιοῦτο,
15   ¹⁵ὅτι χάρις καὶ ἔλεος ἐν τοῖς ἐκλεκτοῖς αὐτοῦ
καὶ ἐπισκοπὴ ἐν τοῖς ὁσίοις αὐτοῦ.
¹⁶κατακρινεῖ δὲ δίκαιος καμὼν τοὺς ζῶντας ἀσεβεῖς

14³ λαοι] αλλοι A*   15² οσιοις] tr. A
15¹ εν>S: cf. 3 9³ | εκλεκτοις . . .   16¹ καμων] θανων ABᶜ

to the moral and spiritual qualities of the human soul.   GIDDY WHIRL:
rembasmos is one of the author's new inventions: an illegitimate formation
from *rembomai*, "to roam or rove about," as used *e. g.* in Prov. 7.12 of the
harlot. The presupposed *rembazein* does not exist at all. This strange word
"points to the insidious and persistent solicitations of desire, which can
make the flesh too strong for the innocent mind." So Gregg, who proposes
to translate "the wandering allurements of desire." Syroh. has "a daz-
zling."   PERVERTS: It is evident that *metalleuei* here is an error for *metal-
lassei*, for the former means "to mine, dig for metals," the latter "to alter,
change." Perhaps the word was associated with *allos* "other." The same
error is repeated in 16.25, leading to the conclusion that the author's
knowledge of Greek was not very profound. Churton thinks that the passage may be regarded as a paraphrase of Isa. 57.1 "the righteous is taken
away from the evil to come,"or with LXX "from the presence of iniquity."
13. MADE PERFECT: The Greek word used to be rendered "dead," and indeed in ecclesiastical Greek it has the meaning of "attaining martyrdom,"
but here, as in Ecclus. 7.32, it denotes "to be perfect." It is analogous to
Heb. *tam*, which means both "be complete, perfect" and "be finished,
destroyed."   FULFILLED LONG TIMES: The Greek phrase is very close to
the Heb. *male yamim* (Gen. 25.24, Lev. 8.33, Num. 6.5, etc.), but although
not found in classical Greek it is considered a good Hellenistic expression,
cf. Ecclus. 26.2; Josephus, *Antiq.*, IV.IV.6; IV Macc. 12.14. The sense is
plain enough: his moral training was completed early in life, and his few
years were as good as very many (Goodrick). Similarly it was said of
Rabbi Bun bar Hiyya, who died young: "In the twenty-eight years of his
life he had learned more than others learn in a hundred years" (Midr.r.
Cant., IV.6).

14. HASTENED HIM AWAY: A forced translation, since *speudein* may be used
transitively of things, but there is no example of its use with a person as
object. Hence R.V. has "hasted he out." Grimm is inclined to emend the
word to read *espasen*. Siegfried is of the opinion that this awkward construction is an imitation of the Hebrew *mahar* with the accusative as in

And the giddy whirl of desire perverts the guileless mind.
[13]Being made perfect in a little while he fulfilled long
times.

[14]For his soul was well-pleasing to God,
Therefore he hastened him away from the midst of
wickedness;
But the nations seeing and not understanding,
Nor taking such a thing to heart,
[15]That grace and mercy are with his chosen,
And his visitation with his holy ones.
[16]But the righteous that is dead shall condemn the
impious that are alive,

Gen. 18.6 or I Kings 22.9. Purinton suggests *hicil* with the direct object understood. For the sense of the passage one should compare Menander 425 and Plautus, *Bacch.*, IV.7.18 "whom the gods love dies young," and many other examples cited by Farrar *ad loc.*　　THE NATIONS: R.V. "the peoples", which may stand for either 'ammim or goyim, cf. Ps. 2.1. The reference is probably to the Gentiles, among whom the renegades were counted. Instead of *hoi laoi*, A reads *alloi*, which Gregg, in order to avoid the anacoluthon, would emend to *anomoi* (an error not uncommon in uncials), "the lawless, the ungodly," a synonym of *asebeis* who are the subject of verses 17 ff. However, our verse looks like a reminiscence of Isa. 6.9: "Go tell this people . . . seeing ye shall see and not understand." GRACE AND MERCY etc.: Almost identical with 3.9, *cf.* note there. VISITATION: in a favorable sense, see 2.20, 3.7. Margoliouth quotes the Armenian version "justice is upon his saints," which he considers as underlying an original Hebrew text.

15. This verse seems to interrupt sense and grammar, hence some prefer to place it after verse 14, where it is more appropriate (Gregg, Holmes). In view of the unnatural Greek style and the startling variation in Pal. Syr. ("He shall judge the righteous and destroy the wicked alive; and youths who go forth for a brief time more than the long time of old men of falsehood") Goodrick is inclined to think that the text has been tampered with.

16. THE RIGHTEOUS THAT IS DEAD: Hence is not subject to temptation and his righteousness is established beyond any doubt. *Kamōn* properly means "he whose sufferings are over," or, as Syroh. renders it, "he that is weary," and is used in Homer for "the dead," and never elsewhere in LXX. Some MSS. have *thanōn* instead of *kamōn*, but the latter is probably genuine as being the more difficult.　　SHALL CONDEMN etc.: "Not with final judgment, but by the daily moral contrast between his life which they count as death, and their moral death which they miscall life" (Gregg). But Goodrick, following Siegfried, takes this to be a reference to final judgment on Judgment Day.

καὶ νεότης τελεσθεῖσα ταχέως πολυετὲς γῆρας ἀδίκου·

[17]ὄψονται γὰρ τελευτὴν σοφοῦ
καὶ οὐ νοήσουσιν τί ἐβουλεύσατο περὶ αὐτοῦ
καὶ εἰς τί ἠσφαλίσατο αὐτὸν ὁ κύριος.

[18]ὄψονται καὶ ἐξουθενήσουσιν·
αὐτοὺς δὲ ὁ κύριος ἐκγελάσεται,

[19]καὶ ἔσονται μετὰ τοῦτο εἰς πτῶμα ἄτιμον
καὶ εἰς ὕβριν ἐν νεκροῖς δι' αἰῶνος,
ὅτι ῥήξει αὐτοὺς ἀφώνους πρηνεῖς
καὶ σαλεύσει αὐτοὺς ἐκ θεμελίων,
καὶ ἕως ἐσχάτου χερσωθήσονται
καὶ ἔσονται ἐν ὀδύνῃ,
καὶ ἡ μνήμη αὐτῶν ἀπολεῖται.

20   [20]ἐλεύσονται ἐν συλλογισμῷ ἁμαρτημάτων αὐτῶν δειλοί,

16² ταχεως>S*t	19² δι>At
18¹ οψονται]+γαρ Sᶜ	20¹ δειλοι] δηλοι Sᶜ

---

17. THEY: R.V. supplies a subject by reading "the ungodly" instead.
SHALL SEE: Namely the wise man's early death, see above verse 7.
WISE MAN: Sofos has the same meaning here as dikaios in the preceding
verse, since the man who has wisdom is necessarily righteous.   HE
TOOK HIM INTO SAFETY: So Isa. 41.10. Itala munierit illum. A.V. has "set
him in safety," R.V. "safely kept him."

18. SHALL LAUGH THEM TO SCORN: The pronoun autous at the beginning of
the line is emphatic: them, in their turn. Ekgelasetai with the accus. is
found also in Ps. 2.4, 37.13, 58.9, etc.

19. THEREAFTER: meta touto, according to Goodrick, must refer to a
future beyond the tomb, on account of the immediate reference to "the
dead," and not to an immediate happening "after all this contempt of the
righteous" (Deane); but Gregg and others maintain that the verse evidently points to a retribution beginning on earth.   DISHONOURED
CARCASS: Closely corresponding to this is Isa. 14.19: "But thou art cast
forth away from the grave . . . as a carcase trodden under foot." Ptōma
is the later Greek equivalent of ptoma nekrōu, and occurs in LXX in Ez.
6.5 and Ps. 110.6. Its Heb. equivalent is nefel, which some commentators
substitute for neṣer in the Isaiah passage, on the basis of LXX and Sym.
Atimon may involve lack of burial, since in ancient times to be unburied
involved dishonor, cf. Ps. 79.2 f., see also Isa. 66.24 and Jer. 22.19.
AN OUTRAGE: So R.V. margin, R.V. has "a reproach," and Goodrick "a
mockery," with reference to Ezek. 32.24 f.   HE SHALL DASH THEM: A
fierce and merciless picture of the punishment of the wicked, which is
reminiscent of Job ch. 18 and the imprecatory Psalms, especially Ps.
137.9   SPEECHLESS: Cf. the account of God's dealing with Heliodorus
in II Macc. 3.27 and 29.   DOWNWARDS: The Greek word, which is an

And youth quickly perfected the many years of an unrighteous man's old age.

17For they shall see the wise man's end,
And shall not understand what the Lord purposed
concerning him,
Nor for what end he took him into safety.
18They shall see and account it as naught,
But the Lord shall laugh them to scorn;
19And thereafter they shall become a dishonoured carcass,
And an outrage among the dead for ever;
For he shall dash them speechless downwards,
And shake them from their foundations;
And to the uttermost shall they be dried up,
And they shall be in anguish,
And their memory shall perish.
20 20In the counting up of their sins they shall come as
cowards,

Ionicism, properly means "headlong" (so Grimm and Goodrick). On the
sense cf. Ezek. 31.16: "I made the nations to shake at the sound of his fall,
when I cast him down to the nether-world with them that descend into
the pit."   SHALL THEY BE DRIED UP: The Greek word occurs only once
in LXX, namely in Prov. 24.31, where it is used of the sluggard's field and
vineyard in the sense "shall be laid waste" or "go to ruin," but it is doubtful if such a term could be applied to persons (Goodrick). It is defended by
Gregg, who avers that the wicked are compared to a parched land, as in
Isa. 19.5 ff., cf. also Ps. 107.33.   THEIR MEMORY SHALL PERISH: This is
the last punishment of the wicked, and is paralleled in Job 18.17. But,
although pictured as a punishment here and elsewhere, yet to be forgotten
is what the wicked anticipate with contentment in 2.4.

20. After the vagueness of verses 18 and 19 we finally get a definite picture
of the wicked being confronted after death with their righteous victim of
former days, now openly justified for his righteousness.   IN THE
COUNTING UP etc.: Many commentators, following Itala and A.V., take
this phrase subjectively: "when they come to count up their own sins";
but this is contrary to the whole tenor of the passage, and, as Farrar puts it
"something more seems to be meant than the appearance of the sinner before the bar of his own conscience." One can hardly doubt that the
episkopê (3.13) or exetasmos (4.6) is referred to (Goodrick). The sins are
personified as in Gen. 4.7, Num. 32.23, etc.   THEY SHALL COME: If the
Judgment Day is here referred to we might better render "they shall
appear there." But many commentators will not admit that the final
judgment is here alluded to. Gregg, for instance, is positive that our

καὶ ἐλέγξει αὐτοὺς ἐξ ἐναντίας τὰ ἀνομήματα αὐτῶν.

5 ¹ Τότε στήσεται ἐν παρρησίᾳ πολλῇ ὁ δίκαιος
κατὰ πρόσωπον τῶν θλιψάντων αὐτὸν
καὶ τῶν ἀθετούντων τοὺς πόνους αὐτοῦ.
²ἰδόντες ταραχθήσονται φόβῳ δεινῷ
καὶ ἐκστήσονται ἐπὶ τῷ παραδόξῳ τῆς σωτηρίας·
³ἐροῦσιν ἐν ἑαυτοῖς μετανοοῦντες
καὶ διὰ στενοχωρίαν πνεύματος στενάξονται καὶ ἐροῦσιν
⁴Οὗτος ἦν, ὃν ἔσχομέν ποτε εἰς γέλωτα
καὶ εἰς παραβολὴν ὀνειδισμοῦ οἱ ἄφρονες·
τὸν βίον αὐτοῦ ἐλογισάμεθα μανίαν
καὶ τὴν τελευτὴν αὐτοῦ ἄτιμον.
5 ⁵πῶς κατελογίσθη ἐν υἱοῖς θεοῦ
καὶ ἐν ἁγίοις ὁ κλῆρος αὐτοῦ ἐστιν;

2² fin.]+αυτου S   3² και ερουσιν]> B†, pr. οι S*†
3¹] εν> S*†   4⁴ ατιμιαν S*†

---

passage "points to a retribution beginning on earth." TO THEIR FACE: Similarly Ps. 50.21. It is interesting that even Gregg is compelled to admit here that "although the writer is careful to abstain from any doctrine of a final judgment, it is probable that he was not unfamiliar with such speculations as those of the Book of Enoch."

1. THEN etc.: Augustine (Ep. 185.41, Contr. Gaud. I.38, etc.) refers this passage to the Last Judgment, but most commentators are opposed to this view. As an instance may serve the dictum of Reuss: "One might conclude that this was a representation of the Last Judgment, as the Jewish theologians contemporary with our Lord represented it. But as this idea does not occur elsewhere, we may be satisfied to see here a poetic tableau of the late repentance of the sinner." Goodrick justly counters: "One would have thought that a scene to which a writer devoted twenty-six verses (4.18–5.23), coupled with his constant references to ἐπισκοπή and ἡμέρα διαγνώσεως, might be considered to form an integral part of his belief, if he has any at all." BOLDNESS: For parrēsia cf. Prov. 13.5. The boldness of the righteous is contrasted with the "speechlessness" and "fear" (4.19 f.) of the wicked. THAT TORMENTED etc.: Itala abstulerunt and Pal. Syr. שלבו, both meaning "plundered."

2. SEEING: The ungodly see the truth concerning the righteous. Cf. I Enoch 108.15. The word recalls their bold challenge "let us see" in 2.17. There is no need to add "it" with R.V. or "him" with the margin. UNEXPECTEDNESS: So Goodrick; R.V. has "marvel"; Deane would render

And their transgressions shall convict them to their
 face.

5 ¹ Then shall the righteous man stand forth with great
 boldness,
 In the face of them that tormented him
 And them that count his labours as naught.
 ²Seeing they shall be dismayed with terrible fear,
 And shall be astounded at the unexpectedness of his
 deliverance.
 ³They shall say within themselves repenting
 And they shall groan for oppression of spirit:
 ⁴This was he whom aforetime we had in derision,
 And for a byword of reproach, we fools;
 His life we accounted madness,
 And his end unhonoured.
 5 ⁵How was he numbered among the sons of God,
 And how is his portion among the saints?

"the unlooked-for allotment of happiness." It should be noted that
paradoxon is rendered in Itala by an unusual word, *subitatio*, which occurs
elsewhere only in African writers. This serves to strengthen the evidence
that the Old Latin version is of African origin.   HIS DELIVERANCE: *I. e.*
the righteous man's deliverance, reading σωτηρίας αὐτοῦ with א, *cf.* III
Macc. 6.33. R.V. has "God's salvation," which is not so evident.

3. OPPRESSION OF SPIRIT: *stenochōria*, literally "torturing confinement,"
occurs several times in LXX. That it seems to have also a physical significance may be seen from IV Macc. 11.11.

4. BYWORD OF REPROACH: R.V. "parable of reproach," imitating the
Greek. For the exact expression see Jer. 24.9, *cf.* also Deut. 28.37, Ps.
69.11, II Chron. 7.20.   WE FOOLS: properly belongs to this verse, as the
rhythm of the Greek shows (so Swete).   MADNESS: *Cf.* 2.15. The
reference is to the refusal of the righteous to purchase material advantage
at the price of apostasy.

5. NUMBERED: Analogous to the register of the inhabitants of the theocratic community (Ps. 69.29) a register is pictured here as existing in the
eternal world.   SONS OF GOD: Some take this to mean "the angels," as in
Job 1.6, 2.1, and 38.7, see also Enoch 104.4; but more likely the reference
here is to "saints" generally, as in Hos. 2.1, where the repentant folk of
Israel are meant. The phrase occurs also in 18.13, but there it denotes the
chosen people of God on earth.   PORTION: or lot, or inheritance, for
klēros means every one of these. The portion of Israel is the Promised

⁶ἄρα ἐπλανήθημεν ἀπὸ ὁδοῦ ἀληθείας,
καὶ τὸ τῆς δικαιοσύνης φῶς οὐκ ἐπέλαμψεν ἡμῖν,
καὶ ὁ ἥλιος οὐκ ἀνέτειλεν ἡμῖν·
⁷ἀνομίας ἐνεπλήσθημεν τρίβοις καὶ ἀπωλείας
καὶ διωδεύσαμεν ἐρήμους ἀβάτους,
τὴν δὲ ὁδὸν κυρίου οὐκ ἐπέγνωμεν.
⁸τί ὠφέλησεν ἡμᾶς ἡ ὑπερηφανία;
καὶ τί πλοῦτος μετὰ ἀλαζονείας συμβέβληται ἡμῖν;
⁹παρῆλθεν ἐκεῖνα πάντα ὡς σκιὰ
καὶ ὡς ἀγγελία παρατρέχουσα·
10   ¹⁰ὡς ναῦς διερχομένη κυμαινόμενον ὕδωρ,
ἧς διαβάσης οὐκ ἔστιν ἴχνος εὑρεῖν
οὐδὲ ἀτραπὸν τρόπιος αὐτῆς ἐν κύμασιν·
¹¹ἢ ὡς ὀρνέου διιπτάντος ἀέρα
οὐθὲν εὑρίσκεται τεκμήριον πορείας,

6² ἐπελαμψεν] επ> BA, +εν At   11¹ διιπταντος B*V(†) (cf. Thack. p.
10³ τροπιος] -πιας S*†, -πεως AS° pl.;   282)] διαπταντος SAB°
τριβων B°†; πορειας V pau.: — 11²

Land, but the word is employed here metaphorically as the inheritance in God which the saints enjoy, *cf.* 3.14, Ps. 16.5, Ecclus. 45.22.

6. THEN: The inferential particle ἄρα is conclusive: "so then after all it is we who were wrong." Thus conceived, the preceding clause—surprise at the good fortune of the righteous—must be regarded as a protasis. So also Itala *ergo.* R.V. "verily" misses this point.   THE PATH OF TRUTH: *I. e.* the path that leads to moral and spiritual truth, or the path that corresponds to true religion with all its observances. The exact phrase occurs in Ps. 119.30 *derek emunah* opposed to the false way *derek sheker.* THE LIGHT OF RIGHTEOUSNESS: *Cf.* II Sam. 22.29, Ps. 119.105. Righteousness is compared to light in Isa. 62.1. Goodrick justly observes that the dogmatic meaning of the passage is most obscure. "Had the words been put into the mouth of heathens they would have been intelligible; but these are Jews, who had enjoyed all the advantages of the Jewish education and the covenanted mercies of God. The text can only mean that they had not been prepared to receive or assimilate such education, being blinded by sensual pleasure."

7. SURFEITED etc.: There is an incongruity in the metaphor, but *cf.* Prov. 14.14. Itala departs slightly from the Greek by reading *lassati sumus.*   THE WAYS OF LAWLESSNESS: *Cf.* Ps. 119.29, where the way of falsehood is contrasted by the way of faithfulness. For ways of destruction see Job 30.12.   PATHLESS DESERTS: Similarly Jer. 12.10 and Ps. 63.1. Itala paraphrases *vias difficiles.* The sense is that their life had no moral purpose and led nowhere, *cf.* Isa. 53.6.   THE WAY OF THE LORD: Equiva-

⁶Then we erred from the path of truth,
And the light of righteousness shone not upon us,
And the sun rose not for us.
⁷We were surfeited with the ways of lawlessness and
    destruction,
And we traversed pathless deserts,
But the way of the Lord we knew not.
⁸What profited us our overweening pride?
And what did riches and vain boasting bring us?
⁹All those things are passed away as a shadow,
And like a message that hurries by.

10 ¹⁰As a ship that passes through billowy water,
Of whose passage there is no trace to be found,
Nor the track of her keel in the waves.
¹¹Or as a bird that flies through the air,
Of whose passage no token is found;

---

lent to the way of knowledge, wisdom, and truth, *cf.* Baruch 3.20.23, also
Job 24.13 and Ps. 95.10.
8. OVERWEENING PRIDE: The Greek word implies pride of self and contempt for others. It is attributed to the people of Sodom in Ecclus. 16.9
and III Macc. 2.5.   VAIN BOASTING: *alazoneia* is glorification of oneself.
In IV Macc. 1.26 it is ranked with covetousness, vainglory, factiousness,
and envy, as a sin of the soul. Itala *divitiarum jactantia* is nothing but a
paraphrase of *ploutos met' alazoneias*.
9-12. A series of similes, borrowed largely from the Scriptures, expressing
the elusive and fugitive nature of life: Man is of no consequence in a world
in which his existence leaves no impression whatever.
9. ARE PASSED AWAY: In Greek the verb stands emphatically at the beginning of the line: "Past are all those things."   A MESSAGE: The abstract *angelia*, which seems to be ambiguous, may stand here for the
concrete "messenger," *cf.* Itala *nuntius*. Similarly Job 9.25 "My days
are swifter than a runner."
10. A SHIP: The reference is to a light skiff of the kind mentioned in Job
9.26 which the writer undoubtedly had in mind. These skiffs, built of a
wooden keel and reeds, are the "vessels of bulrushes," of Isa. 18.2. They
carried but one or two persons, and being light were extremely swift: they
glided over the surface of the water without leaving any trace or impression. *Cf.* also Prov. 30.19, where one of the four wonderful things is the
way of a ship in the midst of the sea.   THE TRACK OF HER KEEL:
atrapon tropios is an instance of epic diction to which the author of Wisdom
is addicted.
11. AS A BIRD: *orneou* is genit. absolute. Similarly Job 9.26 and Prov.
30.19: "the way of an eagle in the air." This is another illustration of

πληγῇ δὲ μαστιζόμενον ταρσῶν πνεῦμα κοῦφον
καὶ σχιζόμενον βίᾳ ῥοίζου
κινουμένων πτερύγων διωδεύθη,
καὶ μετὰ τοῦτο οὐχ εὑρέθη σημεῖον ἐπιβάσεως ἐν αὐτῷ·
¹²ἢ ὡς βέλους βληθέντος ἐπὶ σκοπὸν
τμηθεὶς ὁ ἀὴρ εὐθέως εἰς ἑαυτὸν ἀνελύθη
ὡς ἀγνοῆσαι τὴν δίοδον αὐτοῦ·
¹³οὕτως καὶ ἡμεῖς γεννηθέντες ἐξελίπομεν
καὶ ἀρετῆς μὲν σημεῖον οὐδὲν ἔσχομεν δεῖξαι,
ἐν δὲ τῇ κακίᾳ ἡμῶν κατεδαπανήθημεν.
¹⁴ὅτι ἐλπὶς ἀσεβοῦς ὡς φερόμενος χνοῦς ὑπὸ ἀνέμου
καὶ ὡς πάχνη ὑπὸ λαίλαπος διωχθεῖσα λεπτὴ
καὶ ὡς καπνὸς ὑπὸ ἀνέμου διεχύθη
καὶ ὡς μνεία καταλύτου μονοημέρου παρώδευσεν.
15   ¹⁵ Δίκαιοι δὲ εἰς τὸν αἰῶνα ζῶσιν,

11⁶ εν αυτω] αυτου S*†   14⁴ και]>S*†, η Sᵒ†

---

things that pass in the world without leaving a trace in it.   WHIPPED BY
THE STROKE OF HER PINIONS: A very vigorous expression showing the
writer's command of Greek idiom. Grimm points out that we have here a
very apt metaphor, the life of the wicked having been accompanied with
noise and tumult while they were alive. The aorists are gnomic, the various
actions recurring continually. Deane thinks they represent the rapidity of
the actions described.   BY THE FORCE OF HER RUSHING: *I. e.* by the
force of the rush of the beating wings.

12. AN ARROW: *belous*, too, is a genit. absolute.   CLOSES UP AGAIN: So
R.V., but Siegfried renders "dissolved into itself," Deane "returns to
itself," and Gregg "is released" (as in 16.14). Itala *in se reclusus est.*   IS
NOT TO BE RECOGNIZED: The Greek verb lacks a subject, hence Grimm
would supply τινά, comp. R.V. "men know not," but perhaps this is an
active for a passive (so Goodrick).

13. SO: *houtōs* shows that this is an apodosis to a protasis expressed in
verses 10–12.   CEASED TO BE: The Greek verb is very graphic: "No
sooner were we born than we died, our life in between was not worth calling
one; not only was it as futile and traceless as the three preceding verses
have shown, but it had no token of virtue in it. We wasted it all in friv-
olous wickedness" (Goodrick). Similarly Ps. 90.9.   NO TOKEN OF
VIRTUE: Their only tokens were tokens of their mirth, see above 2.9.

At the close of this verse Itala adds: *Talia dixerunt in inferno hi qui
peccaverunt.* Since this remark has no external support whatever, it must
be assumed that this was a marginal explanatory note that has crept into
the text.

14. Some critics, like Siegfried, are inclined to take this verse as part of

But the light wind being whipped by the stroke of her
pinions,

And divided by the force of her rushing,

Was traversed as her wings moved,

And thereafter no sign was found of her passing through
it.

¹²Or as when an arrow is shot at a mark,

The air being cleft closes up again immediately,

So that its path is not to be recognized.

¹³So also we being born ceased to be,

And had no token of virtue to show,

But in our wickedness were utterly consumed.

¹⁴For the hope of the impious is as chaff borne away by
the wind,

And as thin rime that is chased away by a storm,

And as smoke was it scattered by the wind,

And passed as the remembrance of a guest that tarried
but a day.

15   ¹⁵But the righteous live for ever,

---

the speech of the ungodly, but these are not likely to speak of themselves as "impious." As the addition of Itala in the foregoing verse shows, this is a reflection of the writer concerning the impious.   FOR: In what follows the writer employs four similes to illustrate the truth of his foregoing argument.   THE HOPE: abstract for concrete, the meaning being the object of his hope, namely riches etc.   CHAFF: *Chnous* is often confused with *chous* "dust" (so A.V.), but Itala *lanugo* proves that the first is the correct reading. It occurs frequently in LXX, *cf.* especially Isa. 17.13, 29.5, Hos. 13.3, Ps. 1.4, 35.5, for the expression "chaff carried by the wind."   RIME: *Pachēnē* denotes "hoar-frost," but hoar-frost is not chased away by a storm. A few MSS. have *achne* "foam," so also Pal. Syr. and Itala (*spuma*), but neither is this appropriate in the present connection. Some MSS. have *arachnē*, "spider's web," which is found in LXX of Job 8.14, in a verse immediately succeeding "the hope of the ungodly shall perish."   SMOKE: *Kapnos* is quite clear, yet A.V. margin has "chaff," perhaps with reference to Hos. 13.3, where chaff and smoke are connected. *Cf.* further Ps. 37.20 on the simile.   THE REMEMBRANCE OF A GUEST: The wicked is very significantly compared to a lodger at the wayside inn (*cf.* Jer. 14.8), who is forgotten by the next night when a new traveller claims the attention of the host.

15. THE RIGHTEOUS LIVE FOR EVER: *Cf.* Ecclus. 41.13, II Macc. 7.9 and Philo, *Jos.*, § 43. See also Ber. 17a: "the righteous sit with crowns on their

καὶ ἐν κυρίῳ ὁ μισθὸς αὐτῶν,
καὶ ἡ φροντὶς αὐτῶν παρὰ ὑψίστῳ.
¹⁶διὰ τοῦτο λήμψονται τὸ βασίλειον τῆς εὐπρεπείας
καὶ τὸ διάδημα τοῦ κάλλους ἐκ χειρὸς κυρίου,
ὅτι τῇ δεξιᾷ σκεπάσει αὐτοὺς
καὶ τῷ βραχίονι ὑπερασπιεῖ αὐτῶν.
¹⁷λήμψεται πανοπλίαν τὸν ζῆλον αὐτοῦ
καὶ ὁπλοποιήσει τὴν κτίσιν εἰς ἄμυναν ἐχθρῶν·
¹⁸ἐνδύσεται θώρακα δικαιοσύνην
καὶ περιθήσεται κόρυθα κρίσιν ἀνυπόκριτον·
¹⁹λήμψεται ἀσπίδα ἀκαταμάχητον ὁσιότητα,
20 ²⁰ὀξυνεῖ δὲ ἀπότομον ὀργὴν εἰς ῥομφαίαν,
συνεκπολεμήσει δὲ αὐτῷ ὁ κόσμος ἐπὶ τοὺς παράφρονας.
²¹πορεύσονται εὔστοχοι βολίδες ἀστραπῶν

16³ τη δεξια] δεξια κυριου S†	17² οδοποιησει S*†
16⁴ αυτου S*†	18¹ δικαιοσυνης S
17¹ το ζηλος S*†	

heads and enjoy of the glory of the Shekinah." IN THE LORD: For the varieties of meaning of which ἐν κυρίῳ is capable see Winer, ed. Moulton, p. 486. The meaning here seems to be "their reward is fellowship with God," or perhaps "God is their portion" as in Ps. 73.26 and 119.57, or "in God's keeping" as in Isa. 62.11. Grimm renders "their reward consists in the possession of the Lord," but this cannot be substantiated. CARE: Cf. Ps. 40.17 and 55.23.

16. THE KINGDOM OF SPLENDOUR: basileion in the sense of "kingdom" occurs also in 1.14, but it may sometimes denote "crown" (so R.V.) or "palace," cf. further Preisigke, Wörterbuch der griechischen Papyrusurkunden, s. v. DIADEM OF BEAUTY: diadēma is the Oriental form of crown, "a band of purple silk sewn with pearls" (Farrar). The idea is taken from Isa. 62.3 "a crown of beauty and a royal diadem"). SHIELD THEM: The Greek word means "to champion," lit. to throw one's shield over another, see Zech. 9.15, III Macc. 7.6, cf. also Ps. 18.2 LXX. It should be stated that the critics insist, as usual, that whatever else is referred to here, it cannot be the final judgment.

17. HE SHALL TAKE etc.: This vivid and eloquent passage was evidently inspired by Isa. 59.17. For God as "a man of war" see Ex. 15.3 and elsewhere. Zēlos strictly means "zeal," not "jealousy," but the former is used only of men, whereas the latter is used of God. MAKE ALL CREATION HIS WEAPONS: The Greek verb properly denotes "will be a maker of arms," and apparently the writer misused it. Siegfried "shall arm his creation" assumes the verb hoplizein. For the idea see below verse 20, also 16.17.24 and 19.6. Cf. also Jud. 5.20 "The stars in their courses

And their reward is in the Lord,
And the care of them with the Most High.
¹⁶Therefore they shall receive the kingdom of splendour,
And the diadem of beauty from the Lord's hand
For with his right hand shall he cover them,
And with his arm shall he shield them.
¹⁷He shall take his jealousy as complete armour,
And make all creation his weapons for the repulse of his
foes.
¹⁸He shall clothe himself with righteousness as a breast-
plate,
And put on as a helmet judgment undissembled.
¹⁹He shall take holiness for an invincible shield,
20 ²⁰And sharpen stern anger into a sword,
And with him the world shall fight it out against the
madmen.
²¹Shafts of lightnings shall go forth with true aim,

---

fought against Sisera"; Ecclus. 39.29; Philo. *Moses*, I, 17: "God determined that the land of the wicked should be devastated with the four
elements of which the world is composed."
18. JUDGMENT UNDISSEMBLED: *Krisis anupokritos*, some sort of verbal
oxymoron, implies administration of straightforward justice without
respect of persons. The adjective occurs again in 18.16 in the same sense.
Pal. Syr. literally "without falsehood." A.V. "true judgment" follows
Itala *certum judicium.*
19. HOLINESS: A.V. has "equity" following Itala. *Hosiotēs* denotes here
the absolute impeccability of God, rendering all argument against His
decisions useless; *cf.* Deut. 32.4 and Ps. 145.17. When applied to man it
means absolute faith in and piety towards God, though it also signifies a
pure and saintly life.
20. STERN ANGER: *apotomos*, used five times in this book, cannot be
rendered adequately into English. "The idea is that of an abrupt ending,
as of a cliff ending in a precipice. The Latin *abscisus* quoted by Grimm
from Valer. Max. fairly represents it, and the adverb ἀποτόμως in verse 22
illustrates its force" (Goodrick). Pal. Syr. has "marvellously shall he
sharpen the lance of his anger."   MADMEN: *Parafrones* is a stronger
term than *afrones* used hitherto, and it seems to signify positive madness
on the part of God's opponents. The idea of the last line is the same as that
of verse 17 above.
21. SHAFTS OF LIGHTNINGS: This figure of speech is not uncommon in the
Bible, *cf.* II Sam. 22.15 and its repetition in Ps. 18.15, Hab. 3.11, Zech.

καὶ ὡς ἀπὸ εὐκύκλου τόξου τῶν νεφῶν ἐπὶ σκοπὸν
ἁλοῦνται,

²²καὶ ἐκ πετροβόλου θυμοῦ πλήρεις ῥιφήσονται χάλαζαι·
ἀγανακτήσει κατ' αὐτῶν ὕδωρ θαλάσσης,
ποταμοὶ δὲ συγκλύσουσιν ἀποτόμως·

²³ἀντιστήσεται αὐτοῖς πνεῦμα δυνάμεως
καὶ ὡς λαῖλαψ ἐκλικμήσει αὐτούς·
καὶ ἐρημώσει πᾶσαν τὴν γῆν ἀνομία,
καὶ ἡ κακοπραγία περιτρέψει θρόνους δυναστῶν.

6 ¹ Ἀκούσατε οὖν, βασιλεῖς, καὶ σύνετε·
μάθετε, δικασταὶ περάτων γῆς·
²ἐνωτίσασθε, οἱ κρατοῦντες πλήθους
καὶ γεγαυρωμένοι ἐπὶ ὄχλοις ἐθνῶν·

21² νεφελων S

9.14, II Esdr. 16.13.   FROM A WELL-CURVED BOW OF CLOUDS: So Itala *a bene curvato arcu nubium*. A.V. and R.V. have "from the clouds, as from a well drawn bow," but the reference seems to be to the rainbow, the token of divine mercy (Gen. 9.13), which now is turned into a weapon of destruction.

22. On this verse *cf.* Isa. 28.2 and Ezek. 38.22. Its purport is to demonstrate that all the elements of nature share the wrath of God. Note the omission of ὡς at the beginning of the verse.   SLING: R.V. vaguely "engine of war." *Petrobolon* here is not an adjective, as construed by Itala, but a noun designating a siege-engine used for hurling stones, unlike the catapult which was a large cross-bow. A plural *petrobola* is attested in Josephus.   WATER OF THE SEA: *Cf.* Ps. 18.16. Grimm sees here an allusion to Pharaoh and his host at the Red Sea.   RIVERS SHALL INEXORABLY etc.: Note the play on words in the Greek, which is characteristic of our author. *Sunklusousin* properly means "shall wash over them," "drown them all together." The metaphor is taken from the Scriptures, *cf.* Jud. 5.21. Isa. 43.2, Cant. 8.7.

23. A BREATH OF POWER: Similarly 11.20. A.V. has "a wind of might," R.V. "a mighty blast." Curious is Itala's *spiritus virtutis*.   LIKE A STORM etc.: The same idea is found in Isa. 41.16.   YES: *Kai* in line 3 has the force of an affirmation or asseveration: the destruction depicted in the preceding verses, brought about by the wrath of God, is really the result of the action of the potentates, who by their lawlessness and misdeeds have brought down God's vengeance.   ILL-DEALING: *Kakopragia* in this sense is very rare: its only occurrence is in Josephus, *Antiq.*, II.V.4, where it signifies "misdeed."   OVERTHROW THE THRONES OF POTENTATES: Similarly G in Job 12.18 ff. Making allowance for the

And as from a well-curved bow of clouds, shall they leap
    to the mark.
²²And from a sling hailstones full of wrath shall be
    thrown;
The water of the sea shall rage against them,
And rivers shall inexorably overwhelm them.
²³ A breath of power shall rise up against them,
And like a storm shall winnow them away,
Yes, lawlessness shall lay waste the whole earth,
And ill-dealing overthrow the thrones of potentates.

6 ¹ Hear now, you kings, and understand;
    Learn, you judges of the ends of the earth;
    ²Lend ear, you that have dominion over crowds,
    And that make boast of multitudes of nations.

---

hyperbolic language of our book, *dunastai* might refer to the renegade Jewish officials of chapter 1 (so Goodrick). Grimm thinks the heathen must be
included, and henceforward no doubt this is true; but up to this point
there is nothing that must necessarily refer to pagan rulers.

The last line serves as a transition from the land to its rulers, preparing
the way for the address to rulers and kings at the beginning of chapter 6.

Chapters 6-9 incl. constitute the Book of Wisdom proper with its
distinct Sapiential and Solomonic characteristics. Here Solomon, after an
appeal to the rulers and judges of the earth to recognize their responsibility for the power bestowed upon them, sets forth the essential nature of
Wisdom and acknowledges his complete dependence upon her, winding up
with a prayer of thanksgiving for the gift of heavenly Wisdom. The first
five chapters contain no allusion whatever to the professed Solomonic
origin of the book.

Itala adds the following sentence at the beginning of this chapter:
Melior est sapientia quam vires, et vir prudens quam fortis. This seems to
consist of two biblical sayings: Eccles. 9.16 "Wisdom is better than
strength" and Prov. 24.5 "a wise man is strong."

1. HEAR NOW etc.: *Cf.* 1.1, which consists of a similar address to the judges
of the earth; see also Ps. 2.10.   JUDGES: In the rarer sense of rulers,
which is appropriate here, *cf.* biblical lexica *s. v.* שפט THE ENDS OF THE
EARTH: Similarly I Sam. 2.10, Ps. 2.8, 22.28, etc. *Perata gēs*, like its Hebrew
equivalent *afse eres*, does not have to refer to the real ends of the earth,
but simply to distant parts. The allusion here may very well be to distant
Rome (Goodrick).

2. MULTITUDES OF NATIONS: *Ochlois ethnōn,*"mobs of nations," is an inept

³ὅτι ἐδόθη παρὰ κυρίου ἡ κράτησις ὑμῖν
καὶ ἡ δυναστεία παρὰ ὑψίστου,
ὃς ἐξετάσει ὑμῶν τὰ ἔργα καὶ τὰς βουλὰς διερευνήσει·
⁴ὅτι ὑπηρέται ὄντες τῆς αὐτοῦ βασιλείας οὐκ ἐκρίνατε
ὀρθῶς
οὐδὲ ἐφυλάξατε νόμον
οὐδὲ κατὰ τὴν βουλὴν τοῦ θεοῦ ἐπορεύθητε.

5 ⁵φρικτῶς καὶ ταχέως ἐπιστήσεται ὑμῖν,
ὅτι κρίσις ἀπότομος ἐν τοῖς ὑπερέχουσιν γίνεται.
⁶ὁ γὰρ ἐλάχιστος συγγνωστός ἐστιν ἐλέους,
δυνατοὶ δὲ δυνατῶς ἐτασθήσονται·
⁷οὐ γὰρ ὑποστελεῖται πρόσωπον ὁ πάντων δεσπότης
οὐδὲ ἐντραπήσεται μέγεθος,

3³ διερευν.] εξερ. S
6¹ συγγνωστος AS°: cf. 13 8; ευγνωσ-
τος S*† | ελεου A†

---

2. MULTITUDES OF NATIONS: Ochlois ethnōn,"mobs of nations," is an inept
expression, but having used plēthos in the preceding line the author was at
a loss to seize upon a better synonym. Thus this might be further proof of
his poverty of Greek diction.

It should be stressed that this apostrophe to the rulers of the world was
not intended to be read by them or even known to them, but, like the
utterances of the prophets of yore in denunciation of foreign nations and
their rulers, was aimed for "home consumption," that is for the comfort
and encouragement of Israel against their enemies.

3. YOUR DOMINION etc.: The doctrine that sovereignty is from the Lord is
derived from the Bible, cf. Dan. 2.21, I Chron. 29.12. In Prov. 8.15
Wisdom claims this power for herself: "By me kings reign, and princes
decree justice." According to Josephus, Bellum Judaicum, II. VIII.7, the
Essenes held this doctrine, to justify their passive obedience.   EX-
AMINE: Cf. Ps. 11.4 f. Note that foreign rulers are here represented as
actually receiving their authority from God. This is in consonance with
the rabbinic doctrine that the seventy heathen nations are ruled over by
seventy patron angels (cf. Ginzberg, Legends, I, 181, and especially V,
194 f.), while Michael is the prince of Israel (Dan. 10.13 and 12.1). Cf.
further Ecclus. 17.17 "For every nation he appointed a ruler, and Israel
is the Lord's portion."

4. DID NOT JUDGE ARIGHT: Unfair judgment, consisting in condemning the
innocent and whitewashing the guilty, was a frequent charge levelled at
the rulers and judges in the Bible. Cf. Deut. 16.19, 24.17, Isa. 1.23, Ps.
82.2, Prov. 17.23, etc.   NOR KEPT THE LAW: Not the general principles

³For your dominion was granted to you from the Lord,
And your sovereignty from the Most High,
Who shall examine your works and scrutinize your
    counsels.

⁴For being servants of his kindgom ye did not judge
    aright,
Nor kept the law,
Nor walked according to the will of God.

5   ⁵Terribly and swiftly shall he come upon you,
Because judgment is abrupt in case of them that are
    exalted.

⁶For the lowest is pardonable of grace,
But the mighty shall be mightily tested.

⁷For the Lord of all will not shrink from a countenance,
Nor have respect for greatness,

---

of justice and equity, as understood by A.V., but the Law in the Jewish sense, the Torah with its precepts and statutes and commandments. The objection that *nomos* is used here without the definite article does not hold good: "The Law" indeed, as pointed out by Cornely, had become a separate entity which needed no definite article, *cf.* Isa. 2.3, Hag. 2.11, Mal. 2.6, Ecclus. 24.23 ff.

5. TERRIBLY AND SWIFTLY etc.: This line resembles very closely Prov. 1.27. *Epistēsetai* is used in a hostile sense.   JUDGMENT IS ABRUPT: *Apotomos* is not only "abrupt" but implies also the notion "inexorable," *cf.* 5.22. The sense evidently is that the higher men are placed the more inexorably they will be judged, *cf.* Lev. 4.3, where the sin of the anointed priest is to be expiated by the same sacrifice which was required for the sin of the whole congregation, also Num. 25.4, where the heads of the people are to be hanged for the transgression of the congregation in the matter of Baal-Peor. There are numerous cases of prominent men being severely punished for apparently minor sins, as. *e. g.*, Moses (Num. 20.12), David (II Sam. 24.12), Hezekiah (II Ki. 20.17).

6. PARDONABLE OF GRACE: *I. e.* through grace or because of grace. The sense is plain, but the Greek construction of *sungnōstos eleous* is difficult. Some call it genitive of origin, others genitive of cause; some take it in the sense of "worthy of forgiveness."   TESTED: A.V. has "tormented," following Itala *tormenta patientur*, but this is too strong and not suitable here.

7. This verse is reminiscent of Deut. 1.17, *cf.* also Job 34.19 and Ecclus. 35.12 ff. (32.14 ff.).   SHRINK FROM A COUNTENANCE: The sense seems to be the same as *hikkir panim bamishpat* in Deut. 1.17 and elsewhere. SMALL AND GREAT: This implies that God can raise the lowly and make

ὅτι μικρὸν καὶ μέγαν αὐτὸς ἐποίησεν
ὁμοίως τε προνοεῖ περὶ πάντων,
[8]τοῖς δὲ κραταιοῖς ἰσχυρὰ ἐφίσταται ἔρευνα.
[9]πρὸς ὑμᾶς οὖν, ὦ τύραννοι, οἱ λόγοι μου,
ἵνα μάθητε σοφίαν καὶ μὴ παραπέσητε·
10　[10]οἱ γὰρ φυλάξαντες ὁσίως τὰ ὅσια ὁσιωθήσονται,
καὶ οἱ διδαχθέντες αὐτὰ εὑρήσουσιν ἀπολογίαν.
[11]ἐπιθυμήσατε οὖν τῶν λόγων μου,
ποθήσατε καὶ παιδευθήσεσθε.
[12]　Λαμπρὰ καὶ ἀμάραντός ἐστιν ἡ σοφία
καὶ εὐχερῶς θεωρεῖται ὑπὸ τῶν ἀγαπώντων αὐτὴν
καὶ εὑρίσκεται ὑπὸ τῶν ζητούντων αὐτήν,
[13]φθάνει τοὺς ἐπιθυμοῦντας προγνωσθῆναι.
[14]ὁ ὀρθρίσας πρὸς αὐτὴν οὐ κοπιάσει·
πάρεδρον γὰρ εὑρήσει τῶν πυλῶν αὐτοῦ.

12³ >B*　　　　　　　　　　　14¹ προς] επ BS
13　επιθυμ.]+αυτην S

the great small, see I Sam. 2.7, Ps. 75.8, and elsewhere.　TAKES THOUGHT: *pronoein* undoubtedly refers to divine providence, *pronoia*, in the ordinary sense, whether it be related somehow or not to the philosophical doctrine of Providence of Plato and the Stoics. *Cf.* note on 14.3.

8. A repetition, in different words, of 6b: the mighty shall surely be searched out and tested. The present tense heightens the effect.　A STRICT SCRUTINY: On the impartiality of God's judgment *cf.* II Chron. 19.7 and Ecclus. quoted in the preceding verse.

9. A repetition of the appeal to kings and rulers to learn wisdom at the opening of this chapter.　DESPOTS: *turannos* had a bad sense in Greek literature, implying arbitrary power, though in LXX it means simply "ruler" or "king."　MY WORDS: Solomon is supposed to be the speaker. WISDOM: *Sofia* is still used in the ordinary sense of human wisdom, coupled with understanding of and obedience to God's will. The divine wisdom appears first in verse 12, hence some critics fixed the opening of the second part of our book at that verse.　FALL NOT AWAY: Namely through unjust judgments and personal transgressions. *Parapiptein* implies deviation from the ordained path.

10. SHALL FIND A DEFENSE: So Grimm, who explains it as meaning an excuse for the sins they committed before they knew wisdom, and also for their slips afterwards. A.V. and R.V. "shall find what to answer," following Itala *invenient quid respondeant.*

11. LONG FOR THEM etc.: The same sequence is found in Prov. 4.6. The Greek word alludes not only to mere learning, but also to moral discipline and virtue, *cf.* Ps. 89.12.

Because small and great he made himself,
And alike he takes thought for all.
⁸But over the mighty a strict scrutiny impends.
⁹Unto you, therefore, O despots, are my words,
That you may learn wisdom and fall not away.

10 ¹⁰For they that holily observe holy things shall be made
holy,
And they that have been taught them shall find a
defense.
¹¹Desire you then my words,
Long for them and you shall be taught.
¹²Bright and unfading is Wisdom,
And easily is she beheld of them that love her,
And found of them that seek her.
¹³She forestalls them that desire her eagerly, making
herself known aforehand.
¹⁴He who rises up early for her shall have no travail,
For he shall find her sitting beside his gates.

---

12. Here begins the praise of Wisdom and a description of her qualities,
which extend through the following chapter.   BRIGHT: *lampra* indicates
the luminous nature of Wisdom, which renders her easily attainable in the
gloom of ignorance. *Cf.* Philo, *Leg. Alleg.*, III.59: "What could be more
radiant or more conspicuous than the Divine Logos?"   UNFADING:
amarantos points to the immortality and everlastingness of Wisdom, in
which respect she is on a par with righteousness.   EASILY IS SHE
BEHELD: So LXX of Prov. 3.15.   FOUND OF THEM THAT SEEK HER: This
line, lacking in B, is found in B marg. א A, and is, moreover, translated in
Itala, Pal. Syr. and Arabic. It is a variant of Prov. 8.17 b; *cf.* also Ecclus.
6.27 "seek and she shall be made known unto thee."
13. FORESTALLS: *Fthanein* with the accusative of the persons affected is
normal, but it is generally followed by a participle, not an infinitive, as
here and 4.7. The infinitive here is that of purpose, which in Hellenistic
Greek generally takes the prefix τοῦ. The sense is that Wisdom is ever
anxious to make herself known to men: she cannot enter into them without
being solicited, but she always endeavors to dispose them to welcome her.
Cf. Philo, *Congr.*, § 22, and *Fug.*, § 25; see also Isa. 65.1 and 24.
14. WHO RISES UP EARLY: *Orthrizein* occurs in LXX both in its literal and
metaphorical connotation, *cf.* Ps. 127.2, Ecclus. 4.12 and 6.36.   SITTING
BESIDE HIS GATES: *Paredros* lit. "assessor, counsellor," as in 9.4. The
phrase is reminiscent of Prov. 1.21, 8.3. The task of seeking for wisdom is
quite easy.

15 ¹⁵τὸ γὰρ ἐνθυμηθῆναι περὶ αὐτῆς φρονήσεως τελειότης,
   καὶ ὁ ἀγρυπνήσας δι᾽ αὐτὴν ταχέως ἀμέριμνος ἔσται·
   ¹⁶ὅτι τοὺς ἀξίους αὐτῆς αὐτὴ περιέρχεται ζητοῦσα
   καὶ ἐν ταῖς τρίβοις φαντάζεται αὐτοῖς εὐμενῶς
   καὶ ἐν πάσῃ ἐπινοίᾳ ὑπαντᾷ αὐτοῖς.
   ¹⁷ἀρχὴ γὰρ αὐτῆς ἡ ἀληθεστάτη παιδείας ἐπιθυμία,
   φροντὶς δὲ παιδείας ἀγάπη,
   ¹⁸ἀγάπη δὲ τήρησις νόμων αὐτῆς,
   προσοχὴ δὲ νόμων βεβαίωσις ἀφθαρσίας,
   ¹⁹ἀφθαρσία δὲ ἐγγὺς εἶναι ποιεῖ θεοῦ·
20 ²⁰ἐπιθυμία ἄρα σοφίας ἀνάγει ἐπὶ βασιλείαν.
   ²¹εἰ οὖν ἥδεσθε ἐπὶ θρόνοις καὶ σκήπτροις, τύραννοι λαῶν,
   τιμήσατε σοφίαν, ἵνα εἰς τὸν αἰῶνα βασιλεύσητε.

16¹ αυτη>St   γαρ SAᶜ | αναιρει S*†
20 επιθυμιας S*† (om. σοφιας) | αρα]

---

15. UNDERSTANDING: *Fronēsis* is sometimes identical with wisdom as in 8.21; in 7.7 it is on a par with *pneuma sofias*; in 8.7 it is taught by wisdom as in Prov. 10.23; here it is a moral quality whose completion is the attainment of wisdom. Grimm's rendering "prudence" emphasizes the intellectual quality, hence is not suitable here.   WAKES: literally "to be watchful," *cf.* Prov. 8.24, and the noun *agrupnia* in the sense of "vigilance" is found in Ecclus. 31.1.2, 38.28, 42.10.   WITHOUT CARE: Similarly 7.23, where the term *amerimnos* is used of Wisdom herself. Eusebius in his *Praeparatio Evangelica* 667b records the following saying of Aristobulus of Alexandria (ab. 150 BCE): "They that follow Wisdom consistently shall be free from trouble all their lives."

16. GOES ABOUT etc.: *Cf.* 8.18. The entire passage has its counterpart in Prov. 1.20 ff.   WORTHY OF HER: Through their moral behavior and blameless life. *Cf.* Philo, *Migr.*, § 10 f.: "God draws near to give help to those who are worthy to be helped. And who are they who are worthy to be so blessed? Clearly all who love wisdom and knowledge."   IN EVERY THOUGHT: Itala *in omni providentia* assigns the words to Wisdom, but it is better to refer them to men: "whatever plan a man has in his mind, Wisdom, if he be worthy of her, will set it right for him."   COMES TO MEET THEM: *Cf.* Philo, *Leg. Alleg.*, III, § 76: "Some souls God goes out to meet. What grace it is that He should anticipate our slowness and lead our soul forth into perfect well-doing!"

17. Here begins a figure of speech known as sorites, namely a cumulative series of syllogisms, in which the conclusion of each becomes the premise of the next, until the main conclusion is reached, as follows: The beginning of wisdom is desire of discipline; desire of discipline is love of her; love of her is keeping of her laws; keeping of her laws is assurance of immortality;

15   ¹⁵For to think upon her is perfection of understanding,
        And he that wakes for her sake will soon be without care.
      ¹⁶For she goes about seeking them that are worthy of her,
        And in the paths she graciously appears unto them,
        And in every thought she comes to meet them.
      ¹⁷For the truest beginning of her is the desire for
            instruction,
        And care for instruction is love for her,
      ¹⁸And love for her is keeping of her laws,
        And adherence to the laws the assurance of immortality,
      ¹⁹And immortality makes to be near unto God;
20   ²⁰So then the desire of wisdom leads to a kingdom.
      ²¹If you then delight in thrones and sceptres, you despots
            of the nations,
        Honour wisdom, that you may reign for ever.

---

immortality brings near to God. Logically speaking the conclusion should
be "the desire of wisdom brings near to God," but instead we have in
verse 20 the irrelevant conclusion "the desire of wisdom leads to a kingdom," which is clearly a *non sequitur*. It should be noted that an imperfect sorites is found in Hos. 2.21 ff.   TRUEST BEGINNING: For *archē
sofias cf.* Ps. 111.10, Prov. 1.7, 9.10.
18. IMMORTALITY: *Aftharsia*, means literally "incorruption" (so R.V.),
but is generally used on a par with *athanasia*. Its attainment is not clearly
delineated: in 1.15 it may be attained through justice, in our passage
through adherence to law, in 8.17 through kinship unto wisdom, in 15.3
through knowledge of God's power.
19. The thought that immortality brings one near unto God is familiar to
us from Greek philosophy, but here it occurs for the first time among
Jewish writers. *Cf.* Philo, *Fug.*, § 11: "This is the glorious goal of a deathless life, to be held in a bodiless, fleshless passion and love for God."
20. This verse closes the sorites, which began with verse 17, with an imperfect conclusion, for the desire of wisdom does not necessarily lead to a
kingdom. To obviate this difficulty some commentators suppose that a
heavenly and not an earthly kingdom is meant, or that the reference is to a
spiritual kingship (*cf.* Eccl. 4.13 f. and Philo, *Agr.*, § 10); but the following
line clearly refers to earthly rule.
21. The same thought is expressed in Prov. 8.15 f.: "By me (Wisdom)
kings reign and princes decree justice. By me princes rule and nobles, even
all the judges of the earth."   FOR EVER: This is either hyperbolic, as so often in the Bible (see I Ki. 1.31, Neh. 2.3, Dan. 2.4, etc.), or else an allusion
to the immortality supposed to attend on just deeds and merciful actions.
  Itala exhibits an addition to this verse: *Diligite lumen sapientiae, omnes*

²²τί δέ ἐστιν σοφία καὶ πῶς ἐγένετο, ἀπαγγελῶ
καὶ οὐκ ἀποκρύψω ὑμῖν μυστήρια,
ἀλλὰ ἀπ᾽ ἀρχῆς γενέσεως ἐξιχνιάσω
καὶ θήσω εἰς τὸ ἐμφανὲς τὴν γνῶσιν αὐτῆς
καὶ οὐ μὴ παροδεύσω τὴν ἀλήθειαν.
²³οὔτε μὴν φθόνῳ τετηκότι συνοδεύσω,
ὅτι οὗτος οὐ κοινωνήσει σοφίᾳ.
²⁴πλῆθος δὲ σοφῶν σωτηρία κόσμου,
καὶ βασιλεὺς φρόνιμος εὐστάθεια δήμου.
25　²⁵ὥστε παιδεύεσθε τοῖς ῥήμασίν μου, καὶ ὠφεληθήσεσθε.

7　¹ Εἰμὶ μὲν κἀγὼ θνητὸς ἄνθρωπος ἴσος ἅπασιν
καὶ γηγενοῦς ἀπόγονος πρωτοπλάστου·

23² κοινωνει A　　　　　　　　　1¹ ανθρωπος> B*S†

qui praeestis populis. Most likely this is a marginal gloss or summary of the whole verse which somehow crept into the text itself.

22. WHAT WISDOM IS: The essence of wisdom is indicated in 7.22 ff. HOW SHE CAME INTO BEING: The beginning of wisdom is dealt with in Prov. 8.24 and Job 28.26. Since our author does not fulfill his promise to tell of the beginning of wisdom, it is thought that what he meant to convey was the effect of wisdom upon Solomon, with which the next few chapters deal. MYSTERIES: Namely the mysteries of Wisdom, such as the teachings she imparts (7.17 ff.) and the blessings she confers on her initiated votaries. FROM THE BEGINNING OF CREATION: *Cf.* chapters 10 ff. for the operations of Wisdom from the dawn of human history. See also Prov. 8.22 ff. A.V. renders "from the beginning of her nativity," others "from the beginning of my life." PASS BY: On the use of *parodeuein* in our book see comment on 1.8.

23. JOURNEY ALONG: *sunodeusō* is evidently used in assonance with *parodeusō* in the preceding line. PINING ENVY: Solomon wants to say that he will not associate himself with those learned men who refuse to impart their knowledge to others on one pretext or another. Some exegetes claim that the reference here is to the sophists who had recourse to obscurantism in order to safeguard their prospective profits, *cf.* Philo, *Post. C.,* § 44. Gfrörer (*Philo,* II, 233) sees here a distinct allusion to Philo, Aristeas, Aristobulus, and others, who treated the doctrine of Wisdom as a mystery. "Pining envy," according to him, is a reproach directed against those who prided themselves on the possession of the true interpretation of Scripture. Indeed Philo, though pretending to make all plain, is always posing as a hierophant. It is true that in *Vict. Offer.,* § 12, he protests against the idea of esoteric doctrine, but in *Cherub.,* § 12, he plainly intimates that his doctrine is not for all. THIS: *houtos* probably refers

²²But what wisdom is, and how she came into being, I will
    declare,
And will not conceal from you mysteries,
But will trace her out from the beginning of creation,
And bring into clearness the knowledge of her,
And will not pass by the truth.
²³Neither indeed will I journey along with pining envy,
Because this shall have no fellowship with wisdom.
²⁴But a multitude of wise men is the salvation of the
    world,
And a wise king the soundness of his people.
25   ²⁵And so be you instructed by my words, and you shall be
    benefited.

7   ^I I too, indeed, am a mortal, like to all,
    And offspring of one earthborn, first formed;

---

to *fthonos*, but Itala renders *talis homo*, which is not impossible.   HAVE
NO FELLOWSHIP WITH: *Koinonein* with the dative is in keeping with the
whole metaphor of fellow-travellers walking along a road.
24. A MULTITUDE OF WISE MEN: Contrast Eccl. 1.18: "For in much wisdom
is much vexation; and he that increaseth knowledge increaseth sorrow."
SALVATION: *Sōtēria* here means "the public weal" generally, as in Prov.
11.14.   SOUNDNESS: Itala has *stabilimentum*, A.V. "upholding," R.V.
"tranquillity," Goodrick "establishment." The Greek word *eustatheia* is
commonly used of stability of government, *cf*. II Macc. 14.6. Grimm quotes
the well-known saying of Plato (*Rep*., V.473): "unless philosophers become
kings or kings philosophers, there will never be rest from evils in the
cities."
25. Grimm points out a contradiction between these verses and what pre-
ceded them: the former contemplate a conversion of the heathen rulers to
Wisdom or to the religion of the God of Israel, while the latter (see 5.16
ff.) prophesy the destruction of these heathen powers. But very likely our
author was confused and had no clear idea on the subject. Like the Alexandrine philosophers he is constantly wavering between particularism and
universalism in religion.

In this and the following two chapters the author identifies himself with
King Solomon not as a notable ruler but as a diligent seeker of wisdom.
1. EARTHBORN: *Gēgenēs* refers to Adam as formed "from the earth"
(Gen. 2.7).   FIRST FORMED: *Prōtoplastos* seems to be a new formation
by our author and occurs again in 10.1. It is used abundantly by the

καὶ ἐν κοιλίᾳ μητρὸς ἐγλύφην σὰρξ
²δεκαμηνιαίῳ χρόνῳ παγεὶς ἐν αἵματι
ἐκ σπέρματος ἀνδρὸς καὶ ἡδονῆς ὕπνῳ συνελθούσης.
³καὶ ἐγὼ δὲ γενόμενος ἔσπασα τὸν κοινὸν ἀέρα
καὶ ἐπὶ τὴν ὁμοιοπαθῆ κατέπεσον γῆν
πρώτην φωνὴν τὴν ὁμοίαν πᾶσιν ἴσα κλαίων·
⁴ἐν σπαργάνοις ἀνετράφην καὶ φροντίσιν.
5 ⁵οὐδεὶς γὰρ βασιλέων ἑτέραν ἔσχεν γενέσεως ἀρχήν,
⁶μία δὲ πάντων εἴσοδος εἰς τὸν βίον ἔξοδός τε ἴση.
⁷διὰ τοῦτο εὐξάμην, καὶ φρόνησις ἐδόθη μοι·
ἐπεκαλεσάμην, καὶ ἦλθέν μοι πνεῦμα σοφίας.
⁸προέκρινα αὐτὴν σκήπτρων καὶ θρόνων
καὶ πλοῦτον οὐδὲν ἡγησάμην ἐν συγκρίσει αὐτῆς·

2² υπνου S   5 βασιλευς BS

3³ ισα>S   6 βιον] κοσμον S

4 και]+εν B

Greek and Latin Church Fathers of either Adam or Eve. MOULDED
INTO FLESH: Strictly speaking, *glufein* means "carve" or "engrave"; to
"fashion" or "mould" is *plassein*, cf. Ps. 119.73 and Job 10.8. The man is
here identified with his body, which when formed in the womb received
the loan of a pre-existing soul, cf. 8.19. For a full account of the infusion
of the soul into the embryo at the moment of conception see the rabbinical
quotations in Weber, *Jüdische Theologie*, p. 226, *Cf.* also Ginzberg, *Legends*,
V, 75 ff.

2. TEN MONTHS: Apparently lunar months, which are equal to nine
calendar months. The Greeks and Romans considered ten months as the
period of gestation, cf. Vergil, *Eclogues*, IV. 61: *Matri longa decem tulerunt
fastidia menses*. The Talmud, however, speaks only of nine months for a
normal gestation, cf. Leopold Löw, *Die Lebensalter in der Jüdischen
Literatur*, pp. 47 ff. WITH BLOOD: The reference is to the menstrual
blood, which was supposed to unite with the seed for the formation of the
foetus by a sort of curdling process, cf. Job 10.10: "Hast Thou not poured
me out as milk, and curdled me like cheese?"

3. THE COMMON AIR: *I. e.* common to men and beasts, see Eccles. 3.19.
FELL UPON MY KINDRED EARTH: An old idiomatic expression signifying
"was born, came to life"; cf. Isa. 26.18: "neither have the inhabitants of
the world fallen," which is taken to mean in accordance with the context "been born"; cf. also *ibid*. verse 19: "the earth shall cause shades to
fall," which means "shall bring forth shades." *Homoiopathēs* usually
means "kindred," and here it agrees with *gēgenēs* in verse 1. Solomon
wants to say that earth was his mother no less than of others, and that he
was only common clay. But the sense of the preceding and succeeding

And in the womb of a mother was I moulded into flesh,
²In ten months' time, compact with blood,
By the seed of a man and the pleasure that accompanies
    wedlock.
³And when I was born I drew in the common air,
And fell upon my kindred earth,
Wailing out my first cry like unto all.
⁴In swaddling clothes was I reared and with cares,
5 ⁵For there is no king that had any other beginning of life,
⁶But all men have one entrance into life and a like
    departure.
⁷Wherefore I prayed, and understanding was granted me,
I called, and the spirit of wisdom came unto me.
⁸I preferred her before sceptres and thrones,
And deemed riches as naught in comparison of her.

---

clauses requires that *homoiopathēs* should mean something like "that suffers the same thing at the hands of all her children." The point of the adjective is not to show that Solomon and the earth were related, but Solomon and other men (Gregg). Grimm suggests "equally trodden by all." Churton paraphrases the line "the earth in compassion for my weakness received me into her bosom."

4. WITH CARES: Itala has *curis magnis*. The collocation of swaddling-clothes and cares is very peculiar.

5. BEGINNING OF LIFE: *Genesis* is used not only of actual birth, but also of the life which follows it, cf. Philo, *Opif.*, § 22. Not so Itala *nativitatis initium*.

6. This verse, which states that the beginning and end of life are the same for all, is probably the most pessimistic in our book and very much akin to the Book of Ecclesiastes. It is well illustrated from Ecclus. 40.1 ff.: "A heavy yoke is upon the sons of Adam from the day of their coming forth of their mother's womb until the day for their burial in the mother of all things, etc." Cf. also Job 1.21 and Eccl. 9.3. A very striking parallel to our passage is found in Theodoret, *Orat.*, IX. *de Providentia*.

7. WHEREFORE: Having recognized his own weakness Solomon prayed for wisdom to guide him in the difficult task of government.   UNDERSTAND-ING-SPIRIT OF WISDOM: Grimm labors hard to prove a difference between *fronēsis* and *pneuma sofias*, characterizing the one as "wisdom of God" and the other as "wisdom communicated to a man," but undoubtedly the two are used synonymously for one and the same thing, namely wisdom in general, as usual in the parallelistic construction of the Bible.

8. BEFORE SCEPTRES: In contrast to the kings mentioned in 6.21. Solomon placed wisdom above everything else.   RICHES: *Cf.* I Ki. 3.11. See also Job 28.15 ff.; Prov. 3.14 f., 8.10 f., 16.16.

⁹οὐδὲ ὡμοίωσα αὐτῇ λίθον ἀτίμητον,
ὅτι ὁ πᾶς χρυσὸς ἐν ὄψει αὐτῆς ψάμμος ὀλίγη,
καὶ ὡς πηλὸς λογισθήσεται ἄργυρος ἐναντίον αὐτῆς·
10 ¹⁰ὑπὲρ ὑγίειαν καὶ εὐμορφίαν ἠγάπησα αὐτὴν
καὶ προειλόμην αὐτὴν ἀντὶ φωτὸς ἔχειν,
ὅτι ἀκοίμητον τὸ ἐκ ταύτης φέγγος.
¹¹ἦλθεν δέ μοι τὰ ἀγαθὰ ὁμοῦ πάντα μετ᾽ αὐτῆς
καὶ ἀναρίθμητος πλοῦτος ἐν χερσὶν αὐτῆς·
¹²εὐφράνθην δὲ ἐπὶ πᾶσιν, ὅτι αὐτῶν ἡγεῖται σοφία,
ἠγνόουν δὲ αὐτὴν γενέτιν εἶναι τούτων.
¹³ἀδόλως τε ἔμαθον ἀφθόνως τε μεταδίδωμι,
τὸν πλοῦτον αὐτῆς οὐκ ἀποκρύπτομαι·
¹⁴ἀνεκλιπὴς γὰρ θησαυρός ἐστιν ἀνθρώποις,
ὃν οἱ κτησάμενοι πρὸς θεὸν ἐστείλαντο φιλίαν
διὰ τὰς ἐκ παιδείας δωρεὰς συσταθέντες.
15 ¹⁵ Ἐμοὶ δὲ δῴη ὁ θεὸς εἰπεῖν κατὰ γνώμην
καὶ ἐνθυμηθῆναι ἀξίως τῶν δεδομένων,

9² ψαμμος] pr. ως Sᶜ   14² χρησαμενοι BS*
12² γενεσιν BS   15² δεδομ.] λεγομενων SA

9. A PRICELESS GEM: *Atimētos* is literally "unpriced" or "beyond price," hence "of inestimable value." Cf. III Macc. 3.23. This figure occurs also in rabbinic literature, as, *e. g.*, Gen. r., § 35, end.   IN HER SIGHT: *En opsei autēs* might be rendered "in respect of her," but considering the personification of Wisdom in these chapters it is preferable to say "in her sight" which corresponds to *be'eineiha* in Hebrew. This expression occurs also in 3.4 and 15.19.   AS CLAY: For a depreciation in the value of silver in Solomon's reign *cf.* I Ki. 10.21 and II Chron. 1.15.

10. ABOVE HEALTH: This sentiment is rather exaggerated and hardly fits the real Solomon. Besides, considerable importance was attached to health in ancient as in modern times, *cf.* Ecclus. 30.15 f.: "Health and a good constitution are better than all gold, and a strong body than wealth without measure. There is no riches better than health of body."   NEVER LAID TO REST: *Cf.* verses 29 f. See Philo, *Migr.*, § 8: "Wisdom is the archetypal light of God, whose image and copy is the sun."

11. THERE CAME TO ME: *I. e.* unsolicited, *cf.* I Ki. 3.13 and II Chron. 1.12. RICHES INNUMERABLE: *Cf.* Prov. 3.16. Very peculiarly Itala renders the Greek phrase by *innumerabilis honestas.*

12. WISDOM GUIDES THEM: *I. e.* directs all other good things, such as riches and honors for the benefit of man. As Bois (*Essai*, p. 391) puts it: "Wisdom walks before, and good things follow in her train."   MOTHER: Following the reading of A γενέτιν, though אB have γένεσιν, "origin." Cf. Philo, *Ebr.*, § 8, where Wisdom is called the bride of God and spiritual

⁹Nor did I liken to her a priceless gem,
    For all gold in her sight is as a little sand,
    And as clay shall silver be accounted before her.
10 ¹⁰Above health and comeliness I loved her,
    And preferred to have her rather than light,
    Because the radiance from her is never laid to rest.
    ¹¹But there came to me with her all good things together,
    And riches innumerable in her hands.
    ¹²And I rejoiced in all because wisdom guides them,
    Yet I knew not that she was the mother of these things.
    ¹³Frankly did I learn, ungrudgingly do I impart,
    The riches of her I do not hide away.
    ¹⁴For an unfailing treasure for mankind is she,
    Which they that use do foster friendship towards God,
    Being commended by the gifts that come from her
    training.
15 ¹⁵But to me may God grant to speak according to my mind,
    And to devise worthily of the things that have been
    given me,

---

mother of all things. It should be pointed out that the rule of Solomon was not altogether guided by wisdom, as may be seen from I Ki. 12.4.

13. UNGRUDGINGLY: Cf. 6.23. See also Ecclus. 20.30: "Wisdom that is hid and treasure that is out of sight, what profit is in them both?" Philo (Gig., § 9) says of the sophists: "Is not their disgrace obvious, who call themselves wise, and yet barter wisdom, like auctioneers in the market?"

14. UNFAILING: Aneklipēs for the classical anekleiptos occurs once again in 8.18 and was probably invented by our author.   THEY THAT USE: The use of chrēsthai with an accusative instead of a dative is not classical, and only I Cor. 7.31 supports it.   FOSTER FRIENDSHIP: This Greek expression is likewise unique, the verb being a gnomic aorist. For friendship with God see verse 27 and Philo, Abr., § 46; cf. also Isa. 41.8 and II Chron. 20.7.   COMMENDED: The Greek verb occurs in I Macc. 12.43. GIFTS etc.: Referring probably to the good works that man may do under the influence of Wisdom.

15. MAY GOD GRANT: Dōē is the correct reading, though there seems to have been a variant dedōke, as evidenced by the Complutensian and the Aldine editions and by the renderings of Itala, Arab., etc.   ACCORDING TO MY MIND: So R.V. margin, with a variant "according to his mind." Either reading is superior to R.V. "with judgment" and Goodrick's "as I would."   TO DEVISE: The Greek verb elsewhere means "to be in a passion"; here it is used in the sense of conceiving thoughts (Itala praesumere) and expressing them in worthy language.   THINGS . . .

ὅτι αὐτὸς καὶ τῆς σοφίας ὁδηγός ἐστιν
καὶ τῶν σοφῶν διορθωτής.
¹⁶ἐν γὰρ χειρὶ αὐτοῦ καὶ ἡμεῖς καὶ οἱ λόγοι ἡμῶν
πᾶσά τε φρόνησις καὶ ἐργατειῶν ἐπιστήμη.
¹⁷αὐτὸς γάρ μοι ἔδωκεν τῶν ὄντων γνῶσιν ἀψευδῆ
εἰδέναι σύστασιν κόσμου καὶ ἐνέργειαν στοιχείων,
¹⁸ἀρχὴν καὶ τέλος καὶ μεσότητα χρόνων,
τροπῶν ἀλλαγὰς καὶ μεταβολὰς καιρῶν,
¹⁹ἐνιαυτοῦ κύκλους καὶ ἄστρων θέσεις,
20   ²⁰φύσεις ζῴων καὶ θυμοὺς θηρίων,
πνευμάτων βίας καὶ διαλογισμοὺς ἀνθρώπων,
διαφορὰς φυτῶν καὶ δυνάμεις ῥιζῶν,

---

19 ενιαυτων BSᶜ | αστρων S*†] αστε-   20¹ θυμους] νομους και S*†
    ρων rel.: cf. 29 10 17 13 2 17 5

GIVEN ME: Instead of *dedomenōn* χ A have *legomenōn*, which is supported by all versions except Itala. Grimm claims that the latter reading is a gloss. GUIDE OF WISDOM: So Itala *dux sapientiae*. God is the guide and ultimate source of wisdom, hence Solomon's appeal to God.   DIRECTOR OF THE WISE: Even wise men make mistakes, hence they are directed by God. 16. KNOWLEDGE OF CRAFTS: Ability to design and skill to execute works of art. *Cf.* Ex. 31.3 ff. with reference to Bezaleel.

17. IT WAS HE: αὐτός is the emphatic word here, not ἐμοί as in verse 15. THE ORDERING OF THE WORLD: The same expression occurs in Plato's *Timaeus* 32 c, likewise in connection with the elements.   ELEMENTS: The four elements, earth, air, fire, water, into which substance was resolved by Greek philosophers since Empedocles. Similarly 13.2, 19.18 f. The term *stoicheia*, for these elements was first used by Plato (*Theaet.* 201 E, *Tim.* 48 B), from whom it passed to the Stoics and from them to the Judaeo-Alexandrines and Philo.

18. The first line of this verse seems to refer to chronology and the second to astronomy. Deane very well characterizes this verse as "a poetical circumlocution for the difference and variety of the periods concerned in astronomical chronology." Perhaps Farrar is right in explaining it as reference to the knowledge requisite for constructing an astronomical calendar on sound principles. SOLSTICES: *Tropai*, literally "turnings," and *tropai hēliou*, "the points of midsummer and midwinter," hence solstices or tropics, with or without *hēliou*.   CHANGES OF SEASONS: There are some who think that *metabolai kairōn* might mean "crises in human affairs," justifying the rendering of the Arabic version "vicissitudes of times" for the preceding *tropōn allagas*. An apt parallel is found in our evening prayer: "He who changes the times and causes the seasons to succeed one another."

19. THE CYCLES OF YEARS: *E. g.* the metonic and solar cycles. As Deane

For he too is the guide of wisdom,
And the director of the wise.
16For in his hand are both we and our words;
All sagacity and knowledge of crafts.
17For it was he that gave me an unerring knowledge of the things that be,
To know the ordering of the world and the working of the elements,
18The beginning and end and middle of times,
The turn of the solstices and the changes of seasons,
19The cycles of years and the positions of the stars,
20   20The natures of animals and the tempers of beasts,
The forces of spirits and the reasonings of men,
The species of plants and the virtues of roots.

---

comments, "we must suppose that Pseudo-Solomon claims the knowledge of "cycles" lunar and solar, the intercalary method, the sacred and civil reckonings, etc." POSITIONS OF THE STARS: Probably their relative positions, that is as constellations, cf. Philo, Cong., § 24. The sciences enumerated above, namely mathematics, geometry, and astronomy, were considered as the peculiar study of the Jews during the period of Pseudo-Solomon and after, cf. Edersheim, History of the Jewish Nation, p. 353.
20. The first line has reference to zoology, the second to psychology, and the third to botany. NATURES OF ANIMALS: Zôôn here might include also man. Solomon is supposed to have known the ways and habits of animals generally and to have spoken parables about all sorts of living creatures, cf. I Ki. 5.13 and Josephus, Antiq., VIII.II.5; see also Prov. 1.17, 6.5 ff., 7.22, 26.2.11, 27.8, 28.1.15, 30.15 ff. TEMPERS OF BEASTS: I. e. their disposition and their rages, so Goodrick. R.V. "the ragings of wild beasts" following Itala. FORCES OF SPIRITS: So Goodrick following Grimm. According to Josephus, Antiq., VII.II.5; Solomon had power over spirits and demons. But Itala renders vim ventorum, similarly Pal. Syr., Arab., A.V. and R.V. which translate "forces of wind"; cf. Philo, Opif., § 19, where Solomon is said to have been able to predict storms and winds. The latter interpretation may be supported somewhat by the fact that the belief in demons formed no part of the Alexandrian philosophy. It should be noted that according to Midrash Tehillim 104, 442, angels are wind when sent on missions to earth, in God's presence they are fire. REASONINGS OF MEN: Not "thoughts of men" (R. V., Goodrick), but calculations and judgments necessary to decide perplexing cases, such as are described in I Ki. 3.16 ff. and 10.1 ff. SPECIES OF PLANTS: And probably their medicinal value. VIRTUES OF ROOTS: For Solomon's knowledge of botany and natural history see I Ki. 4.33. Josephus (Antiq., VIII.II.5) tells of the extraction of a demon through a man's nostrils by

²¹ὅσα τέ ἐστιν κρυπτὰ καὶ ἐμφανῆ ἔγνων·
ἡ γὰρ πάντων τεχνῖτις ἐδίδαξέν με σοφία.
²² Ἔστιν γὰρ ἐν αὐτῇ πνεῦμα νοερόν, ἅγιον,
μονογενές, πολυμερές, λεπτόν,
εὐκίνητον, τρανόν, ἀμόλυντον,
σαφές, ἀπήμαντον, φιλάγαθον, ὀξύ,
²³ἀκώλυτον, εὐεργετικόν, φιλάνθρωπον,
βέβαιον, ἀσφαλές, ἀμέριμνον,
παντοδύναμον, πανεπίσκοπον
καὶ διὰ πάντων χωροῦν πνευμάτων
νοερῶν καθαρῶν λεπτοτάτων.
²⁴πάσης γὰρ κινήσεως κινητικώτερον σοφία,
διήκει δὲ καὶ χωρεῖ διὰ πάντων διὰ τὴν καθαρότητα·

21¹ ἐμφανη] αφανη Gra.

the aid of a root discovered by Solomon. As to virtues inherent in herbs
cf. Ecclus. 38.4 ff.
21. SECRET: Namely "the forces of spirits and the reasonings of men"
mentioned in the preceding verse.   MANIFEST: Namely the operations of
nature in its various manifestations.   THE CONTRIVER: So Goodrick,
though *technitis* means "artificer," as rendered by R.V.; but the latter rendering might imply that Wisdom is the actual creator of things. As a matter of fact God Himself is the *technitēs* of the world, as stated in 13.1, while
Wisdom is the intermediary between God and man, like the Logos of Philo.
22. From here to the end of the chapter the nature of Wisdom is described in a series of twenty-one epithets or qualities. The number is sig-
nificant, as it constitutes a multiple of three and seven, both sacred or
mystic numbers symbolizing completeness and perfection. *Cf.* Grimm's
Commentary, p. 157. Reuss, on the other hand, maintains that "it is impossible to see anything here but a chance enumeration dictated by ex-
uberant rhetoric; the epithets succeed one another without order, and,
moreover, are partly synonymous." It is quite possible that on account of
this passage the name *Panaretos Sofia* (The Wisdom which comprises all
virtues) was given to our book by some Church Fathers (Epiphanius and
John of Damascus). Be that as it may, the many-named Wisdom (Philo,
Leg. Alleg., I, § 14) is almost identical with the many-named Logos of the
Stoics.   FOR THERE IS IN HER A SPIRIT: *Estin gar en autē pneuma* is the
received reading found in all manuscripts, yet Eusebius (in *Praeparatio
Evangelica*, VII.XII.4 and XI.XIV.4) quotes a variant *estin gar autē
pneuma*, which would identify Wisdom with the Holy Spirit. For obvious
reasons the Church Fathers favored the latter reading, not realizing that
this was to ascribe the doctrine of the Holy Ghost to an Alexandrian
origin.   QUICK OF UNDERSTANDING: *Noeron* is a technical Stoic term,
meaning "possessed of mind." The Stoics taught that there was a rational

²¹And whatsoever is secret and manifest I learned to
know,
For Wisdom the contriver of all taught me.
²²For there is in her a spirit quick of understanding, holy,
Singly born, manifold, subtile,
Mobile, lucid, unadulterate,
Clear, unharmed, loving what is good, keen,
²³Unhindered, beneficent, kind to man,
Steadfast, unerring, free from care,
All-powerful, all-surveying,
And pervading all spirits
That are quick of understanding, pure, most subtile.
²⁴For Wisdom is more mobile than any motion,
Yes, she pervades and penetrates all things by reason of
her pureness.

---

world-soul, the Logos, of which men are emanations.   HOLY: The word
has a moral significance here, cf. Philo, *Fug.*, § 35. The concept Holy
Spirit occurs three times in the Scriptures, viz. Isa. 63.10.11, Ps. 51.13.
SINGLY BORN: Corresponding to the Stoic belief in one world-soul with
countless manifestations.   SUBTILE: *I. e.* ethereal and spiritual in
essence. *Leptos*, "thin, fine," is applied by Philo (*Leg. Alleg.*, III.59) to the
Logos in the sense of minuteness, transparency, purity.   LUCID:
Tranos (Itala *disertus*) occurs also in 10.21 in the sense of "eloquent."
Others render here "penetrating."   UNHARMED: *I. e.* not liable to suffering or injury.   LOVING WHAT IS GOOD: According to Philo (*Sacr.*,
§ 5), goodness is one of thirty-four qualities attending upon Virtue.
KEEN: *Cf.* Philo, *Q.R.D.H.*, § 26: "God cuts ... with His Logos which acts
upon all things like a knife."
23. KIND TO MAN: Similarly 1.6 and 12.19. This quality, too, is one of
those enumerated by Philo as attending upon Virtue.   ALL-POWERFUL:
Similarly 11.17 and 18.15.   ALL-SURVEYING: Similarly 1.6 ff. and Prov.
15.3. *Cf.* also Philo, *Leg. Alleg.*, III, § 59.   PERVADING ALL SPIRITS:
Really Wisdom cannot enter into all spirits, but into those only which have
the necessary affinity with her, namely those that are quick of thought,
pure and subtile.
24. This verse seems to be an elaboration of the preceding verse: Wisdom
pervades all spirits because she penetrates all things.   MORE MOBILE
etc.: *Kinētikōteron kinēseōs* is quite awkward but very expressive. No
doubt it is in imitation of the Semitic usage of one and the same stem in
both the subject and predicate.   PERVADES AND PENETRATES: These
terms were technical terms in the Stoic philosophy for describing the
diffusion of the world-soul, *cf.* Goodrick *ad loc.*

25 ²⁵ἀτμὶς γάρ ἐστιν τῆς τοῦ θεοῦ δυνάμεως
    καὶ ἀπόρροια τῆς τοῦ παντοκράτορος δόξης εἰλικρινής·
    διὰ τοῦτο οὐδὲν μεμιαμμένον εἰς αὐτὴν παρεμπίπτει.
    ²⁶ἀπαύγασμα γάρ ἐστιν φωτὸς ἀιδίου
    καὶ ἔσοπτρον ἀκηλίδωτον τῆς τοῦ θεοῦ ἐνεργείας
    καὶ εἰκὼν τῆς ἀγαθότητος αὐτοῦ.
    ²⁷μία δὲ οὖσα πάντα δύναται
    καὶ μένουσα ἐν αὐτῇ τὰ πάντα καινίζει
    καὶ κατὰ γενεὰς εἰς ψυχὰς ὁσίας μεταβαίνουσα
    φίλους θεοῦ καὶ προφήτας κατασκευάζει·
    ²⁸οὐθὲν γὰρ ἀγαπᾷ ὁ θεὸς εἰ μὴ τὸν σοφίᾳ συνοικοῦντα.
    ²⁹ἔστιν γὰρ αὕτη εὐπρεπεστέρα ἡλίου
    καὶ ὑπὲρ πᾶσαν ἄστρων θέσιν.
    φωτὶ συγκρινομένη εὑρίσκεται προτέρα·

25² ιλικρινειας A†
29² αστρων BS†] αστερων rel.: cf. 19

---

25. In this verse and in what follows Wisdom is pictured as an emanation
in three distinct metaphors: first as the breath of God, then as an exhala-
tion of His person, and finally as a ray of His brightness. A VAPOUR:
Cf. Ecclus. 24.3, where Wisdom says: "I came out of the mouth of the
most High and covered the earth like a mist." Instead of atmis the Ethiopic
and the Armenian as quoted by Margoliouth (op. cit., p. 285) must have
read aktis, "ray, beam," and if so, aporroia might well mean an emanation
in the form of light, in which case the metaphor would be the same throughout the verse. EMANATION: Aporroia may denote the effluence of
either water or light: for the former see Ecclus. 1.9 and Enoch 49.1; for
the latter see Aquila to Ezek. 1.13 and Athenagoras, Apologia X, who
calls the Holy Spirit the effluence of God, being to Him as the rays are to
the sun. NOTHING DEFILED: Being immaterial she has nothing in her
that can contract stain. Her nature is unadulterated and unpolluted, see
above verse 22.

26. A REFLECTION: The Greek word may denote either the light emitted
from a luminary or the reflection of the luminary. Here the latter is most
appropriate, since the former has been expressed in the preceding verse.
Moreover, here the word is coupled with mirror and image, with both of
which "reflection" harmonizes better than "effulgence" of the R.V. The
word occurs thrice in Philo, once at least clearly in the sense of "reflection"
(Plant., § 12). ETERNAL LIGHT: For God as light see Isa. 60.19 f. But
this light is not material: it is rather what Philo styles asōmatos augē and

25 25For she is a vapour of the power of God,
        And a pure emanation of the glory of the Almighty.
        Therefore nothing defiled creeps into her.
    26For she is a reflection of eternal light,
        And a spotless mirror of the working of God,
        And an image of his goodness.
    27But she being one can do all,
        And abiding in herself makes all things new,
        And generation by generation passing into holy souls,
        Makes them friends of God and prophets.
    28For nothing does God love save him that dwells with
        wisdom.
    29For she is fairer than the sun,
        And above all order of the stars;
        Being compared with light she is found superior.

---

fōs psuchikon, *cf*. below verses 29 and 30.   IMAGE: *eikōn* is frequently
used by Philo of the Logos, as, for instance, in *Fug.*, § 19, and *Conf.
Ling.*, § 28.
27. BEING ONE CAN DO ALL: A variation of the theme of verse 22: Though
Wisdom is one in essence, yet her influence is felt everywhere. Wisdom
herself is immutable, yet she is the cause of all mutation.   MAKES ALL
THINGS NEW: *Cf*. Ps., 104.30. Taken together with the next line it means
"she renews the human race one generation after another, and in each influences holy souls."   FRIENDS OF GOD: This expression is not found in
the Septuagint, but Philo (*Sobr.*, § 11) in quoting Gen. 18.17 adds the
words "my friend." Philo, moreover, has the following saying (*Q.R.D.H.*,
§ 5): "All wise men are friends of God." Perhaps this expression goes
back to Greek philosophy, *cf*. Gregg *ad loc*.   PROPHETS: Meaning
men who interpret God's will, not necessarily men who predict the future
(Deane).
28. DWELLS WITH WISDOM: *Sunoikounta*, recurring in 8.2 and 9.16, is a
metaphor implying matrimonial cohabitation, but this is not surprising
in view of such usages elsewhere. *Cf*. the expression "wedded to evil."
Upon this metaphor of wedlock with Wisdom Dähne (*Geschichtliche
Darstellung der jüdisch-alexandrinischen Philosophie*, II, 170, n. 96) bases
an argument for the Therapeutic authorship of the Book of Wisdom, for
these Egyptian ascetics are said in Philo's *Vit. Cont.*, § 8, to be eager to
cohabit with Wisdom, though such union produces no mortal children.
29. This verse, as hinted above, seems to be an improvement upon the
ambiguity of verse 26.

30   ³⁰τοῦτο μὲν γὰρ διαδέχεται νύξ,
       σοφίας δέ οὐ κατισχύει κακία.

8   ¹διατείνει δὲ ἀπὸ πέρατος ἐπὶ πέρας εὐρώστως
      καὶ διοικεῖ τὰ πάντα χρηστῶς.
      ² Ταύτην ἐφίλησα καὶ ἐξεζήτησα ἐκ νεότητός μου
      καὶ ἐζήτησα νύμφην ἀγαγέσθαι ἐμαυτῷ
      καὶ ἐραστὴς ἐγενόμην τοῦ κάλλους αὐτῆς.
      ³εὐγένειαν δοξάζει συμβίωσιν θεοῦ ἔχουσα,
      καὶ ὁ πάντων δεσπότης ἠγάπησεν αὐτήν·
      ⁴μύστις γάρ ἐστιν τῆς τοῦ θεοῦ ἐπιστήμης
      καὶ αἱρετὶς τῶν ἔργων αὐτοῦ.
5   ⁵εἰ δὲ πλοῦτός ἐστιν ἐπιθυμητὸν κτῆμα ἐν βίῳ,

30² σοφια S*Vt, σοφιαν A | ουκ αντι-   1¹ επι] εις B
σχνει Bt

30. TO THIS: Namely to light.   HAS NO POWER: Katischuein with the genitive does not occur elsewhere.   WISDOM: From its opposition to wickedness it appears that the author here confused divine with human wisdom.

1. Since this verse seems to round off the ideas of the previous verses, it is
generally joined to the preceding chapter.   REACHES: Grimm points out
that the divine activities were viewed by Philo as an extension or out-
reaching of the Being of God. Accordingly, Wisdom must be considered as
an emanation from God.   END: Namely of the world.   ORDERS:
Dioikei, which is said of household management, was a favorite metaphor with the Stoics.
2. I LOVED: The verb used here, filein, lends itself to sexual affection
(The love of God to man and of man to God is generally expressed by
agapan, cf. 7.28). Similarly Ecclus. 15.2: (Wisdom shall) "receive him as a
wife married in her virginity."   AS A BRIDE: This image is necessitated
by the desire of Pseudo-Solomon to express adequately the intimacy and
the productivity of his relation to Wisdom. Cf. Philo, Congr., § 14, where
Wisdom is pictured as mother as well as wife. Philo also describes himself
as having loved in his youth one of the handmaids of Wisdom, Grammar,
who bore children to him, namely, writing, reading, and history. It must
be remembered that Alexandrine writers were given to this mystical use
of sensuous images.   ENAMOURED: Erastes likewise lends itself to a
sensuous interpretation, as in 15.6. Budde (Althebräische Litteratur, p. 279)
finds here an allusion to one of the many allegorical explanations of
Canticles, namely the wooing of Wisdom by Solomon.   BEAUTY:
Meaning virtue. Many commentators adduce a striking parallel from
Xenophon's Memorabilia, II.1.22.

30   ³⁰For to this does night succeed,
     Whereas wickedness has no power against wisdom.

8   ¹   But in full might she reaches from end to end,
        And orders all things graciously.
     ²Her I loved and diligently sought from my youth
        up,
        And sought to take her as a bride for myself,
        And I became enamoured of her beauty.
     ³She glorifies her noble birth as being one that has the
        converse of God,
        And the Lord of all things loved her.
     ⁴For she is initiated into the knowledge of God,
        And chooser of his works.
   5   ⁵But if riches be a possession to be desired in life,

---

3. SHE GLORIFIES HER NOBLE BIRTH: So A.V., R.V., *et al.* Pal. Syr. has
"There is joy and the glory of God in her partnership." Grotius suggested
the following rendering: "She glorifies the nobility of man," *i. e*, however
noble a man may be, the possession of wisdom increases his claim to
respect.   THE CONVERSE OF GOD: *Sumbiōsin* is incongruous here, since
it is used for wedlock. But Wisdom is known as the Bride of God, and a
similar idea is found in Philo, *Ebr.*, § 8: "We shall be justified in calling the
Creator the Father of the world, and His knowledge its Mother, with whom
God dwelt and whom He made mother of the Creation, yet not after the
manner of a man." We must remember that this is the language of symbolism, so familiar to us from the Bible, where the closeness of Yahweh to
Israel is often expressed by the figure of marriage (Isa. 50.1, 62.4; Hos.
2.21 f.).   LOVED HER: Pal Syr. renders "because God is her father, and
the Lord of all loves her," apparently a doublet.

4. INITIATED: *Mustis* is taken by some as *mustagōgos*, not the initiated but
the initiator, and so Itala *doctrix*, but the context, which hinges on the relations of God and Wisdom alone, requires a passive and not active
meaning.   KNOWLEDGE OF GOD: Not knowledge of the being of God, as
proposed by Gfrörer (*Philo*, II, 220), but the knowledge which God
possesses, so Goodrick, et al.   CHOOSER: So Goodrick for *hairetis*, following Itala *electrix*. The idea seems to be that God allowed Wisdom a
voice in deciding the order in which His works should proceed (Gregg).
But some object to this sense on the ground that Wisdom cannot be pictured as choosing or devising what God shall do, and so Speiser and
Torrey, who believe in a Hebrew original of Wisdom, make the suggestion
that the translator mistook Heb. *hoveret*, "associate, companion," for
boheret, "chooser."

τί σοφίας πλουσιώτερον τῆς τὰ πάντα ἐργαζομένης;
⁶εἰ δὲ φρόνησις ἐργάζεται,
τίς αὐτῆς τῶν ὄντων μᾶλλόν ἐστιν τεχνῖτις;
⁷καὶ εἰ δικαιοσύνην ἀγαπᾷ τις,
οἱ πόνοι ταύτης εἰσὶν ἀρεταί·
σωφροσύνην γὰρ καὶ φρόνησιν ἐκδιδάσκει,
δικαιοσύνην καὶ ἀνδρείαν,
ὧν χρησιμώτερον οὐδέν ἐστιν ἐν βίῳ ἀνθρώποις.
⁸εἰ δὲ καὶ πολυπειρίαν ποθεῖ τις,
οἶδεν τὰ ἀρχαῖα καὶ τὰ μέλλοντα εἰκάζει,
ἐπίσταται στροφὰς λόγων καὶ λύσεις αἰνιγμάτων,
σημεῖα καὶ τέρατα προγινώσκει
καὶ ἐκβάσεις καιρῶν καὶ χρόνων.
⁹ἔκρινα τοίνυν ταύτην ἀγαγέσθαι πρὸς συμβίωσιν
εἰδὼς ὅτι ἔσται μοι σύμβουλος ἀγαθῶν

5² πλουσιωτ.] τιμιωτερον St | εργα- 8² εικαζειν BS*
ζομ.] pr. περι S*†

5. MAKES ALL THINGS SERVICEABLE: *Ergazesthai* really means to make money out of a thing, to exploit (so Grimm, Farrar). Here, too, we notice a confusion of divine with human wisdom or prudence, which aims at worldly gain. Cf. Prov. 8.18 and 31.10 ff.

6. UNDERSTANDING: *Fronēsis* is here synonymous with *sofia*. ARTIFICER: Reference might be made to Bezaleel in Ex. 31.2 ff. The meaning seems to be that Wisdom, if it is active at all, must be supreme in any thing to which she puts her hand. *Technitēs* used here of Wisdom is applied to God in 13.1, *q. v.*

7. In this verse Wisdom is represented as the progenitor of the four cardinal virtues of Greek philosophy: Temperance, Prudence, Justice, Fortitude. In a similar vein Philo (*Leg. Alleg.*, 1.19) interprets the four rivers of Paradise allegorically as the four cardinal virtues; *cf.* also Ecclus. 24.25 f. Plato was first to establish and explain these principal virtues, but the Stoics seized upon them and elaborated them at greater length. Thus they are repeatedly dwelt upon in the Stoical book IV Maccabees, which is dated about the same time as the book of Wisdom. In IV Macc. 5.22 f. Piety takes the place of Prudence. RIGHTEOUSNESS: *Dikaiosunē* occurs twice in this verse, but the first refers to the general goodness or moral rectitude of man, while the second denotes justice or fairness as between man and man.

8. MUCH EXPERIENCE: *Polupeiria* is used loosely of insight into the future, as well as of experience of past events. CONJECTURES: So R.V. margin, following A *eikazei* instead of B *eikazein*. The former, it is true, may be the conjecture of a scribe who felt the incongruity of divining

What is richer than wisdom that makes all things
  serviceable?
⁶And if understanding works,
  Who of all beings is a greater artificer than she?
⁷And if a man loves righteousness,
  Her labours are virtues;
  For she teaches temperance and prudence,
  Righteousness and manliness,
  Than which nought in life is more profitable to man.
⁸But if also a man long for much experience,
  She knows the things of old and conjectures the things
    to come;
  She understands the subtilties of speeches and interpre-
    tations of riddles;
  She foresees signs and wonders,
  And the issues of seasons and times.
⁹I determined then to take her to live with me,
  Knowing that she will be to me a counsellor of good
    things,

---

about the past.   SUBTILTIES OF SPEECHES: So R.V., Goodrick "tricks
of arguments," in order to preserve the original force of *strofas*, which is
that of the twistings and turnings of a wrestler. *Cf.* the similar passage in
Ecclus. 39.2 f., said of the wise man: "he will enter in amidst the *strofai*
of parables. He will seek out the hidden meaning of proverbs and be conversant in the dark sayings of parables." The phrase occurs also in the
Septuagint text of Prov. 1.3.   INTERPRETATIONS OF RIDDLES: *Cf.*
Prov. 1.6. *Ainigma* is properly a veiled, allusive, oracular saying. The pro-
pounding and solving of riddles has always been a favorite exercise of
Oriental and Jewish wisdom, *cf.* Jud. 14.12, I Ki. 10.1, Ezek. 17.2 ff., etc.
SIGNS AND WONDERS: occurs frequently in the Scriptures. Wisdom is pictured as having a foreknowledge of natural phenomena, such as eclipses,
storms, earthquakes, etc. *Cf.* Philo *Opif.*, § 19.   SEASONS AND TIMES:
a common phrase in Hellenistic literature. Seasons are climatic periods
of indefinite duration, times are fixed periods depending on the measured
movements of sun and moon (Philo, *ibid.*).

9. TO TAKE HER TO LIVE WITH ME: The idea of marital relationship between Solomon and Wisdom is continued, the same term, *sumbiōsis*,
being used here as in verse 3. *Agagesthai* is an ancient classical expression
for "to lead a bride home" (Lat. *ducere uxorem*), *cf.* Liddell and Scott,
s. v. ἄγω.   A COUNSELLOR OF GOOD THINGS: So A.V. following Pal. Syr.
and Arab. R.V. "one who would give me good thoughts for counsel," and

καὶ παραίνεσις φροντίδων καὶ λύπης.

10 ¹⁰ἕξω δι' αὐτὴν δόξαν ἐν ὄχλοις
καὶ τιμὴν παρὰ πρεσβυτέροις ὁ νέος·
¹¹ὀξὺς εὑρεθήσομαι ἐν κρίσει
καὶ ἐν ὄψει δυναστῶν θαυμασθήσομαι·
¹²σιγῶντά με περιμενοῦσιν καὶ φθεγγομένῳ προσέξουσιν
καὶ λαλοῦντος ἐπὶ πλεῖον
χεῖρα ἐπιθήσουσιν ἐπὶ στόμα αὐτῶν.
¹³ἕξω δι' αὐτὴν ἀθανασίαν
καὶ μνήμην αἰώνιον τοῖς μετ' ἐμὲ ἀπολείψω.
¹⁴διοικήσω λαούς, καὶ ἔθνη ὑποταγήσεταί μοι·
15 ¹⁵φοβηθήσονταί με ἀκούσαντες τύραννοι φρικτοί,
ἐν πλήθει φανοῦμαι ἀγαθὸς καὶ ἐν πολέμῳ ἀνδρεῖος.
¹⁶εἰσελθὼν εἰς τὸν οἶκόν μου προσαναπαύσομαι αὐτῇ·
οὐ γὰρ ἔχει πικρίαν ἡ συναναστροφὴ αὐτῆς
οὐδὲ ὀδύνην ἡ συμβίωσις αὐτῆς,
ἀλλὰ εὐφροσύνην καὶ χαράν.

12³ χειρας S   14 υποταγησονται Sᶜ

margin "hold counsel with me for good things." *Sumboulos* with the genitive of the counsel given occurs in the Septuagint of II Chron. 22.3. A COMFORT: *Parainesis* in this sense is not found elsewhere; evidently it was used for *paramuthia*. Similarly puzzling is Itala *allocutio*.

10. GLORY: *Cf.* Prov. 31.23 LXX. The people will admire the king for his wise decisions and sagacious judgments. See I Ki. 3.28.   MULTITUDES: *Ochloi* is hardly an apt expression here, since it is generally used contemptuously as of a mob, see note on 6.2. Here the sense seems to be "assemblies."   HONOUR WITH THE ELDERS: *I. e.* the elders will approve his judgments in the council.   THOUGH I BE YOUNG: In I Ki. 3.7 Solomon says "I am but a little child," and in I Chron. 22.5 and 29.1 David speaks of him as "young and tender." According to Josephus (*Antiq.*, VIII.VII.8) Solomon died at ninety-four, having reigned eighty years, hence he was fourteen on his accession. Grimm, however, argues from I Ki. 11.4 that he was about twenty-five when he came to the throne. *Cf.* also Ecclus. 47.14 ff., where the wisdom of the young Solomon is contrasted with his folly in his later age. Of course, our author, who has only the ideal Solomon in his mind, abstains from any reference to his seamy side.

11. KEEN: An allusion no doubt to the famous judgment of Solomon in I Ki. 3.16. ff.   POTENTATES: may refer to either the chiefs of his own people or to the foreign rulers with whom he came in contact, such as Hiram of Tyre (I Ki. 5.15 ff.) and the Queen of Sheba (*ibid.* 10.5 ff.)

12. LAY A HAND UPON THEIR MOUTH: So Job 21.5, 29.9, 40.4, and Ecclus.

And a comfort in cares and grief.

10 ¹⁰Through her I shall have glory among multitudes,
And honour with the elders, though I be young.

¹¹Keen shall I be found in judgment,
And in the sight of potentates I shall be admired.

¹²They shall wait on me when I am silent,
And when I speak they shall give heed unto me,
And when I talk at length,
They shall lay a hand upon their mouth.

¹³ Through her I shall have immortality,
And shall leave an eternal memorial to them that come
after me.

¹⁴I shall govern peoples and nations shall be subject unto me.

15 ¹⁵Dreaded tyrants shall fear when they hear of me,
Among people I shall appear good and in war
courageous.

¹⁶When I come home I shall rest with her,
For intercourse with her has no bitterness,
Nor cohabitation with her vexation,
But cheerfulness and joy.

5.12. This gesture is expressive of respectful silence.

13. IMMORTALITY: As the context shows the reference is to subjective immortality, implying undying fame or renown.   AN ETERNAL ME-
MORIAL: *Cf.* Ps. 112.6 "the righteous shall be had in everlasting remembrance."

14. PEOPLES AND NATIONS: λαοί, which in LXX and in the New Testament
is constantly used of Israel, undoubtedly refers to the tribes over whom
Solomon held sway; *ethnē*, on the other hand, must be the Gentiles over
whom Solomon exerted some influence (so Goodrick). Gregg and others
find no distinction between the two, the repetition being due solely to the
requirements of the poetic parallelism, as, for instance, in Ps. 57.10. For
the great sway of Solomon's rule see I Ki. 4.21.

15. DREADED TYRANTS: *Cf.* Ps. 72.10 f. Tyrant here is used not in the
classical sense of "lord, master," but in the later sense of "despot."

16. WHEN I COME HOME: Namely from the state council, burdened with
the cares of state or plans of campaign.   I SHALL REST WITH HER: *Cf.*
Philo, *Migr.*, § 6: "Wisdom is the best dwelling-place of virtuous souls."
INTERCOURSE WITH HER: *Sunanastrophê* denotes social intercourse, see
III Macc. 2.33.   COHABITATION: *Sumbiōsis*, as in vv .3 and 9, means life
under one roof with her.   CHEERFULNESS AND JOY: Philo (*Q.R.D.H.*,
§ 62) compares wisdom to a river full of cheerfulness and joy and all other
blessings.

¹⁷ταῦτα λογισάμενος ἐν ἐμαυτῷ
καὶ φροντίσας ἐν καρδίᾳ μου
ὅτι ἀθανασία ἐστὶν ἐν συγγενείᾳ σοφίας
¹⁸καὶ ἐν φιλίᾳ αὐτῆς τέρψις ἀγαθὴ
καὶ ἐν πόνοις χειρῶν αὐτῆς πλοῦτος ἀνεκλιπὴς
καὶ ἐν συγγυμνασίᾳ ὁμιλίας αὐτῆς φρόνησις
καὶ εὔκλεια ἐν κοινωνίᾳ λόγων αὐτῆς,
περιῄειν ζητῶν ὅπως λάβω αὐτὴν εἰς ἐμαυτόν.
¹⁹παῖς δὲ ἤμην εὐφυὴς
ψυχῆς τε ἔλαχον ἀγαθῆς,
20　²⁰μᾶλλον δὲ ἀγαθὸς ὢν ἦλθον εἰς σῶμα ἀμίαντον.
²¹γνοὺς δὲ ὅτι οὐκ ἄλλως ἔσομαι ἐγκρατής, ἐὰν μὴ ὁ θεὸς δῷ
— καὶ τοῦτο δ᾽ ἦν φρονήσεως τὸ εἰδέναι τίνος ἡ χάρις —,
ἐνέτυχον τῷ κυρίῳ καὶ ἐδεήθην αὐτοῦ
καὶ εἶπον ἐξ ὅλης τῆς καρδίας μου

18² πλουτος] τερψις S*†
18³ ομιλια A
18⁵ λαβω] αγαγω S†

21¹ ουκ αλλως] ου καλως AC†
21² δ ην] δε ην compl., δη S*, δε S°† :
cf. 14 24

---

17. KINSHIP OF WISDOM: *Cf.* Prov. 7.4 *Sungeneia* is used here of the spiritual affinity between Solomon and his bride.
18. IN THE LABOURS etc.: This line is reminiscent of the valiant or industrious woman in Prov. 31.10–31.　　IN COMMON EXERCISE: *Sungumnasia*, a late and rare word, denotes the mutual interaction of the characters of Solomon and his bride, either through speech (Itala *in certamine loquellae*) or through general intercourse.　　IN THE SHARING OF HER TALK: *I. e.* in the sharing of her discourses or disputations, as hinted in the preceding line.　　I WENT ABOUT SEEKING: Contrast 6.16 where Wisdom is the seeker.
19. A CHILD OF FINE PARTS: *I. e.* of good natural disposition. Itala *ingeniosus*. *Eufuês* is used of both spiritual and physical qualities.　　A GOOD SOUL: This seems to imply the pre-existence of the soul, a Greek doctrine current among Alexandrian Jews (see Philo, *Leg. All.*, III.28) but contrary to both Jewish and Christian teachings (see Harnack, *History of Dogma*, I, 318 ff.). Only in later years, in post-biblical times, did the Jews begin to assimilate this foreign element, believing that the souls of all generations were created at the beginning of the world and kept till the time of their birth in a repository (*cf.* G. F. Moore, *Judaism in the First Centuries of the Christian Era*, II, 353, n. 3). Weber (*System der Altsynag. Paläst. Theologie*, p. 217) quotes from Midrash Tanhuma (Pekude 3) to demonstrate the belief that God had created all souls good

¹⁷Considering these things in myself,
And pondering in my heart
That there is immortality in the kinship of wisdom,
¹⁸And in the love of her is good delight,
And in the labours of her hands is unfailing wealth,
And in common exercise with her is understand-
ing,
And great renown in the sharing of her talk,
I went about seeking how I may take her to myself.
¹⁹Now I was a child of fine parts,
And to my lot fell a good soul,
²⁰ ²⁰Or rather being good I came into a body undefiled.
²¹But knowing that I shall not otherwise acquire her
unless God give her,
—And that this was a point of prudence, to know whose
favour it was—,
I interceded with the Lord and begged of him,
And said with my whole heart:

---

from the first, and that these dwelt in a heavenly region and were united
with a body at the time of conception. *Cf.* further on the Jewish idea of
pre-existence the *Jewish Encyclopedia. s. v.* "soul." Some modern Christian
commentators will not admit the idea of pre-existence, and consequently
they interpret this passage somewhat as follows: "I was by nature en-
dowed with good qualities of body and soul, or rather, it was because my
soul was good and pure that a corresponding body was given it, and thus
the εὐφυία was brought about" (Deane). *Cf.* also F. C. Porter (in *Old
Testament and Semitic Studies in Memory of W. R. Harper, I, 207 ff.*), who
endeavors to prove that the pre-existence indicated here is founded not on
Greek speculations but on ancient Hebrew beliefs. This entire problem is
treated in detail by Goodrick in the first Additional Note to his Commentary (pp. 377 ff.).
20. A BODY UNDEFILED: For the body as receptacle of the soul see 9.15
"the corruptible body weighs down the soul."
21. ACQUIRE HER: *Egkratês* without the genitive *autês* following it is no
doubt unusual, but is paralleled by Ecclus. 6.27. Moreover, Syroh. has
distinctly "to be in possession of her," so also the Arabic version, A.V.
and R.V.   I INTERCEDED: *Enetuchon* literally means "I met" (so Goodrick), but it also has the subsidiary meaning "to approach in prayer, to
plead with."   BEGGED OF HIM: Namely for wisdom. This prayer for
wisdom follows in chapter 9.

9 ¹ Θεὲ πατέρων καὶ κύριε τοῦ ἐλέους
ὁ ποιήσας τὰ πάντα ἐν λόγῳ σου
²καὶ τῇ σοφίᾳ σου κατασκευάσας ἄνθρωπον,
ἵνα δεσπόζῃ τῶν ὑπὸ σοῦ γενομένων κτισμάτων
³καὶ διέπῃ τὸν κόσμον ἐν ὁσιότητι καὶ δικαιοσύνῃ
καὶ ἐν εὐθύτητι ψυχῆς κρίσιν κρίνῃ,
⁴δός μοι τὴν τῶν σῶν θρόνων πάρεδρον σοφίαν
καὶ μή με ἀποδοκιμάσῃς ἐκ παίδων σου.

5 ⁵ὅτι ἐγὼ δοῦλος σὸς καὶ υἱὸς τῆς παιδίσκης σου,
ἄνθρωπος ἀσθενὴς καὶ ὀλιγοχρόνιος
καὶ ἐλάσσων ἐν συνέσει κρίσεως καὶ νόμων·
⁶κἂν γάρ τις ᾖ τέλειος ἐν υἱοῖς ἀνθρώπων,
τῆς ἀπὸ σοῦ σοφίας ἀπούσης εἰς οὐδὲν λογισθήσεται.
⁷σύ με προείλω βασιλέα λαοῦ σου
καὶ δικαστὴν υἱῶν σου καὶ θυγατέρων·

1¹ ελεους Cmu.]+σου BSA   6² λογισθησονται S*†
2¹ κατεσκευασας B†

Solomon's Prayer for Wisdom. *Cf.* I Ki. 3.5 ff.
1. GOD OF THE FATHERS: This invocation is based on I Chron. 28.9 and
29.18 ff.   LORD OF MERCY: So most of the ancient versions, but B and
other good manuscripts read "Lord of thy mercy," which hardly makes
sense. Perhaps *sou* was added by mistake from the end of line 2. R.V.
curiously has "Lord who keepest thy mercy." God's mercy is a leading
theme in the prayer of I Ki. 3.6 f.   BY THY WORD: Some writers take
logos here and *sofia* in the next verse to be identical, but there is nothing to
justify such an idea. The fact is that there is no allusion here to the Greek
Logos doctrine of Philo. The phrase is purely Hebraic, and even the
combination of mercy and word may be illustrated from Ps. 33.5 f.
2. THOU FORMEDST MAN: *Kataskeuazein* means "to furnish, equip, organ-
ize" existing matter, *cf.* IV Macc. 2.21.
3. IN SANCTITY AND RIGHTEOUSNESS: *Hosiotês* represents man's duty
towards God, *dikaiosunê* man's duty towards his fellowmen and probably
also towards dumb animals, as enjoined in the Mosaic law.   EXECUTE
JUDGMENT: *Krisin krinê* is a Semitism not uncommon in the Septuagint
and corresponds to Deut. 16.18 and elsewhere.   UPRIGHTNESS OF
SOUL: Equivalent to integrity of character. The expression corresponds exactly to Ps. 119.7, see also I Ki. 3.6.
4. SITS BY THY THRONE: So Itala *adsistricem sedium tuarum*. This metaphor is applied not only to wisdom but also to justice and righteousness,
in Greek as well as in Hebrew. The idea is biblical, *cf.* Prov. 8.30, though

9 ¹ God of the fathers and Lord of mercy,
Who madest all things by thy word,
²And through thy wisdom thou formedst man,
That he should have dominion over the creatures made
by thee,
³And rule the world in sanctity and righteousness,
And execute judgment in uprightness of soul;
⁴Give to me wisdom that sits by thy throne,
And reject me not from among thy children.
5   ⁵For I am thy servant and the son of thy handmaid,
A man weak and short-lived,
And inferior in understanding of judgment and of
laws.
⁶For though one be perfect among the sons of men,
If the wisdom from thee be lacking, he shall be accounted for naught.
⁷Thou didst prefer me as king of thy people
And judge of thy sons and daughters.

---

expressed in pagan language. The Greek plural is the plural of dignity or majesty and recurs in v. 12 and in 18.15.   THY CHILDREN: So A.V., but R.V. and Goodrick "thy servants," as in the next verse. This line reminds one of Ps. 89.38 f.

5. I AM THY SERVANT etc.: Borrowed from Ps. 116.16 and with a slight variation *ibid.* 86.16. The double expression is used to accentuate his dependence on God.   WEAK AND SHORT-LIVED: *Cf.* I Ki. 3.7 and in general I Chron. 29.15. *Oligoxronios* no doubt has reference to the short span of human life which prevents man from attaining to full knowledge of wisdom.   INFERIOR: *elassôn* is used here absolutely (so Pal. Syr. Arab., R.V.), not as a comparative (so Itala, A.V.). According to Goodrick, the phrase is probably bad Greek: *elassôn tês suneseôs* would have been better.   JUDGMENT: Refers to political administration and statecraft. LAWS: Points to judicial equity.

6. PERFECT: *Teleios* (Itala *consummatus*) denotes not so much moral perfection, as the full possession of all natural qualities.   SONS OF MEN: Emphasizing the material side of human nature.   IF THE WISDOM etc.: *Cf.* Philo. *Post. C.*, § 41: "Whence can the thirsty heart of man be filled save from the inexhaustible spring of divine Wisdom?"

7. THOU DIDST PREFER: Thou is emphatic: the responsibility is God's, not Solomon's. *Cf.* I Chron. 28.5.   THY SONS AND DAUGHTERS: This expression is rare and unusual, *cf.* Isa. 4.4 and 43.6, but perhaps there is reference here to the case of the two women in I Ki. 3.16. ff.

⁸εἶπας οἰκοδομῆσαι ναὸν ἐν ὄρει ἁγίῳ σου
καὶ ἐν πόλει κατασκηνώσεώς σου θυσιαστήριον,
μίμημα σκηνῆς ἁγίας, ἣν προητοίμασας ἀπ᾽ ἀρχῆς.
⁹καὶ μετὰ σοῦ ἡ σοφία ἡ εἰδυῖα τὰ ἔργα σου
καὶ παροῦσα, ὅτε ἐποίεις τὸν κόσμον,
καὶ ἐπισταμένη τί ἀρεστὸν ἐν ὀφθαλμοῖς σου
καὶ τί εὐθὲς ἐν ἐντολαῖς σου.

10 ¹⁰ἐξαπόστειλον αὐτὴν ἐξ ἁγίων οὐρανῶν
καὶ ἀπὸ θρόνου δόξης σου πέμψον αὐτήν,
ἵνα συμπαροῦσά μοι κοπιάσῃ,
καὶ γνῶ τί εὐάρεστόν ἐστιν παρὰ σοί.
¹¹οἶδε γὰρ ἐκείνη πάντα καὶ συνίει
καὶ ὁδηγήσει με ἐν ταῖς πράξεσί μου σωφρόνως
καὶ φυλάξει με ἐν τῇ δόξῃ αὐτῆς·
¹²καὶ ἔσται προσδεκτὰ τὰ ἔργα μου,
καὶ διακρινῶ τὸν λαόν σου δικαίως
καὶ ἔσομαι ἄξιος θρόνων πατρός μου.
¹³τίς γὰρ ἄνθρωπος γνώσεται βουλὴν θεοῦ;

12³ θρόνου S*

---

8. THY HOLY MOUNT: Mount Moriah, hallowed by Abraham's sacrifice (Gen. ch. 22) and by the vision of the angel at the threshing-floor of Araunah (II Chron. 3.1.) The expression "holy mount" is quite frequent in the Scriptures.   THE CITY OF THY HABITATION: *I. e.* Jerusalem, the city of David on mount Zion. So Ps. 74.2 *cf.* also Zeitlin's comment on II Macc. 14.35.   Elsewhere "the city of God," see Ps. 46.4, 87.3. A COPY OF THE HOLY TABERNACLE: This seems to refer to Ex. 25.9.40, where God shows Moses the pattern of the tabernacle. See also I Chron. 28.11 f. In the Pal. Talmud Ber. IV, 8c above, we find the following statement: "The earthly Holy of Holies is situated exactly opposite the heavenly Holy of Holies." Most modern commentators, following Gfrörer (*Philo*, I, 228), are of the opinion that the reference here is to the "archetypes of things" as they appear in the Platonic doctrine of ideas. But this assumption is hardly necessary. There may be an allusion here to the talmudic legend (quoted by Kaufman Kohler in the *Jewish Encyclopedia s. v.* "Pre-existence") that seven things had existed before the foundation of the world: the Torah, the Throne of Glory, the Sanctuary, the Patriarchs, Israel, the Messiah, and Repentance. Of these the sanctuary is supposed to have been pre-existent on the basis of Jer. 17.12 "a throne of glory, high from the beginning, is the place of our sanctuary." Accordingly Solomon copied the pre-existent sanctuary in the sense of this Jewish legend, but not in accordance with the Platonic theory of ideas.   FROM THE

⁸Thou badest [me] to build a temple on thy holy mount,
And an altar in the city of thy habitation,
A copy of the holy tabernacle which thou preparedst
    aforehand from the beginning.
⁹And with thee is wisdom that knows thy works,
And was present when thou madest the world,
And knows what is pleasing in thine eyes,
And what is right in thy commandments.
10   ¹⁰Send her forth out of the holy heavens,
And despatch her from the throne of thy glory,
That abiding with me she may toil,
And that I may know what is well pleasing before thee.
¹¹For she knows and understands all things,
And shall guide me in my actions prudently
And guard me in her glory.
¹²So shall my works be acceptable,
And I shall judge thy people righteously,
And I shall be worthy of my father's throne.
¹³For what man shall know the counsel of God,

BEGINNING: *I. e.* from the beginning of Jewish history, not from before the creation of the world, as Gfrörer assumes.
9. WAS PRESENT etc.: Hence wisdom existed from before the creation of the world.   IN THINE EYES: *En ofthalmois sou* is a Hebraism and is used instead of *enōpion sou.*   RIGHT: *euthes* is the Alexandrian form of *euthu* and is generally used for "that which was right in the sight of the Lord."
10. SEND . . . DESPATCH: There is hardly any distinction in sense between the two verbs: the one is a repetition of the other for the sake of parallelism. Itala omits the second altogether, so also A.V.   SHE MAY TOIL: The sense is that she may assist me in my efforts to keep thy laws.
11. GUIDE: used of moral guidance.   IN HER GLORY: Itala *in sua potentia* is far-fetched. Grimm renders "in her brilliance or splendor." Purinton suggests Heb. *hesed*, "loving-kindness," for Greek *doxa*, since the Septuagint renders it so in Isa. 40.6.
12. I SHALL JUDGE: The Greek verb has special reference to the administration of the state.   THRONE: The plural in Greek is a plural of dignity or majesty, as in v. 4 above.
    With this verse Solomon's prayer seems to end. What follows consists of moral reflections.
13. This verse seems to be based on Isa. 40.13, *cf.* further *ibid.* 55.8. It

ἢ τίς ἐνθυμηθήσεται τί θέλει ὁ κύριος;
¹⁴λογισμοὶ γὰρ θνητῶν δειλοί,
καὶ ἐπισφαλεῖς αἱ ἐπίνοιαι ἡμῶν·
15   ¹⁵φθαρτὸν γὰρ σῶμα βαρύνει ψυχήν,
καὶ βρίθει τὸ γεῶδες σκῆνος νοῦν πολυφρόντιδα.
¹⁶καὶ μόλις εἰκάζομεν τὰ ἐπὶ γῆς
καὶ τὰ ἐν χερσὶν εὑρίσκομεν μετὰ πόνου·
τὰ δὲ ἐν οὐρανοῖς τίς ἐξιχνίασεν;
¹⁷βουλὴν δέ σου τίς ἔγνω, εἰ μὴ σὺ ἔδωκας σοφίαν
καὶ ἔπεμψας τὸ ἅγιόν σου πνεῦμα ἀπὸ ὑψίστων;
¹⁸καὶ οὕτως διωρθώθησαν αἱ τρίβοι τῶν ἐπὶ γῆς,
καὶ τὰ ἀρεστά σου ἐδιδάχθησαν ἄνθρωποι,
καὶ τῇ σοφίᾳ ἐσώθησαν.

16¹ μογις SA
16² χερσιν] ποσιν SV†
17² υψηλων S*†

18² και] κ̄ε̄ A†(=κυριε)
18³ σοφια]+σου S

---

stresses the need of communication between God and man which is the
foundation of mysticism.
14. THE REASONINGS OF MORTALS: This is a reminiscence of Ps. 94.11.
TIMOROUS: *Deiloi*, which in older Greek means "cowardly, craven," is
used here in the later sense of "miserable" (so A.V.) or "worthless" (so
Siegfried), exactly as Heb. הבל. No wonder R.V. margin thought it to be
a corruption. OUR DEVICES: *Epinoia* is curiously rendered by Itala
providentiae, which, according to Goodrick, is probably of African usage.
Pal. Syr. reads "their plans."
15. This verse gave rise to considerable discussion. The question was
whether Pseudo-Solomon voiced here the Greek doctrine of dualism which
pronounces matter evil and considers the body as a source of sin and
corruption, cf. Plato, *Phaedo*, XXX.81C, and Philo, *Leg. Alleg.*, I.33,
Q.D.S.I., 32, *Migr.*, 3, *Congr.*, 18. *Somn.*, I.22. Very characteristic is the
following passage of Philo in *Gigant.*, § 7: "The chief cause of ignorance is
the flesh and association with the flesh. Nothing presents such a hindrance
to the growth of the soul as the flesh, for it is a kind of foundation of
ignorance and stupidity, on which all the evils are built . . . souls that bear
the burden of the flesh are weighed down and oppressed till they cannot
look up at the heavens, and have their heads forcibly dragged downwards,
being rooted to the earth like cattle." In fact Philo accepted the epigram
accredited to Heraclitus *sôma sêma*, "the body is a tomb." See further
Deane *ad loc.* and Charles, *Eschatology*, pp. 142 f. But, in spite of the
plausibility of such an assumption, it is better to oppose it with Gregg,
who thinks that the writer goes no further than the Psalmist when he says
(103.14): "He knows our frame; He remembers that we are dust." Gregg
continues: "It is a commonplace of experience that the spirit is willing, but

Or who shall conceive what the Lord wills?

[14]For the reasonings of mortals are timorous,
And our devices are prone to fail.

15 [15]For the corruptible body weighs down the soul,
And the earthy frame lies heavy on a mind that is full
of cares.

[16]And hardly do we guess at things that are upon earth,
And find out with labour the things which are close
at hand,
But the things in heaven who has searched out?

[17]Now who knew thy counsel, except thou gavest wisdom,
And sendest thine holy spirit from on high?

[18]And thus were the paths of those upon the earth made
straight,
And men were taught the things pleasing to thee,
And were saved by wisdom.

---

the flesh is too weak: the writer does not go beyond this, either here, or in
8.20. For one to whom classical literature was open either at first hand or
through Alexandrian teachers, it is remarkable how he has avoided an
error into which Philo fell: this passage presents a typical example of the
distinction between Philo with his speculative bent, and Pseudo-Solomon
with his inflexible religious purpose."   FRAME: *Skênos* is strictly
"tent," hence Itala *inhabitatio* and Goodrick "tabernacle."   FULL OF
CARES: This is the literal rendering of *polufrontida*, but Itala renders
multa cogitantem and A.V. "that museth upon many things" and Goodrick
"much-pondering." The idea is that the mind, in spite of its superiority, is
always hampered and depressed by matter.
16. This verse resumes the thought of v. 13: the impossibility of the
natural fathoming the supernatural. *Cf.* Isa. 55.9 and Job 38.31 f.
THINGS WHICH ARE CLOSE AT HAND: Instead of *ta en chersin* א reads *ta en
posin*, "things which are at our feet," which, as pointed out by Gregg,
causes a singular resemblance between this passage and Diog. Laert.
I.8.34: "Thales fell into a pit when he went out to look at the stars, and an
old woman cried out: If Thales cannot see the things at his feet, does he
expect to learn the things in the heavens?"
17. WISDOM . . . HOLY SPIRIT: There is no distinction between the two, and
the variation of terms is due entirely to poetical parallelism.
18. This last verse, according to Farrar and others, serves to introduce the
historical survey following in the next chapter. According to À Lapide
some began chapter 10 with this verse. Houbigant divided the book here.
SAVED: The reference here is to earthly well-being, not to eternal salvation
in the theological sense.

10 ¹ Αὕτη πρωτόπλαστον πατέρα κόσμου
μόνον κτισθέντα διεφύλαξεν
καὶ ἐξείλατο αὐτὸν ἐκ παραπτώματος ἰδίου
²ἔδωκέν τε αὐτῷ ἰσχὺν κρατῆσαι ἀπάντων.
³ἀποστὰς δὲ ἀπ᾽ αὐτῆς ἄδικος ἐν ὀργῇ αὐτοῦ
ἀδελφοκτόνοις συναπώλετο θυμοῖς.
⁴δι᾽ ὃν κατακλυζομένην γῆν πάλιν ἔσωσεν σοφία
δι᾽ εὐτελοῦς ξύλου τὸν δίκαιον κυβερνήσασα.
5 ⁵αὕτη καὶ ἐν ὁμονοίᾳ πονηρίας ἐθνῶν συγχυθέντων
ἔγνω τὸν δίκαιον καὶ ἐτήρησεν αὐτὸν ἄμεμπτον θεῷ

4¹ εσωσεν] pr. δι Bↀ

5² εγνω] ευρεν Bↀ

This and the following chapters tell of the beneficent action of Wisdom
in Israelitish history, and since they also show the dire effect of idolatry
upon a nation they constitute a serious attempt at a philosophy of history.
An inkling of this is found already in Jud. 2.1 ff., II Ki. 17.7 ff., Neh.
9.9 ff. and elsewhere in the Bible. It should be noted that in interpreting
Israelitish history in this way the writer uses considerable license and employs extra-biblical sources, if not sheer imagination.

1. SHE: Namely Wisdom, with reference to the last line of the preceding chapter. The emphatic pronoun *autê* is used for Wisdom throughout
this chapter.   GUARDED: Both in his good and bad fortune. Even after
his fall Wisdom did not utterly forsake him, but led him forth from his
sin by the way of repentance. Although this is not recorded in the Book of
Genesis it is generally inferred by Jews and Christians alike (*cf.* the
quotations in Deane).   FATHER OF THE WORLD: Namely Adam. In
keeping with this type of writing, no names of historical characters are
given, only indirect allusions. Evidently the book was intended for Jews
only, who knew their people's history.   CREATED ALONE: So Itala *cum
solus esset creatus*. Grimm renders *monon* "unprotected." Some translate
"the alone-created," meaning that Adam alone can claim to have been
created, all others having been born.   DELIVERED: There seems to have
been a tradition that God's curse did not fall upon Adam but upon the
serpent and upon the earth, and that ultimately Adam was restored to
grace and paradise through repentance and humility. See Ginzberg,
Legends, I, 87 ff., and the pertinent note 106 in V, 114 ff.; see also Irenaeus,
Adv. Haer., III. 23, and Tertullian, *de Paen.*, § 12.

2. TO RULE OVER ALL THINGS: R.V. "to get dominion over all things." The
reference is to the authority vested in mankind over all living creatures
(Gen. 1.26 and 28) and renewed after the fall (*ibid.* 9.2). There is a rabbinic
legend to the effect that Adam was enabled to master the world by his
enormous size, strength and knowledge, *cf.* Ginzberg, *Legends*, I, 59 ff.

3. AN UNRIGHTEOUS MAN: Namely Cain, who rejected Wisdom by the

10   1 She guarded the first formed father of the world
            throughout;
         Created alone as he was,
         And delivered him out of his own transgression,
         2And gave him strength to rule over all things.
         3But falling away from her an unrighteous man in his
            anger
         Perished with his fratricidal rage.
         4Through whom when the earth was drowned, wisdom
            again saved it,
         Steering the just one in cheap wood.
   5   5She also, when the nations were confounded in a con-
            spiracy of wickedness,
         Found the just man and preserved him blameless unto
            God,

---

murder of his brother.   PERISHED etc.: Some take it to mean that Cain
perished with Abel by incurring spiritual death in inflicting natural death;
cf. Philo, *Quod Det. Pot.*, § 14 "Cain killed himself not Abel"; see also
Gregg "Cain, in killing his brother, killed his own soul." As to the actual
end of Cain, there are two traditions: according to the Midrash he was the
man killed by accident by Lamech (Gen. 4.23), who mistook him for a
wild beast (see Ginzberg, *Legends*, I, 116); according to the Book of
Jubilees 4.31, he was crushed by a falling house, probably in keeping with
God's promise in Gen. 4.15 that he should not be slain.
4. THROUGH WHOM: It is surprising that Cain is held responsible here for
the flood, while according to Gen. 6.1 ff. the flood was caused by the folly
of the sons of God marrying the daughters of men and by the wickedness
of the earth generally. Perhaps we should read δι' ὅ instead of δι' ὅν with
some MSS. and Grotius, *cf.* the Arab. "on account of that," meaning
that this transgression let loose sin upon the earth.   WAS DROWNED: *Cf.*
Gen. ch. 7.   AGAIN SAVED IT: By saving the living beings in Noah's ark.
Cf. 14.6 where Noah is styled "the hope of the world."   STEERING:
Kubernan is generally used by Stoics in connection with *pronoia*.   THE
JUST ONE: *I. e.* Noah, so called in Gen. 6.9.   CHEAP WOOD: This is not
used contemptuously, but is meant to indicate the small value of even the
huge ark in comparison with the cause of righteousness which was by its
means preserved (Goodrick).
5. CONFOUNDED: An allusion to the confusion of tongues in Gen. 11.1–9.
CONSPIRACY OF WICKEDNESS: Referring no doubt to the concerted action
in building the tower of Babel.   THE JUST MAN: Namely Abraham. This
would seem to imply that Abraham was present at the building of the
tower, but more likely the connection is due to the fact that the story of

καὶ ἐπὶ τέκνου σπλάγχνοις ἰσχυρὸν ἐφύλαξεν.
⁶αὕτη δίκαιον ἐξαπολλυμένων ἀσεβῶν ἐρρύσατο
φυγόντα καταβάσιον πῦρ Πενταπόλεως,
⁷ἧς ἔπι μαρτύριον τῆς πονηρίας
καπνιζομένη καθέστηκε χέρσος,
καὶ ἀτελέσιν ὥραις καρποφοροῦντα φυτά,
ἀπιστούσης ψυχῆς μνημεῖον ἐστηκυῖα στήλη ἁλός.
⁸σοφίαν γὰρ παροδεύσαντες
οὐ μόνον ἐβλάβησαν τοῦ μὴ γνῶναι τὰ καλά,
ἀλλὰ καὶ τῆς ἀφροσύνης ἀπέλιπον τῷ βίῳ μνημόσυνον,
ἵνα ἐν οἷς ἐσφάλησαν μηδὲ λαθεῖν δυνηθῶσιν.
⁹σοφία δὲ τοὺς θεραπεύοντας αὐτὴν ἐκ πόνων ἐρρύσατο.
10 ¹⁰αὕτη φυγάδα ὀργῆς ἀδελφοῦ δίκαιον

---

9 θεραπευσαντας BSᶜᵗ   10⁶ πονους] κοπους SA: cf. 9.17

Abraham begins soon after that of the tower of Babel (Grimm).
AGAINST PITY FOR A SON: This use of *epi* with the dative is classical, see
Liddell-Scott, s. v. The reference is, of course, to the contemplated
sacrifice of Isaac at the command of God (Gen. ch. 22).
6. THE RIGHTEOUS MAN: *I. e.* Lot, who escaped from sinful Sodom (Gen.
19.17 ff.).   DESCENDING FIRE: *Katabasion* is peculiar to this book. Unusual also is the construction with a following genitive.   PENTAPOLIS:
The five cities of the plain: Sodom, Gomorrah, Admah, Zeboüm, and Zoar
(Gen. 14.2). Of these five only the first four were really destroyed by fire,
the last one being spared so that Lot could escape thither (Gen. 19.20 ff.).
It seems to have been customary to speak of five cities as destroyed, *cf.*
for instance, Josephus in *Bell. Jud.*, IV.VIII.4, though elsewhere, in
Antiq., I.XI.4, he mentions Zoar as still existing. Goodrick suggests that
perhaps Bela, another name for Zoar (Gen. 14.2 and 8) was distinct from
Zoar, and might have been one of the five cities that had been destroyed.
7. THAT SMOKES: This phenomenon is mentioned by Philo as still in
existence (*Abr.*, § 27; *Mos.*, II.10). Gregg compares also the Greek *Acts of
Pionius* for an eyewitness account, adding the following explanation:
"Smoke may have issued from the bituminous soil as in the Lydian
Catacecaumene, or the notion may be due to the dense mist which rises
from the basin of the Dead Sea." Actually the story of the still-smoking
land is a legendary exaggeration not uncommon in ancient accounts.
FRUIT OF BLOOM etc.: *Cf.* Deut. 32.32 and the description of Josephus, *Bell.
Jud.*, IV.3.4: "the ashes still grow in their fruits, which fruits have a
colour as if they were fit to be eaten, but if you pluck them with your
hands, they dissolve into smoke and ashes." Josephus refers here to the
apples of Sodom, which became legendary in ancient times. On the nature
of the fruit see Tristram, *Natural History of the Bible*, p. 482.   A PILLAR
OF SALT: Gen. 19.26. Numerous authorities testify to its existence in later
times, notably Josephus (*Antiq.*, I.XI, 4), Irenaeus (*Haer.*, IV.31.3), and

And kept him firm against pity for a son.

[6]She, when the impious were perishing, saved the
righteous man,

Escaping the descending fire on Pentapolis.

[7]Of whose wickedness still exists as a testimony

A waste land that smokes,

And plants that bear fruit of bloom that never ripens;

A pillar of salt standing as a memorial of an unbelieving
soul.

[8]For having passed wisdom by,

They were not only disabled from recognizing the things
that were good,

But also left behind them for human life a memorial of
their folly,

So that they could not even shun detection in what they
failed.

[9]But wisdom delivered out of troubles them that served
her.

10 [10]She guided a righteous man, a fugitive from a brother's
wrath,

---

travellers like Benjamin of Tudela, Maundrell, etc. See Driver in Hastings'
Dictionary of the Bible, III, 152. Such pillars are constantly in course of
formation and destruction, owing to the perpetual decomposition and
liquefaction of the perishable rock at the south end of the Dead Sea
(Goodrick).   A MEMORIAL: *Mnêmeion* is not merely a reminder, but a
concrete monument, especially because of *hestêkuia*. Some render it "a
grave, a tomb": according to the legend, Lot's wife's pillar was her tomb.
UNBELIEVING SOUL: Giving the reason why Lot's wife looked back to the
destroyed cities: she had no trust in God and did not believe in the
destruction of the cities. See Gen. 19.17 and 26.

8. This verse states the sad consequences of mistrust in God and wisdom,
cf. Prov. 1.29 ff. Those who reject wisdom incur a double loss: they
become spiritually blind, and they are held up to the reproach of future
generations, with an unenviable immortality (Gregg).   FOR HUMAN LIFE:
I. e. living men. Itala *hominibus*, so R.V. Goodrick renders "for the world."
SHUN DETECTION: Their fault was glaring and commemorated by a memorial for future generations, and so could not escape its dire consequences.

9. To those that pass by Wisdom the author now contrasts those that
follow Wisdom, describing the benefits they glean therefrom.

10. A RIGHTEOUS MAN: Namely Jacob. The same epithet is applied to
Noah, Abraham, and Lot, while "unrighteous" is used of Cain. To the
heathen Sodomites and Egyptians the epithet "ungodly" is applied.

ὡδήγησεν ἐν τρίβοις εὐθείαις·
ἔδειξεν αὐτῷ βασιλείαν θεοῦ
καὶ ἔδωκεν αὐτῷ γνῶσιν ἁγίων·
εὐπόρησεν αὐτὸν ἐν μόχθοις
καὶ ἐπλήθυνεν τοὺς πόνους αὐτοῦ·
¹¹ἐν πλεονεξίᾳ κατισχυόντων αὐτὸν παρέστη
καὶ ἐπλούτισεν αὐτόν·
¹²διεφύλαξεν αὐτὸν ἀπὸ ἐχθρῶν
καὶ ἀπὸ ἐνεδρευόντων ἠσφαλίσατο·
καὶ ἀγῶνα ἰσχυρὸν ἐβράβευσεν αὐτῷ,
ἵνα γνῷ ὅτι παντὸς δυνατωτέρα ἐστὶν εὐσέβεια.
¹³αὕτη πραθέντα δίκαιον οὐκ ἐγκατέλιπεν,
ἀλλὰ ἐξ ἁμαρτίας ἐρρύσατο αὐτόν·
¹⁴συγκατέβη αὐτῷ εἰς λάκκον
καὶ ἐν δεσμοῖς οὐκ ἀφῆκεν αὐτόν,
ἕως ἤνεγκεν αὐτῷ σκῆπτρα βασιλείας
καὶ ἐξουσίαν τυραννούντων αὐτοῦ·
ψευδεῖς τε ἔδειξεν τοὺς μωμησαμένους αὐτὸν
καὶ ἔδωκεν αὐτῷ δόξαν αἰώνιον.
15   ¹⁵ Αὕτη λαὸν ὅσιον καὶ σπέρμα ἄμεμπτον

12¹ διεφυλ.] και εφυλ. S   14⁴ αυτου] -τον Sᶜ pl.
12⁴ παντως S*¹, παντων Sᶜ¹

IN STRAIGHT PATHS: Literally so, *cf.* Gen. 28.20. Some take it in a
metaphorical sense (Farrar and others).   GOD'S KINGDOM: Perhaps the
reference is to Jacob's dream (Gen. 28.10 ff.), in which God disclosed to
him some of the workings of Providence.   HOLY THINGS: There are
various interpretations: a glimpse of heaven (Farrar), mysteries (Deane),
the supernatural (Grimm), angels, etc. Most likely the reference is to
supernatural mysteries involved in Jacob's wrestling with the angel (Gen.
32.24 ff.) and his prophetic visions (*ibid.* ch. 48 and 49).   THE FRUIT OF
HIS LABOURS: *Ponos* is so rendered also in 8.7 and Ecclus. 14.15.
11. See on this verse Gen. 31.38 ff. Wisdom aided Jacob to prosper in
spite of the machinations of Laban.
12. ENEMIES: Such as Esau and Laban.   LIERS IN WAIT: Probably Esau
who cherished a special hatred for Jacob after he cheated him out of
Isaac's blessing (Gen. 27.41). Others think of the Canaanites who conceived an intense hatred for Jacob after the slaughter of the Shechemites
(Gen. 34.30).   A SORE CONFLICT: This refers no doubt to the struggle of
Jacob with the angel, in which he prevailed (Gen. 32.24 ff.; Hos. 12.5).
13. A RIGHTEOUS ONE: Namely Joseph who was sold by his brothers to the

In straight paths;
Showed him God's kingdom,
And gave him knowledge of holy things;
She prospered him in his toils,
And replenished the fruit of his labours.
[11]In the greed of them that oppressed him she stood by
      him,
And made him rich.
[12]She guarded him throughout from enemies,
And kept him safe from liers in wait,
And a sore conflict she decided for him,
That he might know that piety is stronger than all.
[13]She forsook not a righteous one that was sold,
But delivered him from sin.
[14]Went down with him into a dungeon,
And left him not in bonds,
Until she brought him the sceptre of a kingdom,
And power over them that tyrannized over him,
And proved them false that slandered him,
And gave to him eternal glory.
 15 [15]She delivered a holy people and a blameless seed

Ishmaelites (Gen. 37.27 f.).   FROM SIN: Probably from the sin of co-
habiting with Potiphar's wife (Gen. 39.7 ff.). Less likely is the reading of
R.V. margin "from the sin of his brethren," following Itala *a peccatoribus.*
14. DUNGEON: *Lakkos* may mean "pit" (so Goodrick) and also "dungeon"
(so R.V.), but it is actually used of Joseph's dungeon in Gen. 40.15.
SCEPTRE: The Greek plural *skêptra* is poetical and peculiar to classical
Greek. Similarly *thronoi* in 9.12. With the idea of power entrusted to
Joseph *cf.* Gen. 41.39 ff. and also Philo, *Jos.,* § 21: "Pharaoh made him
second in the kingdom, or rather, to speak the truth, king."   POWER
OVER THEM etc.: Namely over the Egyptians whose officers imprisoned
him.   PROVED THEM FALSE: The reference is no doubt to Potiphar's
wife, see Gen. 39.17 f.   SLANDERED HIM: *Mômasthai* properly means
"to blame," not "to accuse." Itala *maculaverunt,* "defamed." R.V.
"mockingly accused him."   ETERNAL GLORY: The everlasting honor of
being a saviour and benefactor to Egypt and many people (Churton).
15. BLAMELESS SEED: Many commentators adduce Josh. 24.14, Ezek. 20.8
and 23.3, in refutation of this statement. But the author of Wisdom, who
addresses either apostate Jews or heathen rulers, cannot afford to admit
faults in Israel, and so he overlooks them.

ἐρρύσατο ἐξ ἔθνους θλιβόντων·
¹⁶εἰσῆλθεν εἰς ψυχὴν θεράποντος κυρίου
καὶ ἀντέστη βασιλεῦσιν φοβεροῖς ἐν τέρασι καὶ σημείοις.
¹⁷ἀπέδωκεν ὁσίοις μισθὸν κόπων αὐτῶν,
ὡδήγησεν αὐτοὺς ἐν ὁδῷ θαυμαστῇ
καὶ ἐγένετο αὐτοῖς εἰς σκέπην ἡμέρας
καὶ εἰς φλόγα ἄστρων τὴν νύκτα.
¹⁸διεβίβασεν αὐτοὺς θάλασσαν ἐρυθρὰν
καὶ διήγαγεν αὐτοὺς δι' ὕδατος πολλοῦ·
¹⁹τοὺς δὲ ἐχθροὺς αὐτῶν κατέκλυσεν
καὶ ἐκ βάθους ἀβύσσου ἀνέβρασεν αὐτούς.
20 ²⁰διὰ τοῦτο δίκαιοι ἐσκύλευσαν ἀσεβεῖς
καὶ ὕμνησαν, κύριε, τὸ ὄνομα τὸ ἅγιόν σου
τήν τε ὑπέρμαχόν σου χεῖρα ᾔνεσαν ὁμοθυμαδόν·
²¹ὅτι ἡ σοφία ἤνοιξεν στόμα κωφῶν
καὶ γλώσσας νηπίων ἔθηκεν τρανάς.

16² ανεστη βασιλευς S*†, sed post 19, ubi S† per errorem totum uersum 16 repetit, etiam S αντεστη βασιλευσιν

17⁴ φλογας S† | αστρων BS*†] αστερων rel.: cf. 7 19
18¹ θαλ.] pr. εις S
19¹ κατεκλυσαν A†, κατεπαυσεν S*†
19² βαθους αβυσσου] θαμβους S*†

---

16. SERVANT OF THE LORD: *Therapôn kuriou*, alternating in the Septuagint with *doulos theou*, generally refers to Moses, although Aaron is so designated in 18.21. The claim made by some commentators that this designation of Moses proves the connection of the writer with the Therapeutae is hardly worth consideration. TERRIBLE KINGS: The plural is puzzling, since the reference can be only to Pharaoh; but *cf.* Ps. 105.30, 135.9 f. and 136.17 f., where the plural is likewise used under similar circumstances. Perhaps kings outside Egypt are included.

17. THE HOLY: The idealized Israel, *cf.* Deut. 7.6 and elsewhere. A REWARD OF THEIR TOILS: The reference seems to be to the jewels of silver and gold which the Hebrews borrowed from their oppressors (Ex. 12.35 f., *cf.* further Gen. 15.14). Wessely in his Commentary *ad loc.* finds a connection between these words and the legend concerning a lawsuit between the Jews and Egyptians before Alexander the Great. Sanh. 91a relates that the Egyptians appeared before Alexander and demanded that the Jews should return to them the silver and gold which they had borrowed from them. To this the Jewish representative retorted: "Pay us the wages for the labor of 600,000 Jews whom you enslaved in Egypt for four hundred and thirty years." A WONDROUS WAY: *I. e.* a way full of wonders and mir-

From a nation of oppressors.

[16]She entered into the soul of a servant of the Lord,
And stood up against terrible kings in wonders and
signs.

[17]She rendered unto the holy a reward of their toils,
She guided them along a wondrous way,
And became unto them a covering by day,
And a flame of stars by night.

[18]She brought them through the Red Sea,
And led them through much water.

[19]But their enemies she drowned,
And cast them up out of the depths of the abyss.

[20]Therefore the righteous spoiled the impious,
And sang hymns, O Lord, to thy holy name,
And praised with one accord thy defending hand.

[21]For wisdom opened the mouth of the dumb,
And made the tongues of infants clear.

---

acles: crossing the Red Sea, producing water out of the rock, the shower of
manna, the quails, etc. Others take it to refer to the extraordinary and
circuitous route by which the Israelites were led (Cornely etc.).   A
COVERING BY DAY: *Cf.* Ex. 13.21 f., see also Ps. 78.14. The pillar of cloud
was considered not only a guide but also a protection from the heat of the
desert (Num. 10.34, Ps. 105.39). Philo (*Mos.*, I.29) speaks of the cloud as
concealing some ministering angel.

18. *Cf.* Ex. ch. 14.

19. CAST THEM UP: *Anebrasen* is a rare word, but it is precisely
apebrasthysan that Philo uses in connection with the casting up of the
Egyptian corpses. Interesting is the following legend found in Targum
Jonathan to Ex. 15.12: "The sea and the earth had controversy one with
the other. The sea said to the earth: receive thy children; and the earth
said to the sea: receive thy murderers. But the earth willed not to swallow
them, and the sea willed not to overwhelm them . . . Then God swore to
the earth that He would not require them of her in the world to come.
Then did the earth open her mouth and swallow them up."

20. SPOILED: Since the Egyptians were drowned the Israelites could take
their spoil.   SANG HYMNS: Ex. 15.1 ff.   WITH ONE ACCORD: Philo
says (*Mos.*, II.34): "Moses divided the people into two bands of men and
women, to sing in harmony to the Creator-Father; for men's deep voices,
and the clear tones of women, blend in a sweet and melodious strain."

21. MOUTH OF THE DUMB: Clearly an allusion to Ex. 4.10 ff., though the
plural includes others beside Moses.   CLEAR: *Tranos* in this sense
occurs also in LXX of Isa. 35.6.

11 ¹ Εὐόδωσεν τὰ ἔργα αὐτῶν ἐν χειρὶ προφήτου ἁγίου.
²διώδευσαν ἔρημον ἀοίκητον
καὶ ἐν ἀβάτοις ἔπηξαν σκηνάς·
³ἀντέστησαν πολεμίοις καὶ ἐχθροὺς ἠμύναντο.
⁴ἐδίψησαν καὶ ἐπεκαλέσαντό σε,
καὶ ἐδόθη αὐτοῖς ἐκ πέτρας ἀκροτόμου ὕδωρ
καὶ ἴαμα δίψης ἐκ λίθου σκληροῦ.
5 ⁵δι' ὧν γὰρ ἐκολάσθησαν οἱ ἐχθροὶ αὐτῶν,
διὰ τούτων αὐτοὶ ἀποροῦντες εὐεργετήθησαν.
⁶ἀντὶ μὲν πηγῆς ἀενάου ποταμοῦ
αἵματι λυθρώδει ταραχθέντος
⁷εἰς ἔλεγχον νηπιοκτόνου διατάγματος
ἔδωκας αὐτοῖς δαψιλὲς ὕδωρ ἀνελπίστως
⁸δείξας διὰ τοῦ τότε δίψους

11¹ αυτου A | προφητων αγιων A⸶   6² ταραχθεντες B

1. SHE: Namely Wisdom, which is still the subject. Because of this Grimm
joins this verse to chapter 10.   HOLY PROPHET: Namely Moses, cf.
Deut. 34.10, Hos. 12.14. Philo says of Moses (Mos., II.23) that as he was
the greatest king, lawgiver, and high priest, so he was also the most
famous prophet.
2. PITCHED TENTS: Probably a reference to Succoth (Tents), the first station of the Israelites after leaving Egypt, cf. Ex. 12.37. On the institution
of the feast of Succoth see Lev. 23.42 f.
3. ENEMIES . . . FOES: There is no distinction between the two, and the
reduplication is undoubtedly due entirely to poetical variation. The chief
enemies of the Israelites were, of course, the Egyptians, then come the
Amalekites, the Canaanites, the Amorites, the Midianites, the Moabites,
etc.
4. THEY CALLED UPON THEE: This is hardly true: in Ex. 17.3 f. the people
murmured against Moses and were almost ready to stone him. Apparently
Pseudo-Solomon aims to prove the blamelessness of the chosen race.
CRAGGY ROCK: Akrotomos is properly "precipitous," but this does not fit
here. More appropriate is "flinty rock" of A.V. and R.V., which corresponds to the Hebrew in Deut. 8.15. Philo (Leg. Alleg., II.21) comments
"The rock of flint is the Wisdom of God, from which He feeds the souls that
love Him."
5. The meaning of this verse is clear: the Egyptians perished by water, but
water relieved the Israelites' thirst. Pseudo-Solomon is fond of putting
things in this form of retaliation, as may be seen particularly in chapters
16–19. It reminds us of the Mosaic principle "an eye for an eye and a
tooth for a tooth." Cf. also the Talmud Sot. 11a "they were cooked in the
very same pot in which they cooked."

11 ¹She prospered their works by the hand of a holy prophet.
²They journeyed through an uninhabited desert,
And pitched tents in trackless places.
³They withstood enemies and repelled foes.
⁴They thirsted and called upon thee,
And water was given them out of a craggy rock,
And healing of thirst out of hard stone.

5 ⁵For by those things whereby their enemies were punished,
By these they in their need were benefited.
⁶Instead indeed of the fountain of an everflowing river,
Turbid with gory blood,
⁷For a rebuke of the decree for the slaying of babes,
Thou gavest them abundant water beyond all hope,
⁸Showing through their thirst at that time

---

6. This and the next verse are an elaboration of the preceding two verses, the theme being the same: furnishing plentiful water to the parched Israelites.   EVER FLOWING: This epithet contrasts well with the next line which pictures the stream as clotted with gore. The stream is the perennial Nile.   TURBID WITH GORY BLOOD: *Cf.* Ex. 7.19 ff. According to Philo (*Mos.*, I.17) God determined to plague the Egyptians by water because they considered it as the beginning of all creation. Josephus states (*Antiq.*, II.XIV.1) that the Nile water was sweet for the Israelites all the time that it was blood for the Egyptians. Itala renders *humanum sanguinem*.

7. A REBUKE OF THE DECREE: See Ex. 1.15 ff. The Nile was turned to blood because Pharaoh had sinned by the blood of the firstborn. There is a tradition (*Targum* Jonathan to Ex. 2.23) that Pharaoh was afflicted with a leprosy, and he commanded to kill the firstborn of the Israelites that he might bathe himself in their blood. Ex. 1.22 says "Every son that is born ye shall cast into the river." *Cf.* also the Book of Jubilees 48.14 ff.: "All the people that he had led out to pursue Israel the Lord our God cast into the sea, into the depths of the abyss, instead of the children of Israel. For this thing, that the Egyptians had cast their children into the river, he took vengeance on millions of them; and a thousand strong and brave men perished for one suckling that they had cast into the river, of the children of thy people."

8. The idea expressed here, that the Israelites were allowed to thirst for a little in order that they might be able to appreciate the proportionately worse sufferings of the Egyptians, is not in agreement with Deut. 8.3, where the reason given is "that He might make thee know that man doth

πῶς τοὺς ὑπεναντίους ἐκόλασας.

⁹ὅτε γὰρ ἐπειράσθησαν, καίπερ ἐν ἐλέει παιδευόμενοι,
ἔγνωσαν πῶς μετ' ὀργῆς κρινόμενοι ἀσεβεῖς ἐβασανί-
ζοντο·

10 ¹⁰τούτους μὲν γὰρ ὡς πατὴρ νουθετῶν ἐδοκίμασας,
ἐκείνους δὲ ὡς ἀπότομος βασιλεὺς καταδικάζων ἐξήτασας.

¹¹καὶ ἀπόντες δὲ καὶ παρόντες ὁμοίως ἐτρύχοντο·
¹²διπλῆ γὰρ αὐτοὺς ἔλαβεν λύπη
καὶ στεναγμὸς μνημῶν τῶν παρελθόντων·
¹³ὅτε γὰρ ἤκουσαν διὰ τῶν ἰδίων κολάσεων
εὐεργετημένους αὐτούς, ᾔσθοντο τοῦ κυρίου.

¹⁴ὃν γὰρ ἐν ἐκθέσει πάλαι ῥιφέντα ἀπεῖπον χλευάζοντες,
ἐπὶ τέλει τῶν ἐκβάσεων ἐθαύμασαν

9² μετ οργης] εν οργη ΒΑ   13² του κυριου] σου κυριε SᶜV
12² παρελθουσων Β   14² εθαυμαζον Αᵗ

---

not live by bread only, but by every thing that proceedeth out of the
mouth of the Lord doth man live."

9. WHEN THEY WERE TRIED: This is in accordance with Deut. 8.2, though
not with the general tone of the Pentateuch that the Israelites always
tempted God and were punished for it (see, e. g., Ex. 32.28 and Num.
11.33).   THE IMPIOUS WERE TORMENTED: Cf. Deut. 7.15 "He will put
none of the evil diseases of Egypt, which thou knowest, upon thee, but will
lay them upon all that hate thee."
    The A.V. introduces here the third clause of v. 14 without any warrant
from MSS. or versions.
10. God is pictured here as paternal towards Israel but as inimical towards
Egypt. Such doctrine may be consonant with the narrow nationalism or
particularism of Mal. 1.2 f., but is quite contrary to the universalism of the
prophets, see e. g. Ezek. 18.29.
11. The meaning seems to be that the Egyptians suffered both when the
Israelites were with them in Egypt and when they were away from them
in the wilderness: in the first instance because the water of the Nile
became as blood and the Egyptians could not drink it; in the second
because the Israelites were saved by the water of the Red Sea in which the
Egyptians got drowned, or because the Egyptians heard the report that the
thirsty Israelites were saved from death by plentiful water flowing from
the flinty rock in the desert.
12. A DOUBLE GRIEF: The Egyptians were distressed by reports from the
desert, and also by the remembrance of their own folly and its punishment.
A GROANING: The report from the desert concerning Israel's thirst revived
the memories of their own thirst, when the Nile was stricken. Itala

How thou didst punish their adversaries.

⁹For when they were tried, though chastened only in
   mercy,

They understood how being judged in anger the impious
   were tormented.

10   ¹⁰For these as a father admonishing them thou didst
   prove,

But those as a stern king condemning thou didst search
   out.

¹¹Yes, and whether absent or present they were alike
   distressed.

¹²For a double grief took hold on them,

And a groaning over past remembrances.

¹³For when they heard that by their own punishments

The others were being benefited, they learned to know
   the Lord.

¹⁴For the castaway whom aforetime they rejected with
   scorn in the exposure of infants,

In the result of events they admired,

---

gemitus cum memoria praeteritorum follows אA *parelthontôn* instead of
parelthousôn of B.

13. FOR: What irked the Egyptians even more was the fact that Yahweh,
the God of Moses, whom they had despised, had triumphed over the gods
of Egypt.   THEIR OWN PUNISHMENTS: Namely through lack of water.
Perhaps there is an allusion here also to the punishment of the Egyptians
by water, when Israel escaped and their own forces were destroyed in
the Red Sea.

14. FOR THE CASTAWAY: *Ton gar rifenta* forms an anacoluthon with the
following line. A has *hon* instead of *ton*, but this is probably a conscious
correction.   THEY REJECTED WITH SCORN: R.V. has "they left off
mocking," which may be justified linguistically but is not altogether clear
contextually.   IN THE EXPOSURE OF INFANTS: *Ekthesis* is the technical
term for the exposing of a child and occurs again in 18.5. Some MSS. have
en exthesei meaning "hatred," so R.V. Indeed Gregg favors this reading
for the reason that "the exposure of Moses in his infancy is not germane to
the topic in hand, nor has it any connection with the 'mocking' of the
Egyptians: on the other hand, 'cast forth in hatred' refers plainly to
Ex. 10.11–28."   IN THE RESULT OF EVENTS: Literally "at the end of
events," which might mean "on the occasion of the triumphant exodus"
(Goodrick), or still better at the close of the whole series of events which

οὐχ ὅμοια δικαίοις διψήσαντες.

15 ¹⁵ἀντὶ δὲ λογισμῶν ἀσυνέτων ἀδικίας αὐτῶν,
ἐν οἷς πλανηθέντες ἐθρήσκευον ἄλογα ἑρπετὰ καὶ
κνώδαλα εὐτελῆ,
ἐπαπέστειλας αὐτοῖς πλῆθος ἀλόγων ζῴων εἰς ἐκδίκησιν,
¹⁶ἵνα γνῶσιν ὅτι, δι' ὧν τις ἁμαρτάνει, διὰ τούτων
κολάζεται.

¹⁷οὐ γὰρ ἠπόρει ἡ παντοδύναμός σου χεὶρ
καὶ κτίσασα τὸν κόσμον ἐξ ἀμόρφου ὕλης
ἐπιπέμψαι αὐτοῖς πλῆθος ἄρκων ἢ θρασεῖς λέοντας

reached its climax at Massah (Ex. ch. 17). HAVING THIRSTED etc.: The meaning is that the Egyptians suffered a far greater thirst during the plagues (Ex. 7.25) than that suffered by the Israelites at Massah (*ibid.* ch. 17).

15. FOR: *Anti* is rendered more forcefully "in requital" by R.V. UN-RIGHTEOUSNESS: Not only were the Egyptians unrighteous in their actions but also in their creed and cult. SENSELESS REPTILES: The Egyptians are known to have worshipped serpents and creatures of all kinds from the crocodile to the beetle. VILE VERMIN: *Knôdala* is very vague and in-exact, and may have been used for rhetorical purpose only. At any rate, there is no reliable source substantiating this statement that the Egyptians worshipped vermin. Juvenal's account (*Sat.*, XV. 1–15) is certainly prejudiced, and yet there is no mention in it of the worship of vermin. Besides, as stated by Goodrick, to prove our author's theory of punishment of like by like it would be necessary to prove that the Egyptians had wor-shipped such beasts as were sent to plague them—lice, flies, and locusts; but such proof is wanting. On Egyptian idolatry *cf.* Eusebius, *Praep. Evang.*, III.2 f.; Aristid., *Apol.*, ch. XII. For the Jewish view of Egyptian animal-worship see the Sibylline Oracles, III. proem. II. 22 ff. SENSE-LESS BEASTS: The plagues of frogs, lice, flies, and locusts.

16. This verse expresses not only the general idea of retribution "as a man sows so shall he reap" (as, for instance, Ezek. 35.6, Obad. 15, Ps. 109.17, Prov. 5.22, and Job 4.8), but also the notion that the punishment is in-flicted by the very instrument of the transgression. *Cf.* 12.23 and 16.1. Examples of such punishment may be found in the Bible in the case of David, whose adultery and murder were punished by adultery and murder, or in the case of Absalom, who, according to the rabbis, was proud of his hair and hence his hair caused his death. *Cf.* also Ps. 7.16 "He hath digged a pit and hollowed it, and is fallen into the ditch which he made"; so also Ecclus. 27.26. Instances in the Apocrypha are the following: II Macc. 9.6, where Antiochus dies of a disease of the bowels for he had tor-mented other men's bowels with many and strange torments; Jubilees 4.31, where Cain is said to have been killed by a falling stone because he killed his brother with a stone; Testament of the Twelve Patriarchs, Gad,

Having thirsted in another manner than the righteous.

15 ¹⁵But for the foolish reasonings of their unrighteousness,

Led astray by which they worshipped senseless reptiles and vile vermin,

Thou sentest upon them a multitude of senseless beasts for vengeance;

¹⁶That they might know that by what things a man sins, thereby he is punished.

¹⁷For thy all-powerful hand,

That created the world out of formless matter,

Lacked not means to send upon them a multitude of bears or fierce lions,

---

§ 5, where Gad is stricken with a disease of the liver for the duration of eleven months because his liver brought about his hatred of Joseph for eleven months, until he was sold. For the Talmud comp. Mish. Sot. 1.7; introduction to Lam. r., § 21. and for the Midrash see Mekilta for Besh.

17. THY ALL-POWERFUL HAND: Hand here is taken in the same sense as word, and proof is adduced from Isa. 48.13 where "my hand" is rendered by the Targum by "my word." Goodrick is positive that *pantodunamos cheir* of this verse is equivalent to *pantodunamos logos* of 18.15, showing that Wisdom regarded the Logos simply as an exertion of God's power, not as the Philonian Logos.   FORMLESS MATTER: *Amorfos hulê* is a Greek philosophical term, which is entirely foreign to Jewish thought and conception. The Jews believed in creation out of nothing; the Greeks believed in creation out of formless matter which was eternal. On the one hand religious monism (God alone is eternal); on the other philosophic dualism (God and matter are eternal). It is difficult to assume that the author of Wisdom, who was far more Jewish than Philo, would adhere to the Greek view of creation. Undoubtedly the allusion is casual and not dogmatic. Perhaps the phrase stands here as a convenient Greek symbol for *tōhu wa-bōhu* of Gen. 1.2, which is rendered by LXX, *aoratos kai akataskeuastos* (invisible and unorganized). We find the same laxity of expression and ambivalence in Philo, who in one place (*Incor. Mund.*, § 2) affirms Aristotle's dictum "It is impossible for anything to be made out of that which is not," but in another (*Somn.*, I.13) states clearly "God not only brought the world into visible manifestation, but He made things which before were not." It is safe to say that this eclecticism is characteristic of all Jewish Alexandrian writers.   BEARS OR LIONS: Philo (*Mos.*, I.19) poses the question: "Why did God visit the land with such insignificant creatures, and omit to send bears or lions or leopards or other kinds of fierce animals?" The noisome beasts were agents of divine vengeance, see Lev. 26.22; II Kings 2.24 and 17.26; Jer. 8.17; Ezek. 14.21.

¹⁸ἡ νεοκτίστους θυμοῦ πλήρεις θῆρας ἀγνώστους
ἤτοι πυρπνόον φυσῶντας ἄσθμα
ἢ βρόμον λικμωμένους καπνοῦ
ἢ δεινοὺς ἀπ' ὀμμάτων σπινθῆρας ἀστράπτοντας,
¹⁹ὧν οὐ μόνον ἡ βλάβη ἠδύνατο συνεκτρῖψαι αὐτούς,
ἀλλὰ καὶ ἡ ὄψις ἐκφοβήσασα διολέσαι.

20 ²⁰καὶ χωρὶς δὲ τούτων ἑνὶ πνεύματι πεσεῖν ἐδύναντο
ὑπὸ τῆς δίκης διωχθέντες
καὶ λικμηθέντες ὑπὸ πνεύματος δυνάμεώς σου
ἀλλὰ πάντα μέτρῳ καὶ ἀριθμῷ καὶ σταθμῷ διέταξας.
²¹τὸ γὰρ μεγάλως ἰσχύειν σοι πάρεστιν πάντοτε,
καὶ κράτει βραχίονός σου τίς ἀντιστήσεται;
²²ὅτι ὡς ῥοπὴ ἐκ πλαστίγγων ὅλος ὁ κόσμος ἐναντίον σου
καὶ ὡς ῥανὶς δρόσου ὀρθρινὴ κατελθοῦσα ἐπὶ γῆν.

18¹ νεοκτιστου A   19¹ συνεκτριψαι] συν>ASᶜ
18² πυρπνοον] πυρ πνεον S   22² γης Sᶜ
18³ βρομους B†

18. FULL OF RAGE: Some prefer to render "full of poison." BREATHING OUT etc.: The notion of fire-breathing beasts was not uncommon in ancient times, among the Greeks and Romans as well as among the Semites. Cf. the description of Leviathan in Job 41.11 ff. Grimm thinks that the writer drew the separate traits of this picture from the appearance of the crocodile emerging from the water.

19. R.V. renders this verse more freely "which had power not only to consume them by their violence, but to destroy them even by the terror of their sight." The author wants to convey the idea of utter and immediate destruction. SIGHT: Opsis is rendered by Itala aspectus. Farrar thinks that there is an allusion here to the basilisk which was reputed to kill with its glance, but this is very doubtful.

20. THOU DIDST ORDER etc.: The idea expressed here is that God will not unnecessarily interfere with the regular course of nature. Cf. IV Esdr. 4.36 f.: "He has weighed the world in the balance; and by measure has he measured the times, and by number has he numbered the seasons; and He shall not move nor stir them, until the said measure be fulfilled." See also Philo (Somn., II.29): "God and not the mind of man measures, weighs and numbers all things, and circumscribes them with bounds and limits." Charles (Enoch, p.132) remarks: "In apocryphal literature historical events are methodically arranged under artificial categories of measure, number, weight." Cf. further Isa. 40.12 and Job 28.25. A somewhat different explanation of this line is offered by Cornely, who thinks it is intended to give the reason why God merely tormented the Egyptians with vermin

¹⁸Or new-created wild beasts, full of rage, unknown before,
    Either breathing out a blast of fiery breath,
    Or blowing out roarings of smoke,
    Or flashing dreadful sparks from their eyes.
¹⁹Of which not only the harmfulness could despatch them
    at once,
    But even the very sight, by terrifying them, destroy
    them.
20   ²⁰Yes, and without these they might have fallen by a
    single breath,
    Being pursued by justice,
    And scattered by the breath of thy power,
    But thou didst order all things by measure and number
    and weight.
²¹For to be greatly strong is thine at all times,
    And the might of thy arm who shall withstand?
²²For as a turn of the scales is the whole world before thee,
    And as a drop of dew in the dawning that descends upon
    the earth.

---

instead of sending fierce monsters against them or destroying them with a single breath. The Egyptians had not slain the Israelites, but had made their lives miserable; therefore their lives were also made miserable by the plagues, but they were not slain. Not so the Canaanites, for example: they were murderers, hence they were exterminated.

21. FOR: This connects not with the clause immediately preceding, but rather with the whole of verses 17–20. The sense is that God had the power, for He is all-powerful, but He did not exercise it.   THE MIGHT OF THY ARM WHO SHALL WITHSTAND: This phrase combined with the first line of 12.12 is found almost verbatim in Clem. Rom., I Cor. 27, and is considered one of the earliest known patristic quotations from Wisdom. The other is from 2.24.

22. This verse recalls Isa. 40.12 ff., where insignificant man is contrasted with all-powerful God.   A TURN OF THE SCALES: This is the exact meaning of *ropê ek plastingōn*, which Itala renders *momentum staterae*, that is "that which turns the balance." A.V. renders "a little grain of the balance," with "little weight" on the margin. R.V. has "a grain in a balance." Goodrick renders "a sway of the balances." *Cf.* Isa. 40.15 "the small dust of the balance," which LXX renders *ropê zugou*. Undoubtedly the author of Wisdom had this in mind, though Margoliouth thought that Isaiah copied Wisdom!   A DROP OF DEW: Which is tiny and ephemeral. *Cf.* Hos. 6.4 and 13.3.

²³ἐλεεῖς δὲ πάντας, ὅτι πάντα δύνασαι,
καὶ παρορᾷς ἁμαρτήματα ἀνθρώπων εἰς μετάνοιαν.
²⁴ἀγαπᾷς γὰρ τὰ ὄντα πάντα
καὶ οὐδὲν βδελύσσῃ ὧν ἐποίησας·
οὐδὲ γὰρ ἂν μισῶν τι κατεσκεύασας.

25 ²⁵πῶς δὲ διέμεινεν ἄν τι, εἰ μὴ σὺ ἠθέλησας,
ἢ τὸ μὴ κληθὲν ὑπὸ σοῦ διετερήθη;
²⁶φείδῃ δὲ πάντων, ὅτι σά ἐστιν, δέσποτα φιλόψυχε·

12 ¹τὸ γὰρ ἄφθαρτόν σου πνεῦμά ἐστιν ἐν πᾶσιν.
   ² Διὸ τοὺς παραπίπτοντας κατ᾽ ὀλίγον ἐλέγχεις
   καὶ ἐν οἷς ἁμαρτάνουσιν ὑπομιμνῄσκων νουθετεῖς,
   ἵνα ἀπαλλαγέντες τῆς κακίας πιστεύσωσιν ἐπὶ σέ, κύριε.

25¹ διεμεινεν] δι>BA   2³ πιστευσωμεν At
26 εστιν]+παντα A

23. The combination of mercy and power is brought out in 12.16.18.20. For these two attributes of God see Philo, *Sacr.*, § 15. Their earliest occurrence in Hebrew literature is Ps. 62.11 f., see also 101.1; *cf.* also Ecclus. 2.18 and 18.13. THEY MAY REPENT: *Cf.* Ecclus. 17.29. Philo (*Mos.*, I.19) says "God willed rather to admonish the inhabitants of Egypt than to destroy them," and again (*Fug.*, § 18) "God is not inexorable, but kind because of the gentleness of His nature; whoso knows this, though he have sinned, may turn and repent with full hope of amnesty."
24. THOU LOVEST ALL THINGS: *Cf.* Ps. 145.8 f. Philo was convinced that the goodness of God impelled him to the creation of the world, see His *Cherub.*, § 35. WOULDST THOU HAVE FORMED: It is difficult to reconcile the universalism of this verse with the particularism of 12.10 ff. It seems that the author is vacillating between these two extremes, undecided which way to follow.
26. THEY ARE THINE: *Cf.* Ezek. 18.4. An additional reason why God spared such as the Egyptians: He created them and they are His, hence He is merciful towards them. LOVER OF SOULS: R.V. has "lover of men's lives," but margin "lover of men's souls." *Filopsuchos* is hardly the proper word to be used here, since it really means "loving one's life too well," hence "cowardly, dastardly, fainthearted."

1. THINE INCORRUPTIBLE SPIRIT: So A.V. and R.V.; Goodrick prefers to render "thine imperishable spirit." The meaning is clear: All things or persons, both good and bad, exist by the eternal spirit of God; *cf.* similar expressions in Job 33.4 and Ps. 104.30. The only question is whether the writer thinks in Greek or Hebrew terms: if in the former, he may be referring to the Stoic idea of "the soul of the world" (*cf.* 1.7, 7.24, and 8.1), and then the spirit would have to be identified with Wisdom as the agent of the immanence of God; if in the latter, spirit must stand not for a being

²³But thou hast mercy on all because thou hast power over all,

And thou overlookest the sins of men so that they may repent.

²⁴For thou lovest all things that are

And abhorrest nothing which thou madest,

For never wouldst thou have formed anything if thou didst hate it.

25 ²⁵And how would anything have endured, except thou hadst willed it?

Or that which was not bidden by thee be preserved?

²⁶But thou sparest all, because they are thine, O Sovereign Lord, lover of souls.

12 ¹For thine incorruptible spirit is in all things.

²Wherefore thou convictest by little and little them that err,

And reminding them by the very things wherein they sin dost chasten them,

That escaping from their wickedness they may trust in thee, O Lord.

---

distinct from God, but for the creative power of God. *Cf.* Davidson, *Theology of the O. T.*, p. 193.

2. CONVICTEST: So R.V. Other versions have "chasten," "correct," or the like. Itala renders *admones et alloqueris*, similarly Pal. Syr. and Arab. BY LITTLE AND LITTLE: God punishes sinners gently that they may turn and believe in Him. On the longsuffering of God see Am. 4.6 ff.   BY THE VERY THINGS: This is a repetition of the principle enunciated in the case of the Egyptians, that whereby one sins thereby one shall be punished. Plagues of animals were sent upon the Egyptians to teach them that they had sinned through worship of animals.   MAY TRUST IN THEE: The writer regards idolatry as due to moral rather than intellectual deficiency, and holds that moral correction would lead the heathen to the acknowledgment of the true God (Gregg).

The rabbis of the Talmud too thought that God had great pity on the Egyptians, *cf. e. g.* Meg. 10 b: "at the passing of the Red Sea the ministering angels wanted to intone a song, but God said: the works of my hand are sinking into the sea, and you sing songs?" The rabbis go on to give the following reason "for God does not rejoice at the fall of the wicked."

³καὶ γὰρ τοὺς πάλαι οἰκήτορας τῆς ἁγίας σου γῆς
⁴μισήσας ἐπὶ τῷ ἔχθιστα πράσσειν,
ἔργα φαρμακειῶν καὶ τελετὰς ἀνοσίους
5 ⁵τέκνων τε φονὰς ἀνελεήμονας
καὶ σπλαγχνοφάγον ἀνθρωπίνων σαρκῶν θοῖναν καὶ
αἵματος,
ἐκ μέσου μύστας θιάσου
⁶καὶ αὐθέντας γονεῖς ψυχῶν ἀβοηθήτων,
ἐβουλήθης ἀπολέσαι διὰ χειρῶν πατέρων ἡμῶν,
⁷ἵνα ἀξίαν ἀποικίαν δέξηται θεοῦ παίδων
ἡ παρὰ σοὶ πασῶν τιμιωτάτη γῆ.
⁸ἀλλὰ καὶ τούτων ὡς ἀνθρώπων ἐφείσω
ἀπέστειλάς τε προδρόμους τοῦ στρατοπέδου σου σφῆκας,

---

3 παλαι] παλαιους BA
5¹ φονας Fr.] -νεας mss.
5² σπλαγχνοφαγον pau.] -γων BSA
5³ μεσου] μυσου Bᶜ⁺ | μυστας] s
>B*S* | θ(ε)ιασου] θειας σου pau.,

τε θειας σου Bᶜ⁺
6² εβουληθης] εαν βουλ. S*⁺
7¹ ινα] κατα S*⁺
8² τους στρατοπεδους BS

---

3. THE ANCIENT INHABITANTS: The Canaanites, the original inhabitants of the land of Israel. The author passes from the Egyptians to the Canaanites, and stresses the latter by placing them at the beginning of a long sentence of which the verb occurs at the end of v. 6. HOLY LAND: This term, which is common for Palestine in the Middle Ages, occurs only in Zech. 2.16 and II Macc. 1.7 (see Zeitlin's comment there).

4. HATING THEM: This seems to be a contradiction of 11.24 "Never wouldst thou have formed anything if thou didst hate it," but the contradiction is only formal. As Grimm remarks, "the moral earnestness which refuses to relegate the idea of God to a mere abstract speculation, must find an antagonism to man's sin in the divine consciousness, and express this by 'anger' or 'hatred,' or in a milder form as 'displeasure.'" ENCHANTMENTS: An enchanter or sorcerer was one who, by means of the superstitious use of drugs, herbs, spells, etc., produced magical effects, hence the Greek farmakeiōn. Similarly 18.13. Cf. especially Deut. 18.10 ff. RITES: Teletai might possibly refer to the rites of Moloch involving the sacrifice of children, but the word has a technical meaning in LXX, referring to the consecrated prostitutes of both sexes in the Canaanite ritual.

5. MURDERERS OF THEIR CHILDREN: Reading fonas instead of foneas. Sacrifice of children to placate angry gods and obtain favorable oracles from them was a common pernicious practice among the Canaanites, which some early Israelites emulated. Cf. Jud. 11.39 (Jephthah's sacrifice of his daughter), II Ki. 16.3 (Ahab's sacrifice of his son); see also Lev.

³For the ancient inhabitants of thy holy land,
⁴Hating them for doing their most detestable
Works of enchantments and unholy rites,

5   ⁵Merciless murderers of their children,
Yes, an entrail-devourers' banquet of human flesh and
blood,
From the midst of their orgy,
⁶And murderers of children of helpless souls,
Thou didst determine to destroy by the hand of our
fathers,
⁷That the land which with thee is most precious of all
Might receive a worthy settlement of God's children.
⁸But these too as being men thou didst spare,
And sentest wasps as forerunners of thine host,

18.21, Isa. 57.5, Jer. 19.5, and Ps. 106.37. Additional light on child
sacrifice in ancient Palestine has been thrown by recent excavations
there, especially Maclister's discoveries at Gezer. See Otto Eissfeldt,
*Molk als Opferbegriff im Punischen und Hebräischen und das Ende des
Gottes Moloch*, Halle (Saale) 1935.   ENTRAIL-DEVOURERS' BANQUET:
Reading *splanchnofagous* in keeping with *foneas*. This charge of cannibalism finds no corroboration elsewhere, except perhaps in Ezek. 16.20,
which may be figurative only. Unfounded charges of this sort are met with
at all times and climes throughout history, as, for instance, the charge of
"Thyestean banquets" against the primitive Christians or the charge of
ritual murder against the Jews in the Middle Ages and also in modern
times.   FROM THE MIDST OF THEIR ORGY: Reading *ek mesou mustatheias*
with Goodrick. Others read *ek mesou mustas thiasou* "out of the midst of
the idolatrous crew" (A.V.), or *ekmusous mustas thiasou*, "confederates in
an impious fellowship" (R.V., Grimm).
6. TO DESTROY: Two reasons are assigned for the destruction of the
Canaanites: 1) because God loved Israel (Deut. 4.37 f.); 2) because the
Canaanites were very wicked (*ibid*. 9.5).   OUR FATHERS: Whom God
used as instruments (Deut. 7.2).
7. THE LAND: *Cf.* Deut. 11.12. Palestine was God's favorite land, as may
be seen from numerous quotations from the Talmud and Midrash
given in Ginzberg's *Legends* V, 14 ff.   SETTLEMENT: *Apoikia* (A.V.
margin "new inhabitance," R.V. "colony") is hardly the right word here,
since it stands for a party proceeding from the motherland and settling in
a new country. Egypt surely was not the Israelites' motherland. Grimm's
conjecture *epoikia* lacks authority and would be a *hapax legomenon*.
8. WASPS: So A.V. and Goodrick, but R.V. has "hornets" for *sfēkas*,
adopting the traditional rendering of *ṣir'ah* in Ex. 23.28 and Deut. 7.20.

ἵνα αὐτοὺς κατὰ βραχὺ ἐξολεθρεύσωσιν.

⁹οὐκ ἀδυνατῶν ἐν παρατάξει ἀσεβεῖς δικαίοις ὑποχειρίους
    δοῦναι
ἢ θηρίοις δεινοῖς ἢ λόγῳ ἀποτόμῳ ὑφ' ἓν ἐκτρῖψαι,
10 ¹⁰κρίνων δὲ κατὰ βραχὺ ἐδίδους τόπον μετανοίας
οὐκ ἀγνοῶν ὅτι πονηρὰ ἡ γένεσις αὐτῶν
καὶ ἔμφυτος ἡ κακία αὐτῶν
καὶ ὅτι οὐ μὴ ἀλλαγῇ ὁ λογισμὸς αὐτῶν εἰς τὸν αἰῶνα.
¹¹σπέρμα γὰρ ἦν καταραμένον ἀπ' ἀρχῆς,
οὐδὲ εὐλαβούμενός τινα ἐφ' οἷς ἡμάρτανον ἄδειαν ἐδίδους.
¹²τίς γὰρ ἐρεῖ Τί ἐποίησας;
ἢ τίς ἀντιστήσεται τῷ κρίματί σου;
τίς δὲ ἐγκαλέσει σοι κατὰ ἐθνῶν ἀπολωλότων ἃ σὺ
    ἐποίησας;
ἢ τίς εἰς κατάστασίν σοι ἐλεύσεται ἔκδικος κατὰ ἀδίκων
    ἀνθρώπων;

9¹ δουναι] διδοναι S†
10¹ κρινων δε] κεινων γαρ S*†
10⁴ οτι>S*†

11¹ κεκατηραμενον S†: cf. Thack. p.
208/9

Driver (*Deuteronomy*, p. 104) states that there are four species of hornet in Palestine, two of which live underground or in cavities of rocks: the combined attack of a swarm is known to be fatal. It seems that they were especially prevalent in certain places, hence *ir'ah* "hornet-town" is the name of a place in Josh. 15.33 and *Sfêkeia* "waspland" is cited as an ancient name of Cyprus. It should be mentioned that there is also a metaphorical interpretation of the term *ṣir'ah*, which relies on the use of the simile of bees in Deut. 1.44 and "the terror" in Ex. 23.27, but evidently the Book of Wisdom adheres to the literal interpretation.

9. IN BATTLE: *En parataxei* strictly means "in pitched battle." The battles referred to might be that with Amalek (Ex. 17.8 ff.) or that of Ai (Josh. ch. 8).   WORD: À Lapide refers casually to the double meaning of *dbr* in Hebrew, "a word" and "a pestilence," but the latter has no corroboration anywhere.   AT ONCE: ὑφ'ἕν, according to Goodrick, is a most extraordinary phrase, for which no classical or Hellenistic example is quoted. He thinks that it is probably a slang expression which Pseudo-Solomon had picked up, but Itala (*simul*) and Arab. ("in a single moment") understood it.

10. JUDGING THEM: Different reasons are given for the gradual expulsion of the Canaanites: Ex. 23.29 "lest the land become desolate and the beast of the field multiply against thee"; Jud. 2.29 "that by them I may prove Israel, whether they will keep the way of the Lord to walk therein as their

That they might perish by little and little.

⁹Not being unable to make the impious subject to the righteous in battle,

Or with terrible beasts or a stern word to destroy them at once.

10   ¹⁰But judging them by little and little thou gavest them a place of repentance,

Not ignoring that their generation was evil,

And their wickedness inborn,

And that their way of thinking could not change for ever.

¹¹For it was a seed accursed from the beginning,

Nor being afraid of anyone didst thou grant them impunity for the things wherein they sinned.

¹²For who shall say: What hast thou done?

Or who shall oppose thy judgment?

And who shall accuse thee for the perished nations whom thou didst make?

Or who shall come to stand before thee as an avenger for the unrighteous?

---

fathers did keep it, or not." PLACE OF REPENTANCE: The sense seems to be "opportunity of repentance." In this sense the phrase is frequent in Hellenistic Greek, but absent in classical Greek. The term seems to have been transferred bodily from the Latin, cf. Livy, XXIV. 26 locus poenitendi (Goodrick). WICKEDNESS INBORN: This evidently contradicts 1.12 ff., especially v. 16 "ungodly men called death unto them." Some discovered here the doctrine of original sin, but according to Farrar "to talk here of the doctrine of original sin is an anachronism." WAY OF THINKING: Logismos is variously rendered: A.V. following Itala "cogitation," R.V. following Pal. Syr. "manner of thought." See further Gen. 6.5 and 8.21.

11. A SEED ACCURSED: Probably an allusion to the curse of Canaan (Gen. 9.25). NOR BEING AFRAID: The Canaanite stock was doomed as an entity, but room was left for individual amendment, as in the case of Rahab (Josh. ch. 2), whose virtues of faith, hospitality and prophecy delivered her and her family from utter destruction (Clem. Rom., XII). Grimm places v. 11b in the following section.

12. FOR: God's leniency was not due to fear, but to His exalted supremacy. WHO SHALL ACCUSE THEE: There is no one in a position to criticise God for His leniency towards nations. COME TO STAND BEFORE THEE: Perhaps an allusion to the pursuit of a murderer by the avenging kinsman (Num. ch. 35).

¹³οὔτε γὰρ θεός ἐστιν πλὴν σοῦ, ᾧ μέλει περὶ πάντων,
ἵνα δείξῃς ὅτι οὐκ ἀδίκως ἔκρινας,
¹⁴οὔτε βασιλεὺς ἢ τύραννος ἀντοφθαλμῆσαι δυνήσεταί σοι
περὶ ὧν ἐκόλασας.
15 ¹⁵δίκαιος δὲ ὢν δικαίως τὰ πάντα διέπεις
αὐτὸν τὸν μὴ ὀφείλοντα κολασθῆναι καταδικάσαι
ἀλλότριον ἡγούμενος τῆς σῆς δυνάμεως.
¹⁶ἡ γὰρ ἰσχύς σου δικαιοσύνης ἀρχή,
καὶ τὸ πάντων σε δεσπόζειν πάντων φείδεσθαί σε ποιεῖ.
¹⁷ἰσχὺν γὰρ ἐνδείκνυσαι ἀπιστούμενος ἐπὶ δυνάμεως
τελειότητι
καὶ ἐν τοῖς εἰδόσι τὸ θράσος ἐξελέγχεις·
¹⁸σὺ δὲ δεσπόζων ἰσχύος ἐν ἐπιεικείᾳ κρίνεις
καὶ μετὰ πολλῆς φειδοῦς διοικεῖς ἡμᾶς·
πάρεστιν γάρ σοι, ὅταν θέλῃς, τὸ δύνασθαι.
¹⁹ Ἐδίδαξας δέ σου τὸν λαὸν διὰ τῶν τοιούτων ἔργων
ὅτι δεῖ τὸν δίκαιον εἶναι φιλάνθρωπον,
καὶ εὐέλπιδας ἐποίησας τοὺς υἱούς σου
ὅτι διδοῖς ἐπὶ ἁμαρτήμασιν μετάνοιαν.

13² δειξῃς] s>Sᶜ   17² ειδοσι(ν)] pr. σε S*†, +σου Sᵒ,
15³ ηγουμενον S*   pr. ουκ A† | θρασος] κρατος Sᵒ |
16² σε ult.>BS*†   εξελεγχεται S*†
17¹ ισχυς γαρ ενδεικνυς S*†

---

13. ANY GOD BESIDE THEE: *Cf.* Deut. 32.39. There is no other god beside
Yahweh to whom He might have to justify His actions.
14. KING OR TYRANT: There is little difference here between the two,
though in classical Greek tyrant is the upstart in contradistinction to the
hereditary king.   TO CONFRONT THEE: *Antofthalmêsai* is a forcible
though late word (not occurring before Polybius), and is rendered "to
look thee in the face" by R.V.
15. INCONSISTENT: A.V. "not agreeable with thy power," R.V. "alien
from thy power."   TO CONDEMN: God possesses unlimited power, but
He never uses it arbitrarily. *Cf.* Philo, *Mos.*, I.24, and *Leg. Alleg.*, III.34.
See also Ps. 62.13.
16. THY MIGHT: The meaning of this line seems to be that God's justice is
due to His unlimited power. As Farrar puts it very clearly: "Man's injustice is partly due to his feebleness and selfishness, and God being
omnipotent has none of that bias to do wrong which springs from weakness." *Cf.* also Reuss: "Man's power is limited, and he loves to make
others feel it ... God, because His power is unlimited, does not suffer in the

¹³For neither is there any God beside thee that cares for all,

That thou mightest show that thou judgest not un-righteously.

¹⁴Neither is there king or tyrant that shall be able to con-front thee concerning those whom thou hast punished.

¹⁵But being just thou disposest all things justly,

Deeming it inconsistent with thy power

To condemn him who deserves not to be punished.

¹⁶For thy might is the beginning of righteousness,

And that thou art lord of all makes thee to spare all.

¹⁷For thou displayest thy power when disbelieved as to the perfection of thy might,

And in case of them that know thou dost convict their rashness.

¹⁸But thou being master of might judgest with fairness,

And with much leniency dost thou govern us,

For power is at thy command when thou wilt.

¹⁹Now by such works didst thou teach thy people

That the righteous man must needs be a lover of men,

And madest thy sons to be of good hope

That thou grantest repentance for sins.

---

opinion of wise men for using it in moderation." Itala renders *ischus* er-roneously by *virtus*.

17. DISBELIEVED: *Cf.* Ex. 5.2 with regard to Pharaoh.   DOST CONVICT THEIR RASHNESS: When men insolently disregard God's power or even defy it, God puts them to confusion.

18. MASTER OF MIGHT: Itala *dominator virtutis. Cf.* Ps. 78.38.   WITH FAIRNESS: So Goodrick; A.V. "equity"; R.V. "gentleness." The purport of *en epieikeia* is to express moderation of boundless power.   LENIENCY: R.V. "forbearance." God is gentle because He is lenient or forbearing.

19. BY SUCH WORKS: Referring back to 11.15 and 12.8.   DIDST THOU TEACH: Namely the lessons that righteousness is merciful and that re-pentance engenders forgiveness. According to Graetz (*Geschichte*, III, 629, note 3) Pseudo-Solomon here deliberately sets himself to combat the Gentile idea of the Jews as *hostes humani generis*.   THE RIGHTEOUS MAN: *Dikaios* is the strict observer of the ceremonial law as opposed to *filanthrōpos. Cf.* on this point Philo, *Abr.*, § 37.

20   ²⁰εἰ γὰρ ἐχθροὺς παίδων σου καὶ ὀφειλομένους θανάτῳ
μετὰ τοσαύτης ἐτιμωρήσω προσοχῆς καὶ διέσεως
δοὺς χρόνους καὶ τόπον, δι' ὧν ἀπαλλαγῶσι τῆς κακίας,
²¹μετὰ πόσης ἀκριβείας ἔκρινας τοὺς υἱούς σου,
ὧν τοῖς πατράσιν ὅρκους καὶ συνθήκας ἔδωκας ἀγαθῶν
ὑποσχέσεων;
22   Ἡμᾶς οὖν παιδεύων τοὺς ἐχθροὺς ἡμῶν ἐν μυριότητι
μαστιγοῖς,
ἵνα σου τὴν ἀγαθότητα μεριμνῶμεν κρίνοντες,
κρινόμενοι δὲ προσδοκῶμεν ἔλεος.
²³ὅθεν καὶ τοὺς ἐν ἀφροσύνῃ ζωῆς βιώσαντας ἀδίκως
διὰ τῶν ἰδίων ἐβασάνισας βδελυγμάτων·
²⁴καὶ γὰρ τῶν πλάνης ὁδῶν μακρότερον ἐπλανήθησαν
θεοὺς ὑπολαμβάνοντες τὰ καὶ ἐν ζῴοις τῶν αἰσχρῶν
ἄτιμα
νηπίων δίκην ἀφρόνων ψευσθέντες.

20² ετιμωρησας BS | και διεσεως St |
κ. δισεως Vt, κ. διεσωσας pau., κ.
δεησεως B, >A mu.
20³ χρονον A

21¹ μετα ποσης] και μετα πασης Sᶜ(†)
23¹ αφροσυναις St | αδικουσ BS*
24² αισχρων pau.] εσχρων unus cod.,
εχθρων BSA

20. DUE TO DEATH: because of their wickedness and impenitence.   IN-
DULGENCE: Reading dieseôs with א instead of deêseos (supplication) of B
(A omits altogether). The latter is inadmissible despite the reference to
Isa. 65.2 and Prov. 1.24 to justify the idea of supplication of God to
humanity. Some of those who incline to the latter reading adduce the
Heb. tehinah which may mean either "mercy" as in Josh. 11.20 or
"supplication for mercy" as in Ezra 9.8.   TIME AND PLACE: A reads
chronon in the singular, which Grimm prefers on the ground of verbal
assonance so common in Pseudo-Solomon.

21. CAREFULNESS: So R.V.; Goodrick "circumspection." Akribeia here
cannot mean "sharpness, accuracy, precision," since the idea is that of
sparing rather than of exacting the full penalty of the law. Perhaps there is
an allusion here to the continued judgment of Israel by the oppressions of
neighboring nations, as recorded in the Book of Judges.   WHOSE
FATHERS: Abraham, Isaac and Jacob, see Ex. 32.13.

22. THOU SCOURGEST: Properly speaking there is not much of a contrast
between paideuein "chasten" and mastigoun "scourge"; in Prov. 3.12 the
two words are applied to the same form of chastisement, but the author
of Wisdom has a peculiar way of applying terms. Grimm cites II Macc.
6.12 ff. according to which God forbears to punish the other nations till
they fill up the measure of their sins, while the Jews are corrected for the

20 20For if on the enemies of thy servants and on them that
were due to death,
Thou didst take vengeance with so much carefulness
and indulgence,
Giving them time and place to change from their
wickedness;
21With how much carefulness didst thou judge thy sons,
To whose fathers thou gavest oaths and covenants of
good promises?
22Us therefore chastening, thou scourgest our enemies ten
thousandfold,
That when we judge we may ponder on thy goodness,
But when we are judged we may look for pity.
23Wherefore also the unrighteous who lived in folly of life
Thou didst torment through their own abominations.
24For they went astray farther than the ways of error,
Taking as gods those which among the beasts of our
enemies are despised,
Deceived after the manner of foolish infants.

---

slightest sin, so that a delayed vengeance might not be necessary.
23. The author now returns to his favorite theory that the Egyptians
worshipped the very insects by which they were plagued.   WHEREFORE:
Resumes the idea of v. 22a "thou scourgest our enemies."   THE
UNRIGHTEOUS: Namely the Egyptians, as is evident from the reference to
animal worship in v. 24.   FOLLY OF LIFE: Moral folly that leads to
idolatry and atheism.   THEIR OWN ABOMINATIONS: An allusion to the
visitation upon the sacred Nile, the murrain upon the cattle, the plagues of
frogs, lice, flies, etc. bdelugmata is employed by LXX to designate
heathen idols and stands for Heb. to'ebot, or shekeṣ or mezimmah in Jer.
11.15.
24. THE BEASTS OF OUR ENEMIES: So Freudenthal (JQR., III (1891),
744 f.) against all versions rendering echthrōn "their enemies." The latter
is unintelligible: that the Egyptians should worship things which their
enemies, the Israelites, despised was no great proof of folly; but "our
enemies" has reference to the Gentiles and yields good sense. The Egyptians worshipped beasts which even Gentiles like themselves despised—
not merely things like swine which were abhorrent to the Jews. Philo
(Decal., § 16) charges the Egyptians with worshipping oxen, rams, goats,
lions, crocodiles, asps, dogs, cats, wolves, the ibis, hawks, fishes and even
parts of fishes. Cf. also the scornful tirade against Egyptian worship in
Juvenal's Satire XVI.

25 ²⁵διὰ τοῦτο ὡς παισὶν ἀλογίστοις
τὴν κρίσιν εἰς ἐμπαιγμὸν ἔπεμψας.
²⁶οἱ δὲ παιγνίοις ἐπιτιμήσεως μὴ νουθετηθέντες
ἀξίαν θεοῦ κρίσιν πειράσουσιν.
²⁷ἐφ᾽ οἷς γὰρ αὐτοὶ πάσχοντες ἠγανάκτουν,
ἐπὶ τούτοις, οὓς ἐδόκουν θεούς, ἐν αὐτοῖς κολαζόμενοι
ἰδόντες, ὃν πάλαι ἠρνοῦντο εἰδέναι, θεὸν ἐπέγνωσαν
ἀληθῆ·
διὸ καὶ τὸ τέρμα τῆς καταδίκης ἐπ᾽ αὐτοὺς ἐπῆλθεν.

13 ¹ Μάταιοι μὲν γὰρ πάντες ἄνθρωποι φύσει, οἷς παρῆν
θεοῦ ἀγνωσία
καὶ ἐκ τῶν ὁρωμένων ἀγαθῶν οὐκ ἴσχυσαν εἰδέναι τὸν
ὄντα
οὔτε τοῖς ἔργοις προσέχοντες ἐπέγνωσαν τὸν τεχνίτην,

27³ ειδεναι > S
27⁴ αυτων Sᶜᵗ (-τον S*ᵗ)

---

25. This seems to imply that the earlier plagues, such as the frogs, were of a lighter nature, and might be considered as a gentle rebuke of idolatry. The later plagues increased in severity until they culminated in the destruction of the first-born. AS A MOCKERY: Cf. Ex. 10.2 which LXX renders *hosa empepaicha tois Aiguptiois* and R.V. margin "how I have mocked the Egyptians." See Targum Yerushalmi to Gen. 21.9, according to which Ishmael the son of Hagar the Egyptian was cast out because he served foreign idols.

26. BY MOCKERIES OF CORRECTION: The Greek phrase strictly means "by childplay of correction." Itala has *ludibriis et increpationibus*, which may be a hendiadys. For play in connection with God see Philo, *Mos.*, I.38: "The miracle of the smitten rock was God's play, compared with His creative works which are really great."

27. The sense of this verse, according to Churton, is as follows: "The vexation which they felt at these petty chastisements which befell them through their gods constrained them to acknowledge the true God whom they once denied." It is quite evident that *epi* is not used in the same sense in the first two lines. REFUSED: or, as R.V. margin has it, "denied that they knew him." Similarly 16.16. Cf. Ex. 5.2. WHEREFORE: when they recognized the true God and still refused to let the people of Israel go. FINAL CONDEMNATION: This undoubtedly refers to the death of the first-born and the drowning of Pharaoh's host in the Red Sea.

Having dealt with the idols worshipped by the Egyptians the writer

25   25Therefore, as to children without reason,
       Thou didst send thy judgment as a mockery.
         26But they that be not brought to a right mind by
             mockeries of correction
       Shall experience a judgment worthy of God.
         27For through the sufferings whereat they were indig-
             nant,
       Being punished by means of those very creatures whom
             they esteemed gods,
       Knowing him whom before they refused to know, they
             recognized the true God,
       Wherefore also final condemnation came upon them.

13   1   For vain indeed are all men by nature in whom was
             ignorance of God,
           And who from the good things that are seen could not
             know him that is,
           Nor giving heed to his works recognized the work-
             man.

---

goes on to a disquisition on idolatry in general in chapters 13–15. He
divides idolaters into two groups, those who worship nature or natural
phenomena and those who worship animals or manufactured idols. For
the former some excuse might be found; the latter deserve nothing but
contempt and abhorrence.

1. The sense of this verse seems to be: All men must be fools who can
look upon the works of God and not recognize God in them.   VAIN . . .
BY NATURE: Thus differing from those illuminated by wisdom. *Mataioi*
"vain" here corresponds to "miserable" in v. 10 and is repeatedly used of
the folly of idolaters, *cf. e. g.* Jer. 2.5 LXX.   THE GOOD THINGS etc.: The
argument from created things to the character of their creator is met with
in the Bible, see Isa. 42.5, Ps. 19.1, and Job 36.22 ff.   HIM THAT IS:
ton onta is no doubt derived from Ex. 3.14 *egō eimi ho ōn. Cf.* Philo,
Decal., § 13. Philo uses this philosophical term to develop his argument
against anthropomorphism, claiming that God is a pure existence, without
human qualities or modifications. This is not the view of Pseudo-Solomon,
who attributes to God pity and patience (11.23, 12.19, 15.1 ff.) and a
desire to improve the sinner (11.25).   THE WORKMAN: For God as
technitēs cf. Philo, *Q.D.S.I.*, § 6, and *Leg. Alleg.*, III.32. The term is applied also to Wisdom in 8.6, *q. v.*

²ἀλλ' ἢ πῦρ ἢ πνεῦμα ἢ ταχινὸν ἀέρα
ἢ κύκλον ἄστρων ἢ βίαιον ὕδωρ
ἢ φωστῆρας οὐρανοῦ πρυτάνεις κόσμου θεοὺς ἐνόμισαν.
³ὧν εἰ μὲν τῇ καλλονῇ τερπόμενοι ταῦτα θεοὺς ὑπελάμ-
βανον,
γνώτωσαν πόσῳ τούτων ὁ δεσπότης ἐστὶ βελτίων,
ὁ γὰρ τοῦ κάλλους γενεσιάρχης ἔκτισεν αὐτά·
⁴εἰ δὲ δύναμιν καὶ ἐνέργειαν ἐκπλαγέντες,
νοησάτωσαν ἀπ' αὐτῶν πόσῳ ὁ κατασκευάσας αὐτὰ
δυνατώτερός ἐστιν·
5 ⁵ἐκ γὰρ μεγέθους καὶ καλλονῆς κτισμάτων
ἀναλόγως ὁ γενεσιουργὸς αὐτῶν θεωρεῖται.
⁶ἀλλ' ὅμως ἐπὶ τούτοις μέμψις ἐστὶν ὀλίγη,

2² αστερων Sᶜ: cf. 7 19
3¹ ταυτα θεους] θεους Bᵗ, ταυθ S*(ᵗ),
τουθ Sᶜᵗ

4¹ ει] εις ASᶜ | δυναμει και ενεργεια Bᵗ:
cf. Helbing Kasussyntax p. 35
5¹ και καλλονης] tr. BS*, και>A
6¹ επι] ετι Aᵗ

---

2. For the worship of the elements see Philo, Decal., § 12: "Some have deified the four elements, earth, water, air, and fire, and others the sun and the moon and the stars; others the heaven only, and some the whole universe; and the creator, governor, and director they have obscured behind their false ascriptions. For they call the earth Demeter, the sea Poseidon, the air Hera, the sun Apollo, the moon Artemis, and fire Hephaestus." E. Pfleiderer (Heraklit, p. 302), followed by Bois (Essai, p. 293), thinks that Greek philosophy is here referred to: Heraclitus ascribed everything to fire, Thales to water, Anaximenes to air, Pythagoras to heat, and so on. Diogenes Laertius (Proem, VI.6) states that the Magi consider fire, earth, and water as gods, but condemn the worship of images. Herodotus (Hist., I.131) says of the Persians that they worship all the powers of nature. WIND: The Egyptians are known to have worshipped the winds in connection with the annual overflow of the Nile. Mention should be made also of the Greek cult of Aeolus. As to the Persians, cf. the preceding comment. THE CYCLE OF THE STARS: Pythagoras, who regarded heat as the source of life, considered sun, moon and stars as gods (Diog. Laert., II.8, 27). RAGING WATER: The Egyptians worshipped water, see Philo, Mos., I.17. THE LIGHTS OF HEAVEN: Itala renders the Greek phrase "Sun and Moon." The Egyptians worshipped the sun and moon in the form of Isis and Osiris, see Jer. 43.13. That the Israelites themselves were attracted to the worship of the heavenly bodies is apparent from Deut. 4.19, 17.3; II Kings 17.16, 21.3; Jer. 7.18, 8.2, 19.13, 44.15; Zeph. 1.5; Ezek. 8.16. RULERS OF THE WORLD: This applies to all sorts of gods mentioned above, not to sun and moon only. Prutaneis for

²But either fire, or wind, or swift air,
Or the cycle of the stars, or raging water,
Or the lights of heaven, rulers of the world, they thought
to be gods.
³Yet if they delighting in their beauty supposed these
things to be gods,
Let them perceive how much the master of these things
is superior,
For it was the originator of beauty that created them.
⁴But if it was through awe at their power and effect,
Let them understand from them how much more powerful is he that ordered them.

5 ⁵For from the greatness of beauty and of creation
Correspondingly the creator of them is recognized.
⁶But yet for these there is small blame,

"rulers" is an affected word and is characeristic of Pseudo-Solomon.

3. DELIGHTING IN THEIR BEAUTY: The commentators never tire of pointing out that this is a Greek trait, entirely foreign to the Jews. Yet, in view of Ps. ch. 19 and 104, Job ch. 39, and the Song of Songs, it is absurd to maintain that the Jews were altogether blind to the beauties of nature. ORIGINATOR OF BEAUTY: *Cf.* Philo, *Praem. et Poen.*, § 7. On beauty in nature being the revelation of God's majesty see Ginzberg, *Legends*, V, 60.

4. IF IT WAS etc.: Supply "supposed these things to be gods" from v. 3 above. The implication is that some who are not affected by the beauty of nature might be struck by its power and vibrant vitality. HOW MUCH MORE POWERFUL: Just as the creator of beauty must be himself superior in that quality, so the creator of things powerful must be more powerful than they. The artificer is necessarily greater than his work, *cf.* Philo, *Dec.*, § 14.

5. FROM THE GREATNESS OF BEAUTY AND OF CREATION: Undoubtedly the meaning is "from the greatness and beauty of creation," and some commentators accordingly emend the Greek text to read *ek megethous kai kallonês ktismatōn* (Eusebius, Athanasius, Deane, R.V. margin, etc.). CORRESPONDINGLY: So R.V. margin, probably following Jerome's *consequenter* (*ad Damas, ep.*, XXI.10); A.V. "proportionably"; Goodrick "analogously," imitating the Greek, which does not occur in the Septuagint. THE CREATOR: *Genesiourgos* is likewise wanting in the Septuagint.

The argument is similar to that of Job chapters 37–41, but is found also in pagan writers. À Lapide furnishes quotations from Pythagoras, Plato, Xenophon, and Hermes Trismegistus. Gregg remarks that such reasoning only proves the power and beauty of the Creator, but His possession of the higher moral qualities, righteousness and love, must be revealed.

6. FOR THESE: Namely for the worshippers of nature. These men are

καὶ γὰρ αὐτοὶ τάχα πλανῶνται
θεὸν ζητοῦντες καὶ θέλοντες εὑρεῖν·
⁷ἐν γὰρ τοῖς ἔργοις αὐτοῦ ἀναστρεφόμενοι διερευνῶσιν
καὶ πείθονται τῇ ὄψει, ὅτι καλὰ τὰ βλεπόμενα.
⁸πάλιν δ' οὐδ' αὐτοὶ συγγνωστοί·
⁹εἰ γὰρ τοσοῦτον ἴσχυσαν εἰδέναι
ἵνα δύνωνται στοχάσασθαι τὸν αἰῶνα,
τὸν τούτων δεσπότην πῶς τάχιον οὐχ εὗρον;
10　¹⁰ Ταλαίπωροι δὲ καὶ ἐν νεκροῖς αἱ ἐλπίδες αὐτῶν,
οἵτινες ἐκάλεσαν θεοὺς ἔργα χειρῶν ἀνθρώπων,
χρυσὸν καὶ ἄργυρον τέχνης ἐμμελέτημα
καὶ ἀπεικάσματα ζῴων
ἢ λίθον ἄχρηστον χειρὸς ἔργον ἀρχαίας.
¹¹εἰ δὲ καί τις ὑλοτόμος τέκτων εὐκίνητον φυτὸν ἐκπρίσας
περιέξυσεν εὐμαθῶς πάντα τὸν φλοιὸν αὐτοῦ

---

8 συγνωστοι A: cf. 6 6　　　　10³ εμμελετηματα Sᶜ

moved by the world's beauty and endeavor to seek God, but somehow they fail to attain that end.　　THEY TOO: Grimm refers *autoi* to the Jews, who, seeking for God in the wrong way, may go astray; Deane and Bois ascribe it to idolaters, who deserve little reproach, for it was perhaps in seeking for God that they went astray. In either case there is a contradiction of 6.13, which states that any one who seeks wisdom can find her.

9. IF THEY HAD POWER: This takes us back to v. 1 above: there it was said that men failed to rise up to God through His works; here the question is asked: if they could scrutinize God's works, why did they not rise up to God?　　CONJECTURE ABOUT THE WORLD: Itala *aestimare seculum*, A.V. "aim at the world," R.V. "to explore the course of things," Goodrick "to form theories about the world." *Aiōn* is the world in time, while *kosmos* is the world in space. The Hebrew equivalent of *aiōn* is *ólam*. The reference is probably to Greek philosophers and Chaldean star-gazers, *cf.* Philo, *Abr.*, § 15.

10. Here begins a diatribe against idols wrought by human hands, which extends to 14.8 and is considered by some commentators as a separate book in itself. But as a matter of fact it is the logical consequence of the description of the less abominable nature-worship in verses 1–8. For similar invectives against idolatry, *cf.* Deut. 4.28, Isa. 44.9 ff., Jer. 10.3 ff., Ps. 115.4 ff., 135.15 ff. The longest indictment of idolatry is found in the Epistle of Jeremiah (Baruch ch. VI). *Cf.* also the Letter of Aristeas, § 134 ff.　　ON DEAD THINGS: Strictly speaking *en nekrois* means "among the dead men," so Itala and Pal. Syr., hence some commentators interpret

For they too peradventure err,
Seeking God and having the will to find him.
⁷For being conversant with his works they search
diligently,
And believe their sight, that the things seen are
beautiful.
⁸But again even they are not to be excused.
⁹For if they had power to know so much
As to be able to conjecture about the world,
How is it that they did not find sooner the Lord of these
things?

10 ¹⁰But miserable are they and on dead things are their
hopes,
Who called the works of men's hands gods,
Gold and silver, a practice of art,
And likenesses of animals,
Or useless stone, work of an ancient hand.
¹¹Yes, and if some woodcutting craftsman, having sawn
down a handy tree,
Has skilfully stripped away all its bark,

"their hopes of a future life are down among the dead men," namely in
Sheol. Nevertheless most translators prefer to take it in the more suitable
sense of "dead things," adducing as support *nekron* "a dead thing" in
15.17. WORKS OF MEN'S HANDS: *Cf.* Deut. 4.28, II Ki. 19.18, Ps.
115.4, 135.15, and elsewhere. LIKENESSES OF ANIMALS: Like the
golden calf of Aaron (Ex. ch. 32) and the calves of Jeroboam (I Ki. 12.28).
It is quite likely that the author refers to the Egyptian images with human
form and animals' heads. For the animal worship of Egypt see Philo,
Dec., § 16. USELESS STONE: A stone idol, often a meteorite devoid of
shape, *cf.* Ramsay in Hastings' *Dictionary of the Bible*, V, 110 ff.
11. AND IF: This long protasis has its apodosis at the end of verse 13:
"gave it the likeness of the image of a man." The whole passage down to
verse 18 seems to be derived from Isa. 44.9 ff., Jer. 10.3 ff., Baruch ch. 6.
Cf. also Horace (*Satir.*, I.8.1f.):
    Olim truncus eram ficulnus, inutile lignum,
    Cum faber incertus scammum faceretne Priapum,
    Maluit esse deum. Deus inde ego . . .
A HANDY TREE: The Greek is rendered variously: Itala *lignum rectum*, Pal.
Syr. "a tree which was pleasantly moved," Arab. "a fine growing tree,"
Armenian "a fair tree." *Eukinêton* probably means "easily manageable."

καὶ τεχνησάμενος εὐπρεπῶς
κατεσκεύασεν χρήσιμον σκεῦος εἰς ὑπηρεσίαν ζωῆς,
¹²τὰ δὲ ἀποβλήματα τῆς ἐργασίας
εἰς ἑτοιμασίαν τροφῆς ἀναλώσας ἐνεπλήσθη,
¹³τὸ δὲ ἐξ αὐτῶν ἀπόβλημα εἰς οὐθὲν εὔχρηστον,
ξύλον σκολιὸν καὶ ὄζοις συμπεφυκός,
λαβὼν ἔγλυψεν ἐν ἐπιμελείᾳ ἀργίας αὐτοῦ
καὶ ἐμπειρίᾳ συνέσεως ἐτύπωσεν αὐτό,
ἀπείκασεν αὐτὸ εἰκόνι ἀνθρώπου
¹⁴ἢ ζῴῳ τινὶ εὐτελεῖ ὡμοίωσεν αὐτὸ
καταχρίσας μίλτῳ καὶ φύκει ἐρυθήνας χρόαν αὐτοῦ
καὶ πᾶσαν κηλῖδα τὴν ἐν αὐτῷ καταχρίσας
15   ¹⁵καὶ ποιήσας αὐτῷ αὐτοῦ ἄξιον οἴκημα
ἐν τοίχῳ ἔθηκεν αὐτὸ ἀσφαλισάμενος σιδήρῳ.
¹⁶ἵνα μὲν οὖν μὴ καταπέσῃ, προενόησεν αὐτοῦ
εἰδὼς ὅτι ἀδυνατεῖ ἑαυτῷ βοηθῆσαι·
καὶ γάρ ἐστιν εἰκὼν καὶ χρείαν ἔχει βοηθείας.

11³ ευτρεπως S†

12¹ αποβλ.] υπολ(ε)ιμματα A

12² ετοιμ.] υπηρεσιαν A† | αναλωσεως S†

13³ αργιας] εργασιας AS°†

13⁴ συνεσ.] ανεσεως BS*A

14¹ ωμοιωσεν] pr. αφ S

14² χροας S*B°†

14³ fin.]+γηS°

15¹ αυτου>SV†

USEFUL etc.: This is probably intended as a contrast to "useless" in the preceding verse. *Cf.* Baruch 6.59 "It is better to be a vessel in a house profitable for that whereof the owner shall have need, than such false gods."

12. THE REFUSE: *Apoblêmata* means "chips." Italia *reliquii* favors the variant reading of A *hupoleimmata*.   TO DRESS HIS FOOD: A touch of irony is added by the fact that before he makes his idol the man calmly sits down to his dinner. *Cf.* Isa. 44.26.

13. OF THESE: Namely of the chips.   A CROOKED PIECE OF WOOD etc. No possible reason can be assigned why the artisan should purposely choose the most refuse and amorphous fragments to make into idols (Farrar).   WITH DILIGENCE IN HIS IDLENESS: So R.V., but Grimm and Goodrick render less effectively "to occupy his spare time." The A text has *ergasias* "labour" instead of *argias*, but this reading lacks the irony of the paradoxical expression.   WITH THE CAREFULNESS OF HIS LEISURE: Reading *empeiria aneseōs* with most MSS and thus obtaining a contradictory expression similar to that preceding it. So also R.V. "by the skill of

And fashioning it in comely wise,

Has contrived a vessel useful for the service of life,

¹²While spending the refuse of his handiwork

To dress his food he became filled.

¹³But taking the refuse of these which served to no
use,

A crooked piece of wood and full of knots,

He carved it with diligence in his idleness,

And fashioned it with the carefulness of his leisure,

Gave it the likeness of the image of a man,

¹⁴Or to some paltry animal made it like,

Smearing it with vermilion and reddening its surface
with rouge,

And smearing over every blemish that is in it,

15   ¹⁵And making for it a room worthy of it,

Set it in a wall, making it fast with iron;

¹⁶He took thought for it therefore that it might not
fall,

Knowing that it is powerless to help itself,

For indeed it is an image and has need of help.

---

his indolence." Some Greek MSS have *suneseōs* instead of *aneseōs*, and
these are followed by Itala, but this reading again loses in effectiveness by
destroying the paradox and eliminating the sarcasm. Deane interprets
this passage as follows: "with such skill as carelessness gives."

14. VERMILION: *Cf.* Pliny, *H.N.*, XXXV.45, where the statue of Jupiter is
depicted as painted red on festal days, and Ovid, *Fasti*, I.415, where the
statue of Priapus is said to have been painted red. Grimm quotes Pausanias to the effect that the images of Dionysus, Hermes, and Pan were
painted vermilion. Vergil, *Eclogues*, X.25 ff., depicts Pan as "red with
vermilion." Tibullus, II.I.55, speaks not only of red Bacchus, but also of
his rustic worshipper being painted with vermilion.   BLEMISH: So
Goodrick, A.V. "spot," R.V. "stain," Arab, "fills up every hollow and
chink in it with mud." Gregg finds here a touch of sarcasm: "the blem-
ishes are matter of indifference; they are covered over with paint, just as
the marks on white animals brought for sacrifice were chalked over."

15. A ROOM: Probably a niche in the wall, hence the need of fastening it
with iron.

16. MIGHT NOT FALL: *Cf.* Bar. 6.27 "If they fall to the ground at any time
they cannot rise up again of themselves." See also Isa. 46.7 concerning
the helplessness of the image. On the fall of Dagon *cf.* I Sam. ch. 5.

¹⁷περὶ δὲ κτημάτων καὶ γάμων αὐτοῦ καὶ τέκνων προσευ-
χόμενος
οὐκ αἰσχύνεται τῷ ἀψύχῳ προσλαλῶν
καὶ περὶ μὲν ὑγιείας τὸ ἀσθενὲς ἐπικαλεῖται,
¹⁸περὶ δὲ ζωῆς τὸ νεκρὸν ἀξιοῖ,
περὶ δὲ ἐπικουρίας τὸ ἀπειρότατον ἱκετεύει,
περὶ δὲ ὁδοιπορίας τὸ μηδὲ βάσει χρῆσθαι δυνάμενον,
¹⁹περὶ δὲ πορισμοῦ καὶ ἐργασίας καὶ χειρῶν ἐπιτυχίας
τὸ ἀδρανέστατον ταῖς χερσὶν εὐδράνειαν αἰτεῖται.

14 ¹ Πλοῦν τις πάλιν στελλόμενος καὶ ἄγρια μέλλων
διοδεύειν κύματα
τοῦ φέροντος αὐτὸν πλοίου σαθρότερον ξύλον ἐπιβοᾶται.
²ἐκεῖνο μὲν γὰρ ὄρεξις πορισμῶν ἐπενόησεν,
τεχνῖτις δὲ σοφία κατεσκεύασεν·
³ἡ δὲ σή, πάτερ, διακυβερνᾷ πρόνοια,

17¹ προσευχομ.] προς>S   1² πλοιου] ξυλου A
18² ικετευει>St
19² αιτειται] επικαλειται S*t : ex 17³

---

17. PRAYING: He has no shame in praying to a dead thing to grant him a good marriage and a large family. Cf. Isa. 44.17 and Jer. 2.27. Philo says in Dec., § 14: "I know that some who have made images pray and sacrifice to the things they have themselves made, when it would be much better to worship one of their hands, or even their hammers or anvils or tools."   FOR HEALTH: Cf. Bar. 6.36 f. "They can save no man from death . . . they cannot restore a blind man to his sight."

18. This and the following verse present a well balanced series of paradoxes or oxymoron constructions not uncommon in biblical literature. CANNOT EVEN WALK: See Bar. 6.26: "Having no feet they are borne upon shoulders"; cf. also Ps. 115.7. For further ridicule of such motionless gods cf. I Ki. 18.27.

19. HANDIWORK: So R.V. margin; R.V. "getting," Goodrick "trade." The Greek word means literally "trade, business," cf. Ecclus. 38.34. ABILITY: Eudraneia, "corporeal well-being, physical strength," is peculiar to Pseudo-Solomon.

The folly of idolatry and its disastrous effect upon the life of men are illustrated first by seafarers and navigators who trust in a piece of wood.

1. A PIECE OF WOOD: An idol is known to have been affixed at the prow or the stern of ancient vessels. In Acts 28.11 the sign of the ship was the Dioscuri, Castor and Pollux, who were regarded as protectors of voyagers. Herodotus (Hist., III.37), speaking of the image of Hephaestus, compares

¹⁷Yet praying to it about his goods and his marriage and
his children,

He has no shame in addressing the lifeless thing.

Yes, and for health he calls upon that which is weak,

¹⁸And for life beseeches the dead thing,

And for aid supplicates that which is utterly inex-
perienced,

And for a journey that which cannot even walk,

¹⁹And for gain and for handiwork and for success of his
hands

He beseeches ability of that which with its hands is
most unable.

14 ¹   Again, one preparing to sail and about to journey
over raging waves,

Calls upon a piece of wood more rotten than the vessel
that carries him.

²For this the desire of gain devised

And an artificer built it by wisdom.

³But it is thy providence, O Father, that guides,

---

it to the dwarf images of the Pataeci which the Phoenicians carried on
their warships. On invoking gods in a storm *cf*. Jon. 1.5.   MORE
ROTTEN: The meaning implied is that while the wood for the ship is none
too strong to protect life, the idol is actually made out of refuse wood, see
13.13 above.

2. THE DESIRE OF GAIN: Which always accompanies commercial enter-
prise, whether terrestrial or maritime.   AN ARTIFICER BUILT IT BY
WISDOM: Following the reading τεχνίτης σοφίᾳ adopted by Goodrick and
others (so also Itala). Variants are τεχνίτης σοφία, adopted by R.V. "an artificer, even wisdom, built it"; and τεχνῖτις σοφία found in Syroh. and corroborated by Clem. Alex., *Stromata*, VI, 11, *cf*. also 7.22. The real crux here is
this: is the wisdom mentioned here divine or human? If divine, the
question naturally arises: how could a ship sailing under the patronage of a
heathen idol be built under the direction of God's wisdom? One is therefore constrained to conclude with Itala (*artifex sapientia fabricavit sua*)
that the wisdom involved here is human, man's intelligence, which is
exerted on behalf of constructing a sound commercial ship, more lasting
than the idol. Moreover, the man who built the ship was a craftsman, not
a mere woodcutter who in an idle hour hacks refuse wood into an idol.

3. PROVIDENCE: *Pronoia* in the sense of "providence" occurs here (and
also in 17.2) for the first time in the Greek Bible. Some see in it a Platonism

ὅτι ἔδωκας καὶ ἐν θαλάσσῃ ὁδὸν
καὶ ἐν κύμασι τρίβον ἀσφαλῆ
⁴δεικνὺς ὅτι δύνασαι ἐκ παντὸς σῴζειν,
ἵνα κἂν ἄνευ τέχνης τις ἐπιβῇ.

5   ⁵θέλεις δὲ μὴ ἀργὰ εἶναι τὰ τῆς σοφίας σου ἔργα·
διὰ τοῦτο καὶ ἐλαχίστῳ ξύλῳ πιστεύουσιν ἄνθρωποι
ψυχὰς
καὶ διελθόντες κλύδωνα σχεδίᾳ διεσώθησαν.
⁶καὶ ἀρχῆς γὰρ ἀπολλυμένων ὑπερηφάνων γιγάντων
ἡ ἐλπὶς τοῦ κόσμου ἐπὶ σχεδίας καταφυγοῦσα
ἀπέλιπεν αἰῶνι σπέρμα γενέσεως τῇ σῇ κυβερνηθεῖσα
χειρί.
⁷εὐλόγηται γὰρ ξύλον, δι' οὗ γίνεται δικαιοσύνη·

4¹ παντων A   5¹ σου>SV†
4² ινα>S⁰

---

on the part of the author, others take it as an indication of a propensity to Stoic philosophy, pointing to *Kubernan* too as a favorite Stoic expression. But, as pointed out by Goodrick, the Stoic *pronoia* was very little more than the *anima mundi, koinos logos* or *heimarmenê;* the Platonic or rather Socratic πρόνοια, as represented by the teleological argument in Xenophon's *Mem.*, I.IV.2, is really the providence of God, like Wisdom's. And yet, although the word is new in biblical Greek and may have been borrowed from Plato, the idea is old, as may be seen from Ps. 145.9. Drummond (*Philo,* I, 190 ff.) points out that the idea of providence is a natural consequence of Pseudo-Solomon's theological system, such as it is. He does not consider God as merely *ho ōn*, apart from all interference in human affairs, as Philo seems to do, but as a loving father who, "if he had hated anything would not have made it." Philo wrote several books on the subject of divine providence, but his views, as set forth by Drummond, II, 55 ff., are anything but clear and sometimes even self-contradictory. *Cf.* also Wolfson, *Philo,* II, 292 ff. Mention must be made also of Bois (*Essai,* pp. 238 and 264), who sees in *pronoia* nothing more nor less than another designation of Wisdom.   A WAY EVEN IN THE SEA: Refers to the passage of the Red Sea, *cf.* Isa. 43.16, 51.10, Ps. 77.20, 107.30 LXX.

4. FROM ALL: R.V. adds "danger." God is able to save men from all trouble and danger, not so the lifeless idol, *cf.* 13.17 ff.   WITHOUT ART: Itala curiously reads *sine rate* instead of *sine arte*, which may easily be explained as a scribal error, but Coverdale and others accept the former reading which means "without ship" and hence referring to the Red Sea passage. However, as pointed out by Gregg, Pseudo-Solomon can hardly suggest anything so paradoxical as that God could carry men on the sea without vessels.

For thou hast given a way even in the sea,
And in the waves a safe path,
⁴Showing that thou art able to save from all,
So that even without art a man may put to sea.

5   ⁵But thou willest that the works of thy wisdom should
not be idle;
Therefore do men entrust their lives to even the
slenderest timber,
And passing through the surge on a raft are come safely
through.
⁶For in the beginning also, when proud giants perished,
The hope of the world, escaping on a raft,
Left behind for the age a seed of generation, steered by
thy hand.
⁷For blessed is the wood whereby comes righteousness.

5. SHOULD NOT BE IDLE: The meaning seems to be that God will have the
works of wisdom (perhaps equivalent here to nature) distributed for the
good of mankind.   THE SLENDEREST TIMBER: Gregg quotes Diogenes
Laertius (I.8, 103) to the effect that the Scythian philosopher Anacharsis,
having learnt that the thickness of a ship's sides was four fingers' breadth,
said "That is all the distance between the passengers and death."   A
RAFT: The ship is so frail in view of the waves that the author refers to it as
a raft. In v. 6 the same word is used of Noah's ark.   COME SAFELY
THROUGH: *Diesôthêsan* is generally characterized as a gnomic aorist, but
no doubt it is used here as a preparation for the reversion to history in the
next verse.
6. IN THE BEGINNING: *Archês* is not found in this sense, but it is employed
here by analogy with *nuktos* "in the night," *cheimonôs* "in the winter," etc.
THE HOPE OF THE WORLD: Namely Noah and his family.   A RAFT: *Cf.*
the preceding verse. *Schedia* is used of any vessel that is not sound or not
built in accordance with the shipwright's art.   A SEED OF GENERATION:
Itala *semen nativitatis*, seed of a new generation of men. *Cf.* Philo, *Mos.*,
II, § 61, and *Abr.*, § 22.
7. BLESSED IS THE WOOD: This undoubtedly refers to Noah's ark: blessed
is the ark whereby a righteous seed was preserved in the person of Noah,
the righteous man. Some would refer it to Aaron's rod. It was quite
natural that the Church Fathers seized upon this verse as a reference to
the cross, which is often called ξύλον in the New Testament (I Pet. 2.24,
Gal. 3.13, Acts 5.30, 10.39, 13.29). Graetz as naturally stamped it as a
Christian interpolation (*Geschichte*, III, 630).

⁸τὸ χειροποίητον δέ, ἐπικατάρατον αὐτὸ καὶ ὁ ποιήσας
αὐτό,
ὅτι ὁ μὲν ἠργάζετο, τὸ δὲ φθαρτὸν θεὸς ὠνομάσθη.
⁹ἐν ἴσῳ γὰρ μισητὰ θεῷ καὶ ὁ ἀσεβῶν καὶ ἡ ἀσέβεια αὐτοῦ.
10 ¹⁰καὶ γὰρ τὸ πραχθὲν σὺν τῷ δράσαντι κολασθήσεται.
¹¹διὰ τοῦτο καὶ ἐν εἰδώλοις ἐθνῶν ἐπισκοπὴ ἔσται,
ὅτι ἐν κτίσματι θεοῦ εἰς βδέλυγμα ἐγενήθησαν
καὶ εἰς σκάνδαλα ψυχαῖς ἀνθρώπων
καὶ εἰς παγίδα ποσὶν ἀφρόνων.
¹² Ἀρχὴ γὰρ πορνείας ἐπινοια εἰδώλων,
εὕρεσις δὲ αὐτῶν φθορὰ ζωῆς.
¹³οὔτε γὰρ ἦν ἀπ’ ἀρχῆς οὔτε εἰς τὸν αἰῶνα ἔσται·
¹⁴κενοδοξίᾳ γὰρ ἀνθρώπων εἰσῆλθεν εἰς τὸν κόσμον,
καὶ διὰ τοῦτο σύντομον αὐτῶν τὸ τέλος ἐπενοήθη.

8² οτι] και S*†   14¹ εισηλθεν] pr. θανατος S*A

12² ευρεσεις BA† | αυτω S*†

8. THAT WHICH IS MADE WITH HANDS: *Cheiropoiêton* may be taken with *xulon* understood. The adjective itself is employed in LXX to render the Hebrew *elil* "idol," cf. Lev. 26.1, Isa. 2.18, 10.11, 19.1, etc. Margoliouth (*op. cit.*, p. 265) argues that the ark also was made by hand, but cf. Freudenthal's refutation in *JQR.*, III, 722 ff.   ACCURSED: Antithesis to v. 7 beginning with "blessed."

9. THE IMPIOUS AND HIS IMPIETY: The abstract *asebeia* stands almost for the concrete idol, and both doer and deed are equally abominable, cf. Hos. 9.10.

10. THAT WHICH IS MADE etc.: *To prachthen* strictly means "the thing done" and probably refers to the idol, which is almost personified. On the perishing of the idols themselves cf. Isa. 2.18 ff. Margoliouth (*op. cit.*, p. 266) quotes the Midr. Tanhuma on Gen. 47.29: "As the worshipper is punished, so is the thing which he worships." Goodrick further elucidates: "So in old English law, when it was possible, some form of vengeance was exacted from the *corpus delicti* as well as from the murderer." Margoliouth, who argues in favor of a Hebrew original of the Book of Wisdom, further contends that the latter had the words *'ebed and ne'ebad*, which were wrongly translated "doer" and "done," when they should have been rendered "worshipper" and "worshipped," *'ebed* bearing both meanings in Hebrew and Aramaic. This observation, Margoliouth claims, helps to elucidate the preceding verses: "That wood is blessed by which righteousness comes about; but that which is made by the hand is accursed, both it and its maker, because he was making it, and it being corruptible, was named god."

⁸But that which is made with hands is accursed,
    itself and he that made it,
He because he made it, and the corruptible thing
    because it was called god.
⁹For equally hateful to God are the impious and his
    impiety.

10 ¹⁰For that which is made shall be punished with him that
    made it.
¹¹Therefore shall there be a visitation also of the idols of
    the nations,
For as God's creatures they become an abomination,
And stumbling blocks to the souls of men,
And a snare to the feet of the foolish.
¹²For the devising of idols is the beginning of fornication,
And the invention of them the corruption of life.
¹³For they were not from the beginning, nor shall they
    abide for ever.
¹⁴For through the vainglory of men they entered into the
    world,
And therefore was a speedy end devised for them.

---

11. THEREFORE: Explains the preceding verse.   GOD'S CREATURES: Being part of God's creation, which is intended for the good of men, they have been perverted to its destruction.   AN ABOMINATION: Not only in the eyes of God, but, as shown in the following line, a cause of ruin to men. *Bdelugma* seems to be used in LXX for every opprobrious term applied to idols.

12. FORNICATION: A.V. specifies "spiritual fornication," meaning idolatry, but this is hardly necessary, since fornication is a common figure in the Scriptures for abandoning Yahweh for other deities, *cf.* Ex. 34.15 f., Deut. 31.16, and especially Ezek. ch. 16 and 23.   CORRUPTION OF LIFE: In the moral sense, see v. 27.

13. The idols are ephemeral and quickly pass away, *cf.* Deut. 32.17, Isa. 2.18, Zech. 13.2, etc. According to Grimm, Pseudo-Solomon stressed here two points: first, that monotheism was the original religion of man; second, that the Mosaic law was destined to spread over all the earth.

14. ENTERED INTO THE WORLD: This phrase is expressive of crossing the frontiers of a kingdom. The idea is that idols have been introduced into the world in violation of God's order of things.   A SPEEDY END: Man may devise idols (v. 12), but God devises a speedy end to their existence.

15　¹⁵ἀώρῳ γὰρ πένθει τρυχόμενος πατὴρ
　　τοῦ ταχέως ἀφαιρεθέντος τέκνου εἰκόνα ποιήσας
　　τόν ποτε νεκρὸν ἄνθρωπον νῦν ὡς θεὸν ἐτίμησεν
　　καὶ παρέδωκεν τοῖς ὑποχειρίοις μυστήρια καὶ τελετάς·
　　¹⁶εἶτα ἐν χρόνῳ κρατυνθὲν τὸ ἀσεβὲς ἔθος ὡς νόμος
　　ἐφυλάχθη.
　　¹⁷καὶ τυράννων ἐπιταγαῖς ἐθρησκεύετο τὰ γλυπτά,
　　οὓς ἐν ὄψει μὴ δυνάμενοι τιμᾶν ἄνθρωποι διὰ τὸ μακρὰν
　　οἰκεῖν
　　τὴν πόρρωθεν ὄψιν ἀνατυπωσάμενοι
　　ἐμφανῆ εἰκόνα τοῦ τιμωμένου βασιλέως ἐποίησαν,
　　ἵνα ὡς παρόντα τὸν ἀπόντα κολακεύωσιν διὰ τῆς σπουδῆς.
　　¹⁸εἰς ἐπίτασιν δὲ θρησκείας καὶ τοὺς ἀγνοοῦντας
　　ἡ τοῦ τεχνίτου προετρέψατο φιλοτιμία·
　　¹⁹ὁ μὲν γὰρ τάχα κρατοῦντι βουλόμενος ἀρέσαι
　　ἐξεβιάσατο τῇ τέχνῃ τὴν ὁμοιότητα ἐπὶ τὸ κάλλιον·
20　²⁰τὸ δὲ πλῆθος ἐφελκόμενον διὰ τὸ εὔχαρι τῆς ἐργασίας

15³ ποτε] τοτε BS　　　　　　　　20¹ ευχαρες ACt
17⁵ κολακευσωσιν A

15. UNTIMELY GRIEF: *I. e.* grief for an untimely death. This figure of
speech is known as hypallage.　　　AN IMAGE OF A CHILD: Instances of the
worship of deceased children are rather few, the more natural process
being that children venerate their deceased ancestors (*cf.* II Macc. 11.23),
but these few have been collected by À Lapide and copied from him by
succeeding commentators. One of these may be quoted here. Fulgentius
tells of an Egyptian named Syrophanes who erected a statue of his dead
son in his house. To please their master, the members of the family
decorated the statue with flowers, and slaves even fled to it for sanctuary.
Thus the statue gradually became an idol. In connection with this it may
be appropriate to quote also from the Pesikta, ed. Buber, p. 81a: "On the
day that the first-born of one of them died his image was painted in his
house."　　　HONORED AS A GOD: This is very much like the theory of
Euhemerus, who believed that the Greek gods were deified men. *Cf.*
Hastings, *Dictionary of the Bible*, V, 131.

16. CUSTOM WAS KEPT AS A LAW: Refers to the child-worship of the preceding verse which had grown from custom into law: what was begun by a
father among his household is now enforced by a ruler upon his subjects.
There is a contrast here between voluntary worship and dictated worship.

17. BY THE COMMANDS OF DESPOTS: Perhaps this is a reference to Nebuchadnezzar and his great image which he ordered to be worshipped (Dan.
ch. 3). This verse apparently refers to divine honors paid to kings in their

15   ¹⁵For a father afflicted with untimely grief,
      Having made an image of a child quickly reft away,
      Now honoured as a god him which was then a dead man,
      And enjoined upon his dependents mysteries and initia-
        tions.
      ¹⁶Then, in time, being enforced, the impious custom was
        kept as a law,
      ¹⁷And by the commands of despots graven images were
        worshipped;
      Whom men not being able to honour in their presence,
        through distance of dwelling,
      Imagining their likeness from afar,
      Made a visible image of the honoured king,
      That by their zeal they might flatter the absent as
        present.
      ¹⁸But to the exaggeration of worship
      The ambition of the artist urged even the ignorant.
      ¹⁹For he, wishing peradventure to please one in power,
      Forced by his art the likeness into a fairer form.
20   ²⁰But the multitude, allured by the grace of the handiwork,

---

lifetime; *cf.* Ramsay in Hastings, *Dictionary of the Bible*, V, 154, who cites
the case of Lysander, Agesilaus, and the Roman emperors. Augustus was
compelled to protest against his own divine honors. On Caligula's command to erect a statue of himself in the temple of Jerusalem see Josephus,
Antiq., XVIII.VIII.2 ff. On the rise of emperor-worship *cf.* Westcott,
Epistles of St. John, pp. 268 ff.   ABSENT: *scil.* ruler. On the basis of this
word Bousset (*Religion des Judentums*, p. 35) would date our book after
Egypt had come under the Roman Empire.
18. The sense of this verse, according to Gregg, is as follows: "The workman, desiring to secure favor, produced so exquisite a statue, that he
captivated the hearts of a people ever ready to deify any surpassing human excellence; and so those who began with grovelling subservience were
seduced by beauty into actual worship." Herodotus (*Hist.*, V. 47) states
that the Segestans of Sicily actually worshipped as a hero Philip the
pirate, their enemy, because he was so handsome.   THE IGNORANT: *I. e.*
those who do not know what deception is being practiced upon them.
19. TO PLEASE: Painters and sculptors flattered men in power by depicting
them fairer than they naturally were, without any physical defect or
blemish.
20. ALLURED BY THE GRACE: For it is in the nature of men that they deify

τὸν πρὸ ὀλίγου τιμηθέντα ἄνθρωπον νῦν σέβασμα ἐλογίσαντο.

²¹καὶ τοῦτο ἐγένετο τῷ βίῳ εἰς ἔνεδρον,
ὅτι ἢ συμφορᾷ ἢ τυραννίδι δουλεύσαντες ἄνθρωποι
τὸ ἀκοινώνητον ὄνομα λίθοις καὶ ξύλοις περιέθεσαν.

²² Εἶτ' οὐκ ἤρκεσεν τὸ πλανᾶσθαι περὶ τὴν τοῦ θεοῦ
γνῶσιν,
ἀλλὰ καὶ ἐν μεγάλῳ ζῶντες ἀγνοίας πολέμῳ
τὰ τοσαῦτα κακὰ εἰρήνην προσαγορεύουσιν.

²³ἢ γὰρ τεκνοφόνους τελετὰς ἢ κρύφια μυστήρια
ἢ ἐμμανεῖς ἐξάλλων θεσμῶν κώμους ἄγοντες
²⁴οὔτε βίους οὔτε γάμους καθαροὺς ἔτι φυλάσσουσιν,
ἕτερος δ' ἕτερον ἢ λοχῶν ἀναιρεῖ ἢ νοθεύων ὀδυνᾷ.

25 ²⁵πάντα δ' ἐπιμὶξ ἔχει αἷμα καὶ φόνος, κλοπὴ καὶ δόλος,
φθορά, ἀπιστία, τάραχος, ἐπιορκία,

21¹ ενεδρα S*†   24² λοχευων Sᶜ
21³ περιεθηκαν Sᶜ: cf. Thack. p. 255   25¹ επιμιξιν S*(†) (Sᶜ† -ξιαν et om.
22¹ ηρκεσεν]+αυτοις A   εχει)
22² εν μεγαλω] εν> B, μεγαλως S*

---

grace and apotheosize beauty.   AN OBJECT OF WORSHIP: *Sebasma* here
and in 15.17 is a late word, and is used in contrast to God. Philo (*Mon-
arch.*, I.3) condemns the pictorial arts as winning men to idolatry. Elsewhere (*Gigant.*, § 13) he tells how Moses "expelled painting and sculpture from his state, because counterfeiting the nature of truth they devise
deceits and sophisms through the eyes for souls easily deluded."
21. AND THIS: Refers back to verses 15–20. The line itself may be compared to I Ki. 12.30 and 13.34.   IN SLAVERY: By syllepsis the same
verb is used with two substantives of dissimilar character ("calamity"
and "tyranny"), in a sense varying slightly with each.   THE INCOM-
MUNICABLE NAME: The sin consisted in giving the name "god" to things
that are essentially beneath God. *Cf.* Isa. 42.8 "I am the Lord, that is my
name; and my glory will I not give to another, neither my praise to graven
images." See also Philo, *Ebriet.*, § 28.
22. A GREAT WAR: So Goodrick; R.V. has "sore conflict." They live in a
state of war caused by ignorance of their own miserable condition, and yet
call it peace. What this internal state of war is, is enumerated in verses
23 ff. Strikingly similar is Philo (*Conf. Ling.*, § 12): "For they do in peace
everything that is done in war; they plunder, ravage, carry off booty; they
assault, destroy, pollute; they murder treacherously; they murder openly
if they are the more powerful." *Cf.* also Jer. 6.14: "Peace, peace, when

Now counted as an object of worship him that was lately
honored as a man.

²¹And this became a trap to life,

That men, in slavery either to calamity or to tyranny,

Invested stones and stocks with the incommunicable
name.

²²So then it was not enough for them to err concerning the
knowledge of God,

But also, living in the midst of a great war caused by
ignorance,

They call such great evils peace.

²³For either enacting rites of childmurder or secret
mysteries,

Or frantic revels of strange ordinances,

²⁴They keep neither their lives nor marriages pure,

But one either lying in wait for another slays him or
grieves him by adultery.

25   ²⁵And all things are a welter of blood and murder, theft
and deceit,

Corruption, faithlessness, tumult, perjury,

---

there is no peace." E. Pfleiderer (*Heraklit*, p. 316) adduces this passage as
proof of his theory that Pseudo-Solomon held the doctrine of antithesis of
Heraclitus. He considers *eirênê* as a cant term of the mystery-mongers,
and so Margoliouth (*op. cit.*, p. 290) thinks it has some technical significance in connection with religious rites.

23. CHILDMURDER: Refers undoubtedly to the rites of Moloch of ancient
times. Similarly 12.5. *Cf.* Isa. 57.5.   SECRET MYSTERIES: *Cf.* on these
Ramsay in Hastings, *Dict. of the Bible*, V, 124 ff. The Jews had an in-
stinctive hatred of these pagan mysteries.   FRANTIC REVELS: Such as
the Bacchanalian orgies by which the Temple was polluted in the time of
Antiochus (II Macc. 6.1 ff.), or the Phrygian mysteries, or the Babylonian
worship of Aphrodite, and the like. Mysteries and rites derived from
foreign lands were considered abominable.

24. This looks like a description of the immorality in decadent Greece and
Rome, where neither the sacredness of the individual life nor the sanctity
of the marriage tie was observed, and where murder and adultery were
quite common.

25. BLOOD AND MURDER etc.: For a catalogue of the sins in this and the
following verse *cf.* Jer. 7.9 and Hos. 4.2; see also the quotation from Philo's
Conf. Ling. in note on v. 22.

²⁶θόρυβος ἀγαθῶν, χάριτος ἀμνηστία,
ψυχῶν μισμός, γενέσεως ἐναλλαγή,
γάμων ἀταξία, μοιχεία καὶ ἀσέλγεια.
²⁷ἡ γὰρ τῶν ἀνωνύμων εἰδώλων θρησκεία
παντὸς ἀρχὴ κακοῦ καὶ αἰτία καὶ πέρας ἐστίν·
²⁸ἢ γὰρ εὐφραινόμενοι μεμήνασιν ἢ προφητεύουσιν
ψευδῆ
ἢ ζῶσιν ἀδίκως ἢ ἐπιορκοῦσιν ταχέως·
²⁹ἀψύχοις γὰρ πεποιθότες εἰδώλοις
κακῶς ὀμόσαντες ἀδικηθῆναι οὐ προσδέχονται.
30 ³⁰ἀμφότερα δὲ αὐτοὺς μετελεύσεται τὰ δίκαια,
ὅτι κακῶς ἐφρόνησαν περὶ θεοῦ προσέχοντες εἰδώλοις
καὶ ἀδίκως ὤμοσαν ἐν δόλῳ καταφρονήσαντες ὁσιότητος.
³¹οὐ γὰρ ἡ τῶν ὀμνυμένων δύναμις,
ἀλλ' ἡ τῶν ἁμαρτανόντων δίκη
ἐπεξέρχεται ἀεὶ τὴν τῶν ἀδίκων παράβασιν.

26¹ αμνηστια (cf. 19 4)] τ> BS*
30² οτι]+και S*†

26. TROUBLING OF THE GOOD: So R.V. margin following Itala *tumultus honorum*. Similarly Goodrick "Rabbling of good men." This is the better rendering in spite of the fact that *thorubos agathōn* is a peculiar expression not to be found in any good Greek writer. R.V. takes *thorubos* alone, rendering it "turmoil." CONFUSION OF SEX: *Geneseos* is wrongly used here in the sense of *genous*, hence the difficulty experienced by translators and commentators in its rendering. Coverdale has "changing of birth," referring no doubt to the uncertainty of legitimacy which results from adulterous relations. Selden saw in the expression the assumption of feminine costume and manners by men, *cf.* Deut. 22.6. Rabbinic literature points to a somewhat different interpretation: Taking the expression *wa-tishahet-ha-ares* in Gen. 6.11 in the sense of *shihet ibid.* 38.9, it refers it specifically to all sorts of sexual perversion (Sanh. 108a and elsewhere). *Midrash ha-gadol* (ed. Schechter, col. 146) tells of the Sodomites that they had sexual intercourse with all sorts of animals. DISORDER IN MARRIAGE: Not only ubiquitous divorces, but all sorts of irregular unions are meant here, such as the marriage of the Egyptian kings with their sisters. Philo (*Cherub.*, § 27) speaks of "marriages of a day."

27. NAMELESS: It is surprising that Itala renders *anōnumōn* by *infandorum*, "unspeakable," since the word can only mean "unnamed" or "nameless." In support of the former reference might be made to Ex.

²⁶Troubling of the good, forgetfulness of favours,
Pollution of souls, confusion of sex,
Disorder in marriage, adultery and debauchery.
²⁷For the worship of the nameless gods
Is the beginning and cause and end of every evil.
²⁸For either they take pleasure in madness, or prophecy
    lies,
Or live unrighteously, or easily forswear themselves.
²⁹For putting their trust in lifeless idols,
When they have sworn falsely they expect not to be
    punished.
30 ³⁰But for both sins shall justice pursue them,
Because they had evil thoughts of God by giving heed
    to idols,
And swore unrighteously in deceit contemning holiness.
³¹For not the power of them that are sworn by,
But the punishment of them that sin
Pursues ever the transgression of the unrighteous.

23.13, Hos. 2.19, and Ps. 16.4. The latter is equivalent to "without a name," hence "having no real existence," which is most likely here.

28. Enumerates four results of idolatry: madness (Bacchic frenzy), false ideals, injustice, and perjury. *Cf.* Jer. ch. 5, where all these results of idolatry may be found.

29. THEY HAVE SWORN FALSELY: In the same way as among the Jews swearing by God was binding upon all but the wickedest, so among the heathen there were some gods in whose name very few would dare to swear falsely, as, for instance, the Cabiri, see Juvenal III.144 (Gregg). But the Jews considered an oath by an idol as of no consequence.   TO BE PUNISHED: *Adikêthênai* is used loosely for *dikên dounai*.

30. BOTH SINS: Namely giving the name of God to idols and daring to despise the sanctities of life. For the former *cf.* v. 21 above; for the latter see Ezek. 17.18 f.   HOLINESS: An allusion to whatever measure of truth and honor the perjurer might be expected to possess. The writer's argument, according to Gregg, seems to be that even if idols cause no fear, every man ought to carry a fear within him: punishment awaits the man who has stifled that sacred instinct.

31. THE PUNISHMENT etc.: Perjury is followed by vengeance, *cf.* Aristophanes, *Pax*, 1.277; see also Philo, *Jos.*, § 29.   TRANSGRESSION: *Parabasin* is strangely rendered by *praevaricationem* in Itala.

5 ¹ Σὺ δέ, ὁ θεὸς ἡμῶν, χρηστὸς καὶ ἀληθής,
μακρόθυμος καὶ ἐλέει διοικῶν τὰ πάντα.
²καὶ γὰρ ἐὰν ἁμάρτωμεν, σοί ἐσμεν, εἰδότες σου τὸ κράτος·
οὐχ ἁμαρτησόμεθα δέ, εἰδότες ὅτι σοὶ λελογίσμεθα.
³τὸ γὰρ ἐπίστασθαί σε ὁλόκληρος δικαιοσύνη,
καὶ εἰδέναι σου τὸ κράτος ῥίζα ἀθανασίας.
⁴οὔτε γὰρ ἐπλάνησεν ἡμᾶς ἀνθρώπων κακότεχνος ἐπίνοια
οὐδὲ σκιαγράφων πόνος ἄκαρπος,
εἶδος σπιλωθὲν χρώμασιν διηλλαγμένοις,
5 ⁵ὧν ὄψις ἄφροσιν εἰς ὄρεξιν ἔρχεται,
ποθεῖ τε νεκρᾶς εἰκόνος εἶδος ἄπνουν.
⁶κακῶν ἐρασταὶ ἄξιοί τε τοιούτων ἐλπίδων
καὶ οἱ δρῶντες καὶ οἱ ποθοῦντες καὶ οἱ σεβόμενοι.
⁷ Καὶ γὰρ κεραμεὺς ἁπαλὴν γῆν θλίβων ἐπίμοχθον

2¹ αμαρτανωμεν S* | κρατος] κριμα S*†   5¹ αφρονι S* (et A*?) | ορεξιν] ονει-
4³ σπινωθεν S*V†   δος B†

1. BUT THOU: The writer passes now from the lifeless idols to the great
living God of Israel, showing his purifying and restraining influence upon
those who worship Him.   GRACIOUS etc.: The four attributes of God
given here are based on the revelation of Ex. 34.6.
2. EVEN IF WE SIN etc.: Even sin cannot wipe out God's mercy for His
people, who cling to Him under all circumstances on account of His omnipotence and absolute righteousness.   WE SHALL NOT SIN: However,
being accounted God's children they will strive for a perfect life, without
the stain of sin.
3. ROOT: For the use of this word cf. 3.15 and Ecclus. 1.20.
4. THE INSIDIOUS DEVICE OF MEN: Kakotechnos shows that the writer
thinks of art as evil and conducive to idolatry. The impression given here
is that Israel was never entirely seduced by idolatry, since, as stated in
I Ki. 19.18, there was always a remnant that stuck to God. But perhaps the writer has in mind contemporary Jews of the Diaspora, who are
known to have been extremely antagonistic to idolatry.   FRUITLESS
TOIL OF PAINTERS: As pointed out above in 14.20, Philo (Gigant., § 13)
says: "Moses banished from his polity the noble arts of sculpture and
painting: they made a counterfeit presentment of the true, and consequently deceived human souls by deluding the eye." But, as pointed out
by P. Heinisch ad loc., the condemnation of "the fruitless toil of painters"
does not refer to a painted picture but rather to a painted statue. As
cogently stated by Wolfson (Philo, I, 30, n. 22), according to the Talmudic
interpretation of the prohibition against the making of any likeness (Ex.
20.40), this prohibition applies only to carved figures but does not apply to
images not projecting ('Abodah Zarah 43b; Maimonides, Mishneh Torah,

15 ¹ But thou, our God, art gracious and true,
Longsuffering, and in mercy ordering all things.
²For even if we sin we are thine, knowing thy might,
But we shall not sin, knowing that we are accounted
thine.
³For to know thee is perfect righteousness,
And to know thy power is the root of immortality.
⁴For neither were we led astray by the insidious device
of men,
Nor by the fruitless toil of painters,
A form smeared with various colours;
5 ⁵The sight of which for a fool results in desire,
And he lusts for the unbreathing form of a dead image.
⁶Lovers of evil things and worthy of such hopes
Are they that do and they that lust and they that
worship.
⁷For a potter, moulding soft clay painfully,

'*Akum*, III.10). "This interpretation of the law was quite evidently that
which was followed both by the author of the Wisdom of Solomon and by
Philo, as well as also later by the Jews in Duro-Europos, as may be
judged from the paintings in their synagogue" (Du Mesnil du Buisson,
Les Peintures de la Synagogue de Doura-Europos, Roma, 1939).
SMEARED WITH VARIOUS COLORS: *Cf.* 13.14. Statues and images were
usually colored (Plato, *Republic*, IV, 420 c). *Spilôthen* is used here contemptuously: while God never assumed any form or shape (*cf.* Deut.
4.12), the gods of the heathens not only assumed forms, but stained ones
to boot.
5. DESIRE: or lust (R.V.), reading *orexin* with ℵ AC, against *oneidos* (reproach) of B. From sight one comes to desire, and from desire to worship.
Grimm quotes from Arnobius (*Adv. Nat.*, VI.22) the legend of Pygmalion,
king of Cyprus, who fell in love with a statue of Venus.
6. HOPES: May refer to the futile trust in idols, or else to the idols themselves, which are such delusive objects of trust.   THEY THAT DO: or
make them, or fashion them. *Drôntes* is hardly the word to be used here,
but all the ancient versions support it.
7. The writer passes from wooden to ceramic idols, employed especially in
Egypt, and he proceeds to attack the idol-maker rather than the idol
itself.   A POTTER: The maker of the idol is contemptuously called a
potter, just as he is called a carpenter in 13.11 (Gregg). On the work of the
potter *cf.* Isa. 45.9, 64.8, Ecclus. 38.29 f.   MOULDING: *Epimochthon* is
hardly satisfactory, besides being very rare. According to Margoliouth

πλάσσει πρὸς ὑπηρεσίαν ἡμῶν ἓν ἕκαστον·
ἀλλ᾽ ἐκ τοῦ αὐτοῦ πηλοῦ ἀνεπλάσατο
τά τε τῶν καθαρῶν ἔργων δοῦλα σκεύη
τά τε ἐναντία, πάντα ὁμοίως·
τούτων δὲ ἑτέρου τίς ἑκάστου ἐστὶν ἡ χρῆσις,
κριτὴς ὁ πηλουργός.
⁸καὶ κακόμοχθος θεὸν μάταιον ἐκ τοῦ αὐτοῦ πλάσσει πηλοῦ
ὃς πρὸ μικροῦ ἐκ γῆς γενηθεὶς
μετ᾽ ὀλίγον πορεύεται ἐξ ἧς ἐλήμφθη,
τὸ τῆς ψυχῆς ἀπαιτηθεὶς χρέος.
⁹ἀλλ᾽ ἔστιν αὐτῷ φροντὶς οὐχ ὅτι μέλλει κάμνειν
οὐδ᾽ ὅτι βραχυτελῆ βίον ἔχει,
ἀλλ᾽ ἀντερείδεται μὲν χρυσουργοῖς καὶ ἀργυροχόοις
χαλκοπλάστας τε μιμεῖται
καὶ δόξαν ἡγεῖται ὅτι κίβδηλα πλάσσει.
10 ¹⁰σποδὸς ἡ καρδία αὐτοῦ, καὶ γῆς εὐτελεστέρα ἡ ἐλπὶς αὐτοῦ,
πηλοῦ τε ἀτιμότερος ὁ βίος αὐτοῦ,
¹¹ὅτι ἠγνόησεν τὸν πλάσαντα αὐτὸν
καὶ τὸν ἐμπνεύσαντα αὐτῷ ψυχὴν ἐνεργοῦσαν
καὶ ἐμφυσήσαντα πνεῦμα ζωτικόν,

7² εν> B   11¹ πλασ.] ποιησαντα A
7⁶ ετερου BSᶜV†] -ρων S*, εκατερου A,   11³ εμφυσ.]+αυτω Sᶜ
εκατερων compl.

(op. cit., p. 285) the Armenian has "on the wheel," which might lead to epi trochon, but this reading has not the slightest manuscript authority. THE JUDGE: Similarly Jer. 18.4: as seemed good to the potter to make it.

8. TOILING FOR EVIL: So R.V. for kakomochthos, which is a hapax legomenon. Goodrick has "with misdirected toil," following Itala cum labore vano. The underlying meaning is that the clay worker realizes that his is a sham creation: God made man out of clay; the clay turns round and makes a god.   TO RETURN THE LOAN OF HIS SOUL: Similarly in v. 16 below. The idea is clearly expressed in Lucretius III.971: "Life is granted to none in fee-simple, to all in usufruct." Cf. also Philo, Abr., § 44, and Poster. C., § 2. From the use of psuchês here and pneuma in v. 16 it is quite evident that they were to our author only different names of the same thing.

9. HE CONTENDS: or competes. One must remember that the clay idols

Forms each several thing for our service;
But from the same clay he formed
Both the vessels that serve for clean uses
And their opposites, all alike;
But which shall be the use of each of the two
The potter is the judge.

⁸And toiling for evil he forms a vain god out of the same
clay,
Who having but a little before been made of earth,
After a little while goes whence he was taken,
Having been required to return the loan of his soul.

⁹But his anxiety is not that he is certain to fail in power,
Nor that he has a life soon ended,
But he contends with goldsmiths and silversmiths,
And imitates modellers of brass,
And thinks it glory that he moulds counterfeits.

10 ¹⁰His heart is ashes, and his hope more worthless than
earth,
And his life of less account than clay.
¹¹Because he discerned not him that moulded him,
And that inspired him with an active soul,
And breathed into him a vital spirit.

---

were glazed and gilded.   COUNTERFEITS: *Kibdêla* literally "spurious or
adulterated things," hence counterfeits of valuable images. According to
Margoliouth (*op. cit.*, p. 289 f.) this word goes back to an original Heb.
pasal meaning both "spurious" and "unclean" (so Pal. Syr. and Armenian).

10. HIS HEART IS ASHES: This seems to be based on a mistranslation of Isa.
44.20 by LXX *gnōthi hoti spodos hē kardia autōn. Cf.* Ezek. 11.19 and
36.26.   ASHES ... EARTH ... CLAY: All worthless things. The idea expressed is that the whole being of the idolater is inferior to the clay he
uses, though in v. 17 the opposite statement is made.

11. DISCERNED NOT: He wilfully ignored his Maker, *cf.* Isa. 1.3.   SOUL
... SPIRIT: *Psuxê* and *pneuma* are used here, as elsewhere in the book,
promiscuously and without distinction of meaning. This is in accordance
with Jewish thought, but not with Greek philosophy. Some thought of
seeing in this verse the commonly accepted trichotomy of body, soul and
spirit, but more likely the analysis is rhetorical and not to be taken
literally (Cornely).

¹²ἀλλ' ἐλογίσαντο παίγνιον εἶναι τὴν ζωὴν ἡμῶν
καὶ τὸν βίον πανηγυρισμὸν ἐπικερδῆ,
δεῖν γάρ φησιν ὅθεν δή, κἂν ἐκ κακοῦ, πορίζειν.
¹³οὗτος γὰρ παρὰ πάντας οἶδεν ὅτι ἁμαρτάνει
ὕλης γεώδους εὔθραυστα σκεύη καὶ γλυπτὰ δημιουργῶν.
¹⁴πάντες δὲ ἀφρονέστατοι καὶ τάλανες ὑπὲρ ψυχὴν νηπίου
οἱ ἐχθροὶ τοῦ λαοῦ σου καταδυναστεύσαντες αὐτόν,
15 ¹⁵ὅτι καὶ πάντα τὰ εἴδωλα τῶν ἐθνῶν ἐλογίσαντο θεούς
οἷς οὔτε ὀμμάτων χρῆσις εἰς ὅρασιν
οὔτε ῥῖνες εἰς συνολκὴν ἀέρος
οὔτε ὦτα ἀκούειν
οὔτε δάκτυλοι χειρῶν εἰς ψηλάφησιν
καὶ οἱ πόδες αὐτῶν ἀργοὶ πρὸς ἐπίβασιν.
¹⁶ἄνθρωπος γὰρ ἐποίησεν αὐτούς,
καὶ τὸ πνεῦμα δεδανεισμένος ἔπλασεν αὐτούς·
οὐδεὶς γὰρ αὐτῷ ὅμοιον ἄνθρωπος ἰσχύει πλάσαι
θεόν·

12¹ ελογισατο B*Sᶜ
12³ οθεν δη>St
14¹ παντων A | αφρονεστεροι S | ψυχας
νηπιων A
16² δεδανισμενον S*†

16³ αυτω ομοιον ανθρωπος] ανθρωπων
ομοιον A(†) | αυτω — fin.] αν-
θρωπων πλασαι θεον ομοιον ισχυει S*†
(Sᶜ= B, sed αυτων)

---

12. ACCOUNTED: The subject is the idol-maker or the heathen generally.
EXISTENCE . . . LIFE: *Zôê* and *bios* are probably no more than poetical
variations of one and the same thing, namely lifetime or way of life. The
thought expressed is that the idol-maker looks upon our daily life as a
public market, where everyone makes the best bargain he can.   FESTI-
VAL: R.V. and Goodrick have "fair" instead. *Panêgurismos* may signify
both "festival" and "fair." The idea of life as a festival is traced to
Pythagoras (Diog. Laert., VIII.I.6). Similar to it is the saying in the
Talmud (Erub. 54a) "the world that thou leavest is like the house of a
wedding feast." *Cf.* also the description of the traffic of Tyre in Ezek. ch.
27.   WEALTH etc.: *Cf.* Horace, *Ep*.I.I.65: *rem facias, rem; si possis,
recte; si non, quocumque modo rem.*

13. BRITTLE VESSELS AND GRAVEN IMAGES: Both *skeuê* and *glupta* seem to
refer to idols, though some think that the underlying meaning is the same
as in v. 7, namely that the potter makes pots and gods out of the same
clay.

14. MOST FOOLISH OF ALL: Reading with Goodrick *pantôn afronestatoi*; but
B and all versions read *pantes*, and ℵ C have the comparative *afronesteroi*

¹²But accounted our existence to be a sport,
And our life a gainful festival,
For, says he, one must get wealth whencesoever it be,
even out of evil.
¹³For this man above all others knows that he sins,
Fabricating out of earthy matter brittle vessels and
graven images.
¹⁴But most foolish of all, and more wretched than the
soul of a babe,
Are the enemies of thy people that oppress them.

15 ¹⁵For they even accounted all the idols of the nations
gods,
In whom there is no use of eyes for seeing,
Nor nostrils for the drawing of air,
Nor ears to hear,
Nor fingers of hands for feeling,
And their feet are helpless for walking.
¹⁶For a man made them,
And one that had borrowed his soul moulded
them,
For no man is able to mould a god like unto himself.

---

instead of the superlative. According to the latter reading "the enemies of thy people" would refer to all the nations who had ever oppressed Israel, especially the Egyptians, as is clearly indicated from v. 18 onwards. The former reading might be interpreted as an allusion to the despised Jewish apostates of Alexandria.

15. This verse is a free imitation of Ps. 115.4 ff. and 135.15 ff. *Cf.* also Philo, *Decal.*, § 15 (Gregg).   ACCOUNTED ALL THE IDOLS etc.: On the tolerance of Greeks and Romans for foreign cults *cf.* Farrar's note *ad loc.* and Ramsay in Hastings' *Dictionary of the Bible*, V, 151 ff. The Egyptians were not so tolerant towards other gods: they did not include them in their own pantheon, though they recognized that such gods may have power in their own territories.   THE DRAWING: *Sunolkê* is found only in late medical texts, from which it seems to have been adapted by our author.

16. HAD BORROWED HIS SOUL: Similarly, though in different words, verse 8 above. The Syriac reads "a spirit of fraud formed them."   NO MAN IS ABLE etc.: However much the workman may call his work his god, the workman must always be superior to his work. Contrast Ps. 115.8 "they that make them shall be like unto them."

¹⁷θνητὸς δὲ ὢν νεκρὸν ἐργάζεται χερσὶν ἀνόμοις·
κρείττων γάρ ἐστιν τῶν σεβασμάτων αὐτοῦ,
ὧν αὐτὸς μὲν ἔζησεν, ἐκεῖνα δὲ οὐδέποτε. —
¹⁸καὶ τὰ ζῷα δὲ τὰ ἔχθιστα σέβονται·
ἀνοίᾳ γὰρ συγκρινόμενα τῶν ἄλλων ἐστὶ χείρονα·
¹⁹οὐδ' ὅσον ἐπιποθῆσαι ὡς ἐν ζῴων ὄψει καλὰ τυγχάνει
ἐκπέφευγεν δὲ καὶ τὸν τοῦ θεοῦ ἔπαινον καὶ τὴν εὐλογίαν
αὐτοῦ.

16 ¹ Διὰ τοῦτο δι' ὁμοίων ἐκολάσθησαν ἀξίως
καὶ διὰ πλήθους κνωδάλων ἐβασανίσθησαν.
²ἀνθ' ἧς κολάσεως εὐεργετήσας τὸν λαόν σου
εἰς ἐπιθυμίαν ὀρέξεως ξένην γεῦσιν

17³ ων] pr. ανθ S

2¹ ευηργετησεν S*†, -σαν S°†, -σας mu.

2² pr. οις A | γευσεως S*†

---

17. BEING MORTAL: *Thnêtos* is hardly the proper term here, for the meaning implied is not that the man is doomed to die, but that being alive he makes a dead idol.　　BUT THEY NEVER DID: *Cf.* Hab. 2.18 f. The contrast again is between the animate man and the inanimate idol.

18. This and the following verse revert definitely to Egyptian zoolatry, hence they serve as an introduction to ch. 16.　　THE MOST HATEFUL BEASTS: Similarly 12.24. Philo (*Poster. C.*, § 48) states that the Egyptians deify bulls and rams and goats, all of which are useful animals. But they went even further and worshipped wild beasts, such as lions, crocodiles, poisonous asps, dogs, cats, wolves, the ibis and the hawk, etc. (Conybeare, *Vit. Cont.*, p. 261 note).　　IN FOLLY: R.V. "in want of sense," Goodrick "in brutishness." The Egyptians worshipped animal gods which had neither intelligence nor beauty to recommend them.

19. FAIR: The crocodile, for instance, is an unseemly monster, lacking grace and comeliness.　　THEY HAVE ESCAPED etc.: This line lacks clarity. Perhaps our author voiced a legend or tradition according to which the reptiles were excluded from God's blessing and approval. But this would be contradictory to Gen. 1.21.25.30 f.

This and the succeeding chapters deal exclusively with pagan Egypt, the earliest and foremost oppressor of Israel. The purpose of the writer is to show that the Egyptians were punished on the principle of retaliation or like by like (see 11.16, 12.23.27), namely by animals like those they worshipped, and that these animals which were harmful to the Egyptians proved of great benefit to the Israelites. But his diction is often florid and rhetorical, so as to obscure the real meaning of the words and make an analysis of them well-nigh impossible. Roughly these chapters may be

¹⁷But, being mortal, he makes a dead thing with lawless
hands,
For he is better than the things which he worships
Forasmuch as he did live, but they never did.
¹⁸Yes, and they do worship the most hateful beasts,
For being compared in folly they are worse than the
others.
¹⁹Nor are they by any chance fair, so as, in respect to the
appearance of beasts, to be desired,
But they have escaped both the praise of God and his
blessing.

16 ¹ Therefore were they deservedly punished by the like
animals,
And tormented by a multitude of vermin.
²Instead of which punishment, blessing thine own
people,
For the eagerness of their appetite a strange dainty

---

divided into five sections:

16.1–14. The Egyptians were punished by the animals they worshipped:
they worshipped reptiles and were tormented by reptiles; but when these
reptiles were sent against the Israelites in the wilderness it was for no
other purpose than discipline and instruction.

16.15–29. The Egyptians were overcome by fire and water, heat and
cold, whereas these elements were of benefit to Israel.

17.1–18.4. The Egyptians were tormented by darkness, whereas the
pillar of cloud led the Israelites through the wilderness.

18.5–25. Retaliation meted out to the Egyptians: they lost their first-
born because they had killed the male children of the Israelites; they were
drowned in the Red Sea because they had drowned Israel's children in the
Nile; they were finally destroyed through the rescue of one child (Moses).

19.1–21. A comparison between the Egyptians and the Israelites during
the crossing of the Red Sea.

1. DESERVEDLY PUNISHED: For the principle of compensation see further
Philo, *Mos.*, I.17, where the scheme of retaliation of God on the Egyptians
is elaborately worked out. With regard to the system of retribution of the
Rabbis see Weber, *Jüdische Theologie*, p. 244, and George Foot Moore,
Judaism, II, 287 ff.   VERMIN: *Knôdalon* is used of the plagues of lo-
custs, frogs, flies, etc.

2. THEIR APPETITE: The appetite of the Israelites was for flesh, and God
gave them flesh in the form of quail; *cf.* Ps. 78.29.   STRANGE: Because

τροφὴν ἡτοίμασας ὀρτυγομήτραν,
³ἵνα ἐκεῖνοι μὲν ἐπιθυμοῦντες τροφὴν
διὰ τὴν εἰδέχθειαν τῶν ἐπαπεσταλμένων
καὶ τὴν ἀναγκαίαν ὄρεξιν ἀποστρέφωνται,
αὐτοὶ δὲ ἐπ᾽ ὀλίγον ἐνδεεῖς γενόμενοι
καὶ ξένης μετάσχωσι γεύσεως.
⁴ἔδει γὰρ ἐκείνοις μὲν ἀπαραίτητον ἔνδειαν ἐπελθεῖν
τυραννοῦσιν,
τούτοις δὲ μόνον δειχθῆναι πῶς οἱ ἐχθροὶ αὐτῶν ἐβασανί-
ζοντο.
5   ⁵ Καὶ γὰρ ὅτε αὐτοῖς δεινὸς ἐπῆλθεν θηρίων θυμὸς
δήγμασίν τε σκολιῶν διεφθείροντο ὄφεων,
οὐ μέχρι τέλους ἔμεινεν ἡ ὀργή σου·
⁶εἰς νουθεσίαν δὲ πρὸς ὀλίγον ἐταράχθησαν
σύμβολον ἔχοντες σωτηρίας εἰς ἀνάμνησιν ἐντολῆς νόμου
σου·

3¹ τροφης S   3⁴ αυτοι] ουτοι SA : cf. 4
3² ειδεχθειαν C] διχθεισαν B*St, δειχ-   5² διεφθειρ.] δι>S*†
θεισαν AB°

---

they had been living on a vegetable diet for some time.   QUAIL-FOOD:
Ortugomêtra is rendered by Hesychius *ortux hupermegethês*, a bird of
larger size and darker color than the common *ortux*. *Cf.* the article "quails"
in Hastings' *Dictionary of the Bible*, IV, 179. See also Philo, *Mos.*, I.37.
3. THOSE: *Ekeinoi* is, of course, the Egyptians, the people on the other
side of the Red Sea; while *autoi* in l.4 are the Israelites, with whom the
writer henceforth ranges himself.   HIDEOUSNESS: *eidechtheian*, a
hapaxlegomenon, found in C and some cursives and the Syroh., is the
generally accepted reading, as against *deichtheisan* of β ℵ A and Itala,
which makes no sense. The word is said to refer to the frogs in the ovens
and kneading-troughs (Ex. 8.3).   LOATHE: According to the writer, the
Egyptians were punished with animal-plagues in order that they might be
made to loathe the sight of animal food.   BEING IN WANT: The Israelites
are to suffer want in order that their appetite may be stimulated and then
proportionately satisfied. There is nothing in the Scriptures to substantiate
this statement.
4. Very strange is the sentiment voiced here: God made the Israelites
suffer hunger only to show them how the Egyptians had suffered on
account of the frogs.
5. The writer pictures the plague of the fiery serpents as being sent for a
short while only, in order to warn Israel and to show the Egyptians that

Thou didst prepare, quail-food;

3That those, desiring food,

Might, through the hideousness of the things sent among them,

Loathe even their necessary appetite,

While these, being in want for a little while,

Might partake even of a strange dainty.

4For it was needful that inexorable want should come upon those that tyrannized,

But for these only to be shown how their enemies were tormented.

5   5For when upon them came the terrible fury of beasts,

And they were perishing by the bites of writhing serpents,

Thy wrath endured not to the end.

6But for admonition they were dismayed for a little while,

Having a token of salvation to put them in mind of the commandment of thy law.

---

they were worse offenders and therefore deserved worse punishment.
6. FOR ADMONITION: As pointed out above, the writer's standpoint is that the Israelites were not chastised in punishment, but for warning and admonition.   A TOKEN OF SALVATION: *Sumbolon sōtêrias* is probably the brazen serpent which Moses made to save the people, *cf.* Num. 21.9. Some Greek manuscripts, like א A, read *sumboulon* (counsellor), which recalls Philo, *Agric.*, § 22, where the serpent which misled Eve is called *sumboulos anthrōpou.* According to some commentators (Gfrörer, Dähne, Grimm) Pseudo-Solomon regarded the serpent as merely figurative, and they are strengthened in this belief by the fact that Philo considered the serpent as a symbol of *sōfrosunê* (*Leg. Alleg.*, II.20) and *karteria* (Agric., § 22). TO PUT THEM IN MIND: This is best referred to the whole story; both punishment and remedy were to remind them of their complete dependence on God (Goodrick). It may be cogent to quote here the Targum Jonathan (= Targum Yerushalmi) on Num. 21.6: "I have cursed the serpent at the beginning and said to it 'dust shall be thy food' and it was not dissatisfied over it; but I redeemed my people out of Egypt and brought them manna out of heaven and showered them with quail out of the sea and flooded them with water out of the abyss, and again they became dissatisfied with me concerning the manna . . . Therefore let the serpent come that was not dissatisfied over its food and strike this people that is dissatisfied with its food."

⁷ὁ γὰρ ἐπιστραφεὶς οὐ διὰ τὸ θεωρούμενον ἐσῴζετο,
ἀλλὰ διὰ σὲ τὸν πάντων σωτῆρα.

⁸καὶ ἐν τούτῳ δὲ ἔπεισας τοὺς ἐχθροὺς ἡμῶν
ὅτι σὺ εἶ ὁ ῥυόμενος ἐκ παντὸς κακοῦ·

⁹οὓς μὲν γὰρ ἀκρίδων καὶ μυιῶν ἀπέκτεινεν δήγματα,
καὶ οὐχ εὑρέθη ἴαμα τῇ ψυχῇ αὐτῶν,
ὅτι ἄξιοι ἦσαν ὑπὸ τοιούτων κολασθῆναι·

10 ¹⁰τοὺς δὲ υἱούς σου οὐδὲ ἰοβόλων δρακόντων ἐνίκησαν
ὀδόντες,
τὸ ἔλεος γάρ σου ἀντιπαρῆλθεν καὶ ἰάσατο αὐτούς.

¹¹εἰς γὰρ ὑπόμνησιν τῶν λογίων σου ἐνεκεντρίζοντο
καὶ ὀξέως διεσῴζοντο,
ἵνα μὴ εἰς βαθεῖαν ἐμπεσόντες λήθην
ἀπερίσπαστοι γένωνται τῆς σῆς εὐεργεσίας.

¹²καὶ γὰρ οὔτε βοτάνη οὔτε μάλαγμα ἐθεράπευσεν
αὐτούς,
ἀλλὰ ὁ σός, κύριε, λόγος ὁ πάντας ἰώμενος.

¹³σὺ γὰρ ζωῆς καὶ θανάτου ἐξουσίαν ἔχεις

8¹ ημων] σου S*✝   12² παντα   BS   (S°✝ δυναμενος   pro
10² ιασατο] ιατο SV   ιωμενος)

7. As Goodrick says: "The idea is a perfectly natural one; there was no virtue in the brazen serpent as a brazen serpent, but in what it represented and was the symbol of: the life-giving power of God. This has always been the argument of the defenders of images for religious purposes; and if human nature were not prone to attach its adoration to the seen rather than to the unseen it might be valid. But it is to the point that this very serpent, or more likely an imitation of it, had to be destroyed in the reign of Hezekiah because it had become an object of idolatry, II Kings 18.4." The same thought is expressed in the Talmud Rosh hashanah 29a: "Could a serpent kill or revive? But at the time when Israel looked intently towards heaven and subjugated their hearts to their father in heaven they became cured, and if not they fell into decay."

8. The writer assumes that the news of the fortunes of Israel in the wilderness was carried to Egypt from distances of hundreds of miles, cf. Ex. 32.12, Num. 14.13, Deut. 9.28.

9. DID SLAY: This is somewhat hyperbolic: the bites of locusts and flies caused terrific annoyance, but they did not kill. The only allusion to deadly effects is in Ex. 10.17, where Pharaoh calls the locusts "this death." Philo, Mos., I.19, gives a terrifying account of the flies, but never speaks

⁷For he that turned toward it was not saved by that
which was beheld,

But through thee, the saviour of all.

⁸In this too thou didst persuade our enemies

That thou art he that saves from every evil.

⁹For them the bites of locusts and flies did slay,

And there was not found a healing for their life,

For they deserved to be punished by such;

10   ¹⁰Whereas thy sons not even the teeth of poison-darting
dragons overcame,

For thy mercy came forth to meet them and healed
them.

¹¹For to put them in remembrance of thine oracles they
were stung,

And were quickly delivered,

Lest falling into deep forgetfulness,

They should become bereft of thy beneficence.

¹²For it was neither herb nor emollient that cured
them,

But thy word, O Lord, that heals all things.

¹³For thou hast authority over life and death,

---

of them as deadly. Only Josephus (*Antiq.*, II.XIV.3) speaks of the lice as
actually causing death.

10. THY SONS etc.: Pal. Syr. departs from this rendering considerably:
"thy sons rode upon the teeth and heads of dragons."   POISON-
DARTING: The Egyptians died of the mere bite of insects, while Israel
was immune even from venomous serpents, *Cf.* however, Num. 21.6.
Iobola is used of serpents also in Philo, *Mos.*, I.35.

11. ORACLES: *Logia* is used of the oracles of Sinai in Acts 7.38.   BEREFT
OF THY BENEFICENCE: Reading with many exegetes *aperistatoi* instead of
aperispastoi (not drawn hither and thither), which makes no sense here.

12. EMOLLIENT: *Malagma* occurs also in LXX of Isa. 1.6. In support of
this line Philo, *Sacrif.*, § 19, is adduced: "Men do not trust God the
Saviour completely, but have recourse to the aids which nature offers,
doctors, herbs, medical compounds, rigid diet." Contrast the praise of
physicians in Ecclus. 38.1–8.   THY WORD: The word of God here is not
the same as the Philonian Logos: it is simply the utterance of the will of
God, exactly as in Ps. 107.20: "He sent His word and healed them."

13. This and the following two verses seem to be based on Deut. 32.39 and

καὶ κατάγεις εἰς πύλας ᾄδου καὶ ἀνάγεις·
^{14}ἄνθρωπος δὲ ἀποκτέννει μὲν τῇ κακίᾳ αὐτοῦ,
ἐξελθὸν δὲ πνεῦμα οὐκ ἀναστρέφει
οὐδὲ ἀναλύει ψυχὴν παραλημφθεῖσαν.

15   ^{15} Τὴν δὲ σὴν χεῖρα φυγεῖν ἀδύνατόν ἐστιν·
^{16}ἀρνούμενοι γάρ σε εἰδέναι ἀσεβεῖς
ἐν ἰσχύι βραχίονός σου ἐμαστιγώθησαν
ξένοις ὑετοῖς καὶ χαλάζαις καὶ ὄμβροις διωκόμενοι
ἀπαραιτήτοις
καὶ πυρὶ καταναλισκόμενοι.
^{17}τὸ γὰρ παραδοξότατον, ἐν τῷ πάντα σβεννύτι ὕδατι
πλεῖον ἐνήργει τὸ πῦρ,
ὑπέρμαχος γὰρ ὁ κόσμος ἐστὶν δικαίων·
^{18}ποτὲ μὲν γὰρ ἡμεροῦτο φλόξ,
ἵνα μὴ καταφλέξῃ τὰ ἐπ' ἀσεβεῖς ἀπεσταλμένα ζῷα,
ἀλλ' αὐτοὶ βλέποντες εἰδῶσιν ὅτι θεοῦ κρίσει ἐλαύνονται·

14³ αναλυσει S   18² ζωα>S*†
17³ δικαιοις A†

I Sam. 2.6.   THE GATES OF HADES: A variation of the preceding line, the order being reversed. On the gates of Hades see Isa. 38.10, Job 38.17, III Macc. 5.51; cf. also Ps. 9.14 and 107.18.   BRINGEST UP AGAIN: Some commentators see here an allusion to resurrection. The plain meaning is that the Egyptians were actually killed, while the Israelites were only taken as far as the gates of death, and then saved.

14. This verse hardly belongs to the argument, being only an appendix to the declaration of God's power in v. 13. The author wants to say that while God can both kill and restore to life, man can only inflict death but never restore to life (Gregg).   SPIRIT: Probably identical with soul, see 15.11.   TURNS NOT AGAIN: *Anastrefei* is a transitive as in 2.5, but Itala *non revertetur* took it intransitively, so also Pal. Syr. and A.V. Man is powerless in the face of death, cf. Job 7.9 f.   RELEASE: *Analuei* likewise is a transitive here, though Pal. Syr. and A.V. take it as an intransitive as in 2.1.   THAT IS CAPTURED: *Paralêftheisan* is rendered "received" by the versions; R.V. "that Hades hath received" is based on a passage in Polybius, III.XXXIX.2, whose language Pseudo-Solomon emulates. Man cannot rescue his brother (Ps. 49.8), but God can redeem from the hand of Hades (*ibid.* 15 LXX).

15. The author adduces another contrast between the Egyptians and the Israelites: fire and water being employed to punish the former and benefit the latter. The verse resembles very closely Tobit 13.2.   THY HAND:

And leadest down to the gates of Hades and bringest up
again.

[14]But a man slays in his wickedness,
Yet the spirit that is gone forth he turns not again,
Nor does he release the soul that is captured.

15   [15]But thy hand it is impossible to escape,
[16]For impious men, denying knowledge of thee,
Were scourged by the might of thine arm,
Pursued by strange rains and hails and inexorable
showers,
And utterly consumed by fire.
[17]For what was most incredible, in water that quenches
all
The fire had the greater power,
For nature fights for the righteous.
[18]For at one time the flame was tamed,
That it might not burn up the beasts sent against the
impious,
But that they beholding might see that they are pursued
by God's judgment.

Bois (*Essai*, p. 288) considers this an instance of anthropomorphism, but
as a matter of fact it is no more nor less than a metaphor, so common in
the Scriptures, *cf.* especially Am. 9.2.

16. IMPIOUS MEN: Namely the Egyptians.   STRANGE RAINS: *Cf.* Ex.
9.24. They are called strange because rain is rare in Egypt, see Deut.
11.10; also Philo, *Mos.*, III.24.

17. THE FIRE HAD GREATER POWER: *Cf.* Ex. 9.24 quoted above. In the
plague of hail, accompanied by lightning, it appeared that the two
hostile elements, fire and water, were reconciled for the nonce in order to
punish the Egyptians. Philo (*Mos.*, I.20) says: "Compact thunderbolts, of
appalling appearance, ran hither and thither through the hail; and for all
the variance between their natures, the rain did not quench the fire, nor
the fire melt the hail."   NATURE: *Kosmos* here has the same meaning as
ktisis in v. 24 below and in 5.17, namely the creation or the whole order of
nature.

18. The author implies that the frogs and flies lasted until the plague of
hail, and in 19.21 he actually describes the beasts walking in the flames,
but Ex. 8.27 expressly states that they disappeared completely before the
succeeding plagues took place. Perhaps this notion of the simultaneous-
ness of the plagues is based on some unknown legend or tradition.

¹⁹ποτὲ δὲ καὶ μεταξὺ ὕδατος ὑπὲρ τὴν πυρὸς δύναμιν
φλέγει,
ἵνα ἀδίκου γῆς γενήματα διαφθείρῃ.

20 ²⁰ἀνθ᾽ ὧν ἀγγέλων τροφὴν ἐψώμισας τὸν λαόν σου
καὶ ἕτοιμον ἄρτον ἀπ᾽ οὐρανοῦ παρέσχες αὐτοῖς
ἀκοπιάτως
πᾶσαν ἡδονὴν ἰσχύοντα καὶ πρὸς πᾶσαν ἁρμόνιον
γεῦσιν·
²¹ἡ μὲν γὰρ ὑπόστασίς σου τὴν σὴν πρὸς τέκνα ἐνεφάνιζεν
γλυκύτητα,
τῇ δὲ τοῦ προσφερομένου ἐπιθυμίᾳ ὑπηρετῶν
πρὸς ὅ τις ἐβούλετο μετεκιρνᾶτο.
²²χιὼν δὲ καὶ κρύσταλλος ὑπέμεινε πῦρ καὶ οὐκ ἐτήκετο,
ἵνα γνῶσιν ὅτι τοὺς τῶν ἐχθρῶν καρποὺς
κατέφθειρε πῦρ φλεγόμενον ἐν τῇ χαλάζῃ
καὶ ἐν τοῖς ὑετοῖς διαστράπτον·

19² καταφθειρη SA
20² παρεσχες] επεμψας B
20³ ισχοντα Gra.
21¹ υποστασις] υποσταξις Nannius (auctore Fr.), αποσταξις Gra.

22² γνωμεν Sᵒⱡ | εθνων Aⱡ
22³ φλεγον S
22⁴ εν τοις] ξενοις Sᵒⱡ

---

19. ABOVE THE POWER OF FIRE: While in one case the fire was mitigated, in another it became intensified. THE PRODUCTS: Genêmata is used here in the sense of "fruits," as in v. 22, cf. also Ps. 105.32 f. Hence the rendering of Itala nationem is surprising.

20. From here on the author describes the miraculous properties of the manna, which in v. 22 is characterized as "snow and ice." ANGELS' FOOD: Ps. 78.25, where lehem abirim "bread of the mighty," is rendered by the Septuagint arton aggelôn and so Targum. See also Yalkut ha-Makiri, ed. Buber, ad loc., where R. Akiba maintains against R. Ishmael the traditional interpretation of abir "angel." WITHOUT THEIR LABOURING: Philo ibid. calls the manna a food that cost no labor, in contradistinction to corn which has to be cultivated. SUFFICIENT FOR ALL PLEASURE: Reading pros pasan hêdonên ischuonta with Codex 248 and Origen. Without pros, as in the B text, the phrase becomes difficult. The reading of R.V. "having the virtue of every pleasant savour" is based on Itala omne delectamentum in se habentem. The manna is said to have tasted like honey cake in Ex. 16.31, and like fresh oil in Num. 11.8. But a Jewish legend has it that its taste was transformed to suit divers ages and tastes, cf. the comment on the next verse. On the basis of this legend

> [19]But at another time in the midst of water it flames above
>   the power of fire,
> That it may destroy the products of an unrighteous
>   land.
>
> 20 [20]Instead whereof thou feddest thy people with angels'
>   food,
> And sentest ready bread for them from heaven, without
>   their labouring for it,
> Sufficient for all pleasure and agreeing to every taste.
> [21]For thy sustenance manifested thy sweetness towards
>   thy children,
> And ministering to the desire of him that took it
> Was changed to what one desired.
> [22]But snow and ice endured fire and melted not,
> That they might know that fire was destroying the
>   crops of their enemies,
> Flaming amid the hail
> And flashing in the showers.

Margoliouth (*op. cit.*, p. 296) suggested the reading *hēlikian* (age) instead of *hēdonēn* (pleasure).

21. THY SUSTENANCE: So A.V. and Goodrick, but *hupostasis* may also denote "substance," "essence," or "nature" (so R.V., Grimm, Siegfried, Bois, and others). In the latter case the reference is taken to be to the substance of the manna (*cf.* Deane *ad loc.*). Students of Philo take it to refer to the person of the Logos, *cf.* Drummond, II, 160 and 204.   MINISTERING TO THE DESIRE etc.: *Cf.* Yoma 75a; Ex. R., 25.3, on Ex. 16.4; Philo, *Q.D.P.I.*, § 31, where manna is described as a rock out of which two cakes are made, one of honey and one of oil; Jerome on Ps. 147: "If a man desired apples, pears, grapes, bread, flesh, he had the taste of them in the manna." WAS CHANGED: *Metakrinaō* is an unusual word, and its meaning is "to mix" rather than "to change." But one instance of the latter meaning has been adduced from Pausanias.

22. SNOW AND ICE: This is a description of the manna as the writer conceived it, *cf.* 19.21 "the easily-melted ice-like kind of heavenly food." Philo (*Mos.*, I.36) characterizes it "as a dew which had been snowed from heaven, which was neither water, nor hail, nor snow, nor ice," meaning a thing like all of these, but not actually any one of them. *Cf.* Ex. 16.14 "like hoar-frost" and Num. 11.7 LXX "the appearance of ice." See also Ps. 148.8.   MELTED NOT: By hearth-fire, since it did melt under sunlight, see Ex. 16.21. The miracle is that this ice-like substance could be placed in ovens to be cooked (Num. 11.8) and yet not melt.

²³τοῦτο πάλιν δ', ἵνα τραφῶσιν δίκαιοι,
καὶ τῆς ἰδίας ἐπιλέλησται δυνάμεως.
²⁴ Ἡ γὰρ κτίσις σοὶ τῷ ποιήσαντι ὑπηρετοῦσα
ἐπιτείνεται εἰς κόλασιν κατὰ τῶν ἀδίκων
καὶ ἀνίεται εἰς εὐεργεσίαν ὑπὲρ τῶν ἐπὶ σοὶ πεποιθότων.
25   ²⁵διὰ τοῦτο καὶ τότε εἰς πάντα μεταλλευομένη
τῇ παντοτρόφῳ σου δωρεᾷ ὑπηρέτει
πρὸς τὴν τῶν δεομένων θέλησιν,
²⁶ἵνα μάθωσιν οἱ υἱοί σου, οὓς ἠγάπησας, κύριε,
ὅτι οὐχ αἱ γενέσεις τῶν καρπῶν τρέφουσιν ἄνθρωπον,
ἀλλὰ τὸ ῥῆμά σου τοὺς σοὶ πιστεύοντας διατηρεῖ.
²⁷τὸ γὰρ ὑπὸ πυρὸς μὴ φθειρόμενον
ἁπλῶς ὑπὸ βραχείας ἀκτῖνος ἡλίου θερμαινόμενον ἐτήκετο,
²⁸ὅπως γνωστὸν ᾖ ὅτι δεῖ φθάνειν τὸν ἥλιον ἐπ' εὐχαριστίαν
σου
καὶ πρὸς ἀνατολὴν φωτὸς ἐντυγχάνειν σοι·

<table>
<tr><td>24³ επι σοι] εις σε Bⴕ</td><td>27¹ μη>S*ⴕ | φθειρ.] pr. δια S</td></tr>
<tr><td>25¹ εις παντα> Sⴕ</td><td>28¹ η] ην Bⴕ</td></tr>
<tr><td>25³ δεομενων]+σου Sᶜ</td><td>28² προς ανατολην φωτος] προ -λης του</td></tr>
<tr><td>26² καρπων] ανθρωπων Aⴕ</td><td>φ. Sᶜⴕ</td></tr>
</table>

---

23. This verse is still dependent on "know that" of the preceding verse. THIS: Namely the element of fire.   FORGOTTEN: Since the manna was capable of being baked with artificial heat.

24. The underlying idea here is that the Jew never conceived of a purely physical, non-moral world: the universe was forever friendly to the righteous and inimical to the wicked.   STRAINS . . . SLACKENS: A metaphor derived from stringed musical instruments, cf. Philo, *Mut.*, § 13.

25. CHANGING: *Metalleuomenê* stands for *metalloioumenê*—a mistake found also in 4.12, see comment there. While creation as a whole could not change, the elements constituting creation were held to be mutually interchangeable among themselves, cf. Philo, *Mos.*, II.36.   ALL-NOURISHING BOUNTY: Namely the manna. God sustains all, as stated in Ps. 104.27, 136.25, 145.16.

26. IT IS NOT THE GROWTH etc.: These lines are an expansion of Deut. 8.3, where LXX reads "man does not live by bread only, but by every word that proceeds out of the mouth of God." The implication here is the same as in verses 7 and 12 above.   WORD: *Rêma* is used here interchangeably with *logos* in v. 12, proving that the latter has not the same philosophic significance as the Philonic Logos.

²³And this again, that righteous men may be nourished,
    Has forgotten even its own power.
²⁴For creation, ministering to thee its maker,
    Strains itself against the unrighteous for punishment,
    And slackens for beneficence on behalf of them that
        trust in thee.

25   ²⁵Therefore at that time also, changing into all forms,
    It served thine all-nourishing bounty,
    According to the wish of them that needed.
²⁶That thy sons whom thou lovest might learn, O Lord,
    That it is not the growth of the crops that nourishes a
        man,
    But that thy word preserves them that trust thee.
²⁷For that which was not marred by fire,
    Being simply warmed by a faint sunbeam melted away,
²⁸That it might be known that it is needful to anticipate
        the sun for giving thanks to thee,
    And supplicate thee at the dawning of light.

---

27. On this verse *cf.* Ex. 16.21 and Philo, *Mos.*, II.35. A curious tradition is
found in the Targum Yerushalmi to the passage mentioned above: "they
gathered it from dawn till the fourth hour of the day . . . but at the fourth
hour and afterwards the sun grew hot upon it and it melted and became
fountains of water, which flowed down to the great sea, and there came
clean animals and cattle to drink of it, and the Israelites hunted them and
ate them."
28. AT THE DAWNING OF LIGHT: So R.V. and Goodrick following Itala *ad
ortum lucis.* The fact that manna that did not melt in the oven yielded to the
sun's rays, is taken as a symbol of the duty of early prayer. *Pros anatolên
fôtos* could also mean "towards the East," and indeed this interpretation
has been urged by some commentators as proof that Pseudo-Solomon
belonged to the Egyptian sect of Therapeutae who, like the Persians,
prayed towards the rising sun, or to the Palestinian sect of Essenes, of
whom Josephus (*Bell. Jud.*, II.8.5) says "before sunrising they speak not a
word about profane matters, but put up certain prayers which they have
received from their forefathers as if they made a supplication for its
rising." It should also be noted that the daily Jewish prayer of *Shema'*
(Deut. 6.4) was to be recited, according to the Mishnah, when the sun's
rays lighted up the tops of the mountains. However, this interpretation
has no regard for the symbolism of the manna, which was pointed out
above. Drummond is probably right when he remarks (*Philo*, I, 181): "It
is not a violent supposition that some of the Jews in Egypt may have

²⁹ἀχαρίστου γὰρ ἐλπὶς ὡς χειμέριος πάχνη τακήσεται
καὶ ῥυήσεται ὡς ὕδωρ ἄχρηστον.

17 ¹ Μεγάλαι γὰρ σου αἱ κρίσεις καὶ δυσδιήγητοι·
διὰ τοῦτο ἀπαίδευτοι ψυχαὶ ἐπλανήθησαν.

²ὑπειληφότες γὰρ καταδυναστεύειν ἔθνος ἅγιον ἄνομοι
δέσμιοι σκότους καὶ μακρᾶς πεδῆται νυκτὸς
κατακλεισθέντες ὀρόφοις φυγάδες τῆς αἰωνίου προνοίας
ἔκειντο.

³λανθάνειν γὰρ νομίζοντες ἐπὶ κρυφαίοις ἁμαρτήμασιν
ἀφεγγεῖ λήθης παρακαλύμματι
ἐσκορπίσθησαν θαμβούμενοι δεινῶς
καὶ ἰνδάλμασιν ἐκταρασσόμενοι.

⁴οὐδὲ γὰρ ὁ κατέχων αὐτοὺς μυχὸς ἀφόβους διεφύλαττεν,
ἦχοι δ’ ἐκταράσσοντες αὐτοὺς περιεκόμπουν,
καὶ φάσματα ἀμειδήτοις κατηφῆ προσώποις ἐνεφανίζετο.

29¹ χ(ε)ιμερινη S*At   4² δ εκταρ. B*t (cf. 14 24)] δε καταρ.
3³ εσκορπισθ.] pr. δι St, εσκοτισθ. A   ABᶜ, δε ταρ. S
4¹ μυθος A(t) | αφοβως BS

---

adopted so simple and devout a custom as giving thanks before daybreak without submitting themselves to the discipline of a sect."

À Lapide has a voluminous note on the identification of manna with prayer, adducing many instances of such identification from the Church Fathers.

1. From here to 18.4 the third contrast between Israel and Egypt, with regard to light and darkness, is fully dealt with. FOR: *gar* is used very loosely in this chapter, becoming almost meaningless. THY JUDG-MENTS: Not judicial acts, but principles of justice. WENT ASTRAY: The Egyptians lost their way in their effort to persecute the children of Israel.

2. LAWLESS MEN: Namely the Egyptians. PRISONERS OF DARKNESS: Cf. Ex. 10.21 ff. and v. 17 below "one chain of darkness." A LONG NIGHT: Philo (*Mos.*, I.21) says: "It counted as nothing else than one long night, equal to three days and three nights in length." EXILED: like runaway slaves, cowering in secret places. ETERNAL PROVIDENCE: Cf. 14.3 and IV Macc. 13.19. The author speaks of the darkness as if it actually had the effect of screening them from God.

3. TO ESCAPE DETECTION: Another instance of retaliation as set forth in 11.16: they loved darkness in their sins, therefore they were stricken with

²⁹For the hope of the unthankful shall melt away as the
　　winter's hoarfrost,
And run off like useless water.

17　¹　For great are thy judgments and hard to explain;
　　Therefore undisciplined souls went astray.
²For lawless men having thought to hold a holy nation in
　　their power,
Prisoners of darkness and fettered captives of a long
　　night,
Shut in under their roofs lay exiled from eternal
　　providence.
³For thinking to escape detection in their secret sins,
Under a dark veil of forgetfulness,
They were scattered asunder, terribly affrighted
And dismayed by spectres.
⁴For not even the nook that held them kept them from
　　fear,
And echoes dismaying them sounded about them,
And cheerless ghosts with gloomy faces appeared.

---

darkness. *Cf.* Job 24.14.　　FORGETFULNESS: Probably forgetfulness of
God.　　SCATTERED ASUNDER: *eskopisthêsan* of β ℵ and Itala is preferable
to *eskotisthêsan* (were darkened) of AC. The former is commonly used of
the demoralization of an army, which becomes scattered like the sheep of a
flock; similarly the Egyptians became demoralized and scattered, each one
hiding in his own house.　　SPECTRES: *Indalmasin* means "appearances"
or "resemblances" and is rendered by A.V. "apparitions" and by R.V.
"spectral forms." The B text has a gloss *fantasmasin*. As Gregg points out,
"the author, seeking to enhance the terror of the darkness, either supple-
ments the Scriptural account from Midrashic sources by telling of
ghostly apparitions, or is merely recording the hallucinations of the terrified Egyptians."
4. KEPT THEM FROM FEAR: Their own houses offered no protection from the
general terror and chaos: all sorts of sounds and shapes pursued them
everywhere.　　DISMAYING: So Goodrick. A.V. and R.V. adopt the variant *katarassontes*, "rushing down," said of cataracts.　　GHOSTS: *fasmata*
is variously interpreted, *cf.* comment on the preceding verse. According to
Arnold the reference here is to "a sending of messengers of evil" of Ps.
78.49. See also Job 4.13 ff.

5 ⁵καὶ πυρὸς μὲν οὐδεμία βία κατίσχυεν φωτίζειν,
   οὔτε ἄστρων ἔκλαμπροι φλόγες
   καταυγάζειν ὑπέμενον τὴν στυγνὴν ἐκείνην νύκτα.
   ⁶διεφαίνετο δ' αὐτοῖς μόνον
   αὐτομάτη πυρὰ φόβου πλήρης,
   ἐκδειματούμενοι δὲ τῆς μὴ θεωρουμένης ἐκείνης ὄψεως
   ἡγοῦντο χείρω τὰ βλεπόμενα.
   ⁷μαγικῆς δὲ ἐμπαίγματα κατέκειτο τέχνης,
   καὶ τῆς ἐπὶ φρονήσει ἀλαζονείας ἔλεγχος ἐφύβριστος·
   ⁸οἱ γὰρ ὑπισχνούμενοι δείματα καὶ ταραχὰς ἀπελαύνειν
       ψυχῆς νοσούσης,
   οὗτοι καταγέλαστον εὐλάβειαν ἐνόσουν.
   ⁹καὶ γὰρ εἰ μηδὲν αὐτοὺς ταραχῶδες ἐφόβει,
   κνωδάλων παρόδοις καὶ ἑρπετῶν συριγμοῖς ἐκσεσοβημένοι
   διώλλυντο ἔντρομοι

5² ουτε]+πυρογενεις S°†   9¹ ταραχ.] τερατωδες S°V†
6³ μη>A   9² συρισμοις S*A | εκσεσοβ.] εκπεφο-
7¹ κατεκ(ε)ιντο A   βημενοι A

---

5. STRONG ENOUGH TO LIGHT THEM: Philo (Mos., I.21) says that the darkness was so oppressive that it put fires out, or else engulfed them so completely as to neutralize all their light. Josephus (Antiq., II.14.5) has this to
say: "By this darkness the sight of the Egyptians was obstructed, and
their breathing was hindered by the thickness of the air, so that they died
miserably." Cf. also Ibn Ezra's commentary on Ex. 10.21: "they shall
grasp the darkness with their hands, for it will be so thick that neither the
flame of fire nor a light will burn in it."   THE BRILLIANT FLAMES OF THE
STARS: Cf. Targum Yerushalmi on Ex. 10.22 f.: "There was darkness in
Egypt three days. No man saw his brother and none arose from his place
for three days; but among all the sons of Israel there was light that the
wicked among them who died might be buried, and that the righteous
might be occupied with the precepts of the law in their dwellings."
6. It is difficult to tell exactly what the author refers to here, but it is safe
to say that the meaning formulated by Goodrick, based on À Lapide, is
not far from the mark: "Every now and then an electric flash lit up the
darkness and showed the Egyptians the spectral forms of objects (possibly the ghosts) for a moment; when the flash ceased they exaggerated in
the darkness the things they had for an instant beheld." R.V. renders "In
terror they deemed the things which they saw to be worse than that sight
on which they could not gaze," taking opseôs as a genitive of comparison.

5   ⁵And no force of fire was strong enough to light them,
     Nor the brilliant flames of the stars
     Availed to illuminate that hideous night.
     ⁶But there shone upon them only
     A self-kindled flame full of terror,
     And utterly terrified by that sight when they saw it not,
     They deemed the things they beheld worse.
     ⁷But the tricks of magic art lay low,
     And the conviction of the vaunting of their understand-
          ing was ignominious.
     ⁸For they that promised to drive away fears and alarms
          from a sick soul,
     These were sick with ridiculous apprehension.
     ⁹For even if nothing troublesome affrighted them,
     Yet having been scared by the creepings of vermin and
          hissing of reptiles,
     They perished trembling,

7. LAY LOW: Reading *katekeito* with β א and Itala, as against the plural in AC and 248. The latter is adopted by R.V. "they lay helpless, made the sport of magic art"; but it is not likely that a Jew would call the punishment sent by God "magic art." According to the Scriptures the magicians of Egypt were successful at first (Ex. 7.11 and 22), then failed (*ibid.* 8.14), and were miserably discomfited at last (*ibid.* 9.11).   IGNOMINIOUS: The magicians were totally discredited, since they were as powerless as the people against the darkness and the phantoms.

8. APPREHENSION: There is no mention in the Book of Exodus of any attempt by the magicians to dispel the darkness, but, in the words of Farrar, "since they failed in the plague of lice the writer assumes that they failed still more hopelessly during the plague of darkness."

9. EVEN IF NOTHING TROUBLESOME: The magicians are depicted as utterly demoralized and panic-stricken, so that during the darkness, when there was nothing really terrible near them save the darkness, the memory of past plagues caused their imagination to people it with terrors (Gregg). HAVING BEEN SCARED: *Eksesobêmenoi* is a perf. part. and refers back to the time of the plagues of the insects and frogs.   VERMIN: Applied to lice, flies, and locusts, see 16.1.   REPTILES: *Herpeta* has reference to frogs, see 11.15.

Interesting is the loose rendering of Pal. Syr.: "all manner of portents terrified them, flies by defilement, and serpents by irritation; and from birds they fell down and trembled and perished; and from the air which is

καὶ τὸν μηδαμόθεν φευκτὸν ἀέρα προσιδεῖν ἀρνούμενοι.

10   ¹⁰δειλὸν γὰρ ἰδίῳ πονηρία μάρτυρι καταδικαζομένη,
   ἀεὶ δὲ προσείληφεν τὰ χαλεπὰ συνεχομένη τῇ συνειδήσει·
   ¹¹οὐθὲν γάρ ἐστιν φόβος εἰ μὴ προδοσία τῶν ἀπὸ λογισμοῦ
      βοηθημάτων,
   ¹²ἔνδοθεν δὲ οὖσα ἥττων ἡ προσδοκία
   πλείονα λογίζεται τὴν ἄγνοιαν τῆς παρεχούσης τὴν
      βάσανον αἰτίας.
   ¹³οἱ δὲ τὴν ἀδύνατον ὄντως νύκτα
   καὶ ἐξ ἀδυνάτου ᾅδου μυχῶν ἐπελθοῦσαν
   τὸν αὐτὸν ὕπνον κοιμώμενοι

10¹ ιδιω πον. unus cod.] ιδιως πον.   (sim. unus cod.) | μαρτυρει B
BS*A pl., ιδιως πον. ιδιω S°ᵗ   11 προσδοκια S : ex 12

nothing the infidels fled that they might not believe."   REFUSING TO
LOOK ON THE AIR: They kept their eyes closed for fear of unknown horrors.   COULD ON NO SIDE BE ESCAPED: This phrase is quite obscure.
Gregg suggests "the air that needed no escaping from": it was innocent of
harm and contained no horrors, but their imagination peopled it with
such. Another suggestion is to interpret aêr as "darkness," since in
Homer it does signify "a cloud," but Grimm questions this very emphatically.

10. OF ITS OWN NATURE: So Cornely, reading idiōs with AB א and Itala, as
against idiō of some MSS. followed by Grimm and R.V. Bois suggests
eidos, "a cowardly spectacle," but this has no manuscript support whatever.   CONSCIENCE: This is the first occurrence of suneidêsis in the sense
of conscience in biblical Greek. It is found in Eccl. 10.20, but with the
meaning "secret thoughts." Here it is construed as a second self, standing
over against the sinful self. "The word is borrowed from the Stoics, and in
their system stands for a man's judgment upon his act when done, rather
than for the principle which dictates his action. It means con-scientia, his
co-knowledge existing, as the result of reflection, by the side of his
knowledge of the act as done" (Gregg). As might have been expected, the
idea of conscience is very prominent in Philo and, of course, in the New
Testament. For the effect of a guilt-sick conscience cf. Jer. 2.19, Prov.
28.1, and Job 15.20.   FORECASTS: Reading proeilêfen with χ (second
hand), Itala praesumit, A.V. and R.V., as against proseilêfen "takes in
addition" of ABC and א (first hand).

11. This verse, in the form of a sententious saying, expresses the idea that
fear is nothing but the surrender of reason. A guilty conscience upsets the
inner equilibrium, and makes it impossible for a man to look out upon the
world with calm eyes. According to Goodrick, the meaning is that terror
prevents our examining the sources of our fear. "Such an idea was particularly congenial to the popular Stoic school, with its doctrines of 'in-

And refusing to look on the air which could on no side
be escaped.

10 [10]For wickedness is of its own nature cowardly, which
being convicted bears witness thereof,
And being hard pressed by conscience always forecasts
grievous things.

[11]For fear is nothing but abandonment of the succours
that come from reasoning;

[12]For the all too feeble expectation of help from within
Counts the ignorance as worse than the cause that
brings the torment.

[13]But they throughout a night really powerless,
And coming upon them from the depths of powerless
Hades,
Sleeping the same sleep,

---

difference to pain' and 'independence of outward circumstances.' IV
Macc. is a mere fairy tale invented to illustrate the Stoic doctrine of the
superiority of Reason to the Feelings, and classical quotations to this effect are plentiful." Another definition of fear common among Stoic
philosophers was that it was merely "anticipation" or "apprehension," cf.
Philo, *Mut. Nom.*, § 30.

12. Goodrick explains this in connection with the preceding verse:
"Reason in the face of tormenting conscience has surrendered her powers:
the hope from within (which should be founded on reason) is all too feeble.
Man has nothing to rely on, and he naturally counts his ignorance of what
is causing his terrors as the worst of his misfortunes. The passage, in fact,
includes two psychological truths: first, that 'conscience doth make
cowards of us all'; and secondly, that 'dangers unknown are more terrible
than even worse dangers which are understood and can be fathomed.'
According to Gregg, the gist of the last three verses is this: Moral guilt,
when brought home to a man, paralyzes his reasoning faculties; thus fear
is engendered; for, where reason has not full play, ignorance with its
power of exaggeration takes the place of which reason is dispossessed; and
the guilty man is proclaimed a coward.

13. POWERLESS HADES: Hades is the place of death and impotence, hence
the night in which it shrouded the earth partook of the same character.
There are many passages in the Scriptures dealing with the powerlessness
of Sheol, cf. Charles, *Eschatology*, pp. 47. f.　　SLEEPING THE SAME SLEEP:
This is merely rhetorical, since it had been hinted that the Egyptians were
lying and quaking from fear. Perhaps Gregg is right that "the only way of
describing the enforced rest of the Egyptians during a period of seventy-
two hours is to be found in terms of night, *i. e.* sleep."

¹⁴τὰ μὲν τέρασιν ἠλαύνοντο φαντασμάτων,
τὰ δὲ τῆς ψυχῆς παρελύοντο προδοσίᾳ·
αἰφνίδιος γὰρ αὐτοῖς καὶ ἀπροσδόκητος φόβος ἐπεχύθη.

15 ¹⁵εἶθ᾽ οὕτως, ὃς δή ποτ᾽ οὖν ἦν ἐκεῖ καταπίπτων,
ἐφρουρεῖτο εἰς τὴν ἀσίδηρον εἱρκτὴν κατακλεισθείς·
¹⁶εἴ τε γὰρ γεωργὸς ἦν τις ἢ ποιμὴν
ἢ τῶν κατ᾽ ἐρημίαν ἐργάτης μόχθων,
προλημφθεὶς τὴν δυσάλυκτον ἔμενεν ἀνάγκην,
μιᾷ γὰρ ἁλύσει σκότους πάντες ἐδέθησαν·
¹⁷εἴ τε πνεῦμα συρίζον
ἢ περὶ ἀμφιλαφεῖς κλάδους ὀρνέων ἦχος εὐμελὴς
ἢ ῥυθμὸς ὕδατος πορευομένου βίᾳ
ἢ κτύπος ἀπηνὴς καταρριπτομένων πετρῶν
¹⁸ἢ σκιρτώντων ζῴων δρόμος ἀθεώρητος
ἢ ὠρυομένων ἀπηνεστάτων θηρίων φωνὴ
ἢ ἀντανακλωμένη ἐκ κοιλότητος ὀρέων ἠχώ,
παρέλυεν αὐτοὺς ἐκφοβοῦντα.
¹⁹ὅλος γὰρ ὁ κόσμος λαμπρῷ κατελάμπετο φωτὶ
καὶ ἀνεμποδίστοις συνείχετο ἔργοις·
20 ²⁰μόνοις δὲ ἐκείνοις ἐπετέτατο βαρεῖα νὺξ

14³ επεχυθη] επηλθεν BA
16² ερημιας St
17¹ συριζον] pr. δια S*t
18² απηνεστατος A(t)

18⁴ παρελυσεν B S | εκφοβουσα Sᶜt
20¹ επετετατο mu. (cf. Homeri
Odyss. 11, 19)] επετατο BA, επε-
κειτο St, εδεδοτο Vt

14. THEIR SOUL'S SURRENDER: Evidently a reference to v. 12. Itala *animae traductione*, "by treachery of the soul," is a stronger expression and quite feasible here. Pal. Syr. has an extraordinary rendering: "and thou didst seem to be bound when thou wast not in chains." UNEXPECTED FEAR: The fear is elaborated upon in the next four verses. *Cf.* also 18.17. WAS POURED: Reading *epechuthē* with א against the easier *epēlthen* of B.
15. THEN THUS: So Goodrick. When darkness came suddenly over the land, every Egyptian fell down where he was, and stirred not in his terror. A PRISON NOT OF IRON: This rhetorical figure is probably an imitation of Isa. 29.9 "drunken but not with wine."
16. IN A DESERT PLACE: *Erêmian* is hardly appropriate here: what could a laborer do in a desert? Some suggest an emendation: *Eirênên* "in peace."
17. All the sounds of nature became horrible to the Egyptians, even those

¹⁴On the one hand were haunted by portents of ap-
　　paritions,
And on the other were paralyzed by their soul's sur-
　　render,
For sudden and unexpected fear was poured upon
　　them.

15　¹⁵Then thus whosoever there fell down
　　Was kept straitly shut up in a prison not of iron.
¹⁶For whether a man was a husbandman or a shepherd,
　　Or a doer of labours in a desert place,
　　Being overtaken he endured the inevitable fate,
　　For by one chain of darkness all were bound.
¹⁷Whether there were a whistling wind
　　Or a melodious noise of birds around far-spreading
　　　branches,
　　Or a measured sound of water running violently,
　　Or a sharp crash of rocks hurled down,
¹⁸Or an unseen running of bounding animals,
　　Or a voice of most savage beasts roaring,
　　Or an echo resounding from the hollow of the hills,
　　It paralyzed them with terror.
¹⁹For the whole world was illuminated with bright light,
　　And was engaged in unhindered toils.

20　²⁰But over them alone heavy night was spread,

---

that are considered pleasant. The sighing of the wind became like the
hissing of serpents (v. 9), the singing of birds became a shriek, the fall of
waters the roar of a cataract, etc. From the description here it becomes
evident that the writer conceived the darkness as subjective, while the
Scriptural account construed it as objective, *cf.* Ex. 10.23 "all the children
of Israel had light in their dwellings."

18. Here is another class of sounds actually terrible in themselves, which
proved still worse to the helpless Egyptians.　RUNNING OF BOUNDING
ANIMALS: A sudden stampede among the flocks or herds would give rise to
the horrors of 11.17 ff.　AN ECHO RESOUNDING: For the terrifying effect
of an echo in an enclosed space in the dark *cf.* Jud. 7.20.

19. THE WHOLE WORLD: The darkness was local, not universal. It is difficult to explain on rational grounds the effect of the darkness on the
Egyptians and the Israelites as stated in Ex. 10.22 f., but some would see
in the darkness the effect of the electrical wind known as *hamsin* (Gregg).

εἰκὼν τοῦ μέλλοντος αὐτοὺς διαδέχεσθαι σκότους,
ἑαυτοῖς δὲ ἦσαν βαρύτεροι σκότους.

18 ¹ Τοῖς δὲ ὁσίοις σου μέγιστον ἦν φῶς·
ὧν φωνὴν μὲν ἀκούοντες μορφὴν δὲ οὐχ ὁρῶντες,
ὅτι μὲν οὐ κἀκεῖνοι ἐπεπόνθεισαν, ἐμακάριζον,
²ὅτι δ' οὐ βλάπτουσιν προηδικημένοι, ηὐχαρίστουν
καὶ τοῦ διενεχθῆναι χάριν ἐδέοντο.
³ἀνθ' ὧν πυριφλεγῆ στῦλον
ὁδηγὸν μὲν ἀγνώστου ὁδοιπορίας,
ἥλιον δὲ ἀβλαβῆ φιλοτίμου ξενιτείας παρέσχες.
⁴ἄξιοι μὲν γὰρ ἐκεῖνοι στερηθῆναι φωτὸς καὶ φυλακισθῆναι
σκότει
οἱ κατακλείστους φυλάξαντες τοὺς υἱούς σου,
δι' ὧν ἤμελλεν τὸ ἄφθαρτον νόμου φῶς τῷ αἰῶνι δίδοσθαι.

20² αυτου S*†   3³ φιλ. ξεν.] φιλοτιμιας S*†
                            4¹ εκεινου A† | σκοτει] pr. εν B°†,
2¹ ευχαριστουσιν BS†   σκοτους S*†

---

20. WHICH WAS TO RECEIVE THEM: Namely in Hades. *Cf.* v. 14 above, also Ps. 88.12. Hades actually receives souls, see 16.14c, Tobit 14.10.

The sudden introduction of moral darkness in lieu of physical is surprising, and Thackeray (*Journal of Theological Studies*, VI, 234) suggested that εἰκὼν-σκότους may be a Christian interpolation, particularly so because nowhere else in Wisdom do we find any allusion to a hell for the ungodly.

1. THY HOLY ONES: Namely the Israelites, *cf.* 10.15.   HEARING: The Egyptians could not see the Israelites, though they could hear their voices.   HAD NOT SUFFERED: Reading *ou* with A and Itala (so Grimm, Siegfried, Farrar, Gregg, and Goodrick) instead of the meaningless *oun* of B and ℵ (so R.V.). The meaning seems to be that the Egyptians congratulated the Israelites that they had not suffered.

2. GIVE THANKS: A striking use of the historic present: the Egyptians are thankful that the Israelites, although ill-treated by them for many years, did not resort to reprisals when the opportunity offered itself.   FOR THE DIFFERENCE etc.: *I. e.* in their gratitude for having been spared the Egyptians begged of Pharaoh that he would allow the Israelites to depart. But this is not in accord with Scriptures, and the passage remains doubtful. R.V. renders "because they had been at variance with them they made supplication to them," but this does not represent the Greek text. Better is A.V. "besought them pardon for that they had been enemies." Itala has

An image of the darkness which was to receive them;
But to themselves they were heavier than darkness.

18 ¹ But for thy holy ones there was a very great light,
Whose voice indeed hearing, but seeing not their form,
They counted them happy that they had not suffered.
²But for that they do not hurt them, though wronged by
them before, they give thanks;
And for the difference that was made they besought
favour.
³In place of which thou didst provide a pillar blazing
with fire,
A guide indeed of their unknown journey,
And withal a harmless sun for their honourable exile.
⁴For worthy were they to be deprived of light and to be
imprisoned in darkness,
Who kept thy sons shut up,
Through whom the indestructible light of the law was to
be given to the world.

---

ut esset differentia donum petebant. Luther and others render "begged of
them (the Israelites) the favour of their departure," *cf.* Ex. 11.8, 12.33,
also 10.24, but this rendering strains the Greek.
3. IN PLACE OF WHICH: *I. e.* instead of all the terrors of darkness.   A
GUIDE: *Cf.* Targum Jonathan on Ex. 12.37: "The sons of Israel were protected by seven clouds of glory: four on their four sides; one above them,
that neither hail nor rain might fall upon them, nor that they should be
burned by the heat of the sun; one beneath them, that they might not be
hurt by thorns, serpents, or scorpions; and one went before them, to make
the valleys even and the mountains low, and to prepare them a place of
habitation." See also Philo (*Mos.*, I.29): "A cloud, in form like a massive
pillar, went before the people, with a light as of the sun by day and as of
fire by night, that they might not wander, but might follow an unerring
guide."   HARMLESS SUN: Giving light but no scorching heat, see Isa.
49.10. Undoubtedly the writer purports to say that instead of the burning
sun of the Sinai desert the mild rays of the pillar of fire lighted the
Israelites.
4. WORTHY WERE THEY: The Egyptians deserved the plague of darkness,
for, on the basis of the principle enunciated in 11.16, those who had sinned
by shutting Israel in the darkness of captivity, must be punished with
physical darkness.   THE LAW: The law in its widest sense, equivalent to
the religion of Israel, as in Isa. 1.10 and 2.3.   TO THE WORLD: *tô aiôni* is

5   ⁵ Βουλευσαμένους δ' αὐτοὺς τὰ τῶν ὁσίων ἀποκτεῖναι
νήπια
καὶ ἑνὸς ἐκτεθέντος τέκνου καὶ σωθέντος
εἰς ἔλεγχον τὸ αὐτῶν ἀφείλω πλῆθος τέκνων
καὶ ὁμοθυμαδὸν ἀπώλεσας ἐν ὕδατι σφοδρῷ.
⁶ἐκείνη ἡ νὺξ προεγνώσθη πατράσιν ἡμῶν,
ἵνα ἀσφαλῶς εἰδότες οἷς ἐπίστευσαν ὅρκοις ἐπευθυμή-
σωσιν.
⁷προσεδέχθη ὑπὸ λαοῦ σου
σωτηρία μὲν δικαίων, ἐχθρῶν δὲ ἀπώλεια·
⁸ᾧ γὰρ ἐτιμωρήσω τοὺς ὑπεναντίους,
τούτῳ ἡμᾶς προσκαλεσάμενος ἐδόξασας.
⁹κρυφῇ γὰρ ἐθυσίαζον ὅσιοι παῖδες ἀγαθῶν
καὶ τὸν τῆς θειότητος νόμον ἐν ὁμονοίᾳ διέθεντο

5³ το BS*Vꜩ]>Sᶜ, τον Aꜩ, των mu.
5⁴ και] τους δε εχθρους του λαου S*ꜩ
6² επιθυμησωσιν S

8¹ ω Vpl.] ως BSA
9¹ οσιοι>Aꜩ
9² θειοτ.] οσιοτητος S

---

used here exactly as in 14.6. This line recognizes the world-wide mission of
the Jewish people, *cf.* Isa. 42.6, 49.6, Mic. ch. 4, Ps. 22.28, Tobit 13.11.
Philo (*Abr.*, § 19) considers the Jewish people as holding the office of
priest and prophet on behalf of all the human race.
5. From here to v. 25 a fourth contrast is presented between the fortunes
of Israel and Egypt, namely the death of the first-born. Indeed, Gutberlet
notes a threefold contrast: 1. The Egyptians who had killed the male
children of Israel lost their first-born. 2. Those who had drowned Israel's
children in the Nile were themselves drowned in the Red Sea. 3. The rescue
of one child resulted in the destruction of his would-be murderers.   A
SINGLE CHILD etc.: Line 2 is a mere parenthesis, as may be seen also from
the translation of Itala *uno exposito filio et liberato.* The reference is of
course to Moses, see Ex. 2.3. Josephus (*Antiq.*, II.9) states that at the time
of the birth of Moses a wise man had warned Pharaoh that a child would
be born in Israel who, if he were reared, would bring the Egyptian
dominion low, and would raise the Israelites.   EXPOSED: *Ektethentos* is
almost a technical expression for the exposure of an infant with a view to
its death (Goodrick), hence "cast forth" of A.V. and R.V. is insufficient.
CONVICT: Itala renders *elenchos* by *traductio*, which means either "rebuke"
or "conviction." Grimm prefers to connect this phrase with the preceding
line, but as pointed out by Goodrick, the idea of rebuke is more naturally
connected with the destruction of many than the saving of one.
DEPRIVE etc.: See Ex. 12.29. Jubilees 48.14 states: "a thousand strong and
brave men perished for one infant whom they had cast into the river," and

5   5But them who plotted to slay the infants of the holy
       ones,
     And when a single child had been exposed and saved,
     To convict them, thou didst deprive of the multitude of
       their children,
     And all together didst destroy in a mighty flood.
     6That night was known beforehand to our fathers,
     That knowing surely on what oaths they trusted they
       might be cheered.
     7By thy people was expected
     Preservation of the righteous and destruction of their
       enemies;
     8For wherein thou didst punish the adversaries,
     Therein calling us to thee thou didst glorify us.
     9For in secret did the pious children of good men
       sacrifice,
     And with one accord arranged the law of divinity,

---

on the basis of this statement Charles (*Jubilees*, p. lxxiv) proposes the
following translation of our passage: "in retribution for even a single child
that was exposed thou didst take away a multitude," but the question is
whether *elenchos* could bear this meaning.

6. THAT NIGHT: The night was so well known as to need no further definition. *Cf*. Ex. 12.42 LXX.   OUR FATHERS: The writer is strictly impersonal, but here, as in 15.1–4, he identifies himself with the Israelites.
By fathers he means the patriarchs, to whom the deliverance from
Egyptian bondage was revealed (Gen. 15.14, 26.3). The term cannot apply
here to the people generally, since the latter is mentioned in the next
verse.   ON WHAT OATHS etc.: They could rejoice knowing that God's
oath was as sure a ground of satisfaction as the accomplished fact.

7. THE RIGHTEOUS: Meaning the Israelites, "the holy" of verses 1 and 5.
THEIR ENEMIES: *I. e.* the Egyptians.

8. CALLING US TO THEE: God made an appeal to the people through his
intervention on behalf of Israel in the death of the first-born.

9. IN SECRET: Ex. 12.46 implies that the celebration of the Passover, or at
least the sacrifice of the Paschal lamb, was strictly private, in the retire-
ment of the Israelite dwellings.   GOOD MEN: *Agathôn* is masculine, not
neuter. Very likely it refers to the patriarchs of v. 6, whose praises the
Israelites sang that night.   THE LAW OF DIVINITY: This may be the
divine law generally or specifically the divine institution of the Passover,
ton theion nomon. The variant of the Sinaitic *hosiotêtos*, supported by Itala
iustitiae legem, may be a plain gloss for the more difficult *theiotêtos*. But

τῶν αὐτῶν ὁμοίως καὶ ἀγαθῶν
καὶ κινδύνων μεταλήμψεσθαι τοὺς ἁγίους
πατέρων ἤδη προαναμέλποντες αἴνους.

10 ¹⁰ἀντήχει δ' ἀσύμφωνος ἐχθρῶν ἡ βοή,
καὶ οἰκτρὰ διεφέρετο φωνὴ θρηνουμένων παίδων·
¹¹ὁμοίᾳ δὲ δίκῃ δοῦλος ἅμα δεσπότῃ κολασθεὶς
καὶ δημότης βασιλεῖ τὰ αὐτὰ πάσχων,
¹²ὁμοθυμαδὸν δὲ πάντες ἐν ἑνὶ ὀνόματι θανάτου
νεκροὺς εἶχον ἀναριθμήτους·
οὐδὲ γὰρ πρὸς τὸ θάψαι οἱ ζῶντες ἦσαν ἱκανοί,
ἐπεὶ πρὸς μίαν ῥοπὴν ἡ ἐντιμοτέρα γένεσις αὐτῶν
διέφθαρτο.
¹³πάντα γὰρ ἀπιστοῦντες διὰ τὰς φαρμακείας
ἐπὶ τῷ τῶν πρωτοτόκων ὀλέθρῳ ὡμολόγησαν θεοῦ υἱὸν
λαὸν εἶναι.

9⁵ πατερ Sᶜ | προαναμελπόντων BS*† 12⁴ διεφθαρη Β
10² διεφενετο A† | φωνη> B†

more likely *theiotês* here is an affectation of our author for the more simple
theos. ALREADY CHANTING etc.: Reading *proanamelpontes* with A
and some MSS. of א: the Israelites were already united as a nation, and as
such had to chant the traditional glories of the patriarchs. This has
reference to the Hallel psalms, which, according to Pes. 117a, are to be in-
toned on Passover eve. The reading of B *proanamelpontōn* is adopted by
A.V. and R.V.: "the fathers already leading the sacred songs of praise."
This reading seems to be based on a fantastic contrast between the fathers
in Israel rejoicing in song and the lamentation of the Egyptians for their
children. *Êdê* is some source of difficulty. Gregg explains it as follows:
while now the singing was in progress there was heard the discordant cry
from the Egyptians. Grimm interprets thus: even at this time they had already begun to sing something corresponding to the ceremonial Hallel of
later days (Ps. ch. 113–118). Some singing of this sort went on at Hezekiah's Passover (II Chron. 30.21) and at Josiah's Passover (*ibid.* 35.15).
10. A DISCORDANT CRY: Itala *inconveniens vox*. Farrar interprets *asumfônos*
to mean "clashing with the joyful songs of the Israelites," and not merely
discordant in itself. *Cf.* Ex. 11.6 and 12.30; also Philo, *Mos.*, I.24. According to Targum Jonathan on Ex. 12.31 this cry could be heard four hundred
miles away. A PITEOUS VOICE: Reading *fônê* with א A and Itala; B
omits it. *Oiktra* must be taken as an epithet of *boê* or *fônê*, and hence
should not be emended to *oiktros*.
11. *Cf.* Ex. 12.29 and the Targum Yerushalmi to this verse: "from the
firstborn of Pharaoh . . . to the sons of the kings who were captives in

That the saints should share alike
In the same blessings and dangers,
Already chanting the praises of the fathers.

10 [10]But there sounded back a discordant cry of the enemies,
And a piteous voice of lamentation for children was
borne abroad.
[11]But slave together with master being punished with like
punishment,
And the common man suffering the same as the king;
[12]Yet all alike under one form of death
Had corpses without number;
For the living were not even sufficient to bury them,
Since at a single stroke their more precious offspring was
destroyed.
[13]For disbelieving all by reason of the enchantments,
Upon the destruction of the firstborn they confessed the
people to be God's son.

---

the dungeons as hostages, and who, for having rejoiced at the servitude of
Israel, were punished as the Egyptians." The Septuagint makes the
captives feminine, similarly Philo, *Mos.*, I.24.

12. ALL ALIKE: As in v. 5 above, *homothumadon* is used here in an un-
classical sense.   UNDER ONE FORM OF DEATH: So Grimm, Goodrick, *et
al. Onoma* in this sense is unparalleled in both classical and biblical Greek.
Siegfried renders *enheni onomati thanatou* "in one moment," on a par with
pros mian ropên in the last line, but this expresses only the temporal not
the formal phase.   THE LIVING WERE NOT EVEN SUFFICIENT: Perhaps
this is an exaggeration of Num. 33.3 f., which states that when the children
of Israel journeyed from Rameses on the fifteenth day of Nisan, on the
morrow after the passover, the Egyptians were still busy burying their
first-born. *Cf.* also Philo, *Mos.*, I.17. According to the Midrash (*Pesikta
de-Rab Kahana*, ed. Buber, fol. 65a) the first-born themselves killed their
parents because they refused to send the children of Israel out of the land,
the number of the slain parents amounting to 600,000.   AT A SINGLE
STROKE: So R.V., giving the general, though not the literal, sense of
pros mian ropên. Itala renders *uno momento*, so Goodrick.

13. DISBELIEVING ALL: Pharaoh was swayed by the fact that the magicians
could do as Moses had done, see Ex. 7.13 and 22. But the writer ignores
the change in Ex. 8.14.   GOD'S SON: *Cf.* Ex. 4.22. It is not recorded
in the Scriptures that the Egyptians made this claim, but the writer seems
to amplify Ex. 12.31 (Gregg).

¹⁴ἡσύχου γὰρ σιγῆς περιεχούσης τὰ πάντα
  καὶ νυκτὸς ἐν ἰδίῳ τάχει μεσαζούσης
15 ¹⁵ὁ παντοδύναμός σου λόγος ἀπ' οὐρανῶν ἐκ θρόνων
     βασιλείων
   ἀπότομος πολεμιστὴς εἰς μέσον τῆς ὀλεθρίας ἥλατο γῆς
   ξίφος ὀξὺ τὴν ἀνυπόκριτον ἐπιταγήν σου φέρων
¹⁶καὶ στὰς ἐπλήρωσεν τὰ πάντα θανάτου
   καὶ οὐρανοῦ μὲν ἥπτετο, βεβήκει δ' ἐπὶ γῆς.
¹⁷τότε παραχρῆμα φαντασίαι μὲν ὀνείρων δεινῶν ἐξετά-
     ραξαν αὐτούς,
   φόβοι δὲ ἐπέστησαν ἀδόκητοι,
¹⁸καὶ ἄλλος ἀλλαχῇ ῥιφεὶς ἡμίθνητος
   δι' ἣν ἔθνησκον αἰτίαν ἐνεφάνιζεν·
¹⁹οἱ γὰρ ὄνειροι θορυβήσαντες αὐτοὺς τοῦτο προεμήνυσαν,

14² fin.]+τα παντα B*†   17¹ δεινως B†
15³ υποταγην A   18² εθνησκεν BSᶜ | ενεφανιζον A
16² επι>S*V†

---

14. PEACEFUL SILENCE: The description of the mysterious visitation recalls Job 4.13 ff.

15. ALL-POWERFUL WORD: The epithet is applied to Wisdom in 7.23. As to
the noun, it has been claimed by various commentators that it represents
the Philonian Logos. But this cannot be the case for various reasons. In the
first place, we have seen that the divine *logos* has no Greek philosophical
associations in the other passages of this book where it occurs (9.1, 12.9,
16.12). Moreover, the entire chapter is Hebraic in thought, not Greek. In
fact, our passage seems to be based on I. Chron. 21.16, where the agent is
the angel of the Lord. True, Pseudo-Solomon nowhere else speaks of
angels; nevertheless he must have known that angels played an important part in Jewish theology. Again, the function here attributed to
logos is elsewhere assigned to *rêma*, cf. Hos. 6.5. Note also that though the
Targum Jonathan on Ex. 12.29 has "the word of the Lord slew all the
firstborn in the land of Egypt," the text here speaks of God as the agent.
Hence, Gregg concludes, it is plain that the writer had no intention of
hypostatizing the Logos, but had in mind only the customary Jewish
periphrasis for the Lord, *i. e.* the *memra* of Yahweh, meaning the Divine
Being in self-manifestation. Again, if we try to identify God's word with
His wisdom, the application of the Philonian Logos becomes impossible,
since the latter is never represented as the agent of destruction (hence
even Gfrörer, II, 232, refused to identify the *logos* here with that of Philo).
In sum, the personification of *logos* here is purely poetical, as in some biblical narratives in which the agent is now spoken of as God and again as the

^{14}For while peaceful silence enveloped all things,

And night in her own swift course was at midway,

15   ^{15}Thy all-powerful word from heaven, from the royal throne,

A stern warrior leapt into the midst of the doomed land,

Bearing as a sharp sword thine irrevocable command-ment,

^{16}And standing filled all things with death,

And touched the heaven yet trod upon the earth.

^{17}Then on a sudden visions of dreams terribly dismayed them,

And unexpected fears came upon them.

^{18}And one here, another there, thrown down half dead,

Made manifest through what cause he was dying.

^{19}For the dreams that terrified them presaged this,

---

angel of the Lord, *cf.* Gregg's Introduction to his Commentary, pp. XXXVIII f.   ROYAL THRONE: Lit. "thrones," plural of dignity, as in 9.4, Dan. 7.9.   A STERN WARRIOR: The all-powerful word is pictured as a warrior bearing a sword and being sent on an errand of destruction. As stated above, the picture is drawn from I Chron. 21.16.

16. TOUCHED THE HEAVEN etc.: An elaboration of "between the earth and the heaven" of I Chron. 21.16. Similarly Philo, *Confus. Ling.*, § 23, and *Opif.*, § 51.

17. TERRIBLY: Reading *deinōs* with B, but א A have *deinōn* agreeing with *oneirōn* (terrible dreams).

There is hardly any authority for this statement. Arnold thinks it may be a fragment of rabbinic tradition, or a reflection of the well-known super-stition according to which great disasters were heralded by apparitions of the dead.

18. It is not certain whether the first-born or those who died in terror of darkness are meant. In either case it became manifest that their death was due to the wrath of God.   HALF DEAD: *Cf.* Pesikta de-Rab Kahana, ed. Buber, fol. 65a, where it is stated that the first-born did not die suddenly but were stricken with a deadly disease during the evening and were struggling in convulsions all night and died by day. The reason given for this statement is that it is written, We are all dying, *i. e.* the first-born who were about to die said themselves "we are all dying."

19. PRESAGED: Itala *praemonebant*, *i. e.* showed before they died. The revelation by dreams to those about to be punished may be compared with the dream of Nebuchadnezzar in Dan. ch. 2. Pfleiderer would see the influence of the Stoics here, and indeed the Stoics paid much attention to dreams (see Zeller, *Stoics*, p. 355, n. 6), but so did all ancient peoples.

ἵνα μὴ ἀγνοοῦντες δι' ὃ κακῶς πάσχουσιν ἀπόλωνται.

20   ²⁰ Ἥψατο δὲ καὶ δικαίων πεῖρα θανάτου,
καὶ θραῦσις ἐν ἐρήμῳ ἐγένετο πλήθους.
ἀλλ' οὐκ ἐπὶ πολὺ ἔμεινεν ἡ ὀργή·
²¹σπεύσας γὰρ ἀνὴρ ἄμεμπτος προεμάχησεν
τὸ τῆς ἰδίας λειτουργίας ὅπλον
προσευχὴν καὶ θυμιάματος ἐξιλασμὸν κομίσας·
ἀντέστη τῷ θυμῷ καὶ πέρας ἐπέθηκε τῇ συμφορᾷ
δεικνὺς ὅτι σός ἐστιν θεράπων·
²²ἐνίκησεν δὲ τὸν χόλον οὐκ ἰσχύι τοῦ σώματος,
οὐχ ὅπλων ἐνεργείᾳ,
ἀλλὰ λόγῳ τὸν κολάζοντα ὑπέταξεν
ὅρκους πατέρων καὶ διαθήκας ὑπομνήσας.

20¹ πειρα] περι A*†
20³ fin.]+σου S*
21³ προσευχης Sᵉ

22¹ χολον Bauermeister (cf. Fr.)]
οχλον mss.

WITHOUT KNOWING: Not only were the survivors to recognize God's hand, but the victims also.

20. EXPERIENCE OF DEATH: The word implies that the mere taste of death was enough to teach the Israelites the desired lesson.   TOUCHED THE RIGHTEOUS: Namely the Israelites, as in verses 1 and 9 above. The reference is to the plague that befell the Israelites upon their murmuring against Moses and Aaron after the destruction of Korah, Dathan, and Abiram, cf. Num. 16.44 ff., and Philo, Somn., II.35, and Q.R.D.H., 42. DESTRUCTION: Thrausis means literally "breaking" or "smashing," but is used in LXX of Num. 16.46 ff. for "plague."   THE WRATH REMAINED: Cf. 16.5. The plague was indeed stayed, but not before 14,700 perished therein.

21. A BLAMELESS MAN: I. e. Aaron. But why should Aaron be called blameless? Dr. Zeitlin thinks that this is an error based on mistranslation: shalom "peace" was misread shalem "perfect, blameless." In Hebrew literature Aaron is known as a man of peace. Cf. Abot de R. Nathan, 24–5.
SHIELD: So Itala and A.V. for hoplon, which in the singular at least always signifies "shield," never an offensive weapon, as assumed by R.V. Besides, a weapon is entirely inappropriate here, for Aaron did not attack the destroying power, he kept it off, with propitiation of incense.   MINISTRY: Leitourgia is the technical word for the ministration of the priesthood throughout the Bible. Pal. Syr. renders more correctly "priesthood."
PRAYER: Cf. Targum Yerushalmi on Num. 17.12 "Aaron stood in the

That they might not perish without knowing why they
were afflicted.

20   20But an experience of death touched the righteous
also,

And in the desert there was a destruction of a multitude,

But not for long the wrath remained.

21For a blameless man hasted to be their champion,

Bringing the shield of his own ministry,

Prayer and the propitiation of incense;

He opposed the wrath and set a limit to the disaster,

Showing that he was thy servant.

22But he overcame the wrath, not by strength of
body,

Nor by force of arms,

But by word he subdued the chastiser,

Recalling the oaths and covenants of the fathers.

---

midst . . . with the censer and interceded in prayer."   INCENSE: *Cf.*
Num. 17.12. On the efficacy of incense see Lev. 16.12 f.   THY SERVANT:
Aaron proved to the destroyer that he was God's servant by the sacred
ornaments of his office, see v. 24. Note the term *therapôn*, which is of
greater distinction than *doulos*.

22. OVERCAME THE WRATH: Practically all the MSS. and all the versions
read *ochlon* "crowd," which makes no sense. A conjectural emendation, involving only a transposition of letters, was advanced by Bauermeister
and adopted by modern translators and commentators: *cholon* "anger,
wrath." Actual examples of confusion of these two words are cited by
Grimm. Moreover, *cholon* is favored by verses 21 and 23.   BY WORD: His
weapons were spiritual, not physical. By "word" here is meant the word of
intercession, *cf.* next line and Ex. 32.13.   THE CHASTISER: *Kolazonta* is
a personification of the destroying spirit, who elsewhere is called an angel
(IV Macc. 7.11).   RECALLING etc.: Cases of intercession are numerous
in the Scriptures; typical is that of Ex. 32.13. Our writer thinks of Aaron
pleading the merits of the fathers. It should be noted that the rabbis
exalted the merits of the fathers, claiming that they served for the whole
nation, *cf.* Wayyikra rabba, chapter 36.2: "Just as this vine leans upon
dry trees and it is moist so Israel leans upon the merits of their fathers
although they are old."   COVENANTS OF THE FATHERS: Meaning, of
course, covenants concluded with the fathers, as in the case of Abraham
(Gen. 15.7), Isaac (17.19), Jacob (28.13), etc.

²³σωρηδὸν γὰρ ἤδη πεπτωκότων ἐπ' ἀλλήλων νεκρῶν
μεταξὺ στὰς ἀνέκοψε τὴν ὀργὴν
καὶ διέσχισεν τὴν πρὸς τοὺς ζῶντας ὁδόν.
²⁴ἐπὶ γὰρ ποδήρους ἐνδύματος ἦν ὅλος ὁ κόσμος,
καὶ πατέρων δόξαι ἐπὶ τετραστίχου λίθων γλυφῆς,
καὶ μεγαλωσύνη σου ἐπὶ διαδήματος κεφαλῆς αὐτοῦ.
25 ²⁵τούτοις εἶξεν ὁ ὀλεθρεύων, ταῦτα δὲ ἐφοβήθη·
ἦν γὰρ μόνη ἡ πεῖρα τῆς ὀργῆς ἱκανή.

19 ¹ Τοῖς δὲ ἀσεβέσιν μέχρι τέλους ἀνελεήμων θυμὸς
ἐπέστη·
προῄδει γὰρ αὐτῶν καὶ τὰ μέλλοντα,
²ὅτι αὐτοὶ ἐπιτρέψαντες τοῦ ἀπιέναι

23³ διεκοψεν Sᶜ†   25² οργης]+σου S†
24² λιθου BS† | γλυφη S*†
25¹ εφοβηθησαν BS*   2¹ επιστρεψ. BS*

---

23. IN HEAPS: for *sōrēdon* see Philo, *Mos.*, I.17.   PARTED: He cleft a way among the people, keeping the living all on one side of it (Goodrick). Gregg explains it "he cut through it as if he were breaking down a bridge."
24. THE ROBE etc.: The long blue robe of the high priest, fringed with bells and pomegranates. As a matter of fact this robe was not *podêrês* (reaching to the feet), but this is the word applied to it in Ex. 28.4 LXX. The real full-length robe was the white linen garment of I Sam. 2.28, which is there called *ephod*, though the *ephod* proper is known to have been a sort of waistcoat, as described in Ex. 28.6 ff., see William R. Arnold, *Ephod and Ark*, Cambridge 1917, and Hermann Thiersch, *Ependytes und Ehpod*, Stuttgart 1936.   THE WHOLE WORLD: Aaron's garments were symbolic. Jewish tradition had it that each part of the high priest's garments had a mystic signification. *Cf.* Josephus, *Antiq.*, III.VII.7, according to whom the blue vestment denoted the sky, the girdle the ocean, the sardonyx buttons on the priest's shoulders the sun and moon, the mitre or diadem the heaven again. Philo expands this into four full chapters (*Mos.*, III, § 11–14).   THE FOUR-ROWED STONE OF GRAVING: A Hebraism for "the four-rowed graven stone," *i. e.* the four rows of precious stones in the high priest's breastplate, on which see Ex. 28.15 ff. Philo (*Mos.*, II,12) considers it a symbol of the Zodiac, which represents four seasons of three months. Josephus (*Antiq.*, III.7.5) sees in it a symbol of the earth, which is in the middle of the world. On the twelve stones of the breastplate were engraved the names of the twelve patriarchs or tribes of Israel, and these names are "the glories of the fathers," whose acts were symbolized by their names.   THE DIADEM OF HIS HEAD: Refers to the golden *petalon* or

²³For when the dead were already fallen in heaps upon one
  another,
Standing between he cut short the wrath,
And parted the way to the living.
²⁴For on the robe that reached to his feet was the whole
  world,
And the glories of the fathers upon the four-rowed stone
  of graving,
And thy greatness on the diadem of his head.
25   ²⁵To these the destroyer yielded, and these he feared,
For the single experience of wrath was sufficient.

19   ¹   But on the impious until the end there came pitiless
  anger,
For even their future he knew beforehand.
²How themselves having changed their minds about the
  departure,

---

plate fastened on the linen mitre on which were engraved the words
"Holy to the Lord" (Ex. 28.36). According to Josephus (*Antiq.*, III.VII.7)
it symbolizes heaven. To Philo (*Mos.*, II.11 and 14) the tetragrammaton
was to symbolize that the world could only be sustained by the will of God.
25. TO THESE: Namely to the high priest clothed in the symbols of the
world, the fathers, and God, the destroying angel yielded.   HE FEARED:
Reading *efobêthê* with A, Itala, Syroh, and A.V. But against this it is
urged that only an evil spirit could have been terrified by the sacred em-
blems, whereas this was a messenger of God. Hence R.V. and others
follow the reading *efobêthêsan* of B ℵ, Pal. Syr. and Arab., which agrees
better with line 2. Against the plural it may be said that the subject "the
people" has to be supplied, and, further, there is no reason why the people
should have feared the holy garments of the high priest (Holmes).

This chapter deals with the fifth comparison between the Israelites and
Egyptians, the subject being the passage of the Red Sea.
1. THE IMPIOUS: Namely the Egyptians.   UNTIL THE END: Until the
final destruction in the Red Sea.   HE KNEW: The subject is God, supplied out of "anger" in the first line. Cf. Ex. 3.19 and 7.4.
2. HAVING CHANGED THEIR MINDS: Reading *epistrepsantes* with Swete.
The construction with the genitive *tou apeinai* is difficult. Grimm would
read *epistrefesthai* with the genitive, rendering "having thought anxiously
over their departure." R.V. renders "changed their minds to let thy people

ΣΟΦΙΑ ΣΑΛΩΜΩΝΟΣ

καὶ μετὰ σπουδῆς προπέμψαντες αὐτοὺς
διώξουσιν μεταμεληθέντες.
³ἔτι γὰρ ἐν χερσὶν ἔχοντες τὰ πένθη
καὶ προσοδυρόμενοι τάφοις νεκρῶν
ἕτερον ἐπεσπάσαντο λογισμὸν ἀνοίας
καὶ οὓς ἱκετεύοντες ἐξέβαλον, τούτους ὡς φυγάδας
ἐδίωκον.
⁴εἷλκεν γὰρ αὐτοὺς ἡ ἀξία ἐπὶ τοῦτο τὸ πέρας ἀνάγκη
καὶ τῶν συμβεβηκότων ἀμνηστίαν ἐνέβαλεν,
ἵνα τὴν λείπουσαν ταῖς βασάνοις προσαναπληρώσωσιν
κόλασιν,
5 ⁵καὶ ὁ μὲν λαός σου παράδοξον ὁδοιπορίαν πειράσῃ,
ἐκεῖνοι δὲ ξένον εὕρωσι θάνατον.
⁶ὅλη γὰρ ἡ κτίσις ἐν ἰδίῳ γένει πάλιν ἄνωθεν διετυποῦτο
ὑπηρετοῦσα ταῖς σαῖς ἐπιταγαῖς,
ἵνα οἱ σοὶ παῖδες φυλαχθῶσιν ἀβλαβεῖς.

3³ ανοιας> S*†
6² σαις] ιδιαις B

---

go." WITH EAGERNESS: An allusion to the presents which the
Egyptians showered upon the Israelites at their departure, see Ex.
12.35 f.

3. ON THEIR HANDS: *en chersin echontes*, Itala *inter manus habentes*, seems to
be a colloquial expression, and there is hardly any need to suppose that the
actual manual work of embalming is alluded to. COUNSEL OF FOLLY:
An allusion no doubt to the fond expectation of the Egyptians that ignorance of the country would lead the Israelites into a trap, see Ex. 14.2.
Cf. also Targ. Jonathan on Ex. 14.3: "And Pharaoh will say to Dathan and
Abiram, the Israelites who remained in Egypt: The people of the house of
Israel are bewildered in the land, the idol Zaphon had shut them in close
upon the desert."

4. A DESERVED FATE: *Axia anankê* might be taken as a contradiction in
terms, the former implying free will, the latter predestination. But, as
pointed out by Toy (*Encyclopedia Biblica*, col. 5340), *anankê* (necessity) in
Pseudo-Solomon is not the Greek inevitable destiny, but rather the divine
predestination according to desert, or, as Gregg puts it, the inevitable
sequence of cause and effect. MADE THEM FORGET: Blinded them to the
consequences of their sins. THE THINGS etc.: Namely the plagues, and
particularly the death of the first-born.

5. A WONDERFUL JOURNEY: The journey through the desert, characterized
by miracles and wonders. THOSE: Refers to the Egyptians, whose death
was as strange and miraculous as the journey of the Israelites.

And having sent them away with eagerness,
They should pursue them, repenting,
³For while they still had their mournings on their
hands,
And were lamenting over the graves of the dead,
They seized upon another counsel of folly,
And pursued as fugitives those whom they had cast out
with entreaties.
⁴For a deserved fate dragged them on to this end,
And made them forget the things that had befallen
them,
That they might fill up the measure of punishment lacking to their torments.

5   ⁵And that thy people might accomplish a wonderful
journey,
While those might find a strange death.
⁶For the whole creation in its several kinds was fashioned
again anew,
Ministering to thy several commandments,
That thy servants might be kept without hurt.

---

6. The miracle of the passage of the Red Sea is here explained by the
philosophical doctrine of the mutual interchange of the elements. "Nothing new came into being when a miracle occurred: there was only a transmutation of elements," says Gregg, who also quotes Epictetus (III.24):
"This cosmos is one city, and its constituent substance is one, and there
must needs be a certain periodicity and surrender of one thing to another,
some things being dissolved and others combining, some standing still and
others moving"; and again: "This variability is partaken of both by men
and animals; and not only they but the gods and the four elements are
turned up and down in their transmutations, so that earth becomes water,
and water air, and air turns into aether; and the same process of transmutation takes place in the reverse way" (anôthen katô). The quantity of
matter is constant; any partial disturbance is followed by a corresponding
reaction throughout the whole mass. Pfleiderer (Heraklit, p. 325) thinks
that the whole idea is Heraclitic.   WAS FASHIONED AGAIN ANEW: Itala
refigurabatur. Palin anôthen is pleonastic. Anôthen is interpreted either
philosophically "from top to bottom" or theologically "from above."
THY SEVERAL COMMANDMENTS: A.V. has "thy peculiar commandments,"
which Farrar explains as follows: "in the passage of the Red Sea the elements obeyed the special injunctions laid on them instead of following
their normal course."

⁷ἢ τὴν παρεμβολὴν σκιάζουσα νεφέλη,
ἐκ δὲ προϋφεστῶτος ὕδατος ξηρᾶς ἀνάδυσις γῆς ἐθεωρήθη,
ἐξ ἐρυθρᾶς θαλάσσης ὁδὸς ἀνεμπόδιστος
καὶ χλοηφόρον πεδίον ἐκ κλύδωνος βιαίου·
⁸δι᾿ οὗ πανεθνεὶ διῆλθον οἱ τῇ σῇ σκεπαζόμενοι χειρὶ
θεωρήσαντες θαυμαστὰ τέρατα.
⁹ὡς γὰρ ἵπποι ἐνεμήθησαν
καὶ ὡς ἀμνοὶ διεσκίρτησαν
αἰνοῦντές σε, κύριε, τὸν ῥυσάμενον αὐτούς.
10   ¹⁰ἐμέμνηντο γὰρ ἔτι τῶν ἐν τῇ παροικίᾳ αὐτῶν,
πῶς ἀντὶ μὲν γενέσεως ζῴων ἐξήγαγεν ἡ γῆ σκνῖπα,
ἀντὶ δὲ ἐνύδρων ἐξηρεύξατο ὁ ποταμὸς πλῆθος βατράχων.
¹¹εφ᾿ ὑστέρῳ δὲ εἶδον καὶ γένεσιν νέαν ὀρνέων,
ὅτε ἐπιθυμίᾳ προαχθέντες ᾐτήσαντο ἐδέσματα τρυφῆς·
¹²εἰς γὰρ παραμυθίαν ἐκ θαλάσσης ἀνέβη αὐτοῖς ὀρτυγο-
μήτρα.
¹³   Καὶ αἱ τιμωρίαι τοῖς ἁμαρτωλοῖς ἐπῆλθον

7¹] τη την π. σκιαζουση ν. Aǂ: ad 6³   10² σκν(ε)ιπα Bǂ] σκνιφα S*, σκνιφας
tractum   ASᶜ: cf. Ps. 104 31 et Thack. § 7.
7² εθεωρ(ε)ιτο S*Aǂ   18
8¹ πανεθν(ε)ι] παν εθνος S*ABᵒ   10³ ανυδρων Aǂ | πληθος βατραχων]
9³ ρυομενον BS   βατραχους S*ǂ

---

7. A GRASSY PLAIN: This is probably a legendary embellishment of the
Scriptural narrative. M. Gutmann in his German translation of the Book of
Wisdom (Altona 1841) quotes from a Hebrew prayer for the last day of
Passover: "and he rebuked the Red Sea, and the raging waves dried up,
and they (the Israelites) walked through abysses as on paved roads; on
both sides he brought up trees laden with fruit, and he caused sweet
springs to gush out for them in the abyss, and perfume of sweet spices to
spread its scent before them." *Chloêforon pedion* may be a fantastic
description of the actual bottom of the Red Sea, *cf.* Pliny, *Natural History*,
XIII.25.

10. PRODUCTION OF CATTLE: The word *geneseôs* is somewhat ambiguous,
since the earth does not ordinarily generate cattle. A.V. omits the word
altogether. Arnold is probably right in commenting thus: "The ground in
reality does not bring forth flies, much less cattle; the meaning is, and the
sense is much more natural and just, that the ground was so disposed by
God as to be a proper *nidus* for the generation of flies, but did not afford
its usual nourishment for the support and increase of cattle." LICE:
Sknifa is properly singular, though some MSS. have altered it into a plural

⁷The cloud that shadowed the camp,

And dry land seen rising up out of what before was
water,

An unhindered way out of the Red Sea,

And a grassy plain out of the raging wave.

⁸Through which a whole nation did pass, they that were
protected by thy hand,

Beholding marvellous wonders.

⁹For as horses they pastured,

And as lambs they skipped,

Praising thee, O Lord, that delivered them.

10   ¹⁰For they still remembered the things that happened in
their sojourning,

How instead of production of cattle the earth brought
forth lice,

And instead of water-creatures the river vomited forth
a swarm of frogs.

¹¹But later on they beheld also a new production of birds,

When led on by appetite they demanded meats of
delicacy.

¹²For to their comfort there came up for them quails from
the sea.

¹³And the punishments came upon the sinners,

---

sknifas. It is used here generically, as *batrachos* in Ex. 8.6.   WATER-
CREATURES: Itala renders *pro piscibus,* no doubt because fish are the
characteristic product of water, *cf.* Gen. 1.20 f.   VOMITED FORTH:
Properly "belched forth," as rendered by Itala *eructavit, cf.* Ex. 8.3.

11. PRODUCTION: *Genesin* is so rendered also by Itala *creaturam,* which is
certainly better than "race" of R.V., since there was nothing new about
the quails as birds, though their extraordinary quantity was undoubtedly
new. *Cf.* Ex. 16.11 ff. and Num. 11.18 ff.   MEATS OF DELICACY: A
Hebraism for "delicate meats." The writer seems to ignore the biblical
account (Num. 11.4 ff.), treating the sending of the quails as a gracious
answer to a reasonable request.

12. FOR THEIR COMFORT: *Cf.* Philo, *Mos.,* I.37.   QUAILS FROM THE SEA:
See 16.2 f. *Cf.* Num. 11.31. The quails did not originate in the sea, but had
crossed over the sea in one of their annual migrations and then dropped
down tired as soon as they reached the shore.

13. THE SINNERS: Namely the Egyptians, whose punishments form a con-

οὐκ ἄνευ τῶν προγεγονότων τεκμηρίων τῇ βίᾳ τῶν
κεραυνῶν·
δικαίως γὰρ ἔπασχον ταῖς ἰδίαις αὐτῶν πονηρίαις,
καὶ γὰρ χαλεπωτέραν μισοξενίαν ἐπετήδευσαν.
¹⁴οἱ μὲν γὰρ τοὺς ἀγνοοῦντας οὐκ ἐδέχοντο παρόντας·
οὗτοι δὲ εὐεργέτας ξένους ἐδουλοῦντο.
15 ¹⁵καὶ οὐ μόνον, ἀλλ' ἤ τις ἐπισκοπὴ ἔσται αὐτῶν,
ἐπεὶ ἀπεχθῶς προσεδέχοντο τοὺς ἀλλοτρίους·
¹⁶οἱ δὲ μετὰ ἑορτασμάτων
εἰσδεξάμενοι τοὺς ἤδη τῶν αὐτῶν μετεσχηκότας δικαίων
δεινοῖς ἐκάκωσαν πόνοις.
¹⁷ἐπλήγησαν δὲ καὶ ἀορασίᾳ
ὥσπερ ἐκεῖνοι ἐπὶ ταῖς τοῦ δικαίου θύραις,
ὅτε ἀχανεῖ περιβληθέντες σκότει
ἕκαστος τῶν ἑαυτοῦ θυρῶν τὴν δίοδον ἐζήτει.

13² προγεγον.] προ> B   16² των αυτων μετεσχ.] μετεσχ. των St

trast to the comfort of the Israelites.   VIOLENCE OF THE THUNDERS:
This is based on a Jewish tradition that the drowning of the Egyptians
occurred after or during a great war of the elements, cf. Ps. 77.16 ff.;
Targum Yerushalmi on Ex. 14.24 ("the word of the Lord looked forth
upon the host of the Egyptians and cast upon them pitch and fire and
hailstones, etc."); see also Josephus, Antiq., II.XVI.3.   JUSTLY DID
THEY SUFFER: Dramatic justice is a favorite theme of Apocryphal writers,
cf. II Macc. 9.6 and 13.8. The justice of the punishment is shown by comparing it with that of Sodom.   HARSHER HATRED OF STRANGERS: The
comparison is assumed to be with the Sodomites, who were notorious for
their mistreatment of their guests, see Gen. ch. 19 and comment on next
verse. Philo (Mos., I.7) says: "They (the Israelites) came to dwell in
Egypt under guarantee of security, and Pharaoh enslaved them as if they
had been taken captive in war or bought from slave-dealers, and he
treated as slaves those who were not only free but guests, suppliants, and
resident foreigners, with never a thought of his obligation to the god of
freedom, of hospitality, of sanctuary, and of the hearth."
14. CERTAIN PERSONS: Meaning the men of Sodom, which R.V. supplies
in the text. The writer as usual leaves it to his readers to interpret his
allusions.   DID NOT RECEIVE: A hint that the men of Sodom refused to
receive the angel visitors. According to Sanh. 109a they said: "Of what
use are to us traveling strangers? They only come to diminish our money."
THESE: I. e. the Egyptians.   GUESTS THAT DID THEM KINDNESS: That the
Israelites were invited guests in Egypt may be seen from Gen. 45.17 f. The
kindness is an allusion to the benefits they conferred on Egypt through
Joseph and through their own labors in the land of bondage.

Not without signs preceding, in the violence of the
thunders;
For justly did they suffer by their own wickedness,
For they practiced a yet harsher hatred of strangers.
¹⁴For certain persons did not receive them that knew them
not when they came,
But these enslaved guests that did them kindness.

15 ¹⁵And not only so, but whatever visitation there be shall
be theirs,
Since they received hatefully those that were aliens.
¹⁶But they with feastings
Welcoming them that already shared the same rights,
Afflicted them with sore labours.
¹⁷And moreover they were stricken with sightlessness,
As were those at the doors of the righteous man,
When, enveloped in yawning darkness,
Each was seeking for the way through his own doors.

---

15. VISITATION: *Episkopê* is used here in a good sense, as in 3.7 and 4.15.
Goodrick has "allowance" instead.   THEIRS: The reference is to the men
of Sodom, for whom the writer makes excuses and pleads extenuating circumstances. R.V. actually renders "God shall visit the men of Sodom after
another sort."
16. WITH FEASTINGS: The writer seems to embellish the Scriptural account. Undoubtedly he is thinking of Joseph's banquets for his brethren
(Gen. 43.31 ff.) and of the general hospitality shown to the Israelites
(Gen. 47.1 ff.).   THE SAME RIGHTS: Another exaggeration, which may be
justified from Gen. 45.17 ff.
17. The writer reverts to his favorite plague of darkness and again insti-
tutes a correspondence between the men of Sodom and those of Egypt,
the former having lost their sight, the latter having been deprived of light.
SIGHTLESSNESS: *aorasia* is found only in biblical Greek. Philo uses it for the
Egyptian darkness in *Somn.*, I.18.   THE RIGHTEOUS MAN: *I. e.* Lot, *cf.*
10.6.   YAWNING DARKNESS: *Achanei skotei* is variously rendered because
of the uncertainty as to the meaning of *achanês*. Itala renders *subitaneis
tenebris*, Arab. "very deep darkness." Pal. Syr. omits the adjective. The
word is derived from *chanein* "to yawn," "to open the mouth," and may
mean either "speechless" (not opening the mouth) or "yawning wide"
(with *á* emphatic).   THROUGH HIS OWN DOORS: There is no mention anywhere that the Sodomites were groping about to find their own doors,
only that they were seeking to find Lot's door. Perhaps Reuss is right that
in this line the writer returns to the plight of the Egyptians.

¹⁸ Δι᾽ ἑαυτῶν γὰρ γὰ στοιχεῖα μεθαρμοζόμενα,
ὥσπερ ἐν ψαλτηρίῳ φθόγγοι τοῦ ῥυθμοῦ τὸ ὄνομα
διαλλάσσουσιν,
πάντοτε μένοντα ἤχῳ,
ὅπερ ἐστὶν εἰκάσαι ἐκ τῆς τῶν γεγονότων ὄψεως ἀκριβῶς·
¹⁹χερσαῖα γὰρ εἰς ἔνυδρα μετεβάλλετο,
καὶ νηκτὰ μετέβαινεν ἐπὶ γῆς·
20   ²⁰πῦρ ἴσχυεν ἐν ὕδατι τῆς ἰδίας δυνάμεως,
καὶ ὕδωρ τῆς σβεστικῆς φύσεως ἐπελανθάνετο·
²¹φλόγες ἀνάπαλιν εὐφθάρτων ζῴων
οὐκ ἐμάραναν σάρκας ἐμπεριπατούντων,
οὐδὲ τηκτὸν κρυσταλλοειδὲς εὔτηκτον γένος ἀμβροσίας
τροφῆς.

18³ παντα SᵉV† | ηχω] pr. εν SᵉV
19² επι γης] εις γην S*
20¹ ισχυσεν B | δυν.]+επιλελησμενον
A pl.
20² φυσ.] δυναμεως B

21³ τρυφης S*†
Subscr. σοφια σαλωμωνος B†, σοφ.
σαλομωντος S†, σοφ. σολομωνος AV†,
σοφ. σολομωντος C : cf. inscr.

---

18. This verse is difficult grammatically, though its sense seems to be quite clear. The difficulty arises chiefly from the confusion of the comparison with the thing to which it is compared. According to Gregg, the full sentence would read: "For the elements, changing their order one with another, [but continuing always the same, vary their combinations], just as the notes of a psaltery, continuing always the same, each in its several sound, vary the character of the rhythm." The idea is, Gregg continues, that the relations in which a thing stands can modify completely the effect which it produces: the notes of the instrument, in whatever key they are played, are the same notes, but the alteration of their relations seems (but only seems) entirely to have altered their sound. Bois explains it as follows: The musician plays a tune by a certain combination of musical sounds; he lays down his instrument, resumes it, and plays an entirely different tune; yet the sounds are the same, only their combination differs. So God has before Him matter—the *stoicheia*—which He combines in a certain way, and they produce *ktisis*, an orderly creation—the first melody. But then it becomes a question of blessing or punishing. He combines the elements in a different way; there is a new creation—the second melody; but the *fthongoi* are the same. As Gärtner puts it (p. 193): "Through the miracle with which God attacked the creation the harmony of the creation was not disturbed: rather were the elements so arranged as to remain in the same contrast to one another in which nature fixed them, so that the wonderful consequences could ensue. Thus only an en-

¹⁸For the elements being changed in order among them-
selves,
As in a psaltery the notes vary the character of the tune,
Yet always adhering to the sound,
Which one may accurately divine from the sight of
things that have happened.
¹⁹For land creatures were turned into water creatures,
And swimming creatures migrated on the earth.
20 ²⁰Fire had control of its own power in the water,
And water forgot its power of quenching.
²¹Contrariwise, flames wasted not the flesh
Of perishable creatures that walked among them,
Nor was melted the easily-melted ice-like kind of
heavenly food.

---

harmonic transformation of the elements took place, which the simile of
the psaltery purports to illustrate." THE ELEMENTS BEING CHANGED:
Cf. v. 6 above and 16.21.25. See also Philo, *Mos.*, I.17.28; II.12.   A
PSALTERY: Itala *organum*, probably any kind of musical instrument, as
explained by À Lapide. *Cf.* Philo, *Poster. C.*, § 32.   ONE MAY ACCURATELY
DIVINE: As evidence of the philosophical theory of interchange between the
elements the writer proceeds to adduce the various incidents of the
Exodus.
19. The meaning of the first line is that the Israelites and their cattle by
passing through the Red Sea became water creatures. The second line can
only refer to the frogs (Ex. 8.3), which, though amphibious, serve to illustrate the writer's doctrine of transmutation; similarly Philo, *Mos.*,
I.18.
20. This is a rechauffé of 16.17, and the second line is almost a repetition of
the first. On this subject *cf.* Philo, *Mos.*, I.20: "The thunder-bolts, shoot-
ing through the hail, neither melted it nor were put out themselves, for all
the incompatibility of their natures." See also Philo, *Somn.*, I.3: "Springs
of boiling water are known in mid sea, which all the water around them
could not overcome, nor even check in the least degree."
21. This verse, too, is a repetition of 16.18. As stated before, the writer
seems to be under the impression that all the plagues, hail, fire, locusts,
and flies, took place at one and the same time.   NOR WAS MELTED:
Reading *oud' etêkon* with Nannius and all versions, as against *oude
têkton* of all existing MSS. Itala *nec dissolvebant* seems to agree with the
conjectured emendation.   ICE-LIKE: For the forced comparison of
manna to snow and ice see 16.22.   HEAVENLY FOOD: *ambrosias trofês* is a
purpureus pannus "angels' food" *Cf.* 16.20. In the Sibylline Oracles, 3.84,
it is prophesied that manna will be the food of the righteous in heaven.

²² Κατὰ πάντα γάρ, κύριε, ἐμεγάλυνας τὸν λαόν σου
  καὶ ἐδόξασας
  καὶ οὐχ ὑπερεῖδες ἐν παντὶ καιρῷ καὶ τόπῳ παριστάμενος.

---

22. With this verse the book comes to an abrupt conclusion. It summarizes the belief of the writer that history is conducted on behalf of the people of Israel, that Israel is always true to its destiny, and that God is always on the side of Israel.

Various theories have been advanced concerning the abrupt ending. Some have assumed that the book has been mutilated; others that the author failed to complete his design. But there are numerous arguments against such assumptions. In the first place, III Maccabees ends as abruptly as our book, with the words "Blessed be the Saviour of Israel unto all times for ever." Then our author is concerned solely with the history of the Israelites in Egypt, while the subsequent history of Israel does not interest him at all, perhaps because it does not furnish opportunities for

²²For in all things, Lord, thou didst magnify and glorify
   thy people,
And didst not overlook them, standing by them at every
   time and place.

---

the antitheses in which he delights. Having finished with the Egyptians,
against whom for some reason his invectives are directed, he considered
his duty done and penned the last verse as an epilogue to his treatise. But
perhaps more cogent and to the point is the suggestion of Goodrick that
the abrupt termination of the book may be set down to the absolute
weariness of the author with his subject. "Any one who reads carefully the
last chapter or two, with their tautologies in language and their repetitions of matter, will agree that they are the work of a man whose en-
thusiastic rhetoric had found its limit. He has no more to say, and it is a
pity that he did not recognize this before. His vocabulary and his imagination are alike exhausted."

Aaron, 138, 163, 169, 212, 213, 214
Abbahu, Rabbi, 41
Abel, 133
Abraham, 133–34, 135, 213
Absalom, 144
Acts, 65, 68, 166, 169, 189
Adam, 132
Admah, 134
Adultery, 79
Aeolus, 160
Agesilaus, 173
Ahab, 150
Ahikar, 39
Akiba, Rabbi, 192
Albright, 39
Alexandria, 11–12, 15–16, 18, 29, 40
Allegorizing, 30
Ambrosius, 80
Amos, 63, 149, 191
Anacharsis, 169
Anaximenes, 160
Angels, 210
Animal worship, 144, 149, 157, 159, 163, 184, 185
Anonymity, 84
Antiochus, 144
Apocalyptic, 72
Aquila, 116
Arabic, Aramaic, and Armenian versions, 8
Aristeas, 106, 162
Aristobulus, 16, 30, 104, 106
Aristophanes, 177
Aristotle, 145
Arnobius, 179
Arnold, William R., 62, 197, 211, 214, 218
Art, see Painting and sculpture
Astronomy, 112–13
Athanasius, 161
Athenagoras, 116

Augustine, 1, 6, 16, 66, 75, 81, 90
Augustus, 173
Authorized English version, 8

Babel, tower of, 133
Barnabas, 66
Barney, 72
Baruch, 74, 93, 163, 164, 165, 166
Bauermeister, 20, 213
Bela, 134
Benjamin of Tudela, 135
Bertholet, 10, 19, 39
Bissell, E. C., 69
Bois, H., 20, 26, 35, 51, 52, 53, 59, 64, 69, 70, 72, 75, 110, 160, 162, 168, 191, 200, 222
Bousset, W., 173
Bretschneider, Karl Gottlieb, 2, 19, 23, 76
Brooke, 5
Budde, 10, 39, 118
Buisson, du Mesnil du, 179
Bun bar Hiyya, Rabbi, 86
Burkitt, 7

Cain, 70, 132–33, 144
Caligula, 13, 173
Canaanites, 136, 147, 150, 151, 152, 153
Cannibalism, 151
Canticles, 98, 118
Castor and Pollux, 166
Celibacy, 77, 80
Ceriani, A. M., 7
Charles, R. H., 13, 19, 21, 53, 72, 74, 130, 146, 201, 207
Children, dead, worship of, 172; exposure of, 143, 206; punishment of, 83; sacrifice of, 150–51, 175

I Chronicles, 62, 100, 122, 126, 127, 128, 210, 211
II Chronicles, 91, 102, 110, 111, 122, 128, 208
Churton, W. R., 60, 62, 69, 86, 109, 137, 158
Cicero, 54
Clement of Alexandria, 1, 22, 30, 66, 167
Clement of Rome, 147, 153
Conscience, 200, 201
Conybeare, 8, 184
I Corinthians, 111
Cornely, R., 65, 76, 77, 81, 83, 101, 139, 146, 181, 200
Corruption of the body, 34, 52
Coverdale, 168, 176
Creation, 34, 35, 145
Cyprian, 22, 66, 80

Dähne, A. F., 117, 187
Daniel, 33, 63, 74, 100, 105, 172, 211
Darkness, 196 ff.
David, 101, 122, 144
Davidson, 149
Deane, W. J., 12, 26, 56, 57, 61, 64, 66, 73, 82, 88, 90, 94, 112, 117, 125, 130, 132, 136, 161, 162, 165
Death, 58, 59, 60, 83, 85; Book of, 55
de Bruyne, D., 7
Deissmann, Adolf, 25
Deuteronomy, 33, 42, 50, 57, 61, 77-80 (pass.), 91, 97, 100, 101, 126, 134, 138, 140, 141, 142, 150, 151, 152, 154, 160, 162, 163, 171, 176, 179, 188, 189, 191, 194, 195
Diogenes Laertius, 35, 131, 160, 169, 182
Dionysus, 59
Dioscuri, 166
Discipline, 66, 75
Dreams, 211
Driver, 135, 152
Drummond, J., 52, 168, 193, 195
Dualism, 130-31, 145
Ducange, 81

Ecclesiastes, 9-10, 26, 34, 39, 52, 56, 59-65 (pass.), 72, 78, 80, 99, 105, 107, 108, 109, 200
Ecclesiasticus, 14, 36, 39, 56, 57, 62, 63, 65, 67, 70-86 (pass.), 92, 93, 95, 97, 100-4 (pass.), 109, 110, 111, 114, 116, 118, 120, 121, 122, 125, 136, 144, 148, 166, 178, 179, 189
Edersheim, 113
Eichhorn, 19, 22
Eissfeldt, Otto, 151
Eleazar, 65
Elements, 112; transmutation of, 217, 223; worship of, 160
Elijah, 85
Emperor worship, 172-73
Engelbreth, 19, 23
English Revised version, 9
Enoch, 55, 56, 59, 70, 72, 74, 75, 84, 85, 90, 91, 116
Environment, 76
Epictetus, 217
Epicureanism, 12, 34, 59, 61, 63
Epiphanius, 1, 26, 114
Esau, 136
Eschatology, 36, 74, 79
II Esdras, 76, 98
IV Esdras, 146
Essenes, 195
Ethiopic version, 8
Euhemerus, 35, 172
Eunuch, 77-78
Eusebius, 104, 114, 144, 161
Evil, 17, 130
Exodus, 55, 57, 80, 96, 112, 120, 128, 138-44 (pass.), 151, 152, 155, 156, 158, 159, 163, 171, 176, 178, 186, 188, 191, 192, 193, 195, 196, 198, 199, 203, 205-10 (pass.), 213-16 (pass.), 219, 220, 223
Exposure of infants, 143, 206
Ezekiel, 33, 38, 56, 64, 65, 76, 79, 80, 88, 89, 98, 116, 121, 137, 142, 144, 145, 148, 151, 156, 160, 171, 177, 181, 182
Ezra, 76

Faber, J. M., 16
Farrar, F. W., 14, 16–17, 20, 52, 57, 61, 63, 71, 74, 82, 83, 87, 89, 96, 112, 120, 131, 136, 146, 153, 154, 164, 183, 199, 204, 208, 217
Fear, 200–201
Feldmann, F., 6, 20
Flowers, 63–64
Focke, F., 13, 19, 20, 23
Fraenkel, Seckel (Isaac), 9
Freewill, 38
Freudenthal, J., 18, 24, 25, 28, 157, 170
Friedländer, M., 12
Friedmann, 35
Fritzsche, 58
Fulgentius, 172

Gad, 145
Gärtner, 19, 20, 222
Galatians, 169
Gamaliel, R., II, 34
Geiger, 81
Genesis, 36, 37, 42, 50, 61, 70, 72, 78, 84, 86, 87, 89, 98, 107, 117, 128, 132–38 (pass.), 145, 153, 158, 170, 176, 184, 207, 219, 220, 221
German translation, 9
Gezer, 151
Gfrörer, A. Fr., 13, 16, 20, 53, 57, 69, 106, 119, 128, 129, 187, 210
Ginzberg, Louis, H., 85, 100, 108, 132, 133, 151, 161
God, attributes of, 148, 149, 155, 159, 161, 178; conception of, 33, 37, 55, 72, 74, 96, 97; knowledge of, 66; partiality of, to Jews, 41, 142; supremacy of, 153, 154; Wisdom and, 118–19
Gomorrah, 134
Goodrick, A. T. S., 7, 14, 17, 20, 29, 52–55 (pass.), 57, 60–90 (pass.), 92, 94, 97, 99, 107, 111, 113, 114, 115, 119, 121, 123, 125, 127, 130–35 (pass.), 137, 143–56 (pass.), 161–68 (pass.), 170, 174, 176, 180, 182, 184, 187, 188, 193, 195, 197–206 (pass.), 209, 214, 221, 225

Graetz, 6, 13, 69, 71, 77, 155, 169
Grammar, 118
Greek philosophy, viii, 36, 120
Gregg, J. A. F., 5, 13, 27, 31, 51, 58, 62, 64, 66, 70, 71, 72, 75, 82, 83, 86–90 (pass.), 94, 109, 117, 119, 123, 130–35 (pass.), 143, 149, 161, 165, 168, 169, 173, 177, 179, 183, 190, 197, 199–204 (pass.), 208–11 (pass.), 214, 216, 217, 222
Gressmann, Hugo, 38
Grimm, C. L. W., 6, 8, 13, 14, 18, 20, 25, 28, 53, 55, 57–69 (pass.), 73, 75, 76, 78, 80, 82–86 (pass.), 89, 94, 96–99 (pass.), 102, 104, 107, 109, 112, 113, 118, 120, 122, 129, 132, 134, 136, 140, 146, 150, 151, 153, 156, 162, 164, 165, 171, 179, 187, 193, 200, 204, 206, 208, 209, 213, 215
Grotius, 119, 133
Gutberlet, 206
Gutmann, M., 9, 218
Gwilliam, George Henry, 7

Habakkuk, 65, 97, 184
Hades, 58, 59, 60, 201, 204
Haggai, 34, 101
Hallel, 208
Harnack, 124
Hasidim, 70
Headlam, W., 27
Hebrew version, 9
Hebrews, Epistle to, 14, 62, 78
Hedonism, see Epicureanism
Heinisch, Paul, 13, 31, 178
Heliodorus, 88
Hellenism, viii, ix, 15, 25, 29, 37, 49
Heraclitus, 31, 61, 130, 160, 175
Heredity, 76; of sin, 79, 80
Hermes Trismegistus, 161
Herodotus, 160, 166, 173
Hesychius, 186
Hexaplaric text, 7
Heydenreich, 20
Hezekiah, 101
Hillel, 34
Hippolytus, 22

Hiram of Tyre, 122
Holmes, Samuel, 5, 13, 19, 21, 53, 69, 74, 78, 87, 215
Holtzmann, Joseph, 6, 7
Holy Ghost, 114, 115, 116
Homer, 87, 200
Horace, 80, 163, 182
Hosea, 58, 62, 66, 91, 95, 105, 119, 136, 140, 147, 170, 175, 177, 210
Houbigant, Charles Francois, 19, 22, 131

Ibn Ezra, 198
Idolatry, 35, 144, 149, 157, 158, 159 ff., 162 ff., 166 ff., 171, 174; results of, 177
Immortality, 33, 70, 71, 72, 78, 80, 105, 123
Irenaeus, 132, 134
Isaac, 134, 213
Isaiah, 14, 27, 33, 42, 50, 52, 56, 58, 59, 62–69 (*pass.*), 72–78 (*pass.*), 82–89 (*pass.*), 92, 93, 95, 96, 98, 100, 101, 103, 108, 111, 115, 116, 119, 127, 129, 131, 139, 145, 146, 147, 151, 156, 159, 162–66 (*pass.*), 168, 170, 171, 174, 175, 179, 181, 189, 190, 202, 205, 206
Ishmael, Rabbi, 192
Ishmael, son of Hagar, 158
Israel, history of, 132 ff.
Itala, 1, 6–7

Jacob, 135–36, 213
Jephthah, 150
Jeremiah, 38, 53, 54, 60, 65, 79, 80, 82, 88, 91, 92, 95, 128, 145, 151, 157, 160, 162, 163, 166, 174, 175, 177, 180, 200
Jeroboam, 163
Jerome, 1, 6, 16, 25, 161, 193
Jerusalem, 128
Jesus, 66–67, 68
Job, 14, 33, 54, 59–63 (*pass.*), 67, 72, 75, 82, 83, 84, 88–95 (*pass.*), 98, 101, 106, 108, 109, 122, 131, 144, 146, 148, 159, 161, 190, 197, 200, 210

Joel, 55, 74
John, 69
John of Damascus, 114
Jonah, 167
Joseph, 136–37, 145, 220, 221
Josephus, 16, 64, 70, 86, 98, 100, 113, 122, 134, 141, 173, 189, 195, 198, 206, 214, 215, 220
Joshua, 137, 152, 153, 156
Jubilees, 55, 133, 141, 144, 206
Judaism, Alexandrian, 11–12, 18, 29, 40; Pharisaic, 12, 40
Judges, 38, 53, 96, 98, 121, 132, 150, 152, 156, 203
Judgment Day, 79, 89–90
Judith, 64, 81
Justice of God, 154
Justin, 66
Juvenal, 144, 157, 177

Kahana, Abraham, 9, 29
Kautzsch, 13, 20, 50
Kidneys, 53
I Kings, 50, 87, 105, 109, 110, 111, 113, 121, 122, 123, 126, 127, 163, 166, 174, 178
II Kings, 101, 132, 145, 150, 160, 163, 188
Koheleth, 34, 63, 65; *see also* Ecclesiastes
Kohler, Kaufman, 19, 34, 41, 128

Laban, 136
Lactantius, 22, 61
Lagarde, 7, 8
Lamech, 133
Lamentations, 42, 57
À Lapide, C., 68, 131, 152, 161, 172, 196, 198, 223
Law, Mosaic, 66, 100–101, 126, 171
Lévi, 81
Leviticus, 86, 101, 140, 145, 150, 170, 213
Levy, Harry L., ix
Liddell, 121, 134
Life, Book of, 55
Livy, 153

Logos, 17, 52, 103, 114, 115, 117, 126, 145, 189, 194, 210
Lot, 134, 135, 221
Löw, Leopold, 108
Lucretius, 180
Luke, 68, 69
Luther, 16, 79, 205
Lutterbeck, 16
Lysander, 173

Maccabees, books of, 68; I, 19, 70, 72, 111; II, 19, 34, 52, 60, 64, 65, 72, 73, 81, 88, 95, 107, 128, 144, 150, 156, 172, 175, 220; III, 15, 19, 64, 91, 93, 96, 110, 123, 190, 224; IV, 36, 81, 86, 91, 93, 120, 126, 196, 201, 213
McLean, 5
Maclister, 151
Malachi, 41, 55, 65, 73, 74, 76, 101, 142
Manna, 192, 193, 195, 223
Margoliouth, D. S., 5, 8, 18, 23, 24, 25, 40, 52, 78, 87, 116, 147, 170, 175, 179, 181, 193
Marriage, irregular, 176; mixed, 76, 77, 81, 82; unlawful, 79; used as symbol, 118, 119, 121, 124
Massah, 144
Matthew, 68
Maundrell, 135
Menander, 87
Menzel, P., 31, 33
Micah, 206
Midrash, 57, 70, 85, 86, 113, 124, 133, 151, 170, 209
Mishnah, 33, 195
Monism, 145
Monotheism, 171
Moore, G. F., 35, 52, 124, 185
Moriah, Mount, 128
Moses, 4, 42, 101, 138, 139, 140, 143, 174, 178, 187, 206, 212
Moulton, 68, 96

Nachtigal, 9, 19, 34
Nahmanides, 8
Nahum, 60

Nannius, 223
Nathan, Rabbi, 212
Nature, beauty of, 161; sounds of, 202–3; worship of, 160, 162
Nebuchadnezzar, 172, 211
Nehemiah, 76, 105, 132
Nicephorus, 64
Nicolaus de Lyra, 16
Noack, 16
Noah, 133, 135, 169
Numbers, 35, 41, 53, 55, 56, 86, 89, 101, 139, 142, 153, 187, 188, 189, 192, 193, 209, 212, 213, 219

Obadiah, 38, 61, 74, 144
Old age, 84
Origen, 1, 7, 192
Ovid, 165

Painting and sculpture, 174, 178–79
Palestinian version, 7
Parsons, 5
Particularism, 73, 107, 142, 148
Passover, 207, 208
Paul, bishop of Tella, 7
Pausanias, 165, 193
Pentapolis, 134
Perdition, Book of, 55
Personal responsibility, 76
Peshitta, 1, 7, 23
I Peter, 14, 169
II Peter, 68
Peters, N., 23
Pfleiderer, Edmund, 31, 59, 160, 175, 211, 217
Philo, 10, 13–19 (pass.), 26, 35, 37, 49–59 (pass.), 70, 71, 74, 77, 80, 81, 84, 95, 97, 103–6 (pass.), 109–27 (pass.), 130, 131, 133, 134, 137, 139, 140, 141, 145, 146, 148, 154, 155, 157–63 (pass.), 166, 168, 169, 174–201 (pass.), 205–15 (pass.), 219, 220, 221, 223
Plato, 31, 32, 34, 107, 112, 120, 130, 161, 168, 179
Plautus, 87
Pliny, 165, 218
Plumptre, 16

Plutarch, 64
Polybius, 190
Porter, F. C., 32, 125
Potiphar's wife, 137
Pre-existence, 32–33, 108, 128
Preisigke, E., 96
Pritchard, James B., 38
Proverbs, 14, 35, 36, 39, 40, 50, 53, 56, 58, 59, 72–80 (*pass.*), 82, 86, 89, 90, 92, 93, 99–110 (*pass.*), 113, 115, 120, 121, 122, 124, 126, 135, 144, 156, 200
Providence, 35, 102, 167–68
Psalms, 50–56 (*pass.*), 61, 62, 65, 68–76 (*pass.*), 78, 80, 82, 84, 87–100 (*pass.*), 102, 103, 105, 108, 115, 117, 123, 126, 127, 128, 130, 138, 139, 144, 148, 151, 154, 155, 159, 161, 162, 163, 166, 168, 177, 183, 185, 189, 190, 192, 193, 194, 197, 204, 206, 208, 220
Pseudo-Aristobulus, 10, 16
Pseudo-Athanasius, 1
Punishment, of children, 83; of the Egyptians, 139 ff., 144 ff., 149, 184 ff.; of the Israelites, 187; of prominent men, 101; theory of, 75; of the wicked, 71, 88, 89
Purgatory, 83
Purinton, C. E., 24, 87, 129
Pygmalion, 179
Pythagoras, 35, 160, 161, 182

Quail, 185–86, 219

Raba, 33
Rabbinic interpretation, 41–42, 56, 176, 192; *see also* Midrash *and* Talmud
Rahab, 153
Rahlfs, A., 6
Ramsay, 163, 173, 175, 183
Red Sea passage, 217 ff.
Remembrance, Book of, 38, 55
Repentance, 153
Resurrection of the soul, 33–34
Retaliation, 140, 184 ff., 196
Retribution, 35, 38, 144–45, 185

Reusch, 8, 73
Reuss, 54, 55, 61, 68, 90, 114, 154, 221
Revelation, 58, 70
Ringgren, Helmer, 39
Rosenthal, Mr. and Mrs. William, x
Rossi, Azariah dei, 8, 22

Sahidic version, 8
Salt, pillar of, 134, 135
I Samuel, 53, 71, 99, 102, 165, 190, 214
II Samuel, 38, 62, 63, 71, 92, 97, 101
Satan, 70
Schultess, 52
Schürer, E., 13, 14, 18, 22
Scott, 121, 134
Selden, 176
Septuagint, 15, 25
Sexual perversion, 176
Sheba, Queen of, 122
Sheol, 58, 60, 163, 201
Sibylline Oracles, 144, 223
Siegfried, K., 10, 13, 20, 39, 49, 53, 57, 61, 62, 63, 66, 74, 76, 79, 86, 87, 94, 96, 130, 193, 204, 209
Simlai, R., 32
Sin, 38; hereditary, 79, 80; original, 153
Sira, Ben, 16
Sodom, Sodomites, 134, 176, 220, 221
Solomon, 4, 15, 99, 102, 106, 107, 109, 111, 113, 118, 121, 122, 123, 124
Song of Songs, 161
Sophists, 111
Sorites, 104–5
Soul, 61; immortality of, 33, 71 (*see also* Immortality); pre-existence of, 32–33, 108, 124–25; resurrection of, 33–34
Sovereignty from the Lord, doctrine of, 100
Speiser, E. A., 24, 119
Stade, 39, 84
Stein, Menahem, 9, 29
Sterility, 76

Stern, M. E., 9
Stoicism, 31, 34, 54, 114, 115, 118, 120, 168, 200, 211
Succoth, 140
Suffering, 38
Swete, H. B., 5, 91, 215
Symbolism, 118, 119, 121, 124, 214–15
Syriac version, 1, 7
Syro-Hexaplaric text, 7
Syrophanes, 172

Tabernacle, 128
Talmud, 41–42, 70, 81, 84, 108, 128, 140, 145, 149, 151, 178, 182, 188
Targums, Jewish, 7, 139, 141, 145, 158, 187, 192, 195, 198, 205, 208, 210, 212, 216, 220
Tatian, 56
Tertullian, 6, 22, 132
Testament of the Twelve Patriarchs, 144
Thackeray, H. St. John, 13, 26, 204
Thales, 131, 160
Theocritus, 54, 59
Theodoret, 109
Therapeutae, 16, 70, 77, 84, 195
Thielmann, P., 6
Thiersch, Hermann, 214
Tibullus, 165
Tobit, 39, 190, 206
Torrey, 119
Toy, 216
Transmutation, doctrine of, 217, 223
Tregelles, 1
Tristram, 134
Tzschirner, 20

Universalism, 73, 107, 142, 148

Vergil, 108, 165
Virtue, 80–81, 120

Wace, 17, 20
Wahl, 57
Walton's Polyglot, 1, 7
Wayyikra rabba, 213
Weber, F., 19, 20, 56, 66, 108, 124, 185
Wendland, 37
Wessely, Hartwig, 9, 46, 138
Westcott, 173
Winer, 68, 96
Wisdom, attributes of, 51–52, 53, 99 ff., 103 ff., 114 ff.; concept of, 35–37; God and, 118–19; in Israelitish history, 132 ff.; Solomon's prayer for, 126 ff.
Wolf, Edwin, II, ix
Wolfson, H. A., 29, 35, 37, 40, 42, 168, 178

Xenophon, 31, 118, 161, 168

Ibn Yahya, Gedaliah ben Joseph, 16, 22

Zeboïm, 134
Zechariah, 65, 73, 74, 96, 97, 150, 171
Zeitlin, Solomon, ix, 128, 150, 212
Zeller, 32, 33, 34, 211
Zeno, 61
Zephaniah, 160
Zerubbabel, 16
Zoar, 134